BRITISH GOVERNMENT
1914–1953

G. H. L. Le MAY

Former Fellow of Balliol College, Oxford
Professor of Local Government and Public Administrations
in the University of the Witwatersrand, Johannesburg

BRITISH GOVERNMENT

1914 - 1953

Select Documents

METHUEN & CO LTD, LONDON

36 Essex Street, Strand; WC2

First published in 1955

CATALOGUE NO. 5697 U

Printed and bound in Great Britain by
The Camelot Press Ltd., London and Southampton

To
MY MOTHER AND FATHER

ACKNOWLEDGEMENTS

MANY friends and colleagues have, directly and indirectly, helped me in preparing this book. In particular, I should like to thank Mr. D. N. Chester, Professor S. E. Finer, Mr. R. B. McCallum, Mr. H. G. Nicholas, Professor W. A. Robson, Professor K. B. Smellie, and Mr. E. T. Williams, all of whom gave me their criticisms of my synopsis. Mr. Nicholas, and Messrs. Macmillan & Co., Ltd., gave me permission to print an extract from *The General Election of 1950*. Sir David Keir allowed me to see the table of contents of the fourth edition of Keir and Lawson, *Cases in Constitutional Law*. The extracts from official papers are printed with the permission of the Controller of Her Majesty's Stationery Office. Mr. Peter Wait, of the firm of Methuen, first suggested that I should begin this work; and I owe him a deep debt of gratitude, not only for his assistance in collecting material, but for his genial patience. My secretary, Miss Jenifer Nicolson, has given me valuable help in preparing the index.

Above all, I must thank Mr. Asa Briggs. Most of my ideas on the process of government were formulated in discussions with him, first as his pupil and later as his colleague, during the five years which I spent in the University of Oxford.

JOHANNESBURG.
November, 1954.

THE most distinctive indication of the change of outlook of the government of this country in recent times has been its growing preoccupation, irrespective of party, with the management of the life of the people. A study of the Statute Book will show how profoundly the conception of the function of government has altered. Parliament finds itself increasingly engaged in legislation which has for its conscious aim the regulation of the day-to-day affairs of the community and now intervenes in matters formerly thought to be entirely outside its scope.

Report of the Macmillan Committee
on Finance and Industry, 1931.

INTRODUCTION

THE problems of an editor of contemporary documents are similar, in many ways, to those of the contemporary historian. There is, for instance, too much evidence of one kind, and not enough of another. Trends which seem to be dominant, and developments which seem to be critical, in the distorted perspective of the recent past, may well be those which will, in the event, prove minor or insignificant. Documents —especially official papers, which form the greater part of this collection—are by no means a complete record. "We may find many things in rowles," Whitelocke wrote in his diary, "but we knowe not with what passion and what earnestness it was done." But where the contemporary historian, by his own knowledge, and by his interpretation of personal motives, may fill in those gaps where the records are silent, the editor must leave the documents to speak, so far as they can, for themselves.

These documents have been presented with the minimum of explanatory matter. I agree with the views of Mr. Costin and Mr. Steven Watson of those who have "attempted to write the constitutional history of two hundred and fifty years in some century—or score—of breathless pages, and attached it to the front of the selections by way of guide or précis of what is to follow."[1] This is not a supplement to a constitutional history of contemporary Britain, but an attempt to collect materials which may prove helpful when such a history comes to be written. "Most historians of British responsible government have attuned their story to the theme of liberty," Sir Keith Hancock has written. "It might with equal appropriateness be attuned to the theme of efficiency . . ."[2] I have tried, in making my selection, to keep this luminous phrase in mind: and the reader will find, therefore, extracts bearing on the way in which the civil service, in particular, does its business.

There is also a good deal of descriptive matter. It has seemed to me that, in passing judgement on developments in government, we have been using, as a mental standard, a model which has long been obsolete. It is, no doubt, a stimulating mental exercise to compare the conventions of the constitution to-day with those of Lord Palmerston's time, and to conclude, therefore, that we have moved deplorably far from the classical practice of representative democracy; but it adds little to an understanding of the process of government. The theory of British government has never quite kept pace with the practice; but the gap between them, it may be argued, has seldom been quite so

---

[1] W. C. Costin and J. Steven Watson, *The Law and Working of the Constitution* (2 vols. London, 1952), p. vii.

[2] W. K. Hancock and M. M. Gowing, *British War Economy* (London, 1949), p. 88.

wide as it is to-day. The first task, in closing that gap, is to know how the machinery of government actually works; and this collection, it is hoped, will be some contribution to that knowledge.

Although the area and intensity of government action have grown, over the past few generations, the State (if this word may be used loosely to refer to that body which has the final power to make and enforce decisions) has become, at the same time, increasingly remote from the citizen in whose name it claims to function, and increasingly obscure in its inner workings. It may be argued that the two centres of effective power lie in the caucus of the party for the time being in power, on one hand; and somewhere between the political executive (which is linked to the party) and the permanent executive of senior civil servants, on the other. The development of a strict party discipline, the provisions of the Official Secrets Acts, and the extensions of the doctrine of Cabinet secrecy,[1] are making it increasingly difficult for those not in the inner circles of knowledge to do more than speculate on how decisions are, in fact, taken. Nevertheless, a study of such working parts of the machinery of government which are exposed has a definite value if it helps to produce that "intuitive understanding of how things do not happen", which Sir Lewis Namier has called "the crowning attainment of historical study."

Some working parts, however, are not exposed at all. It is not yet possible, for example, to publish official papers showing in detail how Britain was directed from the centre during the Second World War. It is difficult to show the significance, at the present day, of such officials as, for instance, the Secretary of the Cabinet. War and preparation for war have influenced both the structure of government and the technique of administration; they have also left their mark upon the administrative habit of mind. It is too early, still, to say which of these influences will be the most lasting.

[1] This has recently been extended to strange lengths. It is necessary, for instance, for those who wish to read those volumes of the Gladstone Papers in the British Museum in which Mr. Gladstone's notes of Cabinet meetings are preserved, to obtain official permission.

CONTENTS

Section II. PARLIAMENT

SECTION I

Statutes

OFFICIAL SECRETS ACT, 1911
1 and 2 Geo. 5, c. 28

An Act to re-enact the Official Secrets Act, 1889, with Amendments.

[*22nd August 1911.*]

1.—(1) If any person for any purpose prejudicial to the safety or interests of the State—

(*a*) approaches or is in the neighbourhood of, or enters any prohibited place within the meaning of this Act; or

(*b*) makes any sketch, plan, model, or note which is calculated to be or might be or is intended to be directly or indirectly useful to an enemy; or

(*c*) obtains or communicates to any other person any sketch, plan, model, article, or note, or other document or information which is calculated to be or might be or is intended to be directly or indirectly useful to an enemy;

he shall be guilty of felony, and shall be liable to penal servitude for any term not less than three years and not exceeding seven years.

(2) On a prosecution under this section, it shall not be necessary to show that the accused person was guilty of any particular act tending to show a purpose prejudicial to the safety or interests of the State, and, notwithstanding that no such act is proved against him, he may be convicted if, from the circumstances of the case, or his conduct, or his known character as proved, it appears that his purpose was a purpose prejudicial to the safety or interests of the State; and if any sketch, plan, model, article, note, document, or information relating to or used in any prohibited place within the meaning of this Act, or anything in such a place, is made, obtained, or communicated by any person other than a person acting under lawful authority, it shall be deemed to have been made, obtained, or communicated for a purpose prejudicial to the safety or interests of the State unless the contrary is proved.

2.—(1) If any person having in his possession or control any sketch, plan, model, article, note, document, or information which relates to or is used in a prohibited place or anything in such a place, or which has been made or obtained in contravention of this Act, or which has been entrusted in confidence to him by any person holding office under His Majesty or which he has obtained owing to his position as a person who holds or has held office under His Majesty, or as a person who holds or has held a contract made on behalf of His Majesty, or as a person who is or has been employed under a person who holds or has held such an office or contract,—

(*a*) communicates the sketch, plan, model, article, note, document, or information to any person, other than a person to whom he is authorised to communicate it, or a person to whom it is in the interest of the State his duty to communicate it, or

(*b*) retains the sketch, plan, model, article, note, or document in his possession or control when he has no right to retain it or when it is contrary to his duty to retain it:

that person shall be guilty of a misdemeanour.

(2) If any person receives any sketch, plan, model, article, note, document, or information, knowing, or having reasonable ground to believe, at the time when he receives it, that the sketch, plan, model, article, note, document, or information is communicated to him in contravention of this Act, he shall be guilty of a misdemeanour, unless he proves that the communication to him of the sketch, plan, model, article, note, document, or information was contrary to his desire.

(3) A person guilty of a misdemeanour under this section shall be liable to imprisonment with or without hard labour for a term not exceeding two years, or to a fine, or to both imprisonment and a fine.

[§ 3. Definition of "prohibited place".]

4. Any person who attempts to commit any offence under this Act, or incites, or counsels, or attempts to procure another person to commit an offence under this Act, shall be guilty of felony or of a misdemeanour according as the offence in question is felony or misdemeanour, and on conviction shall be liable to the same punishment, and to be proceeded against in the same manner, as if he had committed the offence. . . .

7. If any person knowingly harbours any person whom he knows, or has reasonable grounds for supposing, to be a person who is about to commit or who has committed an offence under this Act, or knowingly permits to meet or assemble in any premises in his occupation or under his control any such persons, or if any person having harboured any such person, or permitted to meet or assemble in any premises in his occupation or under his control any such persons, wilfully refuses to disclose to a superintendent of police any information which it is in his power to give in relation to any such person he shall be guilty of a misdemeanour and liable to imprisonment with or without hard labour for a term not exceeding one year, or to a fine, or to both imprisonment and a fine.

8. A prosecution for an offence under this Act shall not be instituted except by or with the consent of the Attorney-General. . . .

9.—(1) If a justice of the peace is satisfied by information on oath that there is reasonable ground for suspecting that an offence under this Act has been or is about to be committed, he may grant a search warrant authorising any constable named therein to enter at any time any premises or place named in the warrant, if necessary, by force, and to search the premises or place and every person found therein, and to seize any sketch, plan, model, article, note, or document, or anything of a like nature or anything which is evidence of an offence under this Act having been or being about to be committed, which he may find on the premises or place or on any such person, and with regard to or in connexion with which he has reasonable ground for suspecting that an offence under this Act has been or is about to be committed.

(2) Where it appears to a superintendent of police that the case is one of great emergency and that in the interest of the State immediate action is necessary, he may by a written order under his hand give to any constable the like authority as may be given by the warrant of a justice under this section. . . .

13.—(1) This Act may be cited as the Official Secrets Act, 1911.

(2) The Official Secrets Act, 1889, is hereby repealed.

TRADE UNION ACT, 1913
2 and 3 Geo. 5, c. 30

An Act to amend the Law with respect to the objects and powers of Trade Unions.

[*7th March 1913.*]

1.—(1) The fact that a combination has under its constitution objects or powers other than statutory objects within the meaning of this Act shall not prevent the combination being a trade union for the purposes of the Trade Union Acts, 1871-1906, so long as the combination is a trade union as defined by this Act, and, subject to the provisions of this Act as to the furtherance of political objects, any such trade union shall have power to apply the funds of the union for any lawful objects or purposes for the time being authorised under its constitution.

(2) For the purposes of this Act, the expression "statutory objects" means the objects mentioned in section sixteen of the Trade Union Act Amendment Act, 1876, namely, the regulation of the relations between workmen and masters, or between workmen and workmen, or between masters and masters, or the imposing of restrictive conditions

on the conduct of any trade or business, and also the provision of benefits to members.

2.—(1) The expression "trade union" for the purpose of the Trade Union Acts, 1871 to 1906, and this Act, means any combination, whether temporary or permanent, the principal objects of which are under its constitution statutory objects:

Provided that any combination which is for the time being registered as a trade union shall be deemed to be a trade union as defined by this Act so long as it continues to be so registered.

(2) The Registrar of Friendly Societies shall not register any combination as a trade union unless in his opinion, having regard to the constitution of the combination, the principal objects of the combination are statutory objects, and may withdraw the certificate of registration of any such registered trade union if the constitution of the union has been altered in such a manner that, in his opinion, the principal objects of the union are no longer statutory objects, or if in his opinion the principal objects for which the union is actually carried on are not statutory objects.

[(3) Unregistered trade unions may apply to the Registrar for a certificate.]

[(4) Appeal to the High Court against the Registrar's refusal to register a union.]

(5) A certificate of the Registrar that a trade union is a trade union within the meaning of this Act shall, so long as it is in force, be conclusive for all purposes.

3.—(1) The funds of a trade union shall not be applied, either directly or in conjunction with any other trade union, association, or body, or otherwise indirectly, in the furtherance of the political objects to which this section applies (without prejudice to the furtherance of any other political objects), unless the furtherance of those objects has been approved as an object of the union by a resolution for the time being in force passed on a ballot of the members of the union taken in accordance with this Act for the purpose by a majority of the members voting; and where such a resolution is in force, unless, rules, to be approved, whether the union is registered or not, by the Registrar of Friendly Societies, are in force providing—

(*a*) that any payments in the furtherance of those objects are to be made out of a separate fund (in this Act referred to as the political fund of the union), and for the exemption in accordance with this Act of any member of the union from any obligation to contribute to such a fund if he gives notice in accordance with this Act that he objects to contribute; and

(*b*) that a member who is exempt from the obligation to contribute to the political fund of the union shall not be excluded from any benefits of the union, or placed in any respect either directly or indirectly under any disability or at any disadvantage as compared with other members of the union (except in relation to the control or management of the political fund) by reason of his being so exempt, and that contribution to the political fund of the union shall not be made a condition for admission to the union.

(2) If any member of a trade union alleges that he is aggrieved by a breach of any rule made in pursuance of this section, he may complain to the Registrar of Friendly Societies, and the Registrar of Friendly Societies, after giving the complainant and any representative of the union an opportunity of being heard, may, if he considers that such a breach has been committed, make such order for remedying the breach as he thinks just under the circumstances; and any such order of the Registrar shall be binding and conclusive on all parties without appeal and shall not be removable into any court of law or restrainable by injunction, and on being recorded in the county court, may be enforced as if it had been an order of the county court. In the application of this provision to Scotland the sheriff's court shall be substituted for the county court, and "interdict" shall be substituted for "injunction."

(3) The political objects to which this section applies are the expenditure of money—

(*a*) on the payment of any expenses incurred either directly or indirectly by a candidate or prospective candidate for election to Parliament or to any public office, before, during, or after the election in connexion with his candidature or election; or

(*b*) on the holding of any meeting or the distribution of any literature or documents in support of any such candidate or prospective candidate; or

(*c*) on the maintenance of any person who is a member of Parliament or who holds a public office; or

(*d*) in connexion with the registration of electors or the selection of a candidate for Parliament or any public office; or

(*e*) on the holding of political meetings of any kind, or on the distribution of political literature or political documents of any kind, unless the main purpose of the meetings or of the distribution of the literature or documents is the furtherance of statutory objects within the meaning of this Act.

The expression "public office" in this section means the office of member of any county, county borough, district, or parish council, or board of guardians, or of any public body who have power to raise money, either directly or indirectly, by means of a rate.

(4) A resolution under this section approving political objects as an object of the union shall take effect as if it were a rule of the union and

may be rescinded in the same manner and subject to the same provisions as such a rule. . . .

4.—(1) A ballot for the purposes of this Act shall be taken in accordance with rules of the union to be approved . . . by the Registrar of Friendly Societies. . . .

5.—(1) A member of a trade union may at any time give notice . . . that he objects to contribute to the political fund of the union. . . .

(2) On giving notice in accordance with this Act of his objection to contribute, a member of the union shall be exempt, so long as his notice is not withdrawn, from contributing to the political fund of the union as from the first day of January next after the notice is given . . .

[§§ 6 (methods of exemption), 7 (definition of the Registrar of Friendly Societies), 8 (short title), and schedule omitted.]

DEFENCE OF THE REALM CONSOLIDATION ACT, 1914
5 Geo. 5, c. 8

An Act to consolidate and amend the Defence of the Realm Acts.

[*27th November 1914.*]

1.—(1) His Majesty in Council has power during the continuance of the present war to issue regulations for securing the public safety and the defence of the realm, and as to the powers and duties for that purpose of the Admiralty and Army Council and of the members of His Majesty's forces and other persons acting in his behalf; and may by such regulations authorise the trial by courts-martial, or in the case of minor offences by courts of summary jurisdiction, and punishment of persons committing offences against the regulations and in particular against any of the provisions of such regulations designed—

(*a*) to prevent persons communicating with the enemy or obtaining information for that purpose or any purpose calculated to jeopardise the success of the operations of any of His Majesty's forces or the forces of his allies or to assist the enemy; or

(*b*) to secure the safety of His Majesty's forces and ships and the safety of any means of communication and of railways, ports, and harbours; or

(*c*) to prevent the spread of false reports or reports likely to cause disaffection to His Majesty or to interfere with the success of His Majesty's forces by land or sea or to prejudice His Majesty's relations with foreign powers; or

(*d*) to secure the navigation of vessels in accordance with directions given by or under the authority of the Admiralty; or (*e*) otherwise to prevent assistance being given to the enemy or the successful prosecution of the war being endangered.

(2) Any such regulations may provide for the suspension of any restrictions on the acquisition or user of land, or the exercise of the power of making byelaws, or any other power under the Defence Acts, 1842 to 1875, or the Military Lands Acts, 1891 to 1903, and any such regulations or any orders made thereunder affecting the pilotage of vessels may supersede any enactment, order, charter, byelaw, regulation or provision as to pilotage.

(3) It shall be lawful for the Admiralty or Army Council—

(*a*) to require that there shall be placed at their disposal the whole or any part of the output of any factory or workshop in which arms, ammunition, or warlike stores or equipment, or any articles required for the production thereof, are manufactured;

(*b*) to take possession of and use for the purpose of His Majesty's naval or military service any such factory or workshop or any plant thereof;

and regulations under this Act may be made accordingly.

(4) For the purpose of the trial of a person for an offence under the regulations by court-martial and the punishment thereof, the person may be proceeded against and dealt with as if he were a person subject to military law and had on active service committed an offence under section five of the Army Act:

Provided that where it is proved that the offence is committed with the intention of assisting the enemy a person convicted of such an offence by a court-martial shall be liable to suffer death.

(5) For the purpose of the trial of a person for an offence under the regulations by a court of summary jurisdiction and the punishment thereof, the offence shall be deemed to have been committed either at the place in which the same actually was committed or in any place in which the offender may be, and the maximum penalty which may be inflicted shall be imprisonment with or without hard labour for a term of six months or a fine of one hundred pounds, or both such imprisonment and fine; section seventeen of the Summary Jurisdiction Act, 1879, shall not apply to charges of offences against the regulations, but any person aggrieved by a conviction of a court of summary jurisdiction may appeal in England to a court of quarter sessions, and in Scotland under and in terms of the Summary Jurisdiction (Scotland) Acts, and in Ireland in manner provided by the Summary Jurisdiction (Ireland) Acts.

(6) The regulations may authorise a court-martial or court of summary jurisdiction, in addition to any other punishment, to order the forfeiture of any goods in respect of which an offence against the regulations has been committed.

2.—(1) This Act may be cited as the Defence of the Realm Consolidation Act, 1914.

(2) The Defence of the Realm Act, 1914, and the Defence of the Realm (No. 2) Act, 1914, are hereby repealed, but nothing in this repeal shall affect any Orders in Council made thereunder, and all such Orders in Council shall, until altered or revoked by an Order in Council under this Act, continue in force and have effect as if made under this Act.

REPRESENTATION OF THE PEOPLE ACT, 1918
8 Geo. 5, c. 64

Part I

Franchises

1.—(1) A man shall be entitled to be registered as a parliamentary elector for a constituency (other than a university constituency) if he is of full age and not subject to any legal incapacity, and—

(a) has the requisite residence qualification; or
(b) has the requisite business premises qualification.

(2) A man, in order to have the requisite residence qualification or business premises qualification for a constituency—

(a) must on the last day of the qualifying period be residing in premises in the constituency, or occupying business premises in the constituency, as the case may be; and
(b) must during the whole of the qualifying period have resided in premises, or occupied business premises, as the case may be, in the constituency, or in another constituency within the same parliamentary borough or parliamentary county, or within a parliamentary borough or parliamentary county contiguous to that borough or county, or separated from that borough or county by water, not exceeding at the nearest point six miles in breadth, measured in the case of the tidal water from low-water mark.

For the purposes of this subsection the administrative county of London shall be treated as a parliamentary borough.

(3) The expression "business premises" in this section means land or other premises of the yearly value of not less than ten pounds occupied for the purpose of the business, profession, or trade of the person to be registered.

2. A man shall be entitled to be registered as a parliamentary elector for a university constituency if he is of full age and not subject to any legal incapacity, and has received a degree (other than an honorary degree) at any university forming, or forming part of, the constituency, or in the case of the Scottish universities is qualified under section twenty-seven of the Representation of the People (Scotland) Act, 1868, or in the case of the University of Dublin has either received a degree (other than an honorary degree) at the university, or has obtained a scholarship or fellowship in the University whether before or after the passing of this Act.

3. A man shall be entitled to be registered as a local government elector for a local government electoral area, if he is of full age and not subject to any legal incapacity, and—

(a) is on the last day of the qualifying period occupying, as owner or tenant, any land or premises in that area; and

(b) has, during the whole of the qualifying period, so occupied any land or premises in that area, or, if that area is not an administrative county or a county borough, in any administrative county or county borough in which the area is wholly or partly situate:

Provided that—

(i) for the purposes of this section a man who himself inhabits any dwelling-house by virtue of any office, service, or employment, shall, if the dwelling-house is not inhabited by the person in whose service he is in such office, service, or employment, be deemed to occupy the dwelling-house as a tenant; and

(ii) for the purposes of this section the word tenant shall include a person who occupies a room or rooms as a lodger only where such room or rooms are let to him in an unfurnished state.

4.—(1) A woman shall be entitled to be registered as a parliamentary elector for a constituency (other than a university constituency) if she—

(a) has attained the age of thirty years; and

(b) is not subject to any legal incapacity; and

(c) is entitled to be registered as a local government elector in respect of the occupation in that constituency of land or premises (not being a dwelling-house) of a yearly value of not less than five pounds or of a dwelling-house, or is the wife of a husband entitled to be so registered.

(2) A woman shall be entitled to be registered as a parliamentary elector for a university constituency if she has attained the age of thirty years and either would be entitled to be so registered if she were a man, or has been admitted to and passed the final examination, and kept under the conditions required of women by the university the period of residence, necessary for a man to obtain a degree at any university forming, or forming part of, a university constituency which

did not at the time the examination was passed admit women to degrees.

(3) A woman shall be entitled to be registered as a local government elector for any local government electoral area—

(*a*) where she would be entitled to be so registered if she were a man; and

(*b*) where she is the wife of a man who is entitled to be so registered in respect of premises in which they both reside, and she has attained the age of thirty years and is not subject to any legal incapacity.

For the purpose of this provision, a naval or military voter who is registered in respect of a residence qualification which he would have had but for his service, shall be deemed to be resident in accordance with the qualification.

[§ 5 makes special provisions for those on war service.]

6. The qualifying period shall be a period of six months ending either on the fifteenth day of January, or the fifteenth day of July, including in each case the fifteenth day . . .

[§§ 7–9 deal with supplementary provisions as to residence and occupation, the right of those registered to vote, and disqualifications.]

10. A person shall, in addition to and without prejudice to any other qualification, be qualified to be elected a member of the local government authority for any local government electoral area if he is the owner of property held by freehold, copyhold, leasehold or any other tenure within the area of that authority.

[Part II deals with registration. There is to be a spring and autumn register of electors each year, to be compiled by the registration officers of each parliamentary borough and county; appeals from the registration officer's decision shall lie to the county court; the expenses of registration are to be divided between Parliament and local authorities; universities are to compile their own registers.]

PART III

Method and Costs of Elections

20.—(1) At a contested election for a university constituency, where there are two or more members to be elected, any election of the full number of members shall be according to the principle of proportional representation, each elector having one transferable vote as defined by this Act.

(2) (*a*) His Majesty may appoint Commissioners to prepare as soon as may be after the passing of this Act a scheme under which as nearly as possible one hundred members shall be elected to the House of Commons at a general election on the principle of proportional

representation for constituencies in Great Britain returning three or more members. . . .

21.—(1) At a general election all polls shall be held on one day. . . .

[§ 22 lays down penalties for illegal plural voting.]

[§ 23. Ballot papers may be sent to registered absent voters; soldiers, sailors and merchant seamen may vote by proxy.]

[§ 24. Electors employed by the returning officer may vote at the most convenient polling station.]

[§ 25. Candidates may hold meetings in public elementary schools out of school hours.]

[§§ 26–27 require that a candidate shall deposit £150 with the returning officer, which shall be returned to him unless he fails to receive more than one-eighth of the votes cast (or a proportionate number in a constituency returning more than two members). A candidate nominated in more than one constituency may not recover his deposit more than once.]

[§§ 28–32. Duties, payment, etc., of returning officers; polling districts, etc.]

33.—(1) The provisions set out in the Fourth Schedule to this Act shall be substituted for Part IV. and paragraph (3) of Part V. of the First Schedule to the Corrupt and Illegal Practices Prevention Act, 1883 (which relate to the maximum scale of election expenses), and that Act shall have effect accordingly.

[(2) A candidate may send one communication free of charge by post to each elector in his constituency.]

34.—(1) A person other than the election agent of a candidate shall not incur any expenses on account of holding public meetings or issuing advertisements, circulars or publications for the purpose of promoting or procuring the election of any candidate at a parliamentary election, unless he is authorised in writing to do so by such election agent.

(2) If any person acts in contravention of this section, he shall be guilty of a corrupt practice. . . .

Part IV

Redistribution of Seats

37.—(1) Each of the areas mentioned in the First Part of the Ninth Schedule to this Act shall be a parliamentary borough returning the number of members specified opposite thereto in the said Schedule, and where so provided in the Schedule shall be divided into the divisions specified therein, and each such division shall return one member.

[In England, 131 parliamentary boroughs, in 255 divisions; in Wales and Monmouthshire, 6 boroughs in 11 divisions; in Scotland, 13 boroughs in 13 divisions: in all, 299 divisions.]

CBG

(2) Each of the areas mentioned in the first column of the Second Part of the Ninth Schedule to this Act shall be a parliamentary county returning the number of members specified opposite thereto in the said Schedule, and where so provided in the Schedule shall be divided into the divisions specified therein, and each such division shall return one member.

[In England, 46 parliamentary counties, in 230 divisions; in Wales and Monmouthshire, 12 counties in 24 divisions; in Scotland, 21 counties in 38 divisions: in all, 292 divisions.

(3) Each of the universities and combinations of universities mentioned in the Third Part of the Ninth Schedule to this Act shall be a constituency returning the number of members specified opposite thereto in the said Schedule.

[Two members each to be returned by the Universities of Oxford and Cambridge; one each by the Universities of London and Wales; two members by the Victoria University of Manchester and the Universities of Durham, Liverpool, Leeds, Sheffield, Birmingham and Bristol; three members by the Universities of St. Andrews, Glasgow, Aberdeen and Edinburgh: eleven university members in all.]

[Part V (General) and Schedules 1–3 and 5–9 omitted.]

Fourth Schedule

The expenses . . . other than personal expenses and the fee, if any, paid to the election agent (not exceeding in the case of a county election seventy-five pounds and of a borough election fifty pounds . . .) shall not exceed an amount equal—

in the case of a county election to sevenpence for each elector on the register;

in the case of an election for a borough to fivepence for each elector on the register.

RE-ELECTION OF MINISTERS ACT, 1919
9 Geo. 5, c. 2

An Act to make provision for restricting the necessity of the re-election of Members of the House of Commons on acceptance of office, and to make provision as to the right of certain Ministers to sit in the House of Commons.

[*27th February 1919.*]

1.—(1) Notwithstanding anything in any Act, a member of the Commons House of Parliament shall not vacate his seat by reason only of his acceptance of an office of profit if that office is an office the holder of which is capable of being elected to, or sitting or voting in, that House, and if such acceptance has taken place within nine months after the issue of a proclamation summoning a new Parliament:

Provided that this section shall not apply to the acceptance of any office mentioned in the schedule to this Act, nor shall it affect the provisions of any Act imposing a limit on the number of Secretaries or Under Secretaries of State who may sit and vote in the Commons House of Parliament.

(2) Where by virtue of this section a member of the Commons House of Parliament does not vacate his seat by reason of his acceptance of any of the offices mentioned in Schedule H. of the Representation of the People Act, 1867, and Schedule H. of the Representation of the People (Scotland) Act, 1868, and Schedule E. of the Representation of the People (Ireland) Act, 1868, as amended by any subsequent enactment, he shall, for the purposes of section fifty-two, section fifty-one, and section eleven of those Acts, respectively, be treated as if he had been returned as a member to serve in Parliament since the acceptance by him of such office.

(3) This section shall be deemed to have had effect as from the first day of January nineteen hundred and nineteen.

2. Where, before or after the passing of this Act, a member of His Majesty's Privy Council has been or is appointed to be a Minister of the Crown at a salary, without any other office being assigned to him, he shall not by reason thereof be deemed to have been or to be incapable of being elected to or of sitting or voting in the Commons House of Parliament, and the office of such Minister shall be deemed to be an office included in the above-mentioned schedules:

Provided that not more than three Ministers to whom this section applies shall sit as members of that House at the same time.

3. This Act may be cited as the Re-election of Ministers Act, 1919.

Schedule

Excepted Offices

Office of Steward or Bailiff of His Majesty's three Chiltern Hundreds of Stoke, Desborough and Burnham.

Office of Steward or Bailiff of the Manors of East Hendred, Northstead or Hempholme.

MINISTRY OF HEALTH ACT, 1919
9 and 10 Geo. 5, c. 21

1. For the purpose of promoting the health of the people throughout England and Wales, and for the purpose of the exercise of the powers transferred or conferred by this Act, it shall be lawful for His Majesty to appoint a Minister of Health (hereinafter called "the Minister"), who shall hold office during His Majesty's pleasure.

2.—It shall be the duty of the Minister, in the exercise and performance of any powers and duties transferred to or conferred upon him by or in pursuance of this Act, to take all such steps as may be desirable to secure the preparation, effective carrying out and co-ordination of measures conducive to the health of the people, including measures for the prevention and cure of diseases, the avoidance of fraud in connection with alleged remedies therefor, the treatment of physical and mental defects, the treatment and care of the blind, the initiation and direction of research, the collection, preparation, publication, and dissemination of information and statistics relating thereto, and the training of persons for health services.

3.—(1) There shall be transferred to the Minister—

(a) all the powers and duties of the Local Government Board;

(b) all the powers and duties of the Insurance Commissioners and the Welsh Insurance Commissioners;

(c) all the powers of the Board of Education with respect to attending to the health of expectant mothers and nursing mothers and of children who have not attained the age of five years and are not in attendance at schools recognised by the Board of Education;

(d) all the powers and duties of the Board of Education with respect to the medical inspection and treatment of children and young persons under paragraph (b) of subsection (1) of section thirteen of the Education (Administrative Provisions) Act, 1907, as amended and extended by the Education Act, 1918: Provided that, for the purpose of facilitating the effective exercise and performance of these powers and duties, the Minister may make arrangements with the Board of Education respecting the submission and approval of schemes of local education authorities and the payment of grants to local education authorities, so far as such schemes and payment relate to or are in respect of medical inspection and treatment; and the powers and duties of the Minister may under any such arrangements be exercised and performed by the Board on his behalf and with his authority under such conditions as he may think fit;

(e) all the powers of the Privy Council and of the Lord President of the Council under the Midwives Acts, 1902 and 1918;

(f) such powers of supervising the administration of Part I. of the Children Act, 1908 (which relates to infant life protection), as have heretofore been exercised by the Secretary of State:

Provided that—

(i) the power conferred on the Insurance Commissioners by the proviso to subsection (2) of section sixteen of the National Insurance Act, 1911, of retaining and applying for the purposes of research such sums as are therein mentioned shall not be transferred to the Minister, but the duties heretofore performed by the Medical Research Committee shall after the date of the commencement of this Act be carried on by or under the direction of a Committee of the Privy Council appointed by His Majesty for that purpose, and any property held for the purposes of the former Committee shall after that date be transferred to and vested in such persons as the body by whom such duties as aforesaid are carried on may appoint, and be held by them for the purposes of that body; and

(ii) in such matters of a judicial nature under the National Insurance (Health) Acts, 1911 to 1918, as may be prescribed under those Acts, the powers and duties of the Insurance Commissioners and the Welsh Insurance Commissioners by this Act transferred to the Minister shall be exercised by the Minister through a special body or special bodies of persons constituted in such manner as may be so prescribed.

(2) It shall be lawful for His Majesty from time to time by Order in Council to transfer to the Minister—

(*a*) all or any of the powers and duties of the Minister of Pensions with respect to the health of disabled officers and men after they have left the service;

(*b*) all or any of the powers and duties of the Secretary of State under the enactments relating to lunacy and mental deficiency;

(*c*) any other powers and duties in England and Wales of any Government department which appear to His Majesty to relate to matters affecting or incidental to the health of the people.

(3) It shall be lawful for His Majesty from time to time by Order in Council to transfer from the Minister to any other Government department any of the powers and duties of the Minister, whether relating to the relief of the poor or otherwise, which appear to His Majesty not to relate to matters affecting or incidental to the health of the people.

And it is hereby declared that it is the intention of this Act that, in the event of provision being made by Act of Parliament passed in the present or in any future session for the revision of the law relating to the relief of the poor and the distribution amongst other authorities of the powers exerciseable by boards of guardians, there shall be transferred from the Minister to other Government departments such of the powers and duties under the enactments relating to the relief of the poor then vested in the Minister (not being powers or duties relating or incidental to the health of the people) as appear to His Majesty to be such as could be more conveniently exercised and performed by such other departments.

(4) His Majesty may by Order in Council make such incidental, consequential, and supplemental provisions as may be necessary or expedient for the purpose of giving full effect to any transfer of powers or duties by or under this section, including provisions for the transfer of any property, rights, and liabilities held, enjoyed, or incurred by any Government department in connection with any powers or duties transferred, and may make such adaptations in the enactments relating to such powers or duties as may be necessary to make exerciseable by the Minister and his officers or by such other Government department and their officers, as the case may be, the powers and duties so transferred.

(5) In connection with the transfer of powers and duties to or from the Minister by or under this Act, the provisions set out in the First Schedule to this Act shall have effect.

4.—(1) It shall be lawful for His Majesty by Order in Council to establish consultative councils in England and Wales for giving, in accordance with the provisions of the Order, advice and assistance to the Minister in connection with such matters affecting or incidental to the health of the people as may be referred to in such Order.

(2) Every such council shall include women as well as men, and shall consist of persons having practical experience of the matters referred to the Council.

5. The Minister shall, subject to the provisions of this Act, appoint such officers as he may think fit to constitute a Board of Health in Wales through whom he may exercise and perform in Wales in such manner as he may think fit any of his powers and duties; the Board and any officer who is a member thereof shall act under the directions, and comply with the instructions, of the Minister.

[§ 6. Staff and remuneration.]
[§ 7. Seal, style and acts of the Minister.]

8.—(1) Any Order in Council made under this Act may be revoked or varied by a subsequent Order.

(2) Before any Order in Council under this Act (other than an Order appointing a day for the commencement of this Act or any provision thereof) is made, notice of the proposal to make the Order and of the place where copies of a draft of the Order can be obtained shall be published in the London Gazette, and in such other manner as the Minister thinks best adapted for insuring publicity, and a draft of the Order shall be laid before each House of Parliament for not less than thirty days on which such House is sitting.

(3) In the case of a draft of an Order providing for any transfer of powers or duties to or from the Minister under subsections (2) and (3) of section three of this Act, or for the establishment of any consultative council under section four thereof, the Order shall not be made until

both Houses by resolution have approved the draft, nor, if any modifications are agreed to by both Houses, otherwise than as so modified, and in the case of a draft of any other Order which is required to be laid as aforesaid, if either House before the expiration of such thirty days presents an Address to His Majesty against the draft, or any part thereof, no further proceedings shall be taken thereon, without prejudice to the making of any new draft Order.

[§ 9. Modifications of Insurance Acts.]
[§ 10. The Chief Secretary to be the Minister of Health for Ireland.]
[§ 11. Short title, interpretation, etc. Two schedules.]

POLICE ACT, 1919
9 and 10 Geo. 5, c. 46

1.—(1) For the purpose of enabling the members of the police forces of England and Wales to consider and bring to the notice of the police authorities and the Secretary of State all the matters affecting their welfare and efficiency, other than questions of discipline and promotion affecting individuals, there shall be established in accordance with the Schedule[1] to this Act an organisation to be called the Police Federation, which shall act through local and central representative bodies as provided in that schedule.

(2) The Police Federation and every branch thereof shall be entirely independent of and unassociated with any body or person outside the police service.

2.—(1) Subject as aforesaid, it shall not be lawful for a member of a police force to become, or after the expiration of one month from the passing of this Act to be, a member of any trade union, or of any association having for its objects, or one of its objects, to control or influence the pay, pensions, or conditions of service of any police force; and any member of a police force who contravenes this provision shall be disqualified for continuing to be a member of the force; and, if any member of a police force continues to act as such after becoming so disqualified, he shall forfeit all pension rights and be disqualified for being thereafter employed in any police force;

Provided that, where a man was a member of a trade union before becoming a constable, he may, with the consent of the chief officer of police, continue to be a member of that union during the time of his service in the police force.

(2) If any question arises whether any body is a trade union or an association to which this section applies, the question shall be determined by the Minister of Labour.

[1] Schedule omitted.

3. If any person causes, or attempts to cause, or does any act calculated to cause disaffection amongst the members of any police force, or induces, or attempts to induce, or does any act calculated to induce any member of a police force to withhold his services or to commit breaches of discipline, he shall be guilty of a misdemeanour, and shall be liable on conviction on indictment to imprisonment, with or without hard labour, for a term not exceeding two years, or on summary conviction, to imprisonment, with or without hard labour, for a term not exceeding three months, or to a fine not exceeding fifty pounds, or to both such imprisonment and fine, and in either case, if a member of a police force, shall forfeit all pension rights and be disqualified for being a member of any police force: Provided that, where the person convicted of any such offence was a member of a police force and was not sentenced to imprisonment without the option of a fine, the police authority may, if they think fit, pay to him the whole or any part of the rateable deductions which may have been made from his pay.

4.—(1) It shall be lawful for the Secretary of State to make regulations as to the government, mutual aid, pay, allowances, pensions, clothing, expenses and conditions of service of the members of all police forces within England and Wales, and every police authority shall comply with the regulations so made.

(2) A draft of any regulations proposed to be so made as aforesaid shall be submitted to a council, consisting of the joint central committee or a deputation from the joint central committee of the Police Federation and representatives of the chief officers of police and police authorities selected for the purpose by the Secretary of State, after consultation with the County Councils Association and the Association of Municipal Corporations, and before making the regulations the Secretary of State shall consider any representations made by such council.

[§§ 5–6. Pensions.]
[§ 7. Abolition of limits on police rates.]

8.—(1) The amounts payable or transferable by a county council under subsection (2) of section twenty-four of the Local Government Act, 1888, on account of police in respect of the year ending the thirty-first day of March, nineteen hundred and twenty, or any subsequent year shall, instead of being calculated in manner provided in paragraphs (*i*) and (*j*) of that subsection, be the full amounts payable or transferable in accordance with the said paragraphs in respect of the year ending the thirty-first day of March, nineteen hundred and fifteen.

(2) This section shall be construed as one with the Local Government Act, 1888, and shall apply to county borough councils in like manner as it applies to county councils.

9. It shall be lawful for the police authority of any police force, out of the police fund, to make contributions to any provident fund approved by the Secretary of State out of which provision is made for payments to members of the police force on their retirement, or, on their death, to their widows, dependants, or representatives.

10. If any person not being a member of a police force wears without the permission of the police authority the uniform of the police force, or any dress having the appearance or bearing any of the distinctive marks of that uniform, he shall on summary conviction be liable to a fine not exceeding ten pounds:

Provided that this section shall not prevent persons from wearing any uniform or dress in the course of a stage play or music hall or circus performance.

12. This Act shall apply to the City of London Police and to every police force to which the Police Act, 1890, applies. . . .

13.—(1) This Act shall apply to Scotland, with the substitution of references to the Secretary for Scotland for references to the Secretary of State, of references to Scotland for references to England and Wales, and of references to the Police (Scotland) Act, 1890, for references to the Police Act, 1890, and in the case of the schedule, subject to such modifications as the Secretary for Scotland may by order prescribe for the purpose of adapting the provisions of that schedule to the circumstances of Scotland. . . .

14. In making regulations as to government, mutual aid, pay, allowances, pensions, clothing, expenses and conditions of service of members of the police force, the Secretary of State and the Secretary for Scotland shall act in consultation one with another.

15.—(1) This Act may be cited as the Police Act, 1919.

(2) This Act shall not extend to Ireland.

CHURCH OF ENGLAND ASSEMBLY (POWERS) ACT, 1919
9 and 10 Geo. 5, c. 76

Whereas the Convocations of Canterbury and York have recommended in Addresses presented to His Majesty on the tenth day of May nineteen hundred and nineteen, that, subject to the control and authority of His Majesty and of the two Houses of Parliament, powers in regard to legislation touching matters concerning the Church of England shall be conferred on the National Assembly of the Church of England constituted in the manner set forth in identical terms in the Appendix attached to their several Addresses:

And whereas it is expedient, subject to such control and authority as aforesaid, that such powers should be conferred on the Church Assembly so constituted:

Be it therefore enacted . . .

[§ 1. The National Assembly of the Church of England, the Constitution of the Assembly and the Legislative Committee shall be as set out in the Addresses.]

2.—(1) There shall be a Committee of members of both Houses of Parliament styled "The Ecclesiastical Committee."

(2) The Ecclesiastical Committee shall consist of fifteen members of the House of Lords, nominated by the Lord Chancellor, and fifteen members of the House of Commons, nominated by the Speaker of the House of Commons, to be appointed on the passing of this Act to serve for the duration of the present Parliament and thereafter to be appointed at the commencement of each Parliament to serve for the duration of that Parliament.

Any casual vacancy occurring by the reason of the death, resignation, or incapacity of a member of the Ecclesiastical Committee shall be filled by the nomination of a member by the Lord Chancellor or the Speaker of the House of Commons, as the case may be.

(3) The powers and duties of the Ecclesiastical Committee may be exercised and discharged by any twelve members thereof, and the Committee shall be entitled to sit and to transact business whether Parliament be sitting or not, and notwithstanding a vacancy in the membership of the Committee. Subject to the provisions of this Act, the Ecclesiastical Committee may regulate its own procedure.

3.—(1) Every measure passed by the Church Assembly shall be submitted by the Legislative Committee to the Ecclesiastical Committee, together with such comments and explanations as the Legislative Committee may deem it expedient or be directed by the Church Assembly to add.

(2) The Ecclesiastical Committee shall thereupon consider the measure so submitted to it, and may, at any time during such consideration, either of its own motion or at the request of the Legislative Committee, invite the Legislative Committee to a conference to discuss the provisions thereof, and thereupon a conference of the two committees shall be held accordingly.

(3) After considering the measure, the Ecclesiastical Committee shall draft a report thereon to Parliament stating the nature and legal effect of the measure and its views as to the expediency thereof, especially with relation to the constitutional rights of all His Majesty's subjects.

(4) The Ecclesiastical Committee shall communicate its report in draft to the Legislative Committee, but shall not present it to Parliament until the Legislative Committee signify its desire that it should be so presented.

(5) At any time before the presentation of the report to Parliament the Legislative Committee may, either on its own motion or by direction of the Church Assembly, withdraw a measure from further consideration by the Ecclesiastical Committee; but the Legislative Committee shall have no power to vary a measure of the Church Assembly either before or after conference with the Ecclesiastical Committee.

(6) A measure may relate to any matter concerning the Church of England, and may extend to the amendment or repeal in whole or in part of any Act of Parliament, including this Act:

Provided that a measure shall not make any alteration in the composition or powers or duties of the Ecclesiastical Committee, or in the procedure in Parliament prescribed by section four of this Act.

(7) No proceedings of the Church Assembly in relation to a measure shall be invalidated by any vacancy in the membership of the Church Assembly or by any defect in the qualification or election of any member thereof.

4. When the Ecclesiastical Committee shall have reported to Parliament on any measure submitted by the Legislative Committee, the report together with the text of such measure, shall be laid before both Houses of Parliament forthwith, if Parliament be then sitting, or, if not, then immediately after the next meeting of Parliament, and thereupon, on a resolution being passed by each House of Parliament directing that such measure in the form laid before Parliament should be presented to His Majesty, such measure shall be presented to His Majesty, and shall have the force and effect of an Act of Parliament on the Royal Assent being signified thereto in the same manner as to Acts of Parliament:

Provided that, if upon a measure being laid before Parliament the Chairman of Committees of the House of Lords and the Chairman of Ways and Means in the House of Commons acting in consultation, shall be of opinion that the measure deals with two or more different subjects which might be more properly divided, they may, by joint agreement, divide the measure into two or more separate measures accordingly, and thereupon this section shall have effect as if each of the measures resulting from such division had been laid before Parliament as a separate measure.

5. This Act may be cited as the Church of England Assembly (Powers) Act, 1919.

EMERGENCY POWERS ACT, 1920
10 and 11 Geo. 5, c. 55

1.—(1) If at any time it appears to His Majesty that any action has been taken or is immediately threatened by any persons or body of persons of such a nature and on so extensive a scale as to be calculated, by interfering with the supply and distribution of food, water, fuel, or light, or with the means of locomotion, to deprive the community, or any substantial portion of the community, of the essentials of life, His Majesty may, by proclamation (hereinafter referred to as a proclamation of emergency), declare that a state of emergency exists.

No such proclamation shall be in force for more than one month, without prejudice to the issue of another proclamation at or before the end of that period.

(2) Where a proclamation of emergency has been made, the occasion thereof shall forthwith be communicated to Parliament, and, if Parliament is then separated by such adjournment or prorogation as will not expire within five days, a proclamation shall be issued for the meeting of Parliament within five days, and Parliament shall accordingly meet and sit upon the day appointed by that proclamation, and shall continue to sit and act in like manner as if it had stood adjourned or prorogued to the same day.

2.—(1) Where a proclamation of emergency has been made, and so long as the proclamation is in force, it shall be lawful for His Majesty in Council, by Order, to make regulations for securing the essentials of life to the community, and those regulations may confer or impose on a Secretary of State or other Government department, or any other persons in His Majesty's service or acting on His Majesty's behalf, such powers and duties as His Majesty may deem necessary for the preservation of the peace, for securing and regulating the supply and distribution of food, water, fuel, light, and other necessities, for maintaining the means of transit or locomotion, and for any other purposes essential to the public safety and the life of the community, and may make such provisions incidental to the powers aforesaid as may appear to His Majesty to be required for making the exercise of those powers effective:

Provided that nothing in this Act shall be construed to authorise the making of any regulations imposing any form of compulsory military service or industrial conscription:

Provided also that no such regulation shall make it an offence for any person or persons to take part in a strike, or peacefully to persuade any other person or persons to take part in a strike.

(2) Any regulations so made shall be laid before Parliament as soon as may be after they are made, and shall not continue in force after

the expiration of seven days from the time when they are so laid unless a resolution is passed by both Houses providing for the continuance thereof.

(3) The regulations may provide for the trial, by courts of summary jurisdiction, of persons guilty of offences against the regulations; so, however, that the maximum penalty which may be inflicted for any offence against any such regulations shall be imprisonment with or without hard labour for a term of three months, or a fine of one hundred pounds, or both such imprisonment and fine, together with the forfeiture of any goods or money in respect of which the offence has been committed: Provided that no such regulations shall alter any existing procedure in criminal cases, or confer any right to punish by fine or imprisonment without trial.

(4) The regulations so made shall have effect as if enacted in this Act, but may be added to, altered or revoked by resolution of both Houses of Parliament or by regulations made in like manner and subject to the like provisions as the original regulations; and regulations made under this section shall not be deemed to be statutory rules within the meaning of section one of the Rules Publication Act, 1893.

(5) The expiry or revocation of any regulations so made shall not be deemed to have affected the previous operation thereof, or the validity of any action taken thereunder, or any penalty or punishment incurred in respect of any contravention or failure to comply therewith, or any proceeding or remedy in respect of any such punishment or penalty.

3.—(1) This Act may be cited as the Emergency Powers Act, 1920.

(2) This Act shall not apply to Ireland.

OFFICIAL SECRETS ACT, 1920
10 and 11 Geo. 5, c. 75

An Act to amend the Official Secrets Act, 1911.

[*23rd December 1920.*]

1. If any person for the purpose of gaining admission, or of assisting any other person to gain admission, to a prohibited place, within the meaning of the Official Secrets Act, 1911 (hereinafter referred to as "the principal Act"), or for any other purpose prejudicial to the safety or interests of the State within the meaning of the said Acts—

(*a*) uses or wears, without lawful authority, any naval, military, air-force, police, or other official uniform, or any uniform so nearly resembling the same as to be calculated to deceive, or falsely represents himself to be a person who is or has been entitled to use or wear any such uniform; or

(b) orally, or in writing in any declaration or application, or in any document signed by him or on his behalf, knowingly makes or connives at the making of any false statement or any omission; or

(c) forges, alters, or tampers with any passport or any naval, military, air-force, police, or official pass, permit, certificate, licence, or other document of a similar character (hereinafter in this section referred to as an official document), or uses or has in his possession any such forged, altered, or irregular official document; or

(d) personates, or falsely represents himself to be a person holding, or in the employment of a person holding office under His Majesty, or to be or not to be a person to whom an official document or secret official code word or pass word has been duly issued or communicated, or with intent to obtain an official document, secret official code word or pass word, whether for himself or any other person, knowingly makes any false statement; or

(e) uses, or has in his possession or under his control, without the authority of the Government Department or the authority concerned, any die, seal, or stamp of or belonging to, or used, made or provided by any Government Department, or by any diplomatic, naval, military, or air-force authority appointed by or acting under the authority of His Majesty, or any die, seal or stamp so nearly resembling any such die, seal or stamp as to be calculated to deceive, or counterfeits any such die, seal or stamp, or uses, or has in his possession, or under his control, any such counterfeited die, seal or stamp;

he shall be guilty of a misdemeanour.

(2) If any person—

(a) retains for any purpose prejudicial to the safety or interests of the State any official document, whether or not completed or issued for use, when he has no right to retain it, or when it is contrary to his duty to retain it, or fails to comply with any directions issued by any Government Department or any person authorised by such department with regard to the return or disposal thereof; or

(b) allows any other person to have possession of any official document issued for his use alone, or communicates any secret official code word or pass word so issued, or, without lawful authority or excuse, has in his possession any official document or secret official code word or pass word issued for the use of some person other than himself, or on obtaining possession of any official documents by finding or otherwise, neglects or fails to restore it to the person or authority by whom or for whose use it was issued, or to a police constable; or

(*c*) without lawful authority or excuse, manufactures or sells, or has in his possession for sale any such die, seal or stamp as aforesaid;

he shall be guilty of a misdemeanour.

(3) In the case of any prosecution under this section involving the proof of a purpose prejudicial to the safety or interests of the State, subsection (2) of section one of the principal Act shall apply in like manner as it applies to prosecutions under that section.

2.—(1) In any proceedings against a person for an offence under section one of the principal Act, the fact that he has been in communication with, or attempted to communicate with, a foreign agent, whether within or without the United Kingdom, shall be evidence that he has, for a purpose prejudicial to the safety or interests of the State, obtained or attempted to obtain information which is calculated to be or might be or is intended to be directly or indirectly useful to an enemy.

(2) For the purpose of this section, but without prejudice to the generality of the foregoing provision—

(*a*) A person shall, unless he proves the contrary, be deemed to have been in communication with a foreign agent if—

(i) He has, either within or without the United Kingdom, visited the address of a foreign agent or consorted or associated with a foreign agent; or

(ii) Either, within or without the United Kingdom, the name or address of, or any other information regarding a foreign agent has been found in his possession, or has been supplied by him to any other person, or has been obtained by him from any other person:

(*b*) The expression "foreign agent" includes any person who is or has been or is reasonably suspected of being or having been employed by a foreign power either directly or indirectly for the purpose of committing an act, either within or without the United Kingdom, prejudicial to the safety or interests of the State, or who has or is reasonably suspected of having, either within or without the United Kingdom, committed, or attempted to commit, such an act in the interests of a foreign power:

(*c*) Any address, whether within or without the United Kingdom, reasonably suspected of being an address used for the receipt of communications intended for a foreign agent, or any address at which a foreign agent resides, or to which he resorts for the purpose of giving or receiving communications, or at which he carries on any business, shall be deemed to be the address of a foreign agent, and communications addressed to such an address to be communications with a foreign agent.

3. No person in the vicinity of any prohibited place shall obstruct, knowingly mislead or otherwise interfere with or impede, the chief officer or a superintendent or other officer of police, or any member of His Majesty's forces engaged on guard, sentry, patrol, or other similar duty in relation to the prohibited place, and, if any person acts in contravention of, or fails to comply with, this provision, he shall be guilty of a misdemeanour.

[§ 4. The Secretary of State is to have power to require the production of telegrams.]

[§ 5. Those who carry on the business of receiving postal packets are to be registered with the police.]

6. It shall be the duty of every person to give on demand to a chief officer of police, or to a superintendent or other officer of police not below the rank of inspector appointed by a chief officer for the purpose, or to any member of His Majesty's forces engaged on guard, sentry, patrol, or other similar duty, any information in his power relating to an offence or suspected offence under the principal Act or this Act, and, if so required, and upon tender of his reasonable expenses, to attend at such reasonable time and place as may be specified for the purpose of furnishing such information, and, if any person fails to give any such information or to attend as aforesaid, he shall be guilty of a misdemeanour.

[§ 7. Attempts to commit an offence, and incitement of others.]

8.—(1) Any person who is guilty of a felony under the principal Act or this Act shall be liable to penal servitude for a term of not less than three years and not exceeding fourteen years.

(2) Any person who is guilty of a misdemeanour under the principal Act or this Act shall be liable on conviction on indictment to imprisonment, with or without hard labour, for a term not exceeding two years, or, on conviction under the Summary Jurisdiction Acts, to imprisonment, with or without hard labour, for a term not exceeding three months or to a fine not exceeding fifty pounds, or both such imprisonment and fine:

Provided that no misdemeanour under the principal Act or this Act shall be dealt with summarily except with the consent of the Attorney-General.

(3) For the purposes of the trial of a person for an offence under the principal Act or this Act, the offence shall be deemed to have been committed either at the place in which the same actually was committed, or at any place in the United Kingdom in which the offender may be found.

(4) In addition and without prejudice to any powers which a court may possess to order the exclusion of the public from any proceedings if, in the course of proceedings before a court against any person for an

offence under the principal Act or this Act or the proceedings on appeal, or in the course of the trial of a person for felony or misdemeanour under the principal Act or this Act, application is made by the prosecution, on the ground that the publication of any evidence to be given or of any statement to be made in the course of the proceedings would be prejudicial to the national safety, that all or any portion of the public shall be excluded during any part of the hearing, the court may make an order to that effect, but the passing of sentence shall in any case take place in public.

(5) Where the person guilty of an offence under the principal Act or this Act is a company or corporation, every director and officer of the company or corporation shall be guilty of the like offence unless he proves that the act or omission constituting the offence took place without his knowledge or consent.

[§§ 9–11 and two schedules omitted.]

RATING AND VALUATION ACT, 1925
15 and 16 Geo. 5, c. 90

Part I

Rating

1.—(1) The council of every county borough and the council of every urban and rural district shall be the rating authority for the borough or for the county district, and from and after the appointed day no authority or person other than the council shall have power to make or levy any rate within the borough or district.

(2) As from the appointed day all powers and duties of the overseers of the poor in relation to the making, levying, and collection of rates, and of any other person who by virtue of any local Act has powers in that behalf, shall in every rating area be exercised and performed by the rating authority. . . .

2.—(1) As from the date of the first new valuation, the rating authority of each urban rating area, in lieu of the poor rate and any other rate which they have power to make, shall make and levy for their area a consolidated rate which shall be termed "the general rate."

(2) As from the appointed day the rating authority of each rural rating area shall, in lieu of making a poor rate for each parish, make and levy a general rate for the whole of the district.

(3) Subject to the provisions of this Act, every general rate shall be a rate at a uniform amount per pound on the rateable value of each hereditament in the rating area, and shall be made, levied and

collected, and shall be recoverable, in the same manner in which at the commencement of this Act the poor rate may be made, levied, collected and recovered, and all the enactments relating to the poor rate which are in force at the commencement of this Act, including (subject to the provisions of this Act) enactments relating to appeals against a poor rate, shall, so far as not repealed by this Act, apply to the general rate. . . .

Part II

Valuation

39.—(1) If at any time it is shown to the satisfaction of the High Court, on an application made by the Minister, or the council of any county or county borough concerned, that there is reason to apprehend that by reason of default made by any authority, committee or person in complying with any of the provisions of this Part of this Act a valuation list for any area will not be duly prepared in accordance with those provisions so as to come into force on the proper date, the court may appoint such person as they think fit to make and approve the list for the said area or to do any such things as ought to have been done by the authority, committee or person in default. . . .

Part III

General

66.—(1) The Minister may by order make such adaptations in the provisions of any local Act as may seem to him to be necessary in order to make those provisions conform with the provisions of this Act.

(2) Every order made under this section shall be laid before both Houses of Parliament forthwith, and if an Address is presented to His Majesty by either House of Parliament within the next subsequent twenty-eight days on which that House has sat after any such order is laid before it praying that the order may be annulled it shall thenceforth be void, but without prejudice to the validity of anything previously done thereunder or the making of a new order.

67.—(1) If any difficulty arises in connection with the application of this Act to any exceptional area, or the preparation of the first valuation list for any area, or otherwise in bringing into operation any of the provisions of this Act, the Minister may by order remove the difficulty or constitute any assessment committee, or declare any assessment committee to be duly constituted, or make any appointment, or do any other thing, which appears to him necessary or expedient for securing the due preparation of the list or for bringing the said provisions into operation, and any such order may modify the provisions of this Act so far as may appear to the Minister necessary or expedient for carrying the order into effect:

Provided that the Minister shall not exercise the powers conferred by this section after the thirty-first day of March, nineteen hundred and twenty-nine.

(2) Every order made under this section shall be laid before both Houses of Parliament forthwith, and if an Address is presented to His Majesty by either House of Parliament within the next subsequent twenty-eight days on which that House has sat after any such order is laid before it praying that the order may be annulled it shall thenceforth be void, but without prejudice to the validity of anything previously done thereunder or the making of a new order.

(3) In this section the expression "exceptional area" includes any county district which extends into two or more counties or is administered by the council of another district, and any parish which extends into two or more counties or county districts, or which is not within the same district for municipal and sanitary purposes.

[§§ 68–70 and eight schedules omitted.]

BOARDS OF GUARDIANS (DEFAULT) ACT, 1926
16 and 17 Geo. 5, c. 20

1.—(1) Where it appears to the Minister of Health . . . that the board of guardians for any poor law union have ceased, or are acting in a manner as will render them unable, to discharge all or any of the functions exerciseable by the board, the Minister may by order under this Act appoint such person or persons, as he may think fit (whether qualified or not to be guardians for the union), to constitute the board in substitution for the then existing members of the board (who shall on the making of the order vacate their office) for such period, not exceeding twelve months, as may be specified in the order, and the persons so appointed shall be deemed for all purposes to constitute the board. . . .

(2) The Minister may at any time, and from time to time, by order extend, for a period not exceeding six months, the term of office of the appointed guardians.

An order made under this subsection shall be laid before both Houses of Parliament as soon as may be after it is made, and if either House within twenty-one days after the order has been laid before it presents an address to His Majesty praying that the order may be annulled, His Majesty may by Order in Council annul the order and it shall thenceforth be void, but without prejudice to the validity of anything previously done thereunder, or the making of a fresh order.

[Subsections (3) (4) and (5) of § 1, and § 2 omitted.]

LOCAL GOVERNMENT (COUNTY BOROUGHS AND ADJUSTMENTS) ACT, 1926
16 and 17 Geo. 5, c. 38

1.—(1) It shall not be lawful for the Minister of Health by Provisional Order to constitute a borough into a county borough, and accordingly paragraph (*d*) of subsection (1) of section fifty-four of the Local Government Act, 1888, and in subsection (3) of the same section the words "or for constituting a borough into a county borough" shall be repealed.

(2) It shall not be lawful for the council of any borough to promote a Bill for the purpose of constituting the borough into a county borough unless the population of the borough, according to the published returns of the last census, for the time being is seventy-five thousand or upwards.

2.—(1) Where under section fifty-four of the Local Government Act, 1888, a representation is made to the Minister of Health by the council of a county borough for any purpose involving the extension of the area of the county borough, the Minister shall not entertain the representation—

(*a*) unless he is satisfied that the council of the county borough have sent to the councils of the counties, boroughs and districts affected notice of the proposed representation, together with a draft of the order which they desire to have made to give effect to their proposals; and

(*b*) unless no notice of objection to procedure by Provisional Order has been sent to him by any such council within four weeks from the receipt of the notice from the county borough council, or unless every such notice or objection has been withdrawn.

(2) Where in consequence of any such notice of objection or on any other ground the Minister declines to entertain the representation, the application for the Provisional Order shall be deemed and taken to be a petition for leave to bring in a Private Bill . . .:

Provided that the council of a county borough shall forthwith inform all persons who have objected to the Provisional Order and other interested persons of their intention to proceed by way of Private Bill.

[§ 3. Modification of the Borough Funds Acts, 1872 and 1903.]

4. Nothing in the foregoing provisions of this Act shall apply to the union of two county boroughs or affect the powers of the Minister of Health to effect such a union by Provisional Order.

[§ 5 (Amendment to Local Government (Adjustments) Act, 1913) and § 6 (Short title) omitted.]

ROMAN CATHOLIC RELIEF ACT, 1926
16 and 17 Geo. 5, c. 55

An Act to provide for the further relief of His Majesty's Roman Catholic subjects.

[*15th December 1926.*]

1. The enactments specified in the Schedule to this Act are hereby repealed to the extent mentioned in the said Schedule.

2. Nothing herein contained shall affect in any manner whatsoever any power conferred by any Act of Parliament, or by any byelaw made pursuant to any Act of Parliament, upon any local authority in Great Britain to make regulations relating to, or otherwise to control, any meeting or procession in or through any street or other public place whatsoever, or in or through any unfenced ground adjoining or abutting upon any such street or place, nor the power of any local authority conferred by any Act of Parliament to make byelaws relating to any such meeting or procession.

3. Nothing in this Act nor the repeal of any enactments or parts thereof specified in the Schedule thereof shall in any way alter, add to, or abridge the law relating to services, acts, matters or things performed or done in any church or chapel of the established Church of England or relating to clergy or ministers of the said established Church of England, or relating to any right of presentation to any benefice or other ecclesiastical living or office in the established Church of England.

Nothing herein contained shall adversely affect the title to properties which were vested in the Crown by the statute, 1 Eliz., cap. 24.

4. This Act may be cited as the Roman Catholic Relief Act, 1926, and shall not apply to Northern Ireland.

Schedule

Enactments Repealed

Session and Chapter	Short Title	Extent of Repeal
3 & 4 Edw. 6. cap. 10.	. . . . . .	The whole Act.
1 Eliz. cap. 24	. . . . . .	The whole Act, except sections three, ten, twelve and sixteen.
1 Geo. 1. St. 2. cap. 50.	. . . . . .	The whole Act.
31 Geo. 3. cap. 32.	The Roman Catholic Relief Act, 1791.	Sections eleven and seventeen.
10 Geo. 4. cap. 7.	The Roman Catholic Relief Act, 1829.	Section twenty-six, sections twenty-eight to thirty-six inclusive. The Schedule.
2 & 3 Will. 4. cap. 115.	The Roman Catholic Charities Act, 1832.	Section four.
23 & 24 Vict. cap. 134.	The Roman Catholic Charities Act, 1860.	Section seven.

ROYAL AND PARLIAMENTARY TITLES ACT, 1927
17 Geo. 5, c. 4

An Act to provide for the alteration of the Royal Style and Titles and of the Style of Parliament and for purposes incidental thereto.

[*12th April 1927.*]

1. It shall be lawful for His Most Gracious Majesty, by His Royal Proclamation under the Great Seal of the Realm, issued within six months after the passing of this Act, to make such alteration in the style and titles at present appertaining to the Crown as to His Majesty may seem fit.

2.—(1) Parliament shall hereafter be known as and styled the Parliament of the United Kingdom of Great Britain and Northern Ireland; and accordingly, the present Parliament shall be known as the Thirty-fourth Parliament of the United Kingdom of Great Britain and Northern Ireland, instead of the Thirty-fourth Parliament of the United Kingdom of Great Britain and Ireland.

(2) In every Act passed and public document issued after the passing of this Act the expression "United Kingdom" shall, unless the context otherwise requires, mean Great Britain and Northern Ireland.

3. This Act may be cited as the Royal and Parliamentary Titles Act, 1927.

TRADE DISPUTES AND TRADE UNIONS ACT, 1927
17 and 18 Geo. 5, c. 22

1.—(1) It is hereby declared—

(*a*) that any strike is illegal if it—

(i) has any object other than or in addition to the furtherance of a trade dispute within the trade or industry in which the strikers are engaged; and

(ii) is a strike designed or calculated to coerce the Government either directly or by inflicting hardship upon the community; and

(*b*) that any lock-out is illegal if it—

(i) has any object other than or in addition to the furtherance of a trade dispute within the trade or industry in which the employers locking-out are engaged; and

(ii) is a lock-out designed or calculated to coerce the Government either directly or by inflicting hardship upon the community:

and it is further declared that it is illegal to commence, or continue, or to apply any sums in furtherance or support of, any such illegal strike or lock-out. . . .

(2) If any person declares, instigates, incites others to take part in or otherwise acts in furtherance of a strike or lock-out, declared by this Act to be illegal, he shall be liable on summary conviction to a fine not exceeding ten pounds or to imprisonment for a term not exceeding three months, or on conviction on indictment to imprisonment for a term not exceeding two years:

Provided that no person shall be deemed to have committed an offence under this section or at common law by reason only of his having ceased work or refused to continue to work or to accept employment.

(3) Where any person is charged before any court with an offence under this section, no further proceedings in respect thereof shall be taken against him without the consent of the Attorney-General except such as the court may think necessary by remand (whether in custody or on bail) or otherwise to secure the safe custody of the person charged, but this subsection shall not apply to Scotland, or to any prosecution instituted by or on behalf of the Director of Public Prosecutions.

(4) The provisions of the Trade Disputes Act, 1906, shall not, nor shall the second proviso to subsection (1) of section two of the Emergency Powers Act, 1920, apply to any act done in contemplation or furtherance of a strike or lock-out which is by this Act declared to be illegal, and any such act shall not be deemed for the purposes of any enactment to be done in contemplation or furtherance of a trade dispute:

Provided that no person shall be deemed to have committed an offence under any regulations made under the Emergency Powers Act, 1920, by reason only of his having ceased work or having refused to continue to work or to accept employment.

2.—(1) No person refusing to take part or to continue to take part in any strike or lock-out which is by this Act declared to be illegal, shall be, by reason of such refusal or by reason of any action taken by him under this section, subject to expulsion from any trade union or society, or to any fine or penalty, or to deprivation of any right or benefit to which he or his legal personal representatives would otherwise be entitled, or liable to be placed in any respect either directly or indirectly under any disability or at any disadvantage as compared with other members of the union or society, anything to the contrary in the rules of a trade union or society notwithstanding.

(2) No provisions of the Trade Union Acts, 1871 to 1917, limiting the proceedings which may be entertained by any court, and nothing in the rules of a trade union or society requiring the settlement of disputes in any manner shall apply to any proceeding for enforcing any

right or exemption secured by this section, and in any such proceeding the court may, in lieu of ordering a person who has been expelled from membership of a trade union or society to be restored to membership, order that he be paid out of the funds of the trade union or society such sum by way of compensation or damages as the court thinks just.

(3) As respects any strike or lock-out before the passing of this Act but since the first day of May, nineteen hundred and twenty-six, which, according to the law as declared by this Act, was illegal, this section shall have effect as if it had been in operation when the strike or lock-out took place.

3.—(1) It is hereby declared that it is unlawful for one or more persons (whether acting on their own behalf or on behalf of a trade union or of an individual employer or firm, and notwithstanding that they may be acting in contemplation or furtherance of a trade dispute) to attend at or near a house or place where a person resides or works or carries on business or happens to be, for the purpose of obtaining or communicating information or of persuading or inducing any person to work or to abstain from working, if they so attend in such numbers or otherwise in such manner as to be calculated to intimidate any person in that house or place, or to obstruct the approach thereto or egress therefrom, or to lead to a breach of the peace; and attending at or near any house or place in such numbers or in such manner as is by this subsection declared to be unlawful shall be deemed to be a watching or besetting of that house or place within the meaning of section seven of the Conspiracy, and Protection of Property Act, 1875.

(2) In this section the expression "to intimidate" means to cause in the mind of a person a reasonable apprehension of injury to him or to any member of his family or to any of his dependants or of violence or damage to any person or property, and the expression "injury" includes injury to a person in respect of his business, occupation, employment or other source of income, and includes any actionable wrong.

(3) In section seven of the Conspiracy, and Protection of Property Act, 1875, the expression "intimidate" shall be construed as having the same meaning as in this section.

(4) Notwithstanding anything in any Act, it shall not be lawful for one or more persons, for the purpose of inducing any person to work or to abstain from working, to watch or beset a house or place where a person resides or the approach to such a house or place, and any person who acts in contravention of this subsection shall be liable on summary conviction to a fine not exceeding twenty pounds or to imprisonment for a term not exceeding three months.

4.—(1) It shall not be lawful to require any member of a trade union to make any contribution to the political fund of a trade union unless he has at some time after the commencement of this Act and before he is first after the thirty-first day of December, nineteen hundred and twenty-seven, required to make such a contribution delivered at the head office or some branch office of the trade union, notice in writing in the form set out in the First Schedule to this Act of his willingness to contribute to that fund and has not withdrawn the notice in manner hereinafter provided; and every member of a trade union who has not delivered such a notice as aforesaid, or who, having delivered such a notice, has withdrawn it in manner hereinafter provided, shall be deemed for the purposes of the Trade Union Act, 1913, to be a member who is exempt from the obligation to contribute to the political fund of the union, and references in that Act to a member who is so exempt shall be construed accordingly. . . .

(2) All contributions to the political fund of a trade union from members of the trade union who are liable to contribute to that fund shall be levied and made separately from any contributions to the other funds of the trade union and no assets of the trade union, other than the amount raised by such a separate levy as aforesaid, shall be carried to that fund, and no assets of a trade union other than those forming part of the political fund shall be directly or indirectly applied or charged in furtherance of any political object to which section three of the Trade Union Act, 1913, applies; and any charge in contravention of this subsection shall be void.

(3) All rules of a trade union made and approved in accordance with the requirements of section three of the Trade Union Act, 1913, shall be amended so as to conform to the requirements of this Act, and as so amended shall be approved by the Registrar of Friendly Societies. . . .

5.—(1) Amongst the regulations as to the conditions of service in His Majesty's civil establishments there shall be included regulations prohibiting established civil servants from being members, delegates, or representatives of any organisation of which the primary object is to influence or affect the remuneration and conditions of employment of its members, unless the organisation is an organisation of which the membership is confined to persons employed by or under the Crown and is an organisation which complies with such provisions as may be contained in the regulations for securing that it is in all respects independent of, and not affiliated to, any such organisation as aforesaid the membership of which is not confined to persons employed by or under the Crown or any federation comprising such organisations, that its objects do not include political objects, and that it is not associated directly or indirectly with any political party or organisation. . . .

(2) Subject as hereinafter provided, any established civil servant who contravenes the regulations made under this section shall be disqualified for being a member of the Civil Service:

Provided that, in the case of a first offence, a civil servant shall

forthwith be warned by the head of his department, and the said disqualification shall not take effect if within one month after such warning
the civil servant ceases to contravene the said regulations. . . .

6.—(1) It shall not be lawful for any local or other public authority
to make it a condition of the employment or continuance in employment of any person that he shall or shall not be a member of a trade
union, or to impose any condition upon persons employed by the
authority whereby employees who are or who are not members of a
trade union are liable to be placed in any respect either directly or
indirectly under any disability or disadvantage as compared with other
employees.

(2) It shall not be lawful for any local or other public authority to
make it a condition of any contract made or proposed to be made
with the authority, or of the consideration or acceptance of any tender
in connection with such a contract, that any person to be employed
by any party to the contract shall or shall not be a member of a trade
union.

(3) Any condition imposed in contravention of this section shall be
void.

(4) There shall be added to section five of the Conspiracy, and Protection of Property Act, 1875, the following provision, that is to say:—

"If any person employed by a local or other public authority wilfully
breaks a contract of service with that authority, knowing or having
reasonable cause to believe that the probable consequence of his so
doing, either alone or in combination with others, will be to cause
injury or danger or grave inconvenience to the community, he shall
be liable, on summary conviction, to a fine not exceeding ten pounds
or to imprisonment for a term not exceeding three months."

7. Without prejudice to the right of any person having a sufficient
interest in the relief sought to sue or apply for an injunction to restrain
any application of the funds of a trade union in contravention of the
provisions of this Act, an injunction restraining any application of the
funds of a trade union in contravention of the provisions of section
one of this Act may be granted at the suit or upon the application of
the Attorney-General.

In the application of this section to Scotland, there shall be substituted therein for references to an injunction references to an interdict,
and for the reference to the Attorney-General a reference to the Lord
Advocate. . . .

[§ 8 (Short title, etc.) and two schedules omitted.]

AUDIT (LOCAL AUTHORITIES) ACT, 1927
17 and 18 Geo. 5, c. 31

1.—(1) Subject to the provisions of this Act, every person who, at any audit, has been surcharged with an amount exceeding five hundred pounds by a district auditor shall for a period of five years commencing at the expiration of the period allowed for making an appeal or application with respect to the surcharge under the provisions of this Act or, if such an appeal or application is made, commencing on the date on which such an appeal or application is finally disposed of or abandoned or fails by reason of the non-prosecution thereof, be disqualified for being elected or appointed or being a member of any local authority, and if he is a member of a local authority his office shall thereupon become vacant. . . .

(3) If any person acts as a member of any local authority when disqualified under this section, he shall for each offence be liable on summary conviction to a fine not exceeding twenty pounds.

2.—(1) Any person who is aggrieved by a decision of a district auditor on any matter with respect to which he made representations at the audit, and any person aggrieved by a disallowance or surcharge of a district auditor may, where the disallowance or surcharge or other decision relates to an amount exceeding five hundred pounds, appeal to the High Court, and may in any other case appeal either to the High Court or to the Minister of Health . . . and the Court or Minister shall have power to confirm, vary or quash the decision of the auditor with such directions as the Court or Minister thinks fit for giving effect to the decision on appeal, and if the decision of the auditor is quashed, or is varied so as to reduce the amount of the surcharge to five hundred pounds or less, the appellant shall not be subject to the disqualification imposed by this Act. . . .

(2) In the case of a surcharge the person surcharged may, whether or not he appeals under the last preceding subsection, apply to the tribunal (whether the High Court or the Minister) to which he appeals or, if he does not appeal, to the tribunal . . . to which he might have appealed, for a declaration that in relation to the subject matter of the surcharge he acted reasonably or in the belief that his action was authorised by law, and the Court or Minister, if satisfied that there is proper ground for doing so, may make a declaration to that effect, and where such a declaration is made the person surcharged, if by reason of the surcharge he is subject to the disqualification imposed by this Act, shall not be subject to that disqualification, and the Court or Minister may, if satisfied that the person surcharged ought fairly to be excused, relieve him either wholly or partly from personal liability in respect of the surcharge; the decision of the Court or Minister under

this subsection shall be final and shall not be subject to appeal. . .

(4) Where under this section an appeal or application is made to the Minister, the appellant or applicant shall be entitled, if he so desires, to a personal hearing by a person appointed for the purpose by the Minister. . . .

[§ 3 (Recovery of sums certified by the auditor), § 4 (Short title, etc.) and Schedule omitted.]

REPRESENTATION OF THE PEOPLE (EQUAL FRANCHISE) ACT, 1928
18 and 19 Geo. 5, c. 12

1. For the purpose of providing that the parliamentary franchise shall be the same for men and women, subsections (1) and (2) of section four of the Representation of the People Act, 1918 (in this Act referred to as "the principal Act") shall be repealed and the following sections shall be substituted for sections one and two of that Act:—

(Section to be substituted for the said section one.)

" .—(1) A person shall be entitled to be registered as a parliamentary elector for a constituency (other than a university constituency), if he or she is of full age and not subject to any legal incapacity; and

(a) has the requisite residence qualification; or
(b) has the requisite business premises qualification; or
(c) is the husband or wife of a person entitled to be so registered in respect of a business premises qualification.

(2) A person, in order to have the requisite residence qualification or business premises qualification for a constituency—

(a) must on the last day of the qualifying period be residing in premises in the constituency, or occupying business premises in the constituency, as the case may be; and
(b) must during the whole of the qualifying period have resided in premises, or occupied business premises, as the case may be, in the constituency, or in another constituency within the same parliamentary borough or parliamentary county, or within a parliamentary borough or parliamentary county contiguous to that borough or county, or separated from that borough or county by water, not exceeding at the nearest point six miles in breadth, measured in the case of tidal water from low-water mark.

For the purposes of this subsection the administrative county of London shall be treated as a parliamentary borough.

(3) The expression 'business premises' in this section means land or other premises of the yearly value of not less than ten pounds occupied for the purpose of the business, profession, or trade of the person to be registered."

(*Section to be substituted for the said section two.*)

" . A person shall be entitled to be registered as a parliamentary elector for a university constituency if he or she is of full age and not subject to any legal incapacity, and has received a degree (other than an honorary degree) at any university forming, or forming part of, the constituency, or in the case of the Scottish universities is qualified under section twenty-seven of the Representation of the People (Scotland) Act, 1868, or, if a woman, has been admitted to and passed the final examination, and kept under the conditions required of women by the university, the period of residence, necessary for a man to obtain a degree at any university forming, or forming part of, a university constituency which did not at the time the examination was passed admit women to degrees."

2. For the purpose of providing that the local government franchise shall be the same for men and women, subsection (3) of section four of the principal Act shall be repealed, and the following section shall be substituted for section three of that Act:

" . A person shall be entitled to be registered as a local government elector for a local government electoral area if he or she is of full age and not subject to any legal incapacity, and—

(*a*) is on the last day of the qualifying period occupying as owner or tenant any land or premises in that area; and

(*b*) has during the whole of the qualifying period so occupied any land or premises in that area, or, if that area is not an administrative county or a county borough, in any administrative county or county borough in which the area is wholly or partly situate; or

(*c*) is the husband or wife of a person entitled to be so registered in respect of premises in which both the person so entitled and the husband or wife, as the case may be, reside:

Provided that—

(i) for the purposes of this section a person who inhabits any dwelling-house by virtue of any office, service, or employment, shall, if the dwelling-house is not inhabited by the person in whose service he or she is in such office, service, or employment, be deemed to occupy the dwelling-house as a tenant; and

(ii) for the purposes of this section the word tenant shall include a person who occupies a room or rooms as a lodger only where the room or rooms is or are let to that person in an unfurnished state; and

(iii) for the purpose of paragraph (*c*) of this section, a naval or military voter who is registered in respect of a residence qualification which he or she would have had but for his or her service shall be deemed to be resident in accordance with that qualification."

[§ 3. Consequential amendments to 8 Geo. 5, c. 64.]

[§ 4. No person is to vote at a general election for more than one constituency for which he or she has a residence qualification, or for more than one constituency for which he or she has any other qualification.]

[§ 5. The Fourth Schedule to the principal Act . . . shall have effect as if for the word "sevenpence" there were substituted the word "sixpence."]

[§§ 6–8 and one Schedule omitted.]

LOCAL GOVERNMENT ACT, 1929
19 Geo. 5, c. 17

PART I

Poor Law

Transfer and Administration of Functions

1. On the appointed day the functions of each poor law authority, shall, subject to the provisions of this Act and except as otherwise expressly provided by this Act, be transferred to the council of the county or county borough comprising the poor law area for which the poor law authority acts, or, if the poor law area is not wholly comprised within one county or county borough, the functions of the poor law authority so far as they relate to any county or county borough into which the area extends shall be transferred to the council thereof, and as from the appointed day all then existing poor law authorities shall cease to exist.

[§ 2. Duties of local authorities in regard to infant life protection and vaccination.]

3.—(1) Where any two or more councils, whether councils of counties or county boroughs, consider that it is expedient that the areas of the councils should be combined for any purpose connected with the administration of the functions transferred or to be transferred under this part of this Act and make application to the Minister for the purpose, the Minister may make an order for combining the areas of the councils for the purposes named therein.

(2) Where it appears to the Minister that the combination of the areas of any two or more councils . . . would tend to diminish expense, or would otherwise be of public or local advantage, the Minister may

make an order for combining the areas of the councils for the purposes named therein:

Provided that an order shall not be made under this subsection except after a local inquiry, unless all the councils whose areas are to be so combined consent. . . .

(6) An order under this section shall be laid before Parliament as soon as may be after it is made.

4. The council of every county and county borough shall prepare, and within six months after the commencement of this Act submit to the Minister, a scheme (hereinafter referred to as an administrative scheme) of the administrative arrangements proposed to be made for discharging the functions transferred to the council under this Part of this Act. . . .

[§ 5. Provisions as to alternative powers of giving assistance.]

6.—(1) An administrative scheme shall provide for the constitution of a committee of the council (hereinafter referred to as the public assistance committee). . . .

7.—(1) In the case of a county the administrative scheme shall provide—

(*a*) for the division of the county into areas, each area consisting of one or more districts, and for the constitution for each such area of a local sub-committee of the public assistance committee (to be called the guardians committee of the area) consisting of not more than thirty-six nor less than twelve members. . . .

8.—(1) As soon as an administrative scheme has been submitted to the Minister, the council submitting the scheme shall publish in one or more newspapers circulating in their area a notice stating that the scheme has been so submitted and that a copy thereof is open to inspection at a specified place, and that representations thereon may be made to the Minister within four weeks after the publication of the notice, and in the case of a scheme submitted by a county council shall send a copy of the scheme to the council of each district wholly or partly within the county.

(2) No scheme so submitted to the Minister shall be of any effect unless and until it is approved by the Minister, and the Minister, after considering any representations with respect to the scheme which may be submitted to him within four weeks after the publication of such notice as aforesaid by any local authorities and other parties who appear to him to be interested, and after consultation (if and so far as the scheme relates to education) with the Board of Education, may approve the scheme with or without modifications.

(3) If a council fail to submit to the Minister an administrative scheme within the time allowed for the purpose, the Minister may,

after consultation [as in (2)] himself make an administrative scheme [under the conditions in (1)], and shall consider any representations which may be submitted to him . . . , and any scheme so made shall have effect as if it were a scheme submitted by the council and approved by the Minister.

[§§ 9–16 deal with the councils' powers to acquire land, disqualifications for membership of councils, consultations with hospital authorities, assessment committees, recovery of expenses from those maintained in institutions who are able to pay, and the consequential repeal and amendment of certain Acts.]

17. Separate accounts shall be kept by the council of every county borough of their receipts and expenditure in respect of the functions . . . transferred to them under this Part of this Act, . . . and those accounts shall be made up and audited in like manner and subject to the same provisions as in the case of a county council, and the enactments relating to the audit of the accounts of a county council and to all matters incidental thereto and consequential thereon, including penal provisions, shall apply in lieu of the provisions of the Municipal Corporations Act, 1882, relating to accounts and audit.

[§ 18. Application to London.]
[§§ 19–20. Application to guardians appointed, or constituted under a local Act.]

Part II

Registration of Births, Deaths and Marriages

21.—(1) On the appointed day the functions of boards of guardians under the Registration Acts in relation to a registration district and to any sub-districts comprised therein shall—

(*a*) if the registration district is wholly comprised within one county or county borough, be transferred to the council of that county or county borough;

(*b*) if the registration district is not wholly comprised within one county or county borough, be transferred to the council of the county or county borough which is estimated by the Registrar-General to contain on the first day of January preceding the appointed day the larger or largest part of the population of the registration district;

and the functions so transferred are in this Part of this Act referred to as "transferred functions."

[§§ 22–23. Registration officers to become salaried officials.]
[§ 24. Councils to submit to the Minister schemes for dividing their areas into registration districts.]
[§ 25. Salary of the Registrar-General.]
[§ 26. Methods of notifying births and deaths.]
[§ 27. Application to London.]
[§ 28. Construction of previous Acts.]

EBG

Part III

Roads and Town Planning

Roads

29.—(1) The council of every county shall be the highway authority as respects every road in the county which at the appointed day is a main road, or which would, apart from this section, at any time thereafter have become a main road, and every such road and every other road as respects which a county council becomes by virtue of this Part of this Act the highway authority, shall be termed a county road, and all enactments relating to main roads shall as from the appointed day have effect as if for references therein to main roads there were substituted references to county roads. . . .

30.—(1) As from the appointed day, every county council shall be the highway authority as respects such part of the county as is for the time being comprised in any rural district and as respects the highways therein, and as such shall have all such functions under the Highway Acts, 1835 to 1885, as were exercisable by rural district councils who by virtue of the Local Government Act, 1894, became successors of highway boards, and rural district councils shall cease to be highway authorities. . . .

31.—(1) As from the appointed day, the county council shall be the highway authority as respects all classified roads which, immediately before the appointed day, were vested in the councils of urban districts within the county. . . .

32.—(1) Where an urban district has a population exceeding twenty thousand, the urban district council may claim to exercise the functions of maintenance and repair of any county road within their district, and if a claim is made within the time hereinafter limited, then, as from such date as in hereinafter mentioned, the urban district council shall be entitled to exercise those functions, and the road shall vest in that council, and for the purpose of the maintenance, repair and improvement of, and other dealing with, any such road, that council shall have the same functions as if they were as respects that road the highway authority and the road were an ordinary road vested in them. . . .

[§ 33. County councils to contribute towards the maintenance of county roads by urban district councils.]

[§§ 34–36. Maintenance of unclassified roads.]

[§§ 37–39. Miscellaneous.]

Town Planning

40.—(1) Where after the appointed day the council of a county and any local authority or local authorities under the Town Planning

Act, 1925, are desirous of acting jointly in the preparation or adoption of a town planning scheme, they shall be entitled to do so, and the council and the local authority or authorities may concur in appointing out of their respective bodies a joint committee for the purpose, and in conferring, with or without restrictions, on such a joint committee any powers which the local authority or local authorities might exercise for the purpose. . . .

[§ 41. Minister's power to combine two or more councils, after holding a local inquiry, if necessary.]

[§§ 42–45 provide for the relinquishing of powers by district councils to county councils, amendments, etc.]

Part IV

Miscellaneous Local Government Provisions

Rearrangement of County Districts

46.—(1) The Council of every county shall as soon as may be after the commencement of this Act, after conferences with representatives of the councils of the several districts wholly or partly within the county, review the circumstances of all such districts and consider whether it is desirable to effect any of the following changes:

(a) any alteration of definition of the boundaries of any such district or of any parish;

(b) the union of any such district or parish with another such district or parish;

(c) the transfer of any part of such district or parish to another district or parish;

(d) the conversion of any such district or any part thereof, if it is a rural district, into an urban district, or if it is an urban district, into or so as to form part of a rural district;

(e) the formation of any new district or parish;

and shall forthwith after the review is completed as respects the whole or any part of the county, and before the first day of April nineteen hundred and thirty-two, or such later date as the Minister may in any case allow, send to the Minister a report of the review, together with proposals as to the changes, if any, which they consider desirable:

Provided that, before making any such proposals the county council shall consult with the councils of the county boroughs adjoining the county, and the Minister shall give those councils an opportunity of laying before him their views on the proposals made by the county council.

(2) The proposals may include proposals for the transfer of a part of a non-county borough to another district, or of another district or

part of another district to a non-county borough, and, if the council
of the county borough concerned agree, for an alteration of boundaries
between a county borough and the county and any district therein:
but, save as aforesaid, the proposals shall not affect any borough.

(3) As soon as any proposals are made to the Minister, the council
making the proposals shall send copies thereof to the councils of the
several districts affected thereby and shall publish in one or more
newspapers circulating in those districts a notice stating that proposals
have been made and that a copy thereof is open to inspection at a
specified place, and that representations with respect thereto may be
made to the Minister within six weeks after the publication of the
notice.

(4) The Minister shall consider the proposals and any representations with respect to the proposals, or any of them, which may have
been made by any local authorities (including parish councils and
parish meetings) or any local government electors affected thereby,
and either may make an order giving effect to the proposals, or any
of them, with or without modifications, or may refuse to make such an
order:

Provided that, if an objection with respect to any proposal is made
by a local authority affected thereby, and is not withdrawn, the
Minister shall not make an order giving effect to the proposal without
first holding a local inquiry into the objection.

(5) If, either on representations made by a district council or otherwise it appears to the Minister, after consultation with such authorities
as appear to him to be interested, that there is a prima facie case for
making any such change as aforesaid, and that the county authorities
have failed to make a proposal for the purpose within the time allowed,
the Minister shall publish in one or more newspapers circulating in the
districts affected a notice stating that he proposes to make the change,
and that a copy of his proposals is open to inspection at a specified
place, and that representations with respect thereto may be made to
him within six weeks after the publication of the notice; and the
Minister after considering any representations which may be made
within that period, and, if any objections are made by any local
authority and are not withdrawn, after holding a local inquiry with
respect to the proposals to which the objections relate, may make an
order effecting the change or such modified change as appears to him
to be expedient. . . .

(7) An order under this section shall be laid before Parliament as
soon as may be after it is made.

47.—(1) A county council may subsequently whenever they think
it desirable, and shall if so required by the Minister, review generally
the circumstances of the districts within the county, so, however, that
the interval between the original review and the first review under this

section, or between any two reviews under this section, shall in no
case be less than ten years. . . .

[§ 48. Saving of powers under, and amendment to, the Local Government
Act, 1888.]

49.—(1) Where at the commencement of this Act any district or
parish is not wholly comprised within one county, or where a part of a
county is wholly detached therefrom, the county councils concerned
shall as soon as may be take the case into consideration, and if as a
result of such consideration a joint representation is made to the
Minister by those councils, the Minister may, after holding a local
inquiry, except in cases where he is satisfied that an inquiry is unnecessary, by order make such alteration of the counties as may be necessary
to secure that the whole of the district or parish shall be within a single
county, or to provide that such detached part shall be included in or
divided amongst the county or counties surrounding it.

(2) The Minister may, on a joint representation being made by the
council of a county and the council of a county borough, after holding
a local inquiry, except in cases where he is satisfied that an inquiry
is unnecessary, by order alter or define the boundary between the
county and the county council.

(3) An order under this section shall be laid before Parliament as
soon as may be after it is made.

[§ 50. County councils are to review electoral districts.]
[§§ 51–62. Miscellaneous.]
[§ 63. Councils to provide, with the Minister's approval, hospital accommodation for infectious disease.]
[§ 64. The Minister may, on the application of the London County Council,
transfer or delegate functions to metropolitan borough councils. The order is
to be laid before Parliament.]

PART V

Rating and Valuation

Relief from Rates

67.—(1) No person shall, in respect of any period beginning on or
after the appointed day, be liable to pay rates in respect of any agricultural land or agricultural buildings or be deemed to be in occupation
thereof for rating purposes, and notwithstanding anything in the principal Act, or in the Rating and Valuation (Apportionment) Act, 1928,
no such land or buildings shall be included in any rate made in respect
of a period beginning on or after that date.

[(2) Agricultural land shall be deemed to have no rateable value.]
[§ 68. Relief from rates of industrial and freight transport hereditaments.]

Part VI

Exchequer Grants and Other Financial Provisions

Discontinued Grants

85.—(1) The grants set out in the Second Schedule to this Act[1] . . . shall cease to be payable. . . .

General Exchequer Contributions

86.—(1) There shall be paid out of moneys provided by Parliament in respect of . . . each . . . year, an annual contribution towards local government expenses in counties and county boroughs to be called the "General Exchequer Contribution."

(2) The amount of the General Exchequer Contribution shall be periodically revised; the amount first fixed shall be for a period of three years beginning on the appointed day, the amount fixed on the first revision shall be for a period of four years from the expiration of the first period, the amount fixed on any subsequent revision shall be for a period of five years from the expiration of the previous period, and a period for which the General Exchequer Contribution is so fixed is hereinafter referred to as a "fixed grant period."

(3) The amount of the General Exchequer contribution shall be the sum of the following amounts, that is to say:

(*a*) an amount equal to the total losses on account of rates of all counties and county boroughs:

(*b*) an amount equal to the total losses on account of grants of all counties and county boroughs:

(*c*) in respect of each year in the first fixed grant period, five million pounds, and in respect of each year of every following fixed period such amount as Parliament may hereafter determine with respect to the fixed grant period so, however, that the proportion which the General Exchequer Contribution for any fixed grant period bears to the total amount of rate and grant borne expenditure in the penultimate year of the preceding fixed grant period shall never be less than the proportion which the General Exchequer Contribution for the first fixed grant period bore to the total amount of rate and grant borne expenditure in the first year of that fixed grant period. . . .

87.—(1) Towards the General Exchequer Contribution there shall at such times and in such manner as the Treasury may direct be paid out of the Road Fund . . . an annual contribution. . . .

---

[1] Grants payable out of the Consolidated Fund; grants in aid of certain health services; road grants

88.—(1) The General Exchequer Contributions shall be apportioned amongst the several counties and county boroughs in manner hereinafter following, that is to say:

(*a*) during the first four fixed grant periods there shall out of the General Exchequer Contribution for each year be apportioned to each county or county borough an amount equal to the appropriate percentage of the losses on account of rates and grants of the county or county borough:

(*b*) during the first four fixed grant periods the residue, and thereafter the whole, of every General Exchequer Contribution, shall each year be apportioned amongst the several counties and county boroughs in proportion to their weighted populations.

(2) The amount apportioned under this section to a county shall be called "the county apportionment" and the amount so apportioned to a county borough shall be called "the county borough apportionment."

89. Out of the county apportionment of every county other than the county of London there shall be set aside such amount as will be sufficient to pay to the councils of districts situate wholly or partly within the county the sums hereinafter directed to be so set aside; the residue of the county apportionment after such sums as aforesaid have been so set aside, shall be paid to the council of the county and shall be called the "General Exchequer Grant" of that council:

Provided that, if in the case of any county the county apportionment is less than the amount to be so set aside, the deficiency shall be paid out of moneys provided by Parliament, and the sums so paid shall be treated as part of the county apportionment.

[§ 90. Provision for an "additional Exchequer Grant" to counties.]
[§§ 91–94. Grants to county districts.]

95. The whole of every county borough apportionment shall be paid to the council of the county borough and the sum so paid shall be called the "General Exchequer Grant" of that council.

[§§ 96–97. Additional Exchequer Grants to county boroughs.]
[§§ 98–100. Grants to the county of London and the metropolitan boroughs.]
[§§ 101–102. Payments by councils to voluntary associations.]

103. The grants under this Part of this Act shall be payable to the councils entitled thereto at such times and in such manner as the Treasury shall direct.

104. The Minister may reduce the grant payable in respect of any year under this Part of the Act to any council by such amount as he thinks just, if,—

(*a*) he is satisfied, either upon representations made to him by any association or other body of persons experienced or interested in matters relating to public health or without any such representations that the council have failed to achieve or maintain a reasonable standard of efficiency and progress in the discharge of their functions relating to public health services, regard being had to the standards maintained in other areas whose financial resources and other relevant circumstances are substantially similar, and that the health or welfare of the inhabitants of the area of the council or some of them has been or is likely to be thereby endangered; or

(b) he is satisfied that the expenditure of the council has been excessive and unreasonable, regard being had to the financial resources and other relevant circumstances of the area; or

(c) the Minister of Transport certifies that he is satisfied that the council have failed to maintain their roads or any part thereof in a satisfactory condition:

Provided that, whenever the Minister makes such a reduction, he shall make and cause to be laid before Parliament a report stating the amount of the reduction, and the reasons therefor.

108.—(1) The Minister may make regulations for giving effect to the provisions of this Part of this Act. . . .

(4) All regulations made under this Part of this Act shall be laid before Parliament as soon as may be after they are made.

[§§ 109–112 of Part VI and Part VII (Property Liabilities and Officers) omitted.]

Part VIII

General

130.—(1) If any difficulty arises in connection with the application of this Act to any exceptional area, or in bringing into operation any of the provisions of this Act, the Minister may make such order for removing the difficulty as he may judge to be necessary for that purpose, and any such order may modify the provisions of this Act so far as may appear to the Minister necessary for carrying the order into effect:

Provided that the Minister shall not exercise the powers conferred by this section after the thirty-first day of December, nineteen hundred and thirty.

(2) Every order made under this section shall come into operation upon the date specified therein in that behalf, but shall be laid before Parliament as soon as may be after it is made and shall cease to have effect upon the expiration of a period of three months from the date upon which it came into operation, unless at some time before the expiration of that period it has been approved by a resolution passed by each House of Parliament:

Provided that, in reckoning any such period of three months as aforesaid, no account shall be taken of any time during which Parliament is dissolved or prorogued, or during which both Houses are adjourned for more than four days.

[§§ 131–138 and twelve schedules omitted.]

HOUSING ACT, 1930
20 and 21 Geo. 5, c. 39

[Part I of the Act gives local authorities, with the approval of the Minister of Health, powers to require the clearance or improvement of buildings in unhealthy areas, and, in certain circumstances, powers of compulsory purchase.]

11.—(1) The provisions of this section shall have effect with respect to the validity of clearance orders and compulsory purchase orders made under this Act, and the date on which such an order is to come into operation.

(2) So soon as may be after an order has been confirmed by the Minister, the local authority shall publish in a newspaper circulating in their district a notice in the prescribed form stating that the order has been confirmed, and naming a place where a copy of the order as confirmed and of the map referred to therein may be seen at all reasonable hours, and shall serve a like notice on every person who, having given notice to the Minister of his objection to the order, appeared at the public local inquiry in support of his objection.

(3) If any person aggrieved by an order desires to question its validity on the ground that it is not within the powers of this Act or that any requirement of this Act has not been complied with, he may, within six weeks after the publication of the notice of confirmation, make an application for the purpose to the High Court, and where any such application is duly made the court—

(i) may by interim order suspend the operation of the order either generally or in so far as it affects any property of the applicant until the final determination of the proceedings; and

(ii) if satisfied upon the hearing of the application that the order is not within the powers of this Act or that the interests of the applicant have been substantially prejudiced by any requirement of this Act not having been complied with, may quash the order either generally or in so far as it affects any property of the applicant.

(4) Subject to the provisions of the last preceding subsection, an order shall not, either before or after its confirmation, be questioned

by prohibition or certiorari or in any legal proceedings whatsoever, and shall become operative at the expiration of six weeks from the date on which notice of its confirmation is published in accordance with the provisions of subsection (2) of this section.

(5) Except by leave of the Court of Appeal, no appeal shall lie to the House of Lords from a decision of the Court of Appeal in proceedings under this section.

(6) So soon as may be after an order has become operative, the local authority shall serve a copy thereof on every person on whom a notice was served by them of their intention to submit the order to the Minister for confirmation.

IMPORT DUTIES ACT, 1932
22 Geo. 5, c. 8

Most Gracious Sovereign,

We, Your Majesty's most dutiful and loyal subjects, the Commons of the United Kingdom in Parliament assembled, with a view to the restricting in the national interest of the importation of goods into the United Kingdom, to the providing of a remedy in cases where a foreign country discriminates in the matter of importation as against goods produced or manufactured in the United Kingdom, in certain other parts of Your Majesty's dominions or in territories under Your Majesty's protection or in respect of which a mandate is being exercised by Your Majesty's Government of the United Kingdom, and to the making of an addition to the public revenue, have freely and voluntarily resolved to give and grant unto Your Majesty the duties for which provision is hereinafter contained; and do therefore most humbly beseech Your Majesty that it may be enacted, and be it enacted, by the King's most Excellent Majesty, by and with the advice and consent of the Lords Spiritual and Temporal, and Commons, in this present Parliament assembled, and by the authority of the same, as follows:

Part I

General ad valorem Duty and Additional Duties

1.—(1) As from the first day of March, nineteen hundred and thirty-two, there shall, subject to the provisions of this Act, be charged on all goods imported into the United Kingdom, other than goods exempted as hereinafter provided from the provisions of this section, a duty of customs equal to ten per cent. of the value of the goods.

(2) The following goods shall be exempted from the provisions of this section—

(*a*) goods for the time being chargeable with a duty of customs by or under any enactment other than this Act, but not including (subject to the provisions of this Act) any composite goods in the case of which duty is chargeable under any such enactment as aforesaid because some (but not all) of their components are articles so chargeable;

(*b*) goods of any class or description specified in the First Schedule to this Act or added to that Schedule by an order made under the next following subsection.

(3) The Treasury, after receiving a recommendation from the Committee to be constituted under the following provisions of this Act that goods of any class or description ought to be exempted from the provisions of this section, and after consultation with the appropriate department, may by order direct that goods of all or any of the classes or descriptions specified in the recommendation shall be added to the First Schedule to this Act:

Provided that, except in such cases as seem to them of special urgency, the said Committee shall not take into consideration the question whether any recommendation ought to be made under this subsection until the expiration of six months from the passing of this Act.

(4) The duty imposed by this section is in this Act referred to as "the general ad valorem duty." . . .

2.—(1) For the purpose of giving advice and assistance in connection with the discharge by the Treasury of their functions under this Act, there shall be constituted a committee, to be called "the Import Duties Advisory Committee," consisting of a chairman and not less than two or more than five other members to be appointed by the Treasury.

(2) The members of the Committee shall hold office for a period of three years and shall be eligible for re-appointment from time to time on the expiration of their term of office.

If a member becomes, in the opinion of the Treasury, unfit to continue in office or incapable of performing his duties under this Act, the Treasury shall forthwith declare his office to be vacant and shall notify the fact in such manner as they think fit, and thereupon the office shall become vacant.

(3) The Committee shall, as soon as may be after the commencement of this Act, take into consideration the provisions of this Act, and shall, from time to time, take into consideration any representations which may be made to them with respect to matters on which, under the provisions of this Act, action may be taken on a recommendation by

the Committee, and may make recommendations to the Treasury with respect to the matters aforesaid.

(4) The Treasury shall publish in such manner as they think fit any recommendation made to them by the Committee as soon as may be after they have made an order in pursuance of the recommendation or have determined to make no order on the recommendation.

(5) The expenses of the Committee to such an amount as may be approved by the Treasury (including the expenses of their staff and such salaries or other remuneration paid to all or any of the members as the Treasury may determine) shall be paid out of moneys provided by Parliament.

(6) The Committee may make rules—

(*a*) for regulating the proceedings, including the quorum, of the Committee; and

(*b*) for authorising the delegation of any of the functions of the Committee to a sub-committee consisting of members of the Committee.

(7) The Committee, so far as they consider it necessary or desirable so to do for the purpose of the proper discharge of their functions, may by notice in writing require any person to furnish them with returns or other information, or, subject to the payment or tender of the reasonable expenses of his attendance, to attend as a witness before them or before any person authorised by them and to give evidence or to produce documents, and if any person fails without reasonable excuse to comply with the provisions of any such notice, he shall be liable on summary conviction to a fine not exceeding fifty pounds, and in the case of a second or subsequent conviction to a fine not exceeding two hundred pounds:

Provided that the power of the Committee under this subsection to require a person to attend as a witness before a person authorised by them shall not be exercised unless the Committee are satisfied that, having regard to the nature of the proposed inquiry, it can be conducted more conveniently or more efficiently by a person so authorised than by the Committee, and that the person proposed to be authorised possesses the necessary qualifications for the purpose.

(8) The Committee or any person authorised by them shall have power to take evidence on oath, and for that purpose to administer oaths.

3.—(1) Where it appears to the Committee that an additional duty of customs ought to be charged in respect of goods of any class or description which are chargeable with the general ad valorem duty and which, in their opinion, are either articles of luxury or articles of a kind which are being produced or are likely within a reasonable time to be produced in the United Kingdom in quantities which are substantial in relation to United Kingdom consumption, the Committee may recommend to the Treasury that an additional duty ought to be charged on goods of that class or description at such rate as is specified in the recommendation.

(2) In deciding what recommendation, if any, to make for the purposes of this section, the Committee shall have regard to the advisability in the national interest of restricting imports into the United Kingdom and the interests generally of trade and industry in the United Kingdom, including those of trades and industries which are consumers of goods as well as those of trades and industries which are producers of goods.

(3) The Treasury, after receiving a recommendation from the Committee that an additional duty of customs ought to be charged on goods of any class or description, may, if they think fit so to do, and after consultation with the appropriate Department, by order direct that such additional duty of customs as is specified in the order (being a duty at a rate not exceeding the rate specified in the recommendation) shall be charged on the importation into the United Kindom of goods of all or any of the classes or description specified in the recommendation, and an additional duty so directed to be charged shall for all purposes be deemed to be chargeable under this section. . . .

[§§ 4–5. Imperial preference.]

19.—(1) Any order made by the Treasury or the Board of Trade under this Act shall be laid before the Commons House of Parliament as soon as may be after it is made.

(2) Any such order as aforesaid imposing a duty of customs shall cease to have effect on the expiration of a period of twenty-eight days from the date on which it is made, unless at some time before the expiration of that period it has been approved by resolution passed by that House, but without prejudice to anything previously done thereunder or to the making of a new order.

(3) Any such order as aforesaid, other than an order imposing a duty of customs, shall cease to have effect if the Commons House of Parliament within a period of twenty-eight days from the date on which the order is laid before the House, resolves that the order shall be annulled, but without prejudice to anything previously done thereunder or to the making of a new order.

(4) In reckoning any such period of twenty-eight days as aforesaid no account shall be taken of any time during which Parliament is dissolved or prorogued, or during which the Commons House is adjourned for more than four days.

(5) Any such order as aforesaid may be varied or revoked by a subsequent order made in the like manner and subject to the like provisions:

Provided that—

(*a*) this subsection shall not apply to an order made under section one of this Act; and

(*b*) an order made on the recommendation of the Committee may, notwithstanding any further recommendation and without any further recommendation, be revoked or varied by the Treasury as they think fit, after consultation with the appropriate Department, except that the rate of an additional duty shall not be increased above the rate specified in the original recommendation without a further recommendation.

[§§ 20–23 and three schedules omitted.]

LOCAL GOVERNMENT ACT, 1933
23 and 24 Geo. 5, c. 51

PART I

CONSTITUTION AND ELECTIONS

Local Government Areas

1.—(1) For the purpose of local government, England and Wales (exclusive of London) shall be divided into administrative counties and county boroughs, and administrative counties shall be divided into county districts, being either non-county boroughs, urban districts or rural districts, and county boroughs and county districts shall consist of one or more parishes.

[(2) Refers to the First Schedule, enumerating the local government areas.]

(3) Every county borough shall, with respect to the functions which the council of the borough discharge, form a separate administrative area.

Administrative Counties

Constitution of County Councils

2.—(1) For every administrative county there shall be a county council consisting of the chairman, county aldermen and county councillors, and the council shall have all such functions as are vested in the county council by this Act or otherwise.

(2) The county council shall be a body corporate . . . and shall have perpetual succession and a common seal and power to hold land for the purposes of their constitution without licence in mortmain.

[§§ 3–5. Election of the chairman and vice-chairman of the council.]

County Aldermen

6.—(1) The county aldermen shall be elected by the county council from among the county councillors or persons qualified to be county councillors.

(2) The number of county aldermen shall be one-third of the whole number of county councillors or, if that number is not divisible by three, one-third of the highest number below that number which is divisible by three. . . .

(4) In every third year, being the year in which county councillors are elected, one half as near as may be of the whole number of county aldermen, being those who have been county aldermen for the longest time without re-election, shall retire immediately after the election of the new county aldermen, and their places shall be filled by the newly elected county aldermen who shall come into office on that day.

7.—(1) The ordinary election of county aldermen shall be held in every third year, being the year in which county councillors are elected, at the annual meeting of the county council, and shall take place immediately after the election of the chairman. . . .

County Councillors

8.—(1) The county councillors shall be elected by the local government electors for the county in manner provided by this Act.

(2) The term of office of county councillors shall be three years, and they shall retire together in every third year, on the eighth day of March, and their places shall be filled by the newly-elected councillors, who shall come into office on that day.

[§ 9. Elections to be held in March.]

Election of County Councillors

10. For the purpose of the election of county councillors, every county shall be divided into electoral divisions, each returning one councillor, and there shall be a separate election for each electoral division.

[§§ 11–16. Electoral details.]

Boroughs

[§ 17. Name of corporations and constitution of councils of boroughs.]

The Mayor

18.—(1) The mayor shall be elected annually by the council of the borough from among the aldermen or councillors of the borough or persons qualified to be aldermen or councillors of the borough.

(2) The term of office of the mayor shall be one year. . . .

(3) During his term of office, the mayor shall continue to be a member of the council. . . .

(4) The council may pay to the mayor such remuneration as they think reasonable.

(5) The mayor shall have precedence in all places in the borough: Provided that nothing in this sub-section shall prejudicially affect His Majesty's royal prerogative. . . .

(7) The mayor shall, by virtue of his office, be a justice of the peace for the borough. . . .

(8) The mayor of a non-county borough, shall, in addition, during his term of office be a justice of the peace for the county in which the borough is situate. . . .

(9) The mayor, if present, shall be entitled to preside at all meetings of justices of the peace held in the borough. . . .

[§§ 19–20. Election of mayor, and power of mayor to appoint a deputy.]

Aldermen

21.—(1) The aldermen of a borough shall be elected by the council of the borough from among the councillors or persons qualified to be councillors of the borough.

(2) The number of aldermen shall be one-third of the whole number of councillors.

(3) If a councillor is elected to, and accepts the office of, alderman of the borough, his office of councillor shall thereupon become vacant.

(4) The term of office of an alderman of a borough shall be six years, and one half, as near as may be, of the whole number of aldermen, being those who have been aldermen for the longest time without re-election, shall retire in every third year immediately after the election of the new aldermen, and their places shall be filled by the newly-elected aldermen who shall come into office on that day.

Councillors

23.—(1) The councillors of a borough shall be elected by the local government electors for the borough in manner provided by this Act.

(2) The term of office . . . shall be three years, and one third of the whole number of councillors . . . shall retire in every year on the first day of November. . . .

(3) The ordinary day of election of councillors shall be the first day of November.

[§§ 24–30. Electoral details.]

Urban and Rural Districts

31.—(1) For every urban district there shall be an urban district council consisting of the chairman and councillors, and the council shall have all such functions as are vested in the urban district council by this Act or otherwise. . . .

32.—(1) Subject to the provisions of this Act, for every rural district there shall be a rural district council consisting of the chairman and councillors. . . .

[§§ 33–42. Electoral details.]

Rural Parishes

43.—(1) For every rural parish there shall be a parish meeting, and, subject to the provisions of this Act, for every rural parish or group of parishes having a parish council immediately before the commencement of this Act there shall continue to be a parish council.

(2) If a rural parish has not a separate parish council, the county council shall by order establish a parish council for that parish—

(*a*) if the population of the parish is three hundred or upwards; or
(*b*) if, in the case of a parish having a population of two hundred or upwards but under three hundred, the parish meeting of the parish so resolve,

and the county council may, in the case of a parish having a population of less than two hundred, by order establish a parish council for that parish if the parish meeting so resolve. . . .

44.—(1) Where the population of a rural parish having a separate parish council is less than two hundred, the parish meeting may petition the county council for the dissolution of the parish council, and thereupon the county council may by order dissolve the parish council, and from such date as may be specified in the order this Act shall apply to that parish as to a parish not having a separate parish council.

(2) Where a petition for an order under this section is rejected, another petition for the same purpose may not be presented within two years from the presentation of the previous petition.

45.—(1) The parish meeting of a rural parish may apply to the county council for an order grouping the parish with some neighbouring parish or parishes in the same county under a common parish council, and the county council may thereupon make an order (in this Act referred to as "a grouping order") accordingly:

Provided that—

(*a*) no parish shall be so grouped without the consent of the parish meeting of that parish; and
(*b*) unless the county council for special reasons otherwise direct, the grouped parishes shall be within the same rural district. . . .

Part III

COMMITTEES AND JOINT COMMITTEES

General Power of Local Authorities to Appoint Committees

85.—(1) A local authority may appoint a committee for any such general or special purpose as in the opinion of the local authority would be better regulated and managed by means of a committee, and may delegate to a committee so appointed, with or without restrictions or conditions, as they think fit, any functions exercisable by the local authority either with respect to the whole or a part of the area of the local authority, except the power of levying, or issuing a precept for, a rate, or of borrowing money. . . .

(2) A committee appointed under this section (other than a committee for regulating and controlling the finance of the local authority or of their area) may include persons who are not members of the local authority:

Provided that at least two-thirds of the members of every committee shall be members of the local authority. . . .

Finance Committees of County Councils, etc.

86.—(1) A county council shall appoint a finance committee consisting of such number of members of the council as they think fit for regulating and controlling the finance of the county, and shall fix the term of office of the members of the committee.

(2) Subject to the provisions of any enactment relating to the standing joint committee or to any other statutory committee, no costs, debt or liability exceeding fifty pounds shall be incurred by a county council except upon a resolution of the council passed on an estimate submitted by the finance committee.

87.—(1) A rural district council may, at a meeting specially convened for the purpose, appoint for any one or more contributory places within their district a parochial committee consisting either wholly of members of the district council or partly of such members and partly of local government electors for such contributory place or places, as the council may determine. . . .

(2) A rural district council may delegate to a parochial committee, with or without restrictions or conditions, as they think fit, any functions exercisable by them within the contributory place or places for which the committee is formed, except the power of levying a rate or borrowing money.

(3) If a rural district council refuse to appoint a parochial committee for a contributory place after receiving a request to that effect

from the parish council or parish meeting of a parish which is wholly or in part comprised in the contributory place, the parish council or parish meeting may petition the Minister and the Minister may by order direct the rural district council to appoint a parochial committee for that contributory place.

88.—(1) A rural district council may delegate to a parish council any functions which, under the preceding section, may be delegated to a parochial committee, and thereupon that section shall apply as if the parish council were a parochial committee. . . .

Joint Committees

91.—(1) A local authority may concur with any one or more other local authorities in appointing from amongst their respective members a joint committee of those authorities for any purpose in which they are jointly interested, and may delegate to the committee, with or without restrictions or conditions, as they think fit, any functions of the local authority relating to the purpose for which the joint committee is formed, except the power of levying, or issuing a precept for, a rate, or of borrowing money. . . .

[§ 92. Joint committees for parts of parishes.]

[§ 93. Expenses of joint committees to be defrayed by the local authorities by whom the committee is appointed.]

[§§ 94–7. General provisions relating to joint committees.]

[Parts IV (Officers) and V (Offices and Buildings) omitted.]

PART VI

ALTERATION OF AREAS

129.—(1) If, on a petition presented to His Majesty by the council of an urban or rural district praying for the grant of a charter of incorporation, His Majesty, by the advice of His Privy Council, thinks fit by charter to create the district or any part thereof with or without any adjoining area a borough, and to incorporate the inhabitants thereof, it shall be lawful for His Majesty by the charter to extend to that borough and the inhabitants thereof so incorporated the provisions of this Act relating to boroughs.

(2) A petition for a charter of incorporation shall not be presented except upon a resolution passed by a majority of the whole number of members of the council of the district at a meeting specially convened for that purpose, and confirmed by a like majority at a second meeting of the council specially convened for that purpose not earlier than one month after the passing of the resolution. . . .

136. Nothing in this or any other public general Act or in any scheme made under this Part of this Act shall authorise the establishment in a borough of a new separate police force not consolidated with the county police force, unless the population of the area which is created a borough, according to the census last published before the date of the petition for the charter, was twenty thousand or upwards. . . .

139. The council of a borough shall not promote a Bill for the purpose of constituting the borough a county borough, unless the population of the borough is seventy-five thousand or upwards.

[§§ 140–145 (Alterations of Boundaries), § 146 (Review of Areas by County Councils, § 147 (Changes of Name of District or Parish), and §§ 148–155 (Miscellaneous) omitted.]

PART VII

ACQUISITION OF, AND DEALINGS IN, LAND

159.—(1) A county council may be authorised to purchase compulsorily any land, whether situate within or without the county, for the purpose of any of their functions under this or any other public general Act, including any such functions as are exercised through the standing joint committee.

(2) The council of a borough or urban or rural district may be authorised to purchase compulsorily any land, whether situate within or without the area of the local authority, for any of the purposes of the Public Health Acts, 1875 to 1932.

160.—(1) The following provisions of this section shall have effect with respect to the compulsory purchase of land by a local authority in cases where power to authorise the local authority to purchase land compulsorily is conferred—

(a) by this Act; or

(b) by any enactment or statutory order in force immediately before the commencement of this Act and incorporating or applying section one hundred and seventy-six of the Public Health Act, 1875; or

(c) by any enactment passed or statutory order made after the commencement of this Act empowering the Minister to authorise the local authority to purchase land compulsorily by means of a provisional order made by him and confirmed by Parliament.

(2) The local authority shall publish in one or more local newspapers circulating in the locality in which the land proposed to be purchased is situate a notice describing the land and stating the purpose for which the land is required.

(3) The local authority shall serve in the prescribed manner on every owner, lessee and occupier (except tenants for a month or any period

less than a month) of the land proposed to be purchased, a notice in the prescribed form indicating in each case the particular land intended to be purchased and the purpose for which the land is required, and stating that the authority propose to request the Minister to make a provisional order empowering them to purchase the land compulsorily, and specifying the time within which and the manner in which objections can be made to the proposed order.

(4) On compliance with the foregoing provisions of this section, the local authority may request the Minister to make a provisional order empowering them to purchase the land compulsorily.

(5) If no objection is duly made by any of the persons upon whom notices are required to be served, or if all objections so made are withdrawn, the Minister, upon being satisfied that the proper notices have been published and served, may, if he thinks fit, make a provisional order authorising the local authority to purchase compulsorily the land comprised in the order, but in any other case he shall, before making the provisional order, cause a local inquiry to be held, and shall consider any objection not withdrawn and the report of the person who held the inquiry:

Provided that the Minister may require any person who has made an objection to state in writing the grounds thereof, and may make a provisional order without causing a local inquiry to be held, if satisfied that every objection duly made and not withdrawn relates exclusively to matters which can be dealt with by the tribunal by whom the compensation is to be assessed. . . .

[§ 161. Procedure for compulsory purchase of land by means of an order confirmed by the Minister.]

162.—(1) If any person aggrieved by a compulsory purchase order (other than a compulsory purchase order which is provisional only unless and until it is confirmed by Parliament) desires to question its validity, he may, within two months after the publication of the notice of confirmation in accordance with the provisions of the last preceding section, make an application for the purpose to the High Court, and if upon any such application the court are satisfied that the order is invalid, and, where the invalidity of the order arises from a failure to comply with any provision governing the procedure for the making or confirmation thereof, are further satisfied that the interests of the applicant have been substantially prejudiced by that failure, the court may quash the order either generally or in so far as it affects any property of the applicant.

(2) Subject to the provisions of the last preceding subsection a compulsory purchase order shall not, either before or after its confirmation, be questioned by prohibition or certiorari or in any legal proceedings.

(3) Except by leave of the Court of Appeal, no appeal shall lie to the House of Lords from a decision of the Court of Appeal in proceedings under this section.

[§§ 163–179. Miscellaneous provisions relating to the acquisition and disposal of lands.]

[Part VIII (Expenses) and Part IX (Borrowing) omitted.]

Part X

Accounts and Audit

219. The following accounts shall be subject to audit by a district auditor under this Part of this Act, that is to say,—

(a) the accounts of every county council, metropolitan borough council, urban district council, rural district council and parish council, and of every parish meeting for a rural parish not having a parish council;

(b) the accounts of any committee appointed by any such council or parish meeting;

(c) the accounts of any joint committee constituted under Part III of this Act or under any enactment repealed by this Act, of which one or more of the constituent authorities are a county or metropolitan borough or district or parish council or the council of a borough all of whose accounts are subject to audit by a district auditor;

(d) any other accounts which are made subject to audit by a district auditor by virtue of any enactment or statutory order or, in the case of the accounts of the council of a borough, by virtue of a resolution adopting the system of district audit passed by the council in accordance with the provisions of this Part of this Act:

Provided that in relation to any audit of accounts under paragraph (d) of this section this Part of this Act shall have effect subject to the provisions of the relevant enactment or statutory order.

228.—(1) It shall be the duty of the district auditor at every audit held by him—

(a) to disallow every item of account which is contrary to law;

(b) to surcharge the amount of any expenditure disallowed upon the person responsible for incurring or authorising the expenditure;

(c) to surcharge any sum which has not been duly brought into account upon the person by whom that sum ought to have been brought into account;

(d) to surcharge the amount of any loss or deficiency upon any person by whose negligence or misconduct the loss or deficiency has been incurred;

(*e*) to certify the amount due from any person upon whom he has made a surcharge;

(*f*) to certify at the conclusion of the audit his allowance of the accounts, subject to any disallowances or surcharges which he may have made:

Provided that no expenses paid by an authority shall be disallowed by the auditor, if they have been sanctioned by the Minister. . . .

229.—(1) Any person who is aggrieved by a decision of a district auditor . . . may, where the disallowance or surcharge or other decision relates to an amount exceeding five hundred pounds, appeal to the High Court, and may in any other case appeal either to the High Court or to the Minister.

(2) The Court or Minister on such an appeal shall have power to confirm, vary or quash the decision of the auditor, and to remit the case to the auditor with such directions as the Court or Minister thinks fit for giving effect to the decision on appeal. . . .

237.—(1) In every borough there shall, unless and until any such alternative method of audit as hereinafter mentioned is in force at the commencement of this Act or is adopted by the council, be three borough auditors, two elected by the local government electors for the borough, called elective auditors, and one appointed by the mayor, called mayor's auditor. . . .

239.—(1) The council of a borough may, by means of a resolution passed and confirmed in accordance with the provisions of this section, adopt either—

(*a*) the system of district audit; or

(*b*) the system of professional audit. . . .

[Part XI (Local Financial Returns) omitted.]

Part XII

BYELAWS

249.—(1) A county council and the council of a borough may make byelaws for the good rule and government of the whole or any part of the county or borough, as the case may be, and for the prevention and suppression of nuisances therein:

Provided that byelaws made under this section by a county council shall not have effect in any borough.

(2) The confirming authority in relation to byelaws made under this section shall be the Secretary of State, except that as respects byelaws relating to public health or to any other matter which, in the opinion of the Secretary of State and of the Minister [of Health], concerns the functions of the Minister rather than those of the Secretary of State the confirming authority shall be the Minister.

(3) The validity of a byelaw made under this section and confirmed by the Secretary of State or by the Minister shall not be questioned in any legal proceedings on the ground that the Secretary of State or the Minister, as the case may be, is not the confirming authority in relation to that byelaw.

(4) Where by or under any enactment in force in any area provision is made for the prevention and suppression in a summary manner of any nuisance, power to make byelaws under this section for that purpose shall not be exercisable as respects that area.

(5) The council of an urban or rural district shall have power to enforce byelaws made by a county council under this section which are for the time being in force in the district or any part thereof.

[Parts XIII (Local Bills), XIV (Freemen), XV (General Provisions) and eleven Schedules omitted.]

HIS MAJESTY'S DECLARATION OF ABDICATION ACT, 1936
1 Edw. 8, c. 3

An Act to give effect to His Majesty's declaration of abdication; and for purposes connected therewith.

[*11th December 1936.*]

Whereas His Majesty by His Royal Message of the tenth day of December in this present year has been pleased to declare that He is irrevocably determined to renounce the Throne for Himself and His descendants, and has for that purpose executed the Instrument of Abdication set out in the Schedule to this Act, and has signified His desire that effect thereto should be given immediately:

And whereas, following upon the communication to His Dominions of His Majesty's said declaration and desire, the Dominion of Canada pursuant to the provisions of section four of the Statute of Westminster, 1931, has requested and consented to the enactment of this Act, and the Commonwealth of Australia, the Dominion of New Zealand, and the Union of South Africa have assented thereto:

Be it therefore enacted by the King's most Excellent Majesty, by and with the advice and consent of the Lords Spiritual and Temporal, and Commons, in this present Parliament assembled, and by the authority of the same, as follows:

1.—(1) Immediately upon the Royal Assent being signified to this Act the Instrument of Abdication executed by His present Majesty on the tenth day of December, nineteen hundred and thirty-six, set out in the Schedule to this Act, shall have effect, and thereupon His Majesty shall cease to be King and there shall be a demise of the Crown, and accordingly the member of the Royal Family then next in succession to the Throne shall succeed thereto and to all the rights, privileges, and dignities thereunto belonging.

(2) His Majesty, His issue, if any, and the descendants of that issue, shall not after His Majesty's abdication have any right, title or interest in or to the succession to the Throne, and section one of the Act of Settlement shall be construed accordingly.

(3) The Royal Marriages Act, 1772, shall not apply to His Majesty after His abdication nor to the issue, if any, of His Majesty or the descendants of that issue.

2. This Act may be cited as His Majesty's Declaration of Abdication Act, 1936.

Schedule

I, Edward, the Eighth, of Great Britain, Ireland, and the British Dominions beyond the Seas, King, Emperor of India, do hereby declare My irrevocable determination to renounce the Throne for Myself and for My descendants, and My desire that effect should be given to this Instrument of Abdication immediately.

In token whereof I have hereunto set My hand this tenth day of December, nineteen hundred and thirty-six, in the presence of the witnesses whose signatures are subscribed.

EDWARD R.I.

Signed at Fort Belvedere
   in the presence of
      ALBERT.
      HENRY.
      GEORGE.

PUBLIC ORDER ACT, 1936
1 Edw. 8 and 1 Geo. 6, c. 6

1.—(1) Subject as hereinafter provided, any person who in any public place or at any public meeting wears uniform signifying his association with any political organisation or with the promotion of any political object shall be guilty of an offence:

Provided that, if the chief officer of police is satisfied that the wearing of any such uniform as aforesaid on any ceremonial, anniversary, or other special occasion will not be likely to involve risk of public disorder, he may, with the consent of a Secretary of State, by order

permit the wearing of such uniform on that occasion either absolutely
or subject to such conditions as may be specified in the order.

(2) Where any person is charged before any court with an offence
under this section, no further proceedings in respect thereof shall be
taken against him without the consent of the Attorney-General except
such as the court may think necessary by remand (whether in custody
or on bail) or otherwise to secure the due appearance of the person
charged, so, however, that if that person is remanded in custody he
shall, after the expiration of a period of eight days from the date on
which he was so remanded, be entitled to be discharged from custody
on entering into a recognisance without sureties unless within that
period the Attorney-General has consented to such further proceedings
as aforesaid.

2.—(1) If the members or adherents of any association of persons,
whether incorporated or not, are—

(a) organised or trained or equipped for the purpose of enabling them
to be employed in usurping the functions of the police or of the
armed forces of the Crown; or

(b) organised and trained or organised and equipped either for the
purpose of enabling them to be employed for the use or display of
physical force in promoting any political object, or in such manner
as to arouse reasonable apprehension that they are organised and
either trained or equipped for that purpose;

then any person who takes part in the control or management of the
association, or in so organising or training as aforesaid any members
or adherents thereof, shall be guilty of an offence under this section:

Provided that in any proceedings against a person charged with the
offence of taking part in the control or management of such an association as aforesaid it shall be a defence to that charge to prove that he
neither consented to nor connived at the organisation, training, or
equipment of members or adherents of the association in contravention
of the provisions of this section.

(2) No prosecution shall be instituted under this section without the
consent of the Attorney-General.

(3) If upon application being made by the Attorney-General it
appears to the High Court that any association is an association of
which members or adherents are organised, trained, or equipped in
contravention of the provisions of this section, the Court may make
such order as appears necessary to prevent any disposition without
the leave of the Court of property held by or for the association and in
accordance with rules of court may direct an inquiry and report to be
made as to any such property as aforesaid and as to the affairs of the
association and make such further orders as appear to the Court to
be just and equitable for the application of such property in or towards

the discharge of the liabilities of the association lawfully incurred before the date of the application or since that date with the approval of the Court, in or towards the repayment of moneys to persons who became subscribers or contributors to the association in good faith and without knowledge of any such contravention as aforesaid, and in or towards any costs incurred in connection with any such inquiry and report as aforesaid or in winding-up or dissolving the association, and may order that any property which is not directed by the Court to be so applied as aforesaid shall be forfeited to the Crown.

(4) In any criminal or civil proceedings under this section proof of things done or of words written, spoken or published (whether or not in the presence of any party to the proceedings) by any person taking part in the control or management of an association or in organising, training or equipping members or adherents of an association shall be admissible as evidence of the purposes for which, or the manner in which, members or adherents of the association (whether those persons or others) were organised, or trained, or equipped.

(5) If a judge of the High Court is satisfied by information on oath that there is reasonable ground for suspecting that an offence under this section has been committed, and that evidence of the commission thereof is to be found at any premises or place specified in the information, he may, on an application made by an officer of police of a rank not lower than that of inspector, grant a search warrant authorising any such officer as aforesaid named in the warrant together with any other persons named in the warrant and any other officers of police to enter the premises or place at any time within one month from the date of the warrant, if necessary by force, and to search the premises or place and every person found therein, and to seize anything found on the premises or place or on any such person which the officer has reasonable ground for suspecting to be evidence of the commission of such an offence as aforesaid:

Provided that no woman shall, in pursuance of a warrant issued under this subsection, be searched except by a woman.

(6) Nothing in this section shall be construed as prohibiting the employment of a reasonable number of persons as stewards to assist in the preservation of order at any public meeting held upon private premises, or the making of arrangements for that purpose or the instruction of the persons to be so employed in their lawful duties as such stewards, or their being furnished with badges or other distinguishing signs.

3.—(1) If the chief officer of police, having regard to the time or place at which and the circumstances in which any public procession is taking place or is intended to take place and to the route taken or proposed to be taken by the procession, has reasonable ground for apprehending that the procession may occasion serious public disorder, he may give directions imposing upon the persons organising or taking part in the procession such conditions as appear to him necessary for the preservation of public order, including conditions prescribing the route to be taken by the procession and conditions prohibiting the procession from entering any public place specified in the directions:

Provided that no conditions restricting the display of flags, banners, or emblems shall be imposed under this subsection except such as are reasonably necessary to prevent risk of a breach of the peace.

(2) If at any time the chief officer of police is of opinion that by reason of particular circumstances existing in any borough or urban district or in any part thereof the powers conferred on him by the last foregoing subsection will not be sufficient to enable him to prevent serious public disorder being occasioned by the holding of public processions in that borough, district or part, he shall apply to the council of the borough or district for an order prohibiting for such period not exceeding three months as may be specified in the application the holding of all public processions or of any class of public procession so specified either in the borough or urban district or in that part thereof, as the case may be, and upon receipt of the application the council may, with the consent of a Secretary of State, make an order either in terms of the application or with such modifications as may be approved by the Secretary of State.

This subsection shall not apply within the City of London as defined for the purposes of the Acts relating to the City police or within the Metropolitan police district.

(3) If at any time the Commissioner of the City of London police or the Commissioner of police of the Metropolis is of opinion that, by reason of particular circumstances existing in his police area or in any part thereof, the powers conferred on him by subsection (1) of this section will not be sufficient to enable him to prevent serious public disorder being occasioned by the holding of public processions in that area or part, he may, with the consent of the Secretary of State, make an order prohibiting for such period not exceeding three months as may be specified in the order the holding of all public processions or of any class of public procession so specified either in the police area or in that part thereof, as the case may be.

(4) Any person who knowingly fails to comply with any directions given or conditions imposed under this section, or organises or assists in organising any public procession held or intended to be held in contravention of an order made under this section or incites any person to take part in such a procession, shall be guilty of an offence.

4.—(1) Any person who, while present at any public meeting or on the occasion of any public procession, has with him any offensive weapon, otherwise than in pursuance of lawful authority, shall be guilty of an offence.

(2) For the purposes of this section, a person shall not be deemed to be acting in pursuance of lawful authority unless he is acting in his capacity as a servant of the Crown or of either House of Parliament or of any local authority or as a constable or as a member of a recognised corps or as a member of a fire brigade.

5. Any person who in any public place or at any public meeting uses threatening, abusive or insulting words or behaviour with intent to provoke a breach of the peace or whereby a breach of the peace is likely to be occasioned, shall be guilty of an offence.

6. Section one of the Public Meeting Act, 1908, (which provides that any person who at a lawful public meeting acts in a disorderly manner for the purpose of preventing the transaction of the business for which the meeting was called together, or incites others so to act, shall be guilty of an offence) shall have effect as if the following subsection were added thereto—

"(3) If any constable reasonably suspects any person of committing an offence under the foregoing provisions of this section, he may if requested so to do by the chairman of the meeting require that person to declare to him immediately his name and address and, if that person refuses or fails so to declare his name and address or gives a false name and address he shall be guilty of an offence under this subsection and liable on summary conviction thereof to a fine not exceeding forty shillings, and if he refuses or fails so to declare his name and address or if the constable reasonably suspects him of giving a false name and address, the constable may without warrant arrest him."

7.—(1) Any person who commits an offence under section two of this Act shall be liable on summary conviction to imprisonment for a term not exceeding six months or to a fine not exceeding one hundred pounds, or to both such imprisonment and fine, or, on conviction on indictment, to imprisonment for a term not exceeding two years or to a fine not exceeding five hundred pounds, or to both such imprisonment and fine.

(2) Any person guilty of any other offence under this Act shall be liable on summary conviction to imprisonment for a term not exceeding three months or to a fine not exceeding fifty pounds, or to both such imprisonment and fine.

(3) A constable may without warrant arrest any person reasonably suspected by him to be committing an offence under section one, four or five of this Act.

[§ 8. Application to Scotland.]
[§ 9. Interpretation, etc.]

10.—(1) This Act may be cited as the Public Order Act, 1936.

(2) This Act shall not extend to Northern Ireland.

(3) This Act shall come into operation on the first day of January nineteen hundred and thirty-seven.

MINISTERS OF THE CROWN ACT, 1937
1 Edw. 8 and 1 Geo. 6, c. 38

PART I

Salaries and Pension

1.—(1) The annual salaries payable—

(a) to each of the Ministers of the Crown named in Part I of the First Schedule to this Act, shall, subject to the provisions of this Act as to number, be five thousand pounds;

(b) to each of the Ministers of the Crown named in Part II of the said Schedule, shall be three thousand pounds;

(c) to the Minister of the Crown named in Part III of the said Schedule, shall be two thousand pounds.

(2) Subject to the provisions of this Act as to number, the annual salaries payable to the Parliamentary Under-Secretaries to the Departments of State shall—

(a) in the case of the Parliamentary Secretary to the Treasury, be three thousand pounds, and in the case of the Financial Secretary to the Treasury, be two thousand pounds;

(b) in the case of the Secretary for Mines and of the Secretary of the Department of Overseas Trade, be two thousand pounds each;

(c) in the case of each of the Parliamentary Under-Secretaries to the Departments of State specified in the Second Schedule to this Act, other than the Parliamentary Secretaries mentioned in the last foregoing paragraph, be fifteen hundred pounds;

(d) in the case of the Assistant Postmaster-General, be twelve hundred pounds:

Provided that, if and so long as there are two Parliamentary Under-Secretaries to the Foreign Office, to the Admiralty, or to the War Office, the annual salary payable to each of the two Parliamentary Under-Secretaries may be of such amount as may be determined by the Treasury, but so that the aggregate of the annual salaries payable to both of them does not exceed three thousand pounds.

(3) Subject to the provisions of this Act as to number, the annual salaries payable to each of the Junior Lords of the Treasury shall be one thousand pounds.

2.—(1) The number of persons holding office as Secretary of State to whom salaries may be paid under this Act shall not exceed eight.

(2) The number of Parliamentary Under-Secretaries to the Departments of State to whom salaries may be paid under this Act shall—

(*a*) in the case of the Treasury, not exceed two;

(*b*) in the case of the Board of Trade, not exceed three, including the Secretary for Mines and the Secretary of the Department of Overseas Trade;

(*c*) in the case of the Foreign Office, of the War Office, and of the Admiralty, not exceed two;

(*d*) in the case of any other Department of State mentioned in the Second Schedule to this Act, and in the case of the Post Office, not exceed one.

(3) The number of the Junior Lords of the Treasury to whom salaries may be paid under this Act shall not exceed five.

3.—(1) If and so long as any Minister of the Crown to whom this section applies is a member of the Cabinet, there shall be paid to him an additional salary of such amount as together with the salary payable to him in respect of the office held by him will amount to five thousand pounds a year.

(2) The date upon which any Minister of the Crown to whom this section applies becomes or ceases to be a member of the Cabinet shall be published in the London Gazette, and any such notification shall be conclusive evidence for the purposes of this section.

(3) This section applies to any Minister of the Crown named in Part II of the First Schedule to this Act, and to the Chancellor of the Duchy of Lancaster, if, in any case, his salary as such is less than five thousand pounds a year.

4.—(1) There shall be paid to the person who is Prime Minister and First Lord of the Treasury an annual salary of ten thousand pounds.

(2) Any person who, whether before or after the passing of this Act, has been Prime Minister and has as First Lord of the Treasury taken the official oath prescribed by section five of the Promissory Oaths Act, 1868, shall be entitled to a pension of two thousand pounds a year:

Provided that no pension shall be payable under this subsection to any person so long as he is in receipt of any pension under the Political Offices Pension Act, 1869, or any salary payable out of moneys provided by Parliament, the revenues of the Duchy of Lancaster or the Consolidated Fund of the United Kingdom.

5. There shall be paid to the Leader of the Opposition an annual salary of two thousand pounds:

Provided that, if the Leader of the Opposition is in receipt of a pension payable to him under this Act, no salary shall be payable to him under this section, and if he is in receipt of a pension under the Political Offices Pension Act, 1869, the salary payable to him under this section shall be reduced by an amount equal to the amount of that pension.

6.—(1) Subject to the provisions of this Act as to the payment of additional salaries to certain Cabinet Ministers, a person to whom any salary is payable under this Act, shall be entitled to receive only one such salary, but if he is the holder of two or more offices in respect of which a salary is so payable and there is a difference in the salaries payable in respect of those offices, the office in respect of which salary is payable to him shall be that in respect of which the highest salary is payable.

(2) No person in receipt of a salary or pension under this Act shall be entitled to receive any sum out of moneys provided by Parliament by way of salary or allowance in respect of his membership of the House of Commons.

7.—(1) The salaries payable under this Act, except that payable to the Leader of the Opposition, shall be paid out of moneys provided by Parliament.

(2) The salary payable under this Act to the Leader of the Opposition, and any pension payable under this Act to a person who has been Prime Minister and First Lord of the Treasury, shall be charged on and payable out of the Consolidated Fund of the United Kingdom or the growing produce thereof.

8. The amount specified in this Act as being the amount of any salary payable thereunder out of moneys provided by Parliament shall be taken to be the maximum amount so payable, and accordingly, notwithstanding the provisions of this Act as to any such amount, the salary so payable in any year in respect of any office may be of a less amount than that so specified.

Part II

Capacity to Sit in the House of Commons

9.—(1) Subject as hereinafter provided no person to whom a salary is payable under this Act shall by reason of his being the holder of the office or place in respect of which such a salary is payable, be rendered incapable of being elected, or of sitting and voting, as a member of the House of Commons:

Provided that—

(*a*) the number of persons entitled to sit and vote in that House while they are Ministers of the Crown named in Part I of the First Schedule to this Act shall not exceed fifteen;

(*b*) the number of persons entitled to sit and vote in that House while they are Ministers of the Crown named in Part II of the said Schedule shall not exceed three; and

(*c*) the number of persons entitled to sit and vote in that House while they are Parliamentary Under-Secretaries shall not exceed twenty.

(2) If at any time the number of persons who are members of the House of Commons while they are Ministers of the Crown named in Part I or in Part II of the First Schedule to this Act, or while they are Parliamentary Under-Secretaries, exceeds the number respectively entitled under this section to sit and vote in that House, the election of those members shall not be invalidated by reason of the excess, but of the number none except any who held his office and was a member of that House before the excess occurred, shall sit or vote therein until the number of Ministers of the Crown named in the said Part I or in the said Part II or of Parliamentary Under-Secretaries, as the case may be, who are members of the House of Commons has been reduced, by death, resignation or otherwise, to the number entitled under this section to sit and vote in that House.

(3) If any Minister of the Crown named in Part I or in Part II of the First Schedule to this Act or any Parliamentary Under-Secretary sits or votes in the House of Commons at a time when he is not entitled to do so by virtue of this section he shall be liable to a penalty not exceeding five hundred pounds for each day on which he so sits or votes.

PART III

Supplementary

10.—(1) In this Act unless the context otherwise requires the following expressions have the meanings hereby respectively assigned to them, that is to say:—

"Junior Lords of the Treasury" means the Lords Commissioners of the Treasury other than the First Lord and the Chancellor of the Exchequer;

"Leader of the Opposition" means that member of the House of Commons who is for the time being the Leader in that House of the party in opposition to His Majesty's Government having the greatest numerical strength in that House;

"Parliamentary Under-Secretary" means the Parliamentary Secretary and the Financial Secretary to the Treasury, any Parliamentary Under-Secretary of State, the Parliamentary and Financial Secretary to the Admiralty, the Financial Secretary of the War Office, the Civil Lord of the Admiralty, the Parliamentary Secretaries to the Departments of State specified in the Second Schedule to this Act, and the Assistant Postmaster-General; but does not include any Parliamentary Secretary to whom no salary is payable.

(2) For the purposes of this Act, the Secretary of the Department of Overseas Trade shall be deemed to be a Parliamentary Secretary to the Board of Trade, but without prejudice to the provisions of the Overseas Trade Department (Secretary) Act, 1918, relating to the method of his appointment and the functions to be discharged by him.

(3) If any doubt arises as to which is or was at any material time the party in opposition to His Majesty's Government having the greatest numerical strength in the House of Commons, or as to who is or was at any material time the leader in that House of such a party, the question shall be decided for the purposes of this Act by the Speaker of the House of Commons, and his decision, certified in writing under his hand, shall be final and conclusive. . . .

First Schedule

Ministers of the Crown to whom Salaries are payable under this Act

Part I

Chancellor of the Exchequer.
Secretaries of State.
First Lord of the Admiralty.
President of the Board of Trade.
Minister of Agriculture and Fisheries.
President of the Board of Education.
Minister of Health.
Minister of Labour.
Minister of Transport.
Minister for the Co-ordination of Defence.

Part II

Lord President of the Council.
Lord Privy Seal.
Postmaster-General.
First Commissioner of Works.

Part III

Minister of Pensions.

[Second, Third and Fourth Schedules omitted.]

ADMINISTRATION OF JUSTICE (MISCELLANEOUS PROVISIONS) ACT, 1938
1 and 2 Geo. 6, c. 63

7.—(1) The prerogative writs of mandamus, prohibition and certiorari shall no longer be issued by the High Court.

(2) In any case where the High Court would, but for the provisions of the last foregoing subsection, have had jurisdiction to order the issue of a writ of mandamus requiring any act to be done, or a writ of prohibition prohibiting any proceedings or matter, or a writ of certiorari removing any proceedings or matter into the High Court or any division thereof for any purpose, the Court may make an order requiring the act to be done, or prohibiting or removing the proceedings or matter, as the case may be.

(3) The said orders shall be called respectively an order of mandamus, an order of prohibition and an order of certiorari.

(4) No return shall be made to any such order and no pleadings in prohibition shall be allowed, but the order shall be final, subject to any right of appeal therefrom.

(5) In any enactment references to any writ of mandamus, prohibition or certiorari shall be construed as references to the corresponding order and references to the issue or award of any such writ shall be construed as references to the making of the corresponding order.

8. The power of the High Court under any enactment to require justices of the peace or a judge or officer of a county court to do any act relating to the duties of their respective offices, or to require any court of summary jurisdiction or court of quarter sessions to state a case for the opinion of the Court, in any case where immediately before the commencement of this Act the Court had by virtue of any enactment jurisdiction to make a rule absolute or to make an order, as the case may be, for any of those purposes, shall be exercisable by order of mandamus.

9.—(1) Informations in the nature of quo warranto are hereby abolished.

(2) In any case where any person acts in an office in which he is not entitled to act and an information in the nature of quo warranto would, but for the provisions of the last foregoing subsection, have lain against him, the High Court may grant an injunction restraining him from so acting and may (if the case so requires) declare the office to be vacant.

(3) No proceedings for an injunction under this section shall be taken by a person who would not immediately before the commencement of this Act have been entitled to apply for an information in the nature of quo warranto.

EMERGENCY POWERS (DEFENCE) ACT, 1939
2 and 3 Geo. 6, c. 62

1.—(1) Subject to the provisions of this section, His Majesty may by Order in Council make such Regulations (in this Act referred to as "Defence Regulations") as appear to him to be necessary or expedient for securing the public safety, the defence of the realm, the maintenance of public order and the efficient prosecution of any war in which His Majesty may be engaged, and for maintaining supplies and services essential to the life of the community.

(2) Without prejudice to the generality of the powers conferred by the preceding subsection, Defence Regulations may, so far as appears to His Majesty in Council to be necessary or expedient for any of the purposes mentioned in that subsection,—

(*a*) make provision for the apprehension, trial and punishment of persons offending against the Regulations, and for the detention of persons whose detention appears to the Secretary of State to be expedient in the interests of the public safety or the defence of the realm;

(*b*) authorise—

(i) the taking of possession or control, on behalf of His Majesty, of any property or undertaking;

(ii) the acquisition, on behalf of His Majesty, of any property other than land;

(*c*) authorise the entering and search of any premises; and

(*d*) provide for amending any enactment, for suspending the operation of any enactment, and for applying any enactment with or without modification.

(3) Defence Regulations may provide for empowering such authorities, persons or classes of persons as may be specified in the Regulations to make orders, rules and byelaws for any of the purposes for which such Regulations are authorised by this Act to be made, and may contain such incidental and supplementary provisions as appear to His Majesty in Council to be necessary or expedient for the purposes of the Regulations.

(4) A Defence Regulation, and any order, rule or byelaw duly made in pursuance of such a Regulation, shall have effect notwithstanding anything inconsistent therewith contained in any enactment other than this Act or in any instrument having effect by virtue of any enactment other than this Act.

(5) Nothing in this section shall authorise the imposition of any form of compulsory naval, military or air force service or any form of industrial conscription, or the making of provision for the trial by courts

martial of persons not being persons subject to the Naval Discipline
Act, to military law or to the Air Force Act.

(6) In this section the expression "enactment" includes any enactment of the Parliament of Northern Ireland.

2.—(1) The Treasury may by order provide for imposing and
recovering, in connection with any scheme of control contained in or
authorised by Defence Regulations, such charges as may be specified
in the order; and any such order may be varied or revoked by a
subsequent order of the Treasury.

(2) Any charges recovered by virtue of such an order as aforesaid
shall be paid into the Exchequer of the United Kingdom or, if the
order so directs, be paid into such public fund or account as may be
specified in the order.

(3) Any such order as aforesaid shall be laid before the Commons
House of Parliament as soon as may be after it is made, but, notwithstanding anything in subsection (4) of section one of the Rules Publication Act, 1893, shall be deemed not to be a statutory rule to which
that section applies.

(4) Any such order as aforesaid imposing or increasing a charge shall
cease to have effect on the expiration of the period of twenty-eight days
beginning with the day on which the order is made, unless at some
time before the expiration of that period it has been approved by a
resolution of the Commons House of Parliament, without prejudice,
however, to the validity of anything previously done under the order
or to the making of a new order.

In reckoning any period of twenty-eight days for the purposes of this
subsection, no account shall be taken of any time during which Parliament is dissolved or prorogued, or during which the Commons House
is adjourned for more than four days.

(5) Without prejudice to the preceding provisions of this section,
any Defence Regulations may provide—

(a) for charging, in respect of the grant or issue of any licence, permit,
certificate or other document for the purposes of the Regulations,
such fee not exceeding five pounds as may be prescribed under the
Regulations with the approval of the Treasury; and

(b) for imposing and recovering such charges as may be so prescribed
in respect of any services which, in pursuance of such Regulations,
are provided on behalf of His Majesty, or under arrangements
made on behalf of His Majesty, other than services necessary for the
performance of duties imposed by law upon the Crown;

and all sums received by way of such fees or charges as aforesaid shall
be paid into the Exchequer of the United Kingdom or, if the Treasury
so direct, be paid into such public fund or account as they may determine.

3.—(1) Unless the contrary intention appears therefrom, any provisions contained in, or having effect under, any Defence Regulation shall—

(*a*) in so far as they specifically impose prohibitions, restrictions or obligations in relation to ships, vessels or aircraft, or specifically authorise the doing of anything in relation to ships, vessels or aircraft, apply to all ships, vessels or aircraft in or over the United Kingdom and to all British ships or aircraft, not being Dominion ships or aircraft, wherever they may be; and

(*b*) in so far as they impose prohibitions, restrictions or obligations on persons apply (subject to the preceding provisions of this subsection) to all persons in the United Kingdom and all persons on board any British ship or aircraft, not being a Dominion ship or aircraft, and to all other persons being British subjects except persons in any of the following countries or territories, that is to say,—

(i) a Dominion,

(ii) India, Burma and Southern Rhodesia,

(iii) any country or territory to which any provisions of this Act can be extended by Order in Council, and

(iv) any other country or territory, being a country or territory under His Majesty's protection or suzerainty:

Provided that Defence Regulations may make provision whereby the owner, manager or charterer of any British ship or aircraft, being a person resident in the United Kingdom or a corporation incorporated under the law of any part of the United Kingdom, is subjected to restrictions in respect of the employment of persons in any foreign country or territory in connection with the management of the ship or aircraft.

(2) In this section the expression "Dominion ship or aircraft" means a British ship or aircraft registered in a Dominion, not being a ship or aircraft for the time being placed at the disposal of, or chartered by or on behalf of, His Majesty's Government in the United Kingdom; and, for the purposes of subsection (1) of this section, any ship or aircraft registered in India, Burma or Southern Rhodesia, not being a ship or aircraft for the time being placed at the disposal of, or chartered by or on behalf of, His Majesty's Government in the United Kingdom, shall be treated as if it were a Dominion ship or aircraft.

(3) Subsection (1) of this section shall apply in relation to British protected persons, as that subsection applies in relation to British subjects.

4.—(1) His Majesty may by Order in Council direct that the provisions of this Act other than this section shall extend, with such exceptions, adaptations and modifications, if any, as may be specified in the Order,—

(*a*) to the Isle of Man or any of the Channel Islands,

(*b*) to Newfoundland or any colony,

(*c*) to any British protectorate,

(*d*) to any territory in respect of which a mandate on behalf of the
League of Nations has been accepted by His Majesty, and is being
exercised by His Majesty's Government in the United Kingdom,
and

(*e*) (to the extent of His Majesty's jurisdiction therein) to any other
country or territory being a foreign country or territory in which
for the time being His Majesty has jurisdiction;

and, in particular, but without prejudice to the generality of the preceding provisions of this section, such an Order in Council may direct
that any such authority as may be specified in the Order shall be substituted for His Majesty in Council as the authority empowered to
make Defence Regulations for the country or territory in respect of
which the Order is made.

(2) His Majesty may by Order in Council make, or authorise the
making of, provision whereby persons offending against any Defence
Regulations may be apprehended, tried and punished in the United
Kingdom, or any of the countries or territories specified in the preceding subsection, whether section one of this Act extends to that
country or territory or not.

5.—(1) If and so far as the provisions of any Act for purposes of
defence passed by the Parliament of the Commonwealth of Australia
or by the Parliament of the Dominion of New Zealand purport to have
extra-territorial operation as respects—

(*a*) ships or aircraft registered in the said Commonwealth or Dominion,
or

(*b*) the employment of persons in relation to British ships or aircraft
by owners, managers or charterers of such ships or aircraft who are
persons resident in the said Commonwealth or Dominion or corporations incorporated under the law of the said Commonwealth
or Dominion or any part thereof,

the said provisions shall be deemed to have such operation.

(2) No law made for purposes of defence by the Indian Legislature
or the Federal Legislature of India or by the Legislature of Burma
shall, on the ground that it would have extra-territorial operation, be
deemed to be invalid in so far as it makes provision whereby any
owner, manager or charterer of a British ship or aircraft who is a
person resident in India or Burma or a corporation incorporated under
the law of India or Burma or any part thereof, is subjected to restrictions in respect of the employment of persons in relation to the ship
or aircraft.

Nothing in this subsection shall be taken to prejudice the effect of section ninety-nine of the Government of India Act, 1935, or section thirty-three of the Government of Burma Act, 1935.

(3) If and so far as the provisions of any law for purposes of defence made by the Legislature of Southern Rhodesia purport to have extra-territorial operation as respects—

(*a*) aircraft registered in Southern Rhodesia, or
(*b*) the employment of persons in relation to British aircraft by owners, managers or charterers of such aircraft who are persons resident in Southern Rhodesia or corporations incorporated under the law of Southern Rhodesia,

the said provisions shall be deemed to have such operation.

6.—(1) If, as respects any proceedings before a court (whether instituted before or after the commencement of this Act), the court is satisfied that it is expedient, in the interests of the public safety or the defence of the realm so to do, the court—

(*a*) may give directions that, throughout, or during any part of, the proceedings, such persons or classes of persons as the court may determine shall be excluded;
(*b*) may give directions prohibiting or restricting the disclosure of information with respect to the proceedings.

The powers conferred by this subsection shall be in addition to, and not in derogation of, any other powers which a court may have to give such directions as aforesaid.

(2) If any person contravenes any directions given by a court under the preceding subsection, then, without prejudice to the law relating to contempt of court, he shall be liable, on summary conviction, to imprisonment for a term not exceeding three months or to a fine not exceeding one hundred pounds or to both such imprisonment and such fine, or, on conviction on indictment, to imprisonment for a term not exceeding two years or to a fine not exceeding five hundred pounds or to both such imprisonment and such fine.

(3) The operation of subsection (4) of section eight of the Official Secrets Act, 1920, shall be suspended during the continuance in force of this Act.

7. Every document purporting to be an instrument made or issued by any Minister or other authority or person in pursuance of any provision contained in, or having effect under, Defence Regulations, and to be signed by or on behalf of the said Minister, authority or person, shall be received in evidence, and shall, until the contrary is proved, be deemed to be an instrument made or issued by that Minister, authority or person; and primâ facie evidence of any such instrument as aforesaid may, in any legal proceedings (including arbitrations), be given by the production of a document purporting to be certified to be a true copy of the instrument by, or on behalf of, the Minister or other authority or person having power to make or issue the instrument.

8.—(1) Every Order in Council containing Defence Regulations shall be laid before Parliament as soon as may be after it is made; but, notwithstanding anything in subsection (4) of section one of the Rules Publication Act, 1893, such an Order shall be deemed not to be a statutory rule to which that section applies.

(2) If either House of Parliament, within the next twenty-eight days on which that House has sat after such an Order in Council as aforesaid is laid before it, resolves that the Order be annulled, the Order shall thereupon cease to have effect except as respects things previously done or omitted to be done, without prejudice, however, to the making of a new Order.

(3) Any power conferred by the preceding provisions of this Act to make an Order in Council shall be construed as including a power to vary or revoke the Order.

9. The powers conferred by or under this Act shall be in addition to, and not in derogation of, the powers exercisable by virtue of the prerogative of the Crown.

10.—(1) In this Act the expression "Dominion" means any Dominion within the meaning of the Statute of Westminster, 1931, except Newfoundland, and includes any territory administered by His Majesty's Government in such a Dominion.

(2) References in this Act to British aircraft shall be construed as references to aircraft registered in any part of His Majesty's dominions, in any British protectorate or in any territory in respect of which a mandate on behalf of the League of Nations has been accepted by His Majesty and is being exercised by the Government of any part of His Majesty's dominions.

(3) For the avoidance of doubt it is hereby declared that any reference in this Act to Defence Regulations includes a reference to regulations made under any provision of this Act, as extended to any country or territory by an Order in Council under this Act, and that any reference in this Act to any country or territory includes a reference to the territorial waters, if any, adjacent to that country or territory.

11.—(1) Subject to the provisions of this section, this Act shall continue in force for the period of one year beginning with the date of the passing of this Act, and shall then expire:

Provided that, if at any time while this Act is in force, an address is presented to His Majesty by each House of Parliament praying that this Act should be continued in force for a further period of one year from the time at which it would otherwise expire, His Majesty may by Order in Council direct that this Act shall continue in force for that further period.

(2) Notwithstanding anything in the preceding subsection, if His Majesty by Order in Council declares that the emergency that was the occasion of the passing of this Act has come to an end, this Act shall expire at the end of the day on which the Order is expressed to come into operation.

(3) The expiry of this Act shall not affect the operation thereof as respects things previously done or omitted to be done.

12. This Act may be cited as the Emergency Powers (Defence) Act, 1939.

OFFICIAL SECRETS ACT, 1939
2 and 3 Geo. 6, c. 121

1. For section six of the Official Secrets Act, 1920, there shall be substituted the following section:

"**6.**—(1) Where a chief officer of police is satisfied that there is reasonable ground for suspecting that an offence under section one of the principal Act has been committed and for believing that any person is able to furnish information as to the offence or suspected offence, he may apply to a Secretary of State for permission to exercise the powers conferred by this subsection and, if such permission is granted, he may authorise a superintendent of police, or any police officer not below the rank of inspector, to require the person believed to be able to furnish information to give any information in his power relating to the offence or suspected offence, and, if so required and on tender of his reasonable expenses, to attend at such reasonable time and place as may be specified by the superintendent or other officer; and if a person required in pursuance of such an authorisation to give information, or to attend as aforesaid, fails to comply with any such requirement or knowingly gives false information, he shall be guilty of a misdemeanour.

(2) Where a chief officer of police has reasonable grounds to believe that the case is one of great emergency and that in the interest of the State immediate action is necessary, he may exercise the powers conferred by the last foregoing subsection without applying for or being granted the permission of a Secretary of State, but if he does so shall forthwith report the circumstances to the Secretary of State.

(3) References in this section to a chief officer of police shall be construed as including references to any other officer of police expressly authorised by a chief officer of police to act on his behalf for the purposes of this section when by reason of illness, absence, or other cause he is unable to do so."

EMERGENCY POWERS (DEFENCE) ACT, 1940
3 and 4 Geo. 6, c. 20

Whereas by the Emergency Powers (Defence) Act, 1939, His Majesty was enabled to exercise certain powers for the purpose of meeting the emergency existing at the date of the passing of that Act:

And whereas by reason of the development of hostilities since that date it has become necessary to extend the said powers in order to secure that the whole resources of the community may be rendered immediately available when required for purposes connected with the defence of the Realm:

Now therefore be it enacted . . .:—

1.—(1) The powers conferred on His Majesty by the Emergency Powers (Defence) Act, 1939, (hereinafter referred to as the "principal Act") shall, notwithstanding anything in that Act, include power by Order in Council to make such Defence Regulations making provision for requiring persons to place themselves, their services, and their property at the disposal of His Majesty, as appear to him to be necessary or expedient for securing the public safety, the defence of the Realm, the maintenance of public order, or the efficient prosecution of any war in which His Majesty may be engaged, or for maintaining supplies or services essential to the life of the community.

(2) In paragraph (*d*) of subsection (2) of section one of the principal Act and in subsection (4) of that section the expression "enactment" shall mean any enactment passed before the commencement of this Act.

(3) Subsection (1) of section eleven of the principal Act (which relates to the duration of that Act) shall have effect as if for the words "one year", where those words first occur, there were substituted the words "two years."

[§ 2 (Short title and citation) omitted.]

EDUCATION ACT, 1944
6 and 7 Geo. 6, c. 31

1.—(1) It shall be lawful for His Majesty to appoint a Minister (hereinafter referred to as "the Minister"), whose duty it shall be to promote the education of the people of England and Wales and the progressive development of institutions devoted to that purpose, and to secure the effective execution by local authorities, under his control and direction, of the national policy for providing a varied and comprehensive educational service in every area.

(2) The Minister shall for all purposes be a corporation sole under the name of the Minister of Education, and the department of which he is in charge shall be known as the Ministry of Education. . . .

4.—(1) There shall be two Central Advisory Councils for Education, one for England and the other for Wales and Monmouthshire, and it shall be the duty of those Councils to advise the Minister upon such matters connected with educational theory and practice as they think fit, and upon any questions referred to them by him.

(2) The members of each Council shall be appointed by the Minister, and the Minister shall appoint a member of each Council to be Chairman thereof and shall appoint an officer of the Ministry of Education to be secretary thereto. . . .

5. The Minister shall make to Parliament an annual report giving an account of the exercise and performance of the powers and duties conferred and imposed upon him by this Act and of the composition and proceedings of the Central Advisory Councils for Education.

6.—(1) Subject to the provisions of Part I of the First Schedule to this Act,[1] the local education authority for each county shall be the council of the county, and the local education authority for each county borough shall be the council of the county borough.

(2) The local administration of the statutory system of public education shall be conducted in accordance with the provisions of Parts II[2] and III[3] of the said Schedule. . . .

68. If the Minister is satisfied, either on complaint by any person or otherwise, that any local education authority or the managers or governors of any county or voluntary school have acted or are proposing to act unreasonably with respect to the exercise of any power conferred or the performance of any duty imposed by or under this Act, he may, notwithstanding any enactment rendering the exercise of the power or the performance of the duty contingent upon the opinion of the authority or of the managers or governors, give such directions as to the exercise of the power or the performance of the duty as appear to him to be expedient. . . .

99.—(1) If the Minister is satisfied, either upon complaint by any person interested or otherwise, that any local education authority, or the managers or governors of any county school or voluntary school, have failed to discharge any duty imposed upon them by or for the

---

[1] The Minister may appoint joint boards as the local education authority for two or more councils.

[2] Local education authorities are to establish education committees, in accordance with arrangements approved by the Minister.

[3] Local education authorities (except those which are the councils of county boroughs) may make "schemes of divisional administration" and delegate functions to divisional executives.

purposes of this Act, the Minister may make an order declaring the authority, or the managers or governors, as the case may be, to be in default in respect of that duty, and giving such directions for the purpose of enforcing the execution thereof as appear to the Minister to be expedient; and any such directions shall be enforceable, on an application made on behalf of the Minister, by mandamus. . . .

100.—(1) The Minister shall by regulations make provision:

(*a*) for the payment by him to local education authorities of annual grants in respect of the expenditure incurred by such authorities in the exercise of any of their functions relating to education, other than their functions relating to the medical inspection and treatment of pupils. . . .

(2) The Minister of Health shall by regulations make provision for the payment by him to local education authorities of annual grants in aid of the expenditure incurred by such authorities in the exercise of their functions relating to the medical inspection and treatment of pupils. . . .

(3) Any regulations made by the Minister or the Minister of Health under this section may make provision whereby the making of payments by him in pursuance thereof is dependent upon the fulfilment of such conditions as may be determined by or in accordance with the regulations, and may also make provision for requiring local education authorities and other persons to whom payments have been made in pursuance thereof to comply with such requirements as may be so determined. . . .

[§§ 101–122 and nine schedules omitted.]

SUPPLIES AND SERVICES (TRANSITIONAL POWERS) ACT, 1945
9 Geo. 6, c. 10

1.—(1) If it appears to His Majesty to be necessary or expedient that any Defence Regulation to which this section applies should have effect for the purpose of so maintaining controlling and regulating supplies and services as—

(*a*) to secure a sufficiency of those essential to the wellbeing of the community or their equitable distribution or their availability at fair prices; or

(*b*) to facilitate the demobilisation and resettlement of persons and to secure the orderly disposal of surplus material; or

(*c*) to facilitate the readjustment of industry and commerce to the requirements of the community in time of peace; or (*d*) to assist the relief of suffering and the restoration and distribution of essential supplies and services in any part of His Majesty's dominions or in foreign countries that are in grave distress as the result of war;

he may by Order in Council direct that the Regulation shall have effect by virtue of this Act whether or not it is for the time being necessary or expedient for the purposes specified in subsection (1) of section one of the Emergency Powers (Defence) Act, 1939.

(2) An Order in Council made under this section with respect to any Defence Regulation shall provide for the making in the Regulation of such adaptations, if any, as appear to His Majesty to be necessary or expedient for rendering it applicable for the purposes aforesaid.

(3) Where an Order in Council is made under this section with respect to any Defence Regulation, all orders and other instruments made under the Regulation and in force at the date when the Order in Council comes into operation shall continue in force and shall, save as is otherwise expressly provided in the Order in Council, have effect as if they had been made under the Regulation as extended by the Order in Council and as if any references in those orders and instruments to any of the purposes specified in subsection (1) of section one of the Emergency Powers (Defence) Act, 1939, included references to the purposes specified in subsection (1) of this section.

(4) This section applies to any Defence Regulation contained in Part III or Part IV of the Defence (General) Regulations, 1939, at the date of the passing of this Act and to any Defence Regulation specified in the second column of the First Schedule to this Act, and references in any Order in Council made under this section to any such Regulation shall be construed as references to that Regulation as in force at the date on which the Order comes into operation.

2.—(1) The powers conferred on His Majesty by the principal Acts to make such Defence Regulations as appear to him to be necessary or expedient for the purposes specified in subsection (1) of section one of the Emergency Powers (Defence) Act, 1939, shall include power by Order in Council to make such Defence Regulations as appear to him to be necessary or expedient for controlling the prices to be charged for goods of any description or the charges to be made for services of any description, whether or not such Regulations are necessary or expedient for the purposes specified in the said subsection (1).

(2) Without prejudice to the generality of the power conferred by the last foregoing subsection, any Defence Regulation made in pursuance thereof may amend the Goods and Services (Price Control) Acts, 1939 to 1943.

(3) Any Defence Regulation expressed to be made in pursuance of the said power shall have effect by virtue of this Act.

3.—(1) His Majesty, by Order in Council made under this Act, may revoke in whole or in part any Defence Regulation which has effect by virtue of this Act or may vary any such Regulation in such manner as appears to him—

(a) in the case of a Regulation to which section one of this Act applies, to be necessary or expedient for any of the purposes specified in subsection (1) of that section or, while the principal Acts continue in force, for any of the purposes specified in subsection (1) of section one of the Emergency Powers (Defence) Act, 1939, or

(b) in the case of a Regulation made in pursuance of the power conferred by the last foregoing section, to be necessary or expedient for the additional purpose specified in subsection (1) of that section.

(2) Subsection (3) of section eight of the Emergency Powers (Defence) Act, 1939 (which relates to the power to revoke or vary Orders in Council made under that Act) shall not apply to any Defence Regulation which has effect by virtue of this Act.

4.—(1) Every Order in Council made under the principal Acts (or under those Acts as extended by section two of this Act) which contains Defence Regulations, every order or other instrument made under powers conferred by Defence Regulations which is determined in accordance with regulations made under section three of the Rules Publication Act, 1893, to be a statutory rule within the meaning of the said section and to be of the nature of a public Act or which is or is deemed to be a statutory rule to which the Rules Publication Act (Northern Ireland), 1925, applies (being an Order in Council order or instrument made after the passing of this Act), and every Order in Council made under this Act, shall be laid before Parliament as soon as may be after it is made; and if either House of Parliament, within the period of forty days beginning with the day on which any such Order in Council, order or instrument is laid before it, resolves that it be annulled, it shall cease to have effect, but without prejudice to anything previously done thereunder or to the making of any new Order in Council, order or other instrument.

In reckoning any period for the purposes of this subsection no account shall be taken of any time during which Parliament is dissolved or prorogued or during which both Houses are adjourned for more than four days.

(2) Section one of the Rules Publication Act, 1893, shall not apply to any such Order in Council, order or other instrument as aforesaid.

(3) Subsections (1) and (2) of section eight of the Emergency Powers (Defence) Act, 1939, are hereby repealed.

5.—(1) Save as is otherwise expressly provided in the last two foregoing sections of this Act, nothing in this Act shall be construed as restricting the operation of the principal Acts while those Acts remain in force, or as affecting their application to Defence Regulations having effect by virtue of this Act, and any reference in those Acts to the purposes for which Defence Regulations may be made shall, in their application to Defence Regulations having effect by virtue of this Act, be construed as including a reference to the purposes specified in section one or, as the case may be, section two of this Act.

(2) If the principal Acts expire while this Act is in force—

(*a*) the provisions of those Acts, except the provisions specified in the Second Schedule to this Act, shall, notwithstanding their expiry for all other purposes, continue to apply (so far as applicable) while this Act is in force to any Defence Regulation having effect by virtue of this Act, any order or other instrument made under any such Regulation and any scheme of control contained in or authorised by any such Regulation; and

(*b*) any such Regulation and any order or other instrument made under any such Regulation shall have effect, as from the date of the expiry of the said Acts, as if references therein to any of the purposes specified in subsection (1) of section one of the Emergency Powers (Defence) Act, 1939, were omitted therefrom.

(3) Any enactment other than the principal Acts referring to Defence Regulations or to powers conferred under the Emergency Powers (Defence) Act, 1939, shall be construed as including a reference to Defence Regulations having effect by virtue of this Act or, as the case may be, to powers conferred thereby.

(4) Section four of the Emergency Powers (Defence) Act, 1939 (which provides for the application of that Act to colonies and other territories) shall have effect as if the reference to the provisions of that Act included a reference to the foregoing provisions of this Act, and as if the reference to the authority empowered to make Defence Regulations included a reference to the authority empowered to exercise the powers of His Majesty in Council under the foregoing provisions of this Act; and the said section shall, if the principal Acts expire while this Act is in force, continue in force, notwithstanding such expiry, so far as it provides for the extension of the foregoing provisions of this Act to any country or territory mentioned in the said section.

(5) The provisions of Parts II, V and VI of the Requisitioned Land and War Works Act, 1945 (which confer temporary powers to acquire and retain possession of land used for war purposes and to maintain, use and remove war works) shall, subject as hereinafter provided, have effect as if the expression "war period" included any period after the expiry of the Emergency Powers (Defence) Act, 1939, during which this Act is in force and as if the expression "war purposes" included the purposes specified in subsection (1) of section one of this Act, and any

other provisions of the said Requisitioned Land and War Works Act, 1945 (except section forty-five thereof), shall, so far as they relate to the provisions aforesaid, have the like effect:

Provided that no powers shall be exercisable by virtue of this sub-section unless the appropriate Minister has certified—

(a) in a case where the powers arise in consequence of the doing of work on land, that the work was done after the date of the expiry of the Emergency Powers (Defence) Act, 1939, for the purposes specified in subsection (1) of section one of this Act, or that works constructed in the course of the work have been used after the said date for the purposes aforesaid; or

(b) in a case where the powers arise in consequence of the possession or use of land or damage caused by the use of land, that the land has been used after the said date for the purposes aforesaid;

and has served a copy of the certificate, either by delivery or by pre-paid registered letter on any person to whom compensation under paragraph (a) of subsection (1) of section two or subsection (2) of section three of the Compensation (Defence) Act, 1939, is in course of payment in respect of the land to which the certificate relates. . . .

6.—(1) For the purposes of the Ministry of Supply Act, 1939 (which confers powers on the Minister to acquire, produce or dispose of articles required for the public service and to exercise certain other powers in relation to such articles) the expression "articles required for the public service" shall include any supplies which the Minister of Supply is satisfied that it is necessary or expedient to maintain, control or regulate for any of the purposes specified in subsection (1) of section one of this Act, and the expression "works required for the public service" shall be construed accordingly.

(2) Notwithstanding anything in proviso (i) to subsection (1) of section two of the Ministry of Supply Act, 1939, the powers of the Minister of Supply under that subsection may, so long as this Act continues in force, be exercised in relation to the supply to any other government department of any articles required by that department for the purpose of the discharge of its functions, whether or not the powers of that department in relation to the supply of those articles are for the time being transferred to or made exercisable by the Minister under section three of the Ministry of Supply Act, 1939.

(3) Notwithstanding anything in proviso (ii) to the said subsection (1) of section two, the powers of the said Minister under that subsection of manufacturing or otherwise producing articles may continue to be exercised so long as this Act continues in force in respect of any articles whatsover required for the public service within the meaning of the Ministry of Supply Act, 1939, as amended by this Act.

(4) Notwithstanding anything in section fourteen of the Ministry of

HBG

Supply Act, 1939, the provisions of sections seven to thirteen thereof shall continue in force so long as this Act continues in force.

7. There shall be defrayed out of moneys provided by Parliament any expenses incurred by any Minister of the Crown in consequence of the passing of this Act, and any increase attributable to the passing of this Act in any sums authorised or required by any other enactment to be paid out of moneys provided by Parliament.

8.—(1) Subject as hereinafter provided this Act shall continue in force for the period of five years after the passing thereof and shall then expire:

Provided that, if at any time while this Act is in force, an Address is presented to His Majesty by each House of Parliament praying that this Act should be continued in force for a further period of one year from the time at which it would otherwise expire, His Majesty may by Order in Council direct that this Act shall continue in force for that further period.

(2) Subsection (2) of section thirty-eight of the Interpretation Act, 1889, shall apply upon the expiry of this Act as if this Act had then been repealed.

9. Nothing in this Act shall restrict the powers of the Parliament of Northern Ireland to make laws with respect to any matter with respect to which that Parliament has power to make laws, and any laws made by that Parliament with respect to any such matters shall have effect notwithstanding anything in any Defence Regulation having effect by virtue of this Act and applicable to Northern Ireland, or in any order or other instrument made under such a Regulation.

10.—(1) This Act may be cited as the Supplies and Services (Transitional Powers) Act, 1945.

(2) In this Act the expression "Defence Regulation" means a Regulation made under the Emergency Powers (Defence) Act, 1939, or under that Act as extended by any subsequent enactment (including this Act), and the expression "the principal Acts" means the Emergency Powers (Defence) Acts, 1939 to 1945.

[Two schedules omitted.]

MINISTERS OF THE CROWN (TRANSFER OF FUNCTIONS) ACT, 1946
9 and 10 Geo. 6, c. 31

General Power to redistribute Functions of Ministers

1.—(1) His Majesty may by Order in Council provide for the transfer to any Minister of the Crown of any functions theretofore exercisable by another Minister of the Crown.

(2) His Majesty may by Order in Council provide for the dissolution of the Government Department in the charge of any Minister of the Crown and the transfer to or distribution among such other Minister or Ministers of the Crown as may be specified in the Order of any functions theretofore exercisable by the Minister in charge of that Department.

(3) An Order in Council under this section may contain such incidental, consequential and supplemental provisions as may be necessary or expedient for the purpose of giving full effect to the Order, including provisions—

(*a*) for the transfer of any property, rights and liabilities held, enjoyed or incurred by any Minister of the Crown in connection with any functions transferred or distributed;

(*b*) for the carrying on and completion by or under the authority of the Minister to whom any functions are transferred of anything commenced by or under the authority of a Minister of the Crown before the date when the Order takes effect;

(*c*) for such adaptations of the enactments relating to any functions transferred as may be necessary to enable them to be exercised by the Minister to whom they are transferred and his officers;

(*d*) for making in the enactments regulating the number of offices in respect of which salaries may be paid or the number of office holders who may be elected, and sit and vote, as members of the House of Commons such modifications as may be expedient by reason of any transfer of functions or dissolution of a Department effected by the Order, so, however, that such modifications shall not increase the amount of any salary which may be paid or the aggregate number of persons to whom such salaries may be paid under such enactments or the aggregate number of persons capable thereunder of being elected, and of sitting and voting, as aforesaid;

(*e*) for the substitution of the Minister to whom functions are transferred for any other Minister of the Crown in any instrument, contract, or legal proceedings made or commenced before the date when the Order takes effect.

(4) Where by any Order made under this section provision is made for the transfer of functions in respect of which any Minister may sue or be sued by virtue of any enactment, the Order shall make any provision which may be required for enabling the Minister to whom those functions are transferred to sue or be sued in like manner.

(5) A certificate issued by a Minister of the Crown that any property vested in any other Minister immediately before an Order under this section takes effect has been transferred by virtue of the Order to the Minister issuing the certificate shall be conclusive evidence of the transfer.

2. If His Majesty is pleased by Order in Council to direct that any change shall be made in the style and title of a Minister of the Crown, the Order may contain provisions substituting the new style and title—

(*a*) in the enactments (including such enactments as are mentioned in paragraph (*d*) of subsection (3) of the last foregoing section) relating to the Minister;

(*b*) in any instrument, contract, or legal proceedings made or commenced before the date when the Order takes effect.

3.—(1) No Order in Council which provides for the dissolution of a Government Department shall be made under this Act unless, after copies of the draft thereof have been laid before Parliament, each House presents an Address to His Majesty praying that the Order be made.

(2) An Order in Council under this Act, not being an Order made in pursuance of such an Address as aforesaid, shall not come into operation until copies thereof have been laid before Parliament, and if either House, within the period of forty days beginning with the day on which a copy thereof is laid before it, resolves that an Address be presented to His Majesty praying that the Order in Council be annulled, no further proceedings shall be taken thereunder after the date of the resolution, and His Majesty may by Order in Council revoke the Order, so, however, that any such resolution and revocation shall be without prejudice to the validity of anything previously done thereunder or to the making of a new Order.

In reckoning any such period of forty days, no account shall be taken of any time during which Parliament is dissolved or prorogued or during which both Houses are adjourned for more than four days.

(3) Notwithstanding anything in subsection (4) of section one of the Rules Publication Act, 1893, an Order under this Act shall be deemed not to be, or to contain, statutory rules to which that section applies.

(4) Any Order under this Act may be varied or revoked by a subsequent Order thereunder made in the like manner and subject to the like conditions, so however that the variation or revocation of an Order providing for the dissolution of a Government Department shall not affect the dissolution thereof.

(5) No provision in any Act passed before the commencement of this Act shall be construed as limiting the powers conferred by this Act.

(6) Nothing in this Act shall prejudice any power exercisable by virtue of the prerogative of the Crown in relation to the functions of Ministers of the Crown.

(7) Any reference in the foregoing provisions of this Act to a Minister of the Crown shall include a reference to Ministers acting jointly.

[§§ 4–7, and the First Schedule, provide for the continuance of the office and functions of the Ministers of Food, Labour and National Service, and Transport, and the Secretary of the Department of Overseas Trade.]

STATUTORY INSTRUMENTS ACT, 1946
9 and 10 Geo. 6, c. 36

An Act to repeal the Rules Publication Act, 1893, and to make further provision as to the instruments by which statutory powers to make orders, rules, regulations and other subordinate legislation are exercised.

[26th March 1946.]

1.—(1) Where by this Act or any Act passed after the commencement of this Act power to make, confirm or approve orders, rules, regulations or other subordinate legislation is conferred on His Majesty in Council or on any Minister of the Crown then, if the power is expressed—

(*a*) in the case of a power conferred on His Majesty, to be exercisable by Order in Council;

(*b*) in the case of a power conferred on a Minister of the Crown, to be exercisable by statutory instrument,

any document by which that power is exercised shall be known as a "statutory instrument" and the provisions of this Act shall apply thereto accordingly.

(2) Where by any Act passed before the commencement of this Act power to make statutory rules within the meaning of the Rules Publication Act, 1893, was conferred on any rule-making authority within the meaning of that Act, any document by which that power is exercised after the commencement of this Act shall, save as is otherwise provided by regulations made under this Act, be known as a "statutory instrument" and the provisions of this Act shall apply thereto accordingly.

2.—(1) Immediately after the making of any statutory instrument, it shall be sent to the King's printer of Acts of Parliament and numbered in accordance with regulations made under this Act, and except in such cases as may be provided by any Act passed after the commencement of this Act or prescribed by regulations made under this Act, copies thereof shall as soon as possible be printed and sold by the King's printer of Acts of Parliament.

(2) Any statutory instrument may, without prejudice to any other mode of citation, be cited by the number given to it in accordance with the provisions of this section, and the calendar year.

[§ 3. Supplementary provisions as to publication.]

4.—(1) Where by this Act or any Act passed after the commencement of this Act any statutory instrument is required to be laid before Parliament after being made, a copy of the instrument shall be laid before each House of Parliament and, subject as hereinafter provided, shall be so laid before the instrument comes into operation:

Provided that if it is essential that any such instrument should come into operation before copies thereof can be so laid as aforesaid, the instrument may be made so as to come into operation before it has been so laid; and where any statutory instrument comes into operation before it is laid before Parliament, notification shall forthwith be sent to the Lord Chancellor and to the Speaker of the House of Commons drawing attention to the fact that copies of the instrument have yet to be laid before Parliament and explaining why such copies were not so laid before the instrument came into operation.

(2) Every copy of any such statutory instrument sold by the King's printer of Acts of Parliament shall bear on the face thereof—

(a) a statement showing the date on which the statutory instrument came or will come into operation; and

(b) either a statement showing the date on which copies thereof were laid before Parliament or a statement that such copies are to be laid before Parliament.

(3) Where any Act passed before the date of the commencement of this Act contains provisions requiring that any Order in Council or other document made in exercise of any power conferred by that or any other Act be laid before Parliament after being made, any statutory instrument made in exercise of that power shall by virtue of this Act be laid before Parliament and the foregoing provisions of this section shall apply thereto accordingly in substitution for any such provisions as aforesaid contained in the Act passed before the said date.

5.—(1) Where by this Act or any Act passed after the commencement of this Act, it is provided that any statutory instrument shall be subject to annulment in pursuance of resolution of either House of Parliament, the instrument shall be laid before Parliament after being made and the provisions of the last foregoing section shall apply thereto accordingly, and if either House, within the period of forty days beginning with the day on which a copy thereof is laid before it, resolves that an Address be presented to His Majesty praying that the instrument be annulled, no further proceedings shall be taken thereunder after the date of the resolution, and His Majesty may by Order in Council revoke the instrument, so however, that any such resolution and revocation shall be without prejudice to the validity of anything previously done under the instrument or to the making of a new statutory instrument.

(2) Where any Act passed before the date of the commencement of this Act contains provisions requiring that any Order in Council or other document made in exercise of any power conferred by that or

any other Act shall be laid before Parliament after being made and shall cease to be in force or may be annulled, as the case may be, if within a specified period either House presents an address to His Majesty or passes a resolution to that effect, then, subject to the provisions of any Order in Council made under this Act, any statutory instrument made in exercise of the said power shall by virtue of this Act be subject to annulment in pursuance of a resolution of either House of Parliament and the provisions of the last foregoing subsection shall apply thereto accordingly in substitution for any such provisions as aforesaid contained in the Act passed before the said date.

6.—(1) Where by this Act or any Act passed after the commencement of this Act it is provided that a draft of any statutory instrument shall be laid before Parliament, but the Act does not prohibit the making of the instrument without the approval of Parliament, then, in the case of an Order in Council the draft shall not be submitted to His Majesty in Council, and in any other case the statutory instrument shall not be made, until after the expiration of a period of forty days beginning with the day on which a copy of the draft is laid before each House of Parliament, or, if such copies are laid on different days, with the later of the two days, and if within that period either House resolves that the draft be not submitted to His Majesty or that the statutory instrument be not made, as the case may be, no further proceedings shall be taken thereon, but without prejudice to the laying before Parliament of a new draft.

(2) Where any Act passed before the date of the commencement of this Act contains provisions requiring that a draft of any Order in Council or other document to be made in exercise of any power conferred by that or any other Act shall be laid before Parliament before being submitted to His Majesty, or before being made, as the case may be, and that it shall not be so submitted or made if within a specified period either House presents an address to His Majesty or passes a resolution to that effect, then, subject to the provisions of any Order in Council made under this Act, a draft of any statutory instrument made in exercise of the said power shall by virtue of this Act be laid before Parliament and the provisions of the last foregoing subsection shall apply thereto accordingly in substitution for any such provisions as aforesaid contained in the Act passed before the said date.

7.—(1) In reckoning for the purposes of either of the last two foregoing sections any period of forty days, no account shall be taken of any time during which Parliament is dissolved or prorogued or during which both Houses are adjourned for more than four days.

(2) In relation to any instrument required by any Act, whether passed before or after the commencement of this Act, to be laid before the House of Commons only, the provisions of the last three foregoing sections shall have effect as if references to that House were therein

substituted for references to Parliament and for references to either House and each House thereof.

(3) The provisions of sections four and five of this Act shall not apply to any statutory instrument being an order which is subject to special Parliamentary procedure, or to any other instrument which is required to be laid before Parliament, or before the House of Commons, for any period before it comes into operation.

8.—(1) The Treasury may, with the concurrence of the Lord Chancellor and the Speaker of the House of Commons, by statutory instrument make regulations for the purposes of this Act, and such regulations may, in particular:—

(*a*) provide for the different treatment of instruments which are of the nature of a public Act, and of those which are of the nature of a local and personal or private Act;

(*b*) make provision as to the numbering, printing, and publication of statutory instruments including provision for postponing the numbering of any such instrument which does not take effect until it has been approved by Parliament, or by the House of Commons, until the instrument has been so approved;

(*c*) provide with respect to any classes or descriptions of statutory instrument that they shall be exempt, either altogether or to such extent as may be determined by or under the regulations, from the requirement of being printed and of being sold by the King's printer of Acts of Parliament, or from either of those requirements;

(*d*) determine the classes of cases in which the exercise of a statutory instrument by any rule-making authority constitutes or does not constitute the making of such a statutory rule as is referred to in subsection (2) of section one of this Act, and provide for the exclusion from that subsection of any such classes;

(*e*) provide for the determination by a person or persons nominated by the Lord Chancellor and the Speaker of the House of Commons of any question—

(i) as to the numbering, printing, or publication of any statutory instrument or class or description of such instruments:

(ii) whether or to what extent any statutory instrument or class or description of such instruments is, under the regulations, exempt from any such requirement as is mentioned in paragraph (*c*) of this subsection:

(iii) whether any statutory instrument or class or description of such instruments is in the nature of a public Act or of a local and personal or private Act:

(iv) whether the exercise of any power conferred by an Act passed before the commencement of this Act is or is not the exercise of a power to make a statutory rule.

(2) Every statutory instrument made under this section shall be subject to annulment in pursuance of a resolution of either House of Parliament.

9.—(1) If with respect to any power to confirm or approve orders, rules, regulations or other subordinate legislation conferred on a Minister of the Crown by any Act passed before the commencement of this Act, it appears to His Majesty in Council that, notwithstanding that the exercise of that power did not constitute the making of a statutory rule within the meaning of the Rules Publication Act, 1893, it is expedient that the provisions of this Act should apply to documents by which that power is exercised, His Majesty may by Order in Council direct that any document by which that power is exercised after such date as may be specified in the Order shall be known as a "statutory instrument" and the provisions of this Act shall apply thereto accordingly.

(2) If with respect to any Act passed before the commencement of this Act it appears to His Majesty in Council that by reason of the exceptional nature of any provisions of that Act the application of subsection (2) of section five or subsection (2) of section six of this Act to statutory instruments made under any provisions of that Act would be inexpedient, His Majesty may by Order in Council direct that those subsections shall not apply to statutory instruments made under those provisions, or shall apply thereto subject to such modifications as may be specified in the Order.

(3) A draft of any Order in Council proposed to be made under this section shall be laid before Parliament.

10.—(1) This Act shall come into operation on such date as His Majesty may by Order in Council appoint:

Provided that, without prejudice to the provisions of section thirty-seven of the Interpretation Act, 1889, the last foregoing section and, in relation to any Order in Council made thereunder, the provisions of sections six and seven of this Act shall come into operation on the passing of this Act.

(2) The Order in Council made under this section shall be laid before Parliament after being made.

11.—(1) For the purposes of this Act, any power to make, confirm or approve orders, rules, regulations or other subordinate legislation conferred on the Treasury, the Admiralty, the Board of Trade or any other government department shall be deemed to be conferred on the Minister of the Crown in charge of that department.

(2) If any question arises whether any board, commissioners or other body on whom any such power as aforesaid is conferred are a government department within the meaning of this section, or what Minister of the Crown is in charge of them, that question shall be referred to and determined by the Treasury.

12.—(1) The Rules Publication Act, 1893, is hereby repealed.

(2) The publication in the London, Edinburgh or Belfast Gazette

of a notice stating that a statutory instrument has been made, and specifying the place where copies thereof may be purchased, shall be sufficient compliance with the provisions of any enactment, whether passed before or after the commencement of this Act, requiring that instrument to be published or notified in that Gazette.

13.—(1) This Act may be cited as the Statutory Instruments Act, 1946.

(2) This Act shall apply to any statutory instrument made by His Majesty in Council or by any Minister of the Crown (not being a rule-making authority within the meaning of the Rules Publication Act (Northern Ireland), 1925) in so far as it extends to Northern Ireland, but except as aforesaid this Act shall not extend to Northern Ireland.

TRADE DISPUTES AND TRADE UNIONS ACT, 1946
9 and 10 Geo. 6, c. 52

Be it enacted by the King's most Excellent Majesty, by and with the advice and consent of the Lords Spiritual and Temporal, and Commons, in this present Parliament assembled, and by the authority of the same, as follows:

1. The Trade Disputes and Trade Unions Act, 1927 (in this Act referred to as "the Act of 1927") is hereby repealed, and, subject to the transitional provisions set out in the Schedule to this Act, every enactment and rule of law amended or otherwise affected by that Act shall, as from the commencement of this Act, have effect as if the Act of 1927 had not been passed.

2. This Act may be cited as the Trade Disputes and Trade Unions Act, 1946.

COAL INDUSTRY NATIONALISATION ACT, 1946
9 and 10 Geo. VI, c. 59

An Act to establish public ownership and control of the coal-mining industry and certain allied activities; and for purposes connected therewith.

[12th July 1946.]

The National Coal Board

1.—(1) There shall be a National Coal Board which shall, on and after the primary vesting date, be charged with the duties of—

(*a*) working and getting the coal in Great Britain, to the exclusion (save as in this Act provided) of any other person;

(*b*) securing the efficient development of the coal-mining industry; and

(*c*) making supplies of coal available, of such qualities and sizes, in such quantities and at such prices, as may seem to them best calculated to further the public interest in all respects, including the avoidance of any undue or unreasonable preference or advantage.

(2) The functions of the National Coal Board (in this Act referred to as "the Board") shall include the carrying on of all such activities as it may appear to the Board to be requisite, advantageous or convenient for them to carry on for or in connection with the discharge of their duties under the preceding subsection, and in particular, but without prejudice to the generality of this section,—

(*a*) searching and boring for coal in Great Britain, to the exclusion of any other person;

(*b*) treating, rendering saleable, supplying and selling coal;

(*c*) producing, manufacturing, treating, rendering saleable, supplying and selling products of coal;

(*d*) producing or manufacturing any goods or utilities which are of a kind required by the Board for or in connection with the working and getting of coal or any other of their activities, or which can advantageously be produced or manufactured by the Board by reason of their having materials or facilities for the production or manufacture thereof in connection with the working and getting of coal or any other of their activities, and supplying and selling goods or utilities so produced or manufactured;

(*e*) any activities which can advantageously be carried on by the Board with a view to making the best use of any of the assets vested in them by this Act;

(*f*) activities conducive to advancing the skill of persons employed or to be employed for the purposes of any of the activities aforesaid, or the efficiency of equipment and methods to be used therefor, including the provision by the Board themselves, and their assisting the provision by others, of facilities for training, education and research.

(3) The Board shall have power to do any thing and to enter into any transaction (whether or not involving the expenditure, borrowing in accordance with the provisions of this Act in that behalf or lending of money, the acquisition of any property or rights, or the disposal of any property or rights not in their opinion required for the proper discharge of their functions) which in their opinion is calculated to facilitate the proper discharge of their duties under subsection (1) of this section or the carrying on by them of any such activities as aforesaid, or is incidental or conducive thereto.

(4) The policy of the Board shall be directed to securing, consistently with the proper discharge of their duties under subsection (1) of this section,—

(a) the safety, health and welfare of persons in their employment;

(b) the benefit of the practical knowledge and experience of such persons in the organisation and conduct of the operations in which they are employed;

(c) that the revenues of the Board shall not be less than sufficient for meeting all their outgoings properly chargeable to revenue account (including, without prejudice to the generality of that expression, provisions in respect of their obligations under sections twenty-eight and twenty-nine of this Act) on an average of good and bad years.

2.—(1) The Board shall be a body corporate by the name of "the National Coal Board", with perpetual succession and a common seal and power to hold land without licence in mortmain.

(2) The Board shall consist of a chairman and eight other members.

(3) The chairman and other members of the Board shall be appointed by the Minister of Fuel and Power (in this Act referred to as "the Minister") from amongst persons appearing to him to be qualified as having had experience of, and having shown capacity in, industrial, commercial or financial matters, applied science, administration, or the organisation of workers.

(4) A person shall be disqualified for being appointed or being a member of the Board so long as he is a member of the Commons House of Parliament.

(5) The Minister shall appoint one of the members of the Board to act as deputy chairman.

(6) There shall be paid to the members of the Board such salaries and allowances as may be determined by the Minister with the approval of the Treasury, and, on the retirement or death of any of them as to whom it may be so determined to make such provision, such pensions and gratuities to them or to others by reference to their service as may be so determined.

The said salaries and allowances, and any such pensions and gratuities as aforesaid, shall be paid out of the revenues of the Board.

(7) The Minister may make regulations with respect to—

(a) the appointment of, and the tenure and vacation of office by, the members of the Board;

(b) the quorum, proceedings and meetings of the Board, and determinations of the Board; and

(c) the execution of instruments and the mode of entering into contracts by and on behalf of the Board, and the proof of documents purporting to be executed, issued or signed by the Board or a member, officer or servant thereof.

(8) Subject to the provisions of any regulations made under the last preceding subsection, the Board shall have power to regulate their own procedure.

3.—(1) The Minister may, after consultation with the Board, give to the Board directions of a general character as to the exercise and performance by the Board of their functions in relation to matters appearing to the Minister to affect the national interest, and the Board shall give effect to any such directions.

(2) In framing programmes of reorganisation or development involving substantial outlay on capital account, the Board shall act on lines settled from time to time with the approval of the Minister.

(3) In the exercise and performance of their functions as to training, education and research, the Board shall act on lines settled as aforesaid.

(4) The Board shall afford to the Minister facilities for obtaining information with respect to the property and activities of the Board, and shall furnish him with returns, accounts and other information with respect thereto and afford to him facilities for the verification of information furnished, in such manner and at such times as he may require.

4.—(1) There shall be established for the purposes mentioned in this section two consumers' councils, to be known respectively as the Industrial Coal Consumers' Council and the Domestic Coal Consumers' Council.

(2) Each of the said councils shall consist of such number of persons as the Minister may think fit, appointed by him to represent the Board, and—

(*a*) in the case of the Industrial Coal Consumers' Council, after consultation with such bodies representative of the interests concerned as the Minister thinks fit, to represent consumers of coal, coke and manufactured fuel respectively, for industrial purposes or other purposes involving supply in bulk, and persons engaged in organising or effecting the sale or supply, whether for home use or for export, of coal, coke and manufactured fuel respectively, for those purposes;

(*b*) in the case of the Domestic Coal Consumers' Council, after consultation with such bodies representative of the interests concerned as the Minister thinks fit, to represent consumers of coal, coke and manufactured fuel respectively, for domestic purposes and other purposes not falling within the preceding paragraph, and persons engaged in organising or effecting the sale or supply of coal, coke and manufactured fuel respectively, for those purposes.

In formulating his proposals for appointments to each of the said councils, the Minister shall have particular regard to nominations made to him by the said bodies representative of the interests concerned of persons recommended by them as having both adequate knowledge of the requirements of those interests and also qualifications for exercising a wide and impartial judgment on the matters to be dealt with by the council generally.

(3) The Industrial Coal Consumers' Council shall be charged with the duties—

(a) of considering any matter affecting the sale or supply, whether for home use or for export, of coal, coke or manufactured fuel for the purposes mentioned in paragraph (a) of subsection (2) of this section which is the subject of a representation made to them by consumers for those purposes of coal, coke or manufactured fuel, as the case may be, or which appears to them to be a matter to which consideration ought to be given apart from any such representation, and, where action appears to them to be requisite as to any such matter, of notifying their conclusions to the Minister;

(b) of considering, and reporting to the Minister on, any such matter which may be referred to them by the Minister.

(4) The Domestic Coal Consumers' Council shall be charged with the like duties in relation to the sale or supply of coal, coke and manufactured fuel for the purposes mentioned in paragraph (b) of subsection (2) of this section.

(5) On the notification or making to the Minister by either of the said councils of their conclusions or report on any matter, if it appears to him, after consultation with the Board, that a defect is disclosed in the Board's general arrangements for the production, sale or supply of coal, coke or manufactured fuel, as the case may be, he may give to the Board such directions as he may think requisite for remedying the defect, and the Board shall give effect to any such directions. . . .

(8) Each of the said councils shall make an annual report to the Minister, and the Minister shall lay the reports before both Houses of Parliament.

[§§ 5–25. Detailed provisions for the transfer of assets to the Board, compensation, etc.]

[§ 26. The Minister may make advances to the Board for capital expenditure.]

[§ 27. The Board may, with the Minister's consent, borrow sums not exceeding £10,000,000 at any one period.]

[§ 28. Payments by the Board to the Minister to recoup expenses incurred by the Crown during the process of nationalisation, and of interest on advances.]

29.—(1) The Board shall establish a reserve fund.

(2) The management of the said fund, the sums to be carried from time to time to the credit thereof, and the application thereof, shall be as the Board may determine:

Provided that—

(*a*) no part of the said fund shall be applied otherwise than for purposes of the Board; and

(*b*) the power of the Minister to give directions to the Board shall extend to the giving of them, with the approval of the Treasury, of directions as to any matter relating to the establishment or management of the said fund, the carrying of sums to the credit thereof, or the application thereof, notwithstanding that the directions may be of a specific character.

30. Any excess of the Board's revenues for any financial year of the Board over their outgoings for that year properly chargeable to revenue account (including, without prejudice to the generality of that expression, provisions in respect of their obligations under the two last preceding sections) shall be applied for such purposes as the Board may determine:

Provided that—

(*a*) no part of any such excess shall be applied otherwise than for purposes of the Board; and

(*b*) the power of the Minister to give directions to the Board shall extend to the giving to them, with the approval of the Treasury, of directions as to the application of any such excess, notwithstanding that the directions may be of a specific character.

31.—(1) The Board shall keep proper accounts and other records in relation thereto, and shall prepare in respect of each financial year of the Board a statement of accounts in such form as the Minister may direct, being a form which shall conform with the best commercial standards and which shall distinguish the colliery activities and each of the main ancillary activities of the Board.

(2) The accounts of the Board shall be audited by auditors to be appointed annually by the Minister.

(3) So soon as the accounts of the Board have been audited, they shall send a copy of the statement of accounts referred to in subsection (1) of this section to the Minister together with a copy of any report made by the auditors on that statement or on the accounts of the Board.

(4) The Minister shall lay a copy of every such statement and report before each House of Parliament.

[§§ 32–33. Provisions as to stock.]

34.—(1) The Treasury may issue to the Minister out of the Consolidated Fund such sums as are necessary to enable him to make money payments, and advances to the Board, under this Act.

(2) For the purpose of providing sums (or any part of sums) to be

issued under the preceding subsection, or of providing for the replacement of all or any part of sums so issued, the Treasury may, at any time, if they think fit, raise money in any manner in which they are authorised to raise money under the National Loans Act, 1939, and any securities created and issued to raise money under this subsection shall be deemed for all purposes to have been created and issued under that Act.

[§§ 35–45. Account of Minister's receipts; provisions regarding superannuation, welfare of miners, research, etc.]

46.—(1) It shall be the duty of the Board to enter into consultation with organisations appearing to them to represent substantial proportions of the persons in the employment of the Board, or of any class of such persons, as to the Board's concluding with those organisations agreements providing for the establishment and maintenance of joint machinery for—

(*a*) the settlement by negotiation of terms and conditions of employment, with provision for reference to arbitration in default of such settlement in such cases as may be determined by or under the agreements; and

(*b*) consultation on—
    (i) questions relating to the safety, health or welfare of such persons;
    (ii) the organisation and conduct of the operations in which such persons are employed and other matters of mutual interest to the Board and such persons arising out of the exercise and performance by the Board of their functions.

(2) The Board shall deposit with the Minister and the Minister of Labour and National Service copies of any such agreement as aforesaid entered into by the Board and of any instrument varying the terms of any such agreement.

47. Nothing in this Act shall be deemed to exempt the Board from liability for any tax, duty, rate, levy, or other charge whatsoever, whether general or local.

[§ 48. Transfer of certain liabilities from colliery concerns to the Board.]

49.—(1) The Public Authorities Protection Act, 1893, and section twenty-one of the Limitation Act, 1939, shall not apply to any action, prosecution or proceeding against the Board, or for or in respect of any act, neglect or default done or committed by a servant or agent of the Board in his capacity as a servant or agent of theirs.

(2) In their application to any such action as aforesaid sections two and three of the Limitation Act, 1939 (which relate to the limitation of actions of contract and tort, and certain other actions) shall have

effect with the substitution for references therein to six years of references to three years.

(3) No right adverse to the title of the Board to any coal or mine of coal shall be capable of being acquired under the Limitation Act, 1939.

(4) For the avoidance of doubt it is hereby declared that the authorisations conferred on the Board by section one of this Act, whilst discharging them in the exercise and performance of the functions therein mentioned from limitations to which they might otherwise have been subject arising from the law relating to the capacity of statutory corporations, are not to be construed as authorising disregard of any enactment or any act or omission unlawful on any other ground.

[§ 50. The Board not required to insure against liabilities for workmen's compensation.]

[§§ 51–53. Board's documents as public records, etc.]

54.—(1) The Board shall, as soon as possible after the end of each financial year of the Board make to the Minister a report on the exercise and performance by them of their functions during that year and on their policy and programmes, and the Minister shall lay a copy of every such report before each House of Parliament.

(2) The report for any year shall set out any direction given by the Minister to the Board during that year unless the Minister has notified to the Board his opinion that it is against the national interest so to do.

[§§ 55–61. General provisions regarding disclosures of information relating to individual businesses, penalties for false information, prosecutions, arbitration, etc.]

62.—(1) Regulations made (whether by the Minister or by the Treasury) for the purposes of any provision of this Act (in this section referred to, in relation to the regulations in question, as "the authorising enactment") may, in addition to providing for any matters specified in the authorising enactment, provide—

(a) for imposing limits of time within which things to be done for the purposes of the regulations must be done, with or without power to any authority therein specified to extend limits imposed;

(b) for punishing persons offending against provisions of the regulations;

(c) for the determination of questions of fact or of law which may arise in giving effect to the regulations, and as to evidence for that purpose, and for regulating (otherwise than in relation to any court proceedings) any matters relating to the practice and procedure to be followed in connection with the determination of such questions, including provision as to parties and their representation and provision for the right to appear and be heard (as well in court proceedings as otherwise) of the Minister, District Valuation Boards, referees, or other authorities, and as to awarding costs of proceedings for the determination of such questions, determining the amount thereof and the enforcement of awards thereof;

(*d*) for amending or repealing enactments inconsistent with the provision to be made for the purposes of the authorising enactment, and for applying enactments with or without modification; and

(*e*) for any incidental or supplementary matters for which it appears to the Minister to be necessary or expedient for the purposes of the authorising enactment to provide:

Provided that any punishment imposed by virtue of paragraph (*b*) of this subsection shall not exceed that provided for by section fifty-eight of this Act or, in the case of a fine imposed in respect of each day on which a person is in default, five pounds.

(2) Regulations made (whether by the Minister or by the Treasury) under this Act shall be laid before Parliament as soon as may be after they are made, and if either House of Parliament within the period of forty days beginning with the day on which any such regulations are laid before it resolves that the regulations be annulled, the regulations shall thereupon become void, without prejudice, however, to the validity of anything previously done thereunder or to the making of new regulations.

In reckoning any such period of forty days as aforesaid, no account shall be taken of any time during which Parliament is dissolved or prorogued, or during which both Houses are adjourned for more than four days.

(3) Notwithstanding anything in subsection (4) of section one of the Rules Publication Act, 1893, regulations made (whether by the Minister or by the Treasury) under this Act shall be deemed not to be, or to contain, statutory rules to which that section applies.

[§ 63. Interpretation of expressions.]
[§ 64. Application to Scotland.]

65.—(1) This Act may be cited as the Coal Industry Nationalisation Act, 1946.

(2) This Act shall not extend to Northern Ireland. . . .

[Four schedules omitted.]

NATIONAL HEALTH SERVICE ACT, 1946
9 and 10 Geo. 6, c. 81

Part I

CENTRAL ADMINISTRATION

1.—(1) It shall be the duty of the Minister of Health (hereafter in this Act referred to as "the Minister") to promote the establishment in England and Wales of a comprehensive health service designed to secure improvement in the physical and mental health of the people of England and Wales and the prevention, diagnosis and treatment of illness, and for that purpose to provide or secure the effective provision of services in accordance with the following provisions of this Act.

(2) The services so provided shall be free of charge, except where any provision of this Act expressly provides for the making and recovery of charges.

2.—(1) There shall be constituted . . . a council, to be called the Central Health Services Council and hereafter in this Act referred to as "the Central Council", and it shall be the duty of the Central Council to advise the Minister upon such general matters relating to the services provided under this Act, or any services provided by local health authorities in their capacity as such authorities, as the Council think fit and upon any questions referred to them by him relating to those services. . . .

(3) The Minister may, after consultation with the Central Council, by order constitute standing advisory committees for the purpose of advising him and the Central Council on such of the services aforesaid as may be specified in the order. . . .

(5) The Central Council shall make an annual report to the Minister on their proceedings and on the proceedings of any standing advisory committee constituted under this section, and the Minister shall lay that report before Parliament with such comments (if any) as he thinks fit:

Provided that, if the Minister, after consultation with the Central Council, is satisfied that it would be contrary to the public interest to lay any such report, or a part of any such report, before Parliament, he may refrain from laying that report or part. . . .

Part II

HOSPITAL AND SPECIALIST SERVICES

Provision of Services by Minister

3.—(1) As from the appointed day, it shall be the duty of the Minister to provide throughout England and Wales, to such extent as he considers necessary to meet all reasonable requirements, accommodation and services of the following descriptions, that is to say:

(*a*) hospital accommodation;
(*b*) medical, nursing and other services required at or for the purposes of hospitals;
(*c*) the service of specialists, whether at a hospital, a health centre provided under Part III of this Act or a clinic or, if necessary on medical grounds, at the home of the patient;

and any accommodation and services provided under this section are in this Act referred to as "hospital and specialist services".

(2) Regulations may provide for the making and recovery by the Minister of such charges as may be prescribed—

(*a*) in respect of the supply, as part of the hospital and specialist services, of any appliance which is, at the request of the person supplied, of a more expensive type than the prescribed type, or in respect of the replacement or repair of any such appliance. . . . .

[§§ 4–5. Payments by private patients.]

Transfer of Hospitals to the Minister

6.—(1) Subject to the provisions of this Act, there shall, on the appointed day, be transferred to and vest in the Minister by virtue of this Act all interests in or attaching to premises forming part of a voluntary hospital or used for the purposes of a voluntary hospital. . . .

(2) Subject to the provisions of this Act, there shall also, on the appointed day, be transferred to and vest in the Minister by virtue of this Act all hospitals vested in a local authority immediately before the appointed day. . . .

[§ 7. Endowments of voluntary hospitals.]
[§ 8. Exception for medical and dental schools.]
[§§ 9–10. Supplementary provisions.]

11.—(1) The Minister shall by order constitute . . . boards, to be called Regional Hospital Boards, for such areas as he may by order determine, for the purpose of exercising functions with respect to the administration of hospital and specialist services in those areas. . . .

(3) Every Regional Hospital Board shall, within such period as the Minister may by direction specify, submit to the Minister a scheme for the appointment by them of committees, to be called Hospital Management Committees, for the purpose of exercising functions with respect to the management and control of individual hospitals or groups of hospitals, other than teaching hospitals, providing hospital and specialist services in the area of the Board. . . .

12.—(1) Subject to the exercise of functions by Hospital Management Committees . . . , it shall be the duty of a Regional Hospital Board, subject to and in accordance with regulations and such directions as may be given by the Minister, generally to administer on behalf of the Minister the hospital and specialist services provided in their area. . . .

[§§ 13–14. Legal status of boards and committees; conditions of service of hospital officers.]

[§ 15. Incorporation of medical schools in London.]

[§§ 16–18. The Minister may provide research, bacteriological and blood transfusion services.]

Part III

HEALTH SERVICES PROVIDED BY LOCAL HEALTH AUTHORITIES

19.—(1) Subject to the provisions of this section, the local authority for the purposes of this Part of this Act, who shall be called the "local health authority", shall for each county be the council of the county and for each county borough be the council of the county borough.

[(2) The Minister may combine authorities into joint boards.]

20.—(1) Every local health authority shall, within such period as the Minister may by direction specify, submit to the Minister proposals for carrying out their duties under the next following eight sections of this Act. . . .

(3) The Minister may approve the proposals with or without modifications (which may include additions or exceptions), and it shall be the duty of the local health authority to carry out their duties under the next following eight sections of this Act in accordance with the proposals submitted and approved for their area under this section, subject to any modifications made by subsequent proposals so submitted and approved. . . .

[§§ 21–28. Local authorities shall provide health centres; make arrangements for the care of mothers and young children; provide midwifery services; provide for home nursing; make arrangements for vaccination and immunisation; ensure that ambulances are available; and provide for preventive measures and the care of convalescents.]

[§ 29. A local authority may provide domestic help for households in which there is an invalid.]

[Parts IV (General Services) and V (Mental Health Services) omitted.]

Part VI

GENERAL

Financial Provisions

52.—(1) Any expenses incurred by the Minister in the exercise of his functions under this Act, the Lunacy and Mental Treatment Acts,

1890 to 1930, or the Mental Deficiency Acts, 1913 to 1938, shall be defrayed out of moneys provided by Parliament.

(2) All sums received by the Minister under this Act, except sums required to be transferred to the Hospital Endowments Fund, shall be paid into the Exchequer.

53.—(1) In respect of the period beginning with the appointed day and ending with the thirty-first day of March next following and each subsequent period of twelve months, there shall be paid out of moneys provided by Parliament to every local health authority a grant in respect of the expenditure, estimated in the prescribed manner, incurred by the authority in carrying out their functions as a local health authority, whether under this Act or any other enactment, and the grant shall be payable in accordance with regulations made by the Minister with the approval of the Treasury:

Provided that the total amount of the grant payable to any local health authority in respect of any such period shall not exceed three-quarters of the total expenditure estimated as aforesaid of that authority and shall not be less than three-eighths of that expenditure.

[§§ 54–56. Payments to Regional Hospital Boards, etc., accounts, etc.]

Administrative Provisions

57.—(1) Where the Minister is of opinion, on complaint or otherwise, that any Regional Hospital Board, Board of Governors of a teaching hospital, Hospital Management Committee, Executive Council, Ophthalmic Services Committee or local health authority, or the Medical Practices Committee or the Dental Estimates Board have failed to carry out any functions conferred or imposed on them by or under this Act, or have in carrying out those functions failed to comply with any regulations or directions relating thereto, he may after such inquiry as he may think fit make an order declaring them to be in default.

(2) Except where the body in default is a local health authority, the members of the body shall forthwith vacate their office and the order shall provide for the appointment, in accordance with the provisions of this Act, of new members of the body, and may contain such provisions as seem to the Minister expedient for authorising any person to act in the place of the body in question pending the appointment of the new members.

(3) If the body in default is a local health authority, the order shall direct them, for the purposes of remedying the default, to discharge such of their functions, in such manner and within such time or times, as may be specified in the order, and if the authority fail to comply with any direction given under this subsection, within the time limited for compliance therewith, the Minister, in lieu of enforcing the order

by mandamus or otherwise, may make an order transferring to himself such of the functions of the authority as he thinks fit.

(4) Any expenses certified by the Minister to have been incurred by him in discharging functions transferred to him under this section from a local health authority shall on demand be paid to him by that authority and shall be recoverable by him from them as a debt due to the Crown. . . .

[§§ 58–80 and ten schedules omitted.]

CROWN PROCEEDINGS ACT, 1947
10 and 11 Geo. 6, c. 44

1. Where any person has a claim against the Crown after the commencement of this Act, and, if this Act had not been passed, the claim might have been enforced, subject to the grant of His Majesty's fiat, by petition of right, or might have been enforced by a proceeding provided by any statutory provision repealed by this Act, then, subject to the provisions of this Act, the claim may be enforced as of right, and without the fiat of His Majesty, by proceedings taken against the Crown for that purpose in accordance with the provisions of this Act.

2.—(1) Subject to the provisions of this Act, the Crown shall be subject to all those liabilities in tort to which, if it were a private person of full age and capacity, it would be subject:

(*a*) in respect of torts committed by its servants or agents;
(*b*) in respect of any breach of those duties which a person owes to his servants or agents at common law by reason of being their employer; and
(*c*) in respect of any breach of the duties attaching at common law to the ownership, occupation, possession or control of property:

Provided that no proceedings shall lie against the Crown by virtue of paragraph (*a*) of this subsection in respect of any act or omission of a servant or agent of the Crown unless the act or omission would apart from the provisions of this Act have given rise to a cause of action in tort against that servant or agent or his estate.

(2) Where the Crown is bound by a statutory duty which is binding also upon persons other than the Crown and its officers, then, subject to the provisions of this Act, the Crown shall, in respect of a failure to comply with that duty, be subject to all those liabilities in tort (if any) to which it would be so subject if it were a private person of full age and capacity.

(3) Where any functions are conferred or imposed upon an officer of the Crown as such either by any rule of the common law or by statute, and that officer commits a tort while performing or purporting to perform those functions, the liabilities of the Crown in respect of the tort shall be such as they would have been if those functions had been conferred or imposed solely by virtue of instructions lawfully given by the Crown.

(4) Any enactment which negatives or limits the amount of the liability of any Government department or officer of the Crown in respect of any tort committed by that department or officer shall, in the case of proceedings against the Crown under this section in respect of a tort committed by that department or officer, apply in relation to the Crown as it would have applied in relation to that department or officer if the proceedings against the Crown had been proceedings against that department or officer.

(5) No proceedings shall lie against the Crown by virtue of this section in respect of anything done or omitted to be done by any person while discharging or purporting to discharge any responsibilities of a judicial nature vested in him, or any responsibilities which he has in connection with the execution of judicial process.

(6) No proceedings shall lie against the Crown by virtue of this section in respect of any act, neglect or default of any officer of the Crown, unless that officer has been directly or indirectly appointed by the Crown and was at the material time paid in respect of his duties as an officer of the Crown wholly out of the Consolidated Fund of the United Kingdom, moneys provided by Parliament, the Road Fund, or any other Fund certified by the Treasury for the purposes of this subsection or was at the material time holding an office in respect of which the Treasury certify that the holder thereof would normally be so paid.

[§§ 3–9. Provisions regarding industrial property, the law as to indemnity, contributory negligence, etc., Crown ships, docks and harbours, etc.]

10.—(1) Nothing done or omitted to be done by a member of the armed forces of the Crown while on duty as such shall subject either him or the Crown to liability in tort for causing the death of another person, or for causing personal injury to another person, in so far as the death or personal injury is due to anything suffered by that other person while he is a member of the armed forces of the Crown if—

(*a*) at the time when that thing is suffered by that other person, he is either on duty as a member of the armed forces of the Crown or is, though not on duty as such, on any land, premises, ship, aircraft or vehicle for the time being used for the purposes of the armed forces of the Crown; and (*b*) the Minister of Pensions certifies that his suffering that thing has been or will be treated as attributable to service for the purposes of entitlement to an award under the Royal Warrant, Order in Council or Order of His Majesty relating to the disablement or death of members of the force of which he is a member:

Provided that this subsection shall not exempt a member of the said forces from liability in tort in any case in which the court is satisfied that the act or omission was not connected with the execution of his duties as a member of those forces.

(2) No proceedings in tort shall lie against the Crown for death or personal injury due to anything suffered by a member of the armed forces of the Crown if—

(*a*) that thing is suffered by him in consequence of the nature or condition of any such land, premises, ship, aircraft or vehicle as aforesaid, or in consequence of the nature or condition of any equipment or supplies used for the purposes of those forces; and
(*b*) the Minister of Pensions certifies as mentioned in the preceding subsection;

nor shall any act or omission of an officer of the Crown subject him to liability in tort for death or personal injury, in so far as the death or personal injury is due to anything suffered by a member of the armed forces of the Crown being a thing as to which the conditions aforesaid are satisfied.

(3) The Admiralty or a Secretary of State, if satisfied that it is the fact:—

(*a*) that a person was or was not on any particular occasion on duty as a member of the armed forces of the Crown; or
(*b*) that at any particular time any land, premises, ship, aircraft, vehicle, equipment or supplies was or was not, or were or were not, used for the purposes of the said forces;

may issue a certificate certifying that to be the fact; and any such certificate shall, for the purposes of this section, be conclusive as to the fact which it certifies.

11.—(1) Nothing in Part I of this Act shall extinguish or abridge any powers or authorities which, if this Act had not been passed, would have been exercisable by virtue of the prerogative of the Crown, or any powers or authorities conferred on the Crown by any statute, and, in particular, nothing in the said Part I shall extinguish or abridge any powers or authorities exercisable by the Crown, whether in time of peace or of war, for the purpose of the defence of the realm or of training, or maintaining the efficiency of, any of the armed forces of the Crown.

(2) Where in any proceedings under this Act it is material to determine whether anything was properly done or omitted to be done in the exercise of the prerogative of the Crown, the Admiralty or a Secretary of State may, if satisfied that the act or omission was necessary for any such purpose as is mentioned in the last preceding subsection, issue a certificate to the effect that the act or omission was necessary for that purpose; and the certificate shall, in those proceedings, be conclusive as to the matter so certified.

[§ 12. Transitional provisions.]
[§§ 13–15. Proceedings in the High Court and in county courts.]

16. The Crown may obtain relief by way of interpleader proceedings, and may be made a party to such proceedings, in the same manner in which a subject may obtain relief by way of such proceedings or be made a party thereto, and may be made a party to such proceedings notwithstanding that the application for relief is made by a sheriff or other like officer; and all rules of court and county court rules relating to interpleader proceedings shall, subject to the provisions of this Act, have effect accordingly.

17.—(1) The Treasury shall publish a list specifying the several Government departments which are authorised departments for the purposes of this Act, and the name and address for service of the person who is, or is acting for the purposes of this Act as, the solicitor for each such department, and may from time to time amend or vary the said list. . . .

(2) Civil proceedings by the Crown may be instituted either by an authorised Government department in its own name, whether that department was or was not at the commencement of this Act authorised to sue, or by the Attorney General.

(3) Civil proceedings against the Crown shall be instituted against the appropriate authorised Government department, or, if none of the authorised Government departments is appropriate or the person instituting the proceedings has any reasonable doubt whether any and if so which of those departments is appropriate, against the Attorney General.

(4) Where any civil proceedings against the Crown are instituted against the Attorney General, an application may at any stage of the proceedings be made to the court by or on behalf of the Attorney General to have such of the authorised Government departments as may be specified in the application substituted for him as defendant to the proceedings; and where any such proceedings are brought against an authorised Government department, an application may at any stage of the proceedings be made to the court on behalf of that department to have the Attorney General or such of the authorised Government departments as may be specified in the application substituted for the applicant as the defendant to the proceedings.

Upon any such application the court may if it thinks fit make an order granting the application on such terms as the court thinks just; and on such an order being made the proceedings shall continue as if they had been commenced against the department specified in that behalf in the order, or, as the case may require, against the Attorney General.

(5) No proceedings instituted in accordance with this Part of this Act by or against the Attorney General or an authorised Government department shall abate or be affected by any change in the person holding the office of Attorney General or in the person or body of persons constituting the department.

[§§ 18–39 omitted.]

40.—(1) Nothing in this Act shall apply to proceedings by or against, or authorise proceedings in tort to be brought against His Majesty in His private capacity.

(2) Except as therein otherwise expressly provided, nothing in this Act shall:—

(*a*) affect the law relating to prize salvage, or apply to proceedings in causes or matters within the jurisdiction of the High Court as a prize court or to any criminal proceedings; or

(*b*) authorise proceedings to be taken against the Crown under or in accordance with this Act in respect of any alleged liability of the Crown arising otherwise than in respect of His Majesty's Government in the United Kingdom, or affect proceedings against the Crown in respect of any such alleged liability as aforesaid; or

(*c*) affect any proceedings by the Crown otherwise than in right of His Majesty's Government in the United Kingdom; or

(*d*) subject the Crown to any greater liabilities in respect of the acts or omissions of any independent contractor employed by the Crown than those to which the Crown would be subject in respect of such acts or omissions if it were a private person; or

(*e*) subject the Crown, in its capacity as a highway authority, to any greater liability than that to which a local authority is subject in that capacity; or

(*f*) affect any rules of evidence or any presumption relating to the extent to which the Crown is bound by any Act of Parliament. . . .

and, without prejudice to the general effect of the foregoing provisions, Part III of this Act shall not apply to the Crown except in right of His Majesty's Government in the United Kingdom.

(3) A certificate of a Secretary of State:—

(*a*) to the effect that any alleged liability of the Crown arises otherwise than in respect of His Majesty's Government in the United Kingdom;

(*b*) to the effect that any proceedings by the Crown are proceedings otherwise than in right of His Majesty's Government in the United Kingdom;

shall, for the purposes of this Act, be conclusive as to the matter so certified. . . .

(5) This Act shall not operate to limit the discretion of the court to grant relief by way of mandamus in cases in which such relief might have been granted before the commencement of this Act, notwithstanding that by reason of the provisions of this Act some other and further remedy is available.

[§§ 41–54 and two schedules omitted.]

SUPPLIES AND SERVICES (EXTENDED PURPOSES) ACT, 1947
10 and 11 Geo. 6, c. 55

An Act to extend the purposes of the Supplies and Services (Transitional Powers) Act, 1945.

[*13th August 1947.*]

Whereas under the Supplies and Services (Transitional Powers) Act, 1945, Defence Regulations appearing to His Majesty to be necessary or expedient for the purposes mentioned in subsection (1) of section one of that Act (being purposes connected mainly with the orderly transition from war to peace, the maintenance of a sufficiency of supplies essential to the well-being of the community and the allocation of available supplies and services during the transition) were continued in force by virtue of that Act:

And whereas, by reason of the war and the dislocation of trade consequent thereon, supplies and services available are, or are likely shortly to become, insufficient for meeting the essential needs of the community, and it has become necessary that the use of the powers conferred by those Regulations should be directed more particularly to increasing production and redressing the balance of trade:

Now, therefore, be it enacted by the King's most Excellent Majesty, by and with the advice and consent of the Lords Spiritual and Temporal, and Commons, in this present Parliament assembled, and by the authority of the same, as follows:—

1.—(1) The Regulations which at the date of the passing of this Act have effect by virtue of the Supplies and Services (Transitional Powers) Act, 1945 (hereafter in this Act referred to as "the Act of 1945"), and any orders or other instruments in force thereunder, shall, in so far as their operation is limited, expressly or by implication, to the purposes mentioned in subsection (1) of section one of that Act, be extended so as to be applicable for the following additional purposes, that is to say:—

(*a*) for promoting the productivity of industry, commerce and agriculture;

(*b*) for fostering and directing exports and reducing imports, or imports of any classes, from all or any countries and for redressing the balance of trade; and

(*c*) generally for ensuring that the whole resources of the community are available for use, and are used, in a manner best calculated to serve the interests of the community;

and accordingly any references in the said Regulations, orders and other instruments to the purposes mentioned in subsection (1) of section one of that Act shall be construed as including references to the purposes aforesaid:

Provided that nothing in this Act shall be held to authorise the suppression or suspension of any newspaper, periodical, book or other publication.

(2) In section three of the Act of 1945 (which confers powers to revoke and vary Regulations having effect by virtue of that Act) references to the purposes specified in subsection (1) of section one of that Act shall be construed as including references to the purposes specified in the preceding subsection.

(3) In paragraph (*d*) of subsection (2) of section one of the Emergency Powers (Defence) Act, 1939, as applied by section five of the Act of 1945 to Regulations having effect by virtue of that Act, and in subsection (4) of that section as so applied, the expression "enactment" shall mean any enactment passed before the commencement of this Act, other than the Act of 1945 and the provisions of the Emergency Powers (Defence) Acts, 1939 and 1940, applied by section five of the Act of 1945.

(4) His Majesty may by Order in Council direct that the preceding provisions of this section shall apply, with such exceptions, adaptations, and modifications, if any, as may be specified in the Order, in relation to—

(*a*) any Regulation having effect by virtue of the Act of 1945 in or in respect of any of the countries or territories specified in section four of the Emergency Powers (Defence) Act, 1939, and any orders or other instruments made thereunder; and

(*b*) any power to vary such Regulations.

2. This Act may be cited as the Supplies and Services (Extended Purposes) Act, 1947.

LOCAL GOVERNMENT ACT, 1948
11 and 12 Geo. 6, c. 26

PART I

Exchequer Grants and Other Financial Provisions (England and Wales)

Discontinued Grants

1. Save as otherwise provided by this Part of this Act—

(a) no Exchequer grant shall be payable under the Local Government Acts, 1929 to 1946, for the year 1948–49 or any subsequent year; and

(b) the third fixed grant period shall for the purposes of all enactments be terminated at the end of March, nineteen hundred and forty-eight.

Exchequer Grants to Counties and County Boroughs

2.—(1) Where for the year 1948–49 or any subsequent year the rateable value for a county or county borough is less than the standard rateable value for that county or county borough (as defined by the subsequent provisions of this Part of this Act), there shall be paid out of moneys provided by Parliament to the council of the county or county borough a grant equal to the relevant fraction (as so defined) of the amount of the difference.

(2) The said difference is in the subsequent provisions of this Part of this Act referred to as the rateable value credited to the county or county borough.

(3) Grants under this section are in the subsequent provisions of this Part of this Act referred to as "Exchequer Equalisation Grants."

3.—(1) The standard rateable value for a county or county borough for the purposes of the preceding provisions of this Part of this Act is the amount which bears to the weighted population of that county or county borough for the year in question that same proportion as the sum which is to be taken for the purposes of this subsection as the rateable value for England and Wales for that year bears to the aggregate of the weighted populations of all the counties and county boroughs in England and Wales for that year.

(2) In this section, the expression "the weighted population" in relation to a county or county borough means the population thereof plus the number of children under fifteen years of age therein and, in the case of a county the population whereof divided by the road-mileage thereof is less than seventy, plus also one-third of the additional population needed in order that the population thereof divided by the road-mileage thereof should be seventy.

(3) The sum which is to be taken for the purposes of subsection (1) of this section as the rateable value for England and Wales for any year is the rateable value for England and Wales for that year, increased, in the case of any year subsequent to the year 1948–49, to such extent, if any, as the Minister may direct in relation to that subsequent year.

(4) The power conferred on the Minister by the last preceding subsection to direct such increases as are therein referred to shall, as respects any year, be used for the purpose and only for the purpose of securing that the proportion which the aggregate of the rateable values credited to all the counties and county boroughs in England and Wales bears to the rateable value for England and Wales shall be as nearly as may be the same for that year as for the year 1948–49; but the Minister shall not use the said power as respects any year unless the effect of the use thereof would be to increase the aggregate of the rateable values credited to all counties and county boroughs in England and Wales for that year by at least one per cent.

4.—(1) The relevant fraction for a county or county borough for the purposes of the preceding provisions of this Part of this Act is the fraction arrived at by dividing the relevant local expenditure for the year in question by the sum of the following amounts, that is to say, the rateable value credited to the county or county borough for that year and the product of a rate of one pound in the pound for the county or county borough for that year.

(2) In this section, the expression "the relevant local expenditure" means so much of the total expenditure for the year—

(*a*) in the case of a county, of the council of the county and of the other local authorities in the county; and

(*b*) in the case of a county borough, of the council of the county borough,

as would have to be met out of rates levied within the county or county borough if no Exchequer Grants under this Part of this Act and (so far as any such Grant is relevant to the year in question) no Exchequer Grants payable for any previous year under the Local Government Acts, 1929 to 1946, were payable, and if no grants had been made out of moneys provided by Parliament to local authorities by the Minister by way of special assistance in respect of their financial difficulties arising out of the war.

(3) Where, by virtue of a precept or other instrument, not being a precept or instrument issued by a county council, any sum falls to be paid by a local authority to any other authority, the amount payable shall be treated for the purposes of subsection (2) of this section as expenditure of the first-mentioned authority.

(4) The provisions of subsection (2) of this section shall, as respects

the year 1948–49, have effect subject to the special provisions relating to Exchequer Grants for that year contained hereafter in this Part of this Act.

[§ 5. Exchequer Transitional Grants for the first five years.]

6.—(1) The Minister may, subject to the provisions of this section, reduce any Exchequer Equalisation Grant or Exchequer Transitional Grant payable to a council by such amount as he thinks just, if—

(a) he is satisfied, either upon representations made to him or without any such representations, that the council have failed to achieve or maintain a reasonable standard of efficiency and progress in the discharge of their functions, regard being had to the standards maintained in other areas; or

(b) he is satisfied that the expenditure of the council has been excessive and unreasonable, regard being had to the financial resources and other relevant circumstances of the area.

(2) Before reducing any grant by virtue of this section, the Minister shall make and cause to be laid before Parliament a report stating the amount of the reduction, and the reasons therefor, and he shall not make the reduction until the said report is approved by a resolution of the Commons House of Parliament.

7.—(1) The amount of any grant payable out of moneys provided by Parliament under subsection (1) of section fifty-three of the National Health Service Act, 1946, to a local health authority shall, in lieu of being determined by regulations under the said subsection (1), be one-half of the expenditure in respect of which the grant is made. . . .

[§ 8. Payments to voluntary associations.]

9.—(1) Before the beginning of the year 1948–49 and each subsequent year, the Minister shall estimate for the year in relation to every county district in England and Wales the amount following, that is to say, the amount which is equal to the fraction hereinafter specified of the aggregate of the Exchequer Equalisation Grants which will become payable for that year to the councils of counties in England and Wales outside London, and the council of each county shall pay to the council of each county district in the county the amount so estimated by the Minister in relation to that district.

(2) That said fraction is—

(a) in the case of any county district other than a rural district, one-half of the population of the county district; and

(b) in the case of a rural district, one-quarter of the population of the rural district, divided, in any case, by the aggregate of the population of all counties in England and Wales outside London.

(3) Any payment under this section may, if the councils concerned so agree, be effected in whole or in part by making the appropriate deduction from the amount due under a precept.

[§ 10. Payments to metropolitan boroughs.]
[§§ 11–16 (Miscellaneous) and Part II (Scotland) omitted.]

PART III

Valuation and Rating Procedure

General

33.—(1) Valuation lists shall, instead of being prepared and amended by the bodies and at the times, in accordance with the conditions and subject to the rights as to objection and appeal specified in the Rating and Valuation Acts, 1925 to 1940, and the Rating and Valuation (Metropolis) Acts, 1869 to 1940, be prepared and amended by valuation officers of the Commissioners of Inland Revenue at the times, in accordance with the conditions and subject to the rights as to objection and appeal specified in this Part of this Act; and

(a) assessment committees, county valuation committees and the central valuation committee shall cease to exist; and
(b) save as hereafter provided in this Part of this Act, rating authorities shall have no functions in relation to the preparation and amendment of valuation lists.

(2) Nothing in this section affects any rights of a rating authority as a person who is aggrieved by anything done or omitted to be done by the valuation officer in a valuation list or draft valuation list in relation to any hereditament.

(3) In this Part of this Act, the expression "the valuation officer", in relation to a valuation list, means such officer of the Commissioners of Inland Revenue as may for the time being be authorised by the Commissioners to act (either generally or for the particular purpose in question) as the valuation officer in relation to that list.

[§ 34. Provisions for new valuation lists at five-yearly intervals.]
[§§ 35–43. Preparation and revision of, and objections to, valuation lists.]

44.—(1) Local valuation courts constituted as hereinafter provided shall be convened as often as may be necessary for the purpose of hearing and determining appeals under the preceding provisions of this Part of this Act against draft valuation lists and against objections to proposals for the alteration of valuation lists. . . .

(3) Every such court shall consist of—

(*a*) either the chairman of the local valuation panel or the deputy chairman (or, if more than one, one of the deputy chairmen) thereof; and

(*b*) two other members of the panel selected in accordance with the scheme under which the panel is constituted.

45.—(1) It shall be the duty of the council of every county and county borough to make and submit to the Minister a scheme for the constitution of a local valuation panel for the county or county borough or two or more local valuation panels for areas which together comprise the whole of the county or county borough:

Provided that any two or more councils, whether councils of counties or of county boroughs, may, and, if so directed by the Minister, shall, make and submit to the Minister a joint scheme for the constitution of a local valuation panel or local valuation panels for the whole of their respective areas, or for areas which together comprise the whole of their respective areas. . . .

[§§ 46–48. Membership, staff, expenses, procedure, etc., of panels and valuation courts.]

49.—(1) Any person who, in pursuance of the last preceding section, appeared before a local valuation court on the hearing of an appeal and is aggrieved by the decision of the court thereon may, within twenty-one days from the date of the decision, appeal to the county court for the county court district in which the hereditament in question is situated, or, where the hereditament extends into more than one county court district, to the county court for any one of the county court districts in which any part of the hereditament is situated, and the court, after hearing such of the persons as appeared as aforesaid as desire to be heard, may give any directions which the local valuation court might have given. . . .

50.—(1) Notwithstanding anything in the preceding provisions of this Part of this Act, the persons who would be entitled to appear and be heard before any local valuation court or any county court may by agreement in writing agree to refer to arbitration any matter which would but for the agreement fall to be heard or determined by that local valuation court or county court, and the matter shall be referred to arbitration accordingly.

(2) The Arbitration Acts, 1889 to 1934, shall apply to any such arbitration.

[§§ 51–73 (provisions regarding rates, inspection, etc.) and Part IV (valuation of dwelling houses) omitted.]

PART V

Rating of Transport and Electricity Authorities

General

85.—(1) Save as is otherwise provided in this Part of this Act, no premises which are or form part of either—

(*a*) a railway or canal hereditament (as defined for the purposes of this Part of this Act); or

(*b*) a hereditament occupied by the British Electricity Authority, an Area Electricity Board or the North of Scotland Hydro-Electric Board,

shall be liable to be rated or be included in any valuation list or in any rate, and the British Transport Commission, the British Electricity Authority and the North of Scotland Hydro-Electric Board shall, in the year 1948–49 and all subsequent years, make such payments for the benefit of local authorities as are provided for by the subsequent provisions of this Part of this Act in lieu of the rates which would, apart from the provisions of this Part of this Act, be payable to rating authorities in respect of those hereditaments. . . .

[§§ 93–99. Provisions by which the amounts of payments are to be calculated and adjusted.]

100.—(1) The sums falling to be paid under the preceding provisions of this Part of this Act for the benefit of local authorities in England and Wales shall be paid to the Minister, and the sums falling to be paid under the said provisions for the benefit of local authorities in Scotland shall be paid to the Secretary of State.

(2) The sums so paid to the Minister for any year shall, subject to the provisions of this Part of this Act relating to liabilities of the Railway Assessment Authority and the Anglo-Scottish Railways Assessment Authority, be distributed by him, at such times as he may determine, in the manner following, that is to say—

(*a*) the sums shall first be allocated among the rating authorities in England and Wales in proportion to the rateable values for their respective areas for that year;

(*b*) in the case of the council of a county borough, the amount so allocated to that council shall be paid to that council;

(*c*) in the case of any other rating authority, the amount so allocated to that authority shall be paid as to one-third thereof to that authority and as to two-thirds thereof to the council of the county of which the area of that authority forms part.

(3) The sums so paid to the Secretary of State for any year shall be distributed by him according to their respective rateable valuations among the rating authorities—

(a) throughout Scotland;
(b) in that part of Scotland which is not included in the North of
    Scotland District; and
(c) in the said District,

according as the said sums represent sums paid to the Secretary of
State by the British Transport Commission, the British Electricity
Authority and the North of Scotland Hydro-Electric Board.

[§§ 101–148 and two schedules omitted.]

NATIONAL ASSISTANCE ACT, 1948
11 and 12 Geo. 6, c. 29

PART I

INTRODUCTORY

1. The existing poor law shall cease to have effect, and shall be
replaced by the provisions of Part II of this Act as to the rendering,
out of moneys provided by Parliament, of assistance to persons in
need, the provisions of Part III of this Act as to accommodation and
other services to be provided by local authorities, and the related
provisions of Part IV of this Act.

PART II

NATIONAL ASSISTANCE

The National Assistance Board

2.—(1) The Assistance Board shall be known as the National
Assistance Board, and in addition to the functions for the time being
exercisable under any other enactment shall exercise the functions conferred on them by the following provisions of this Act.

(2) The National Assistance Board (hereafter in this Act referred
to as "the Board") shall exercise their functions in such manner as
shall best promote the welfare of persons affected by the exercise
thereof.

(3) For the purpose of securing the prompt discharge of their functions under this Act, the Board shall by regulations provide for the
local administration of their said functions, and in particular, but subject to any arrangements for the discharge thereof by officers of
another Government department or of a local authority, for the discharge by local officers of the Board of the functions of the Board in

relation to applications for assistance and the decision of all questions arising thereon.

(4) Annual reports on the activities of the Board shall be made by the Board to the Minister of National Insurance, and the said Minister shall lay each report of the Board under this subsection before Parliament.

(5) The constitution and proceedings of the Board shall continue to be governed by the provisions set out in the First Schedule to this Act, being the provisions in that behalf of the Unemployment Assistance Act, 1934.

3.—(1) For the purpose of securing that full use is made of the advice and assistance, both on general questions and on difficult individual cases, of persons having local knowledge and experience in matters affecting the functions of the Board, the Board shall arrange for the establishment of advisory committees throughout Great Britain to act for such areas as the Board think fit.

(2) The Board shall pay to members of advisory committees appointed by the Board such travelling and other allowances (including compensation for loss of remunerative time) as the Board, after consultation with the Minister of National Insurance and with the consent of the Treasury, may determine.

Giving of Assistance by Board

4. It shall be the duty of the Board in accordance with the following provisions of this Part of this Act to assist persons in Great Britain who are without resources to meet their requirements, or whose resources (including benefits receivable under the National Insurance Acts, 1946) must be supplemented in order to meet their requirements.

5.—(1) The question whether a person is in need of assistance, and the nature and extent of any assistance to be given to him, shall, subject to the provisions of this Act as to appeals, be decided by the Board.

(2) The Minister of National Insurance shall in accordance with the provisions of the next following section make regulations as to the computation of requirements and resources for the purposes of this Part of this Act and as to the decision of any such question as aforesaid, and the Board shall give effect to the relevant provisions of the regulations.

(3) Regulations under this section may make different provision for different classes of cases, and in particular shall make special provision for blind persons and persons who have suffered a loss of income in order to undergo treatment for tuberculosis of the respiratory system.

(4) Regulations under this section shall include provision for securing that the rules as to disregarding certain assets set out in the Second Schedule to this Act shall be observed in computing resources.

6.—(1) The Board shall as soon as may be after the passing of this Act, and thereafter from time to time as occasion may require, prepare and submit to the Minister of National Insurance (in this section referred to as "the Minister") draft regulations under the last foregoing section.

(2) The Minister shall consider any draft submitted to him under the last foregoing subsection and shall make draft regulations either in the form of the draft as submitted or with such variations and amendments as he thinks fit.

(3) Where the Minister makes any draft regulations otherwise than in the form of the draft submitted to him, then before making the draft regulations he shall inform the Board of the variations and amendments which he intends to make, the Board shall report to him thereon, and he shall consider the report.

(4) Any draft regulations made by the Minister under this section shall be laid before Parliament as soon as may be after they are made, and, if the draft regulations so laid are made otherwise than in the form submitted to the Minister, there shall also be laid before Parliament a statement of the Minister's reasons for, and a copy of the report of the Board on, the variations and amendments made by him.

(5) If each House resolves that draft regulations made by the Minister under this section be approved, the Minister shall in the terms of the draft make regulations under the last foregoing section to take effect on such date as may be specified in the regulations.

[§§ 7–13. Details of assistance, disqualifications, etc.]

14.—(1) Where a person applying for, or in receipt of, assistance is aggrieved by a decision of the Board . . . he may appeal to the Appeal Tribunal. . . .

(4) On an appeal under this section the Appeal Tribunal may confirm the decision of the Board appealed against or substitute therefore any decision which the Board could have made under this Part of this Act, and any decision of the Tribunal shall be conclusive for all purposes. . . .

[§ 15. Supplementary provisions for assistance.]
[§§ 16–20. Re-establishment and reception centres.]

Part III

LOCAL AUTHORITY SERVICES

Provision of Accommodation

21.—(1) It shall be the duty of every local authority, subject to and in accordance with the provisions of this Part of this Act, to provide—

(a) residential accommodation for persons who by reason of age, infirmity or any other circumstances are in need of care and attention which is not otherwise available to them;

(*b*) temporary accommodation for persons who are in urgent need thereof, being need arising in circumstances which could not reasonably have been foreseen or in such other circumstances as the authority may in any particular case determine.

(2) In the exercise of their said duty a local authority shall have regard to the welfare of all persons for whom accommodation is provided, and in particular to the need for providing accommodation of different descriptions suited to different descriptions of such persons as are mentioned in the last foregoing subsection.

(3) A local authority shall exercise their functions under this section in accordance with a scheme made thereunder.

(4) Accommodation provided by a local authority in the exercise of their said functions shall be provided in premises managed by the authority or, to such extent as may be specified in the scheme under this section, in such premises managed by another local authority as may be agreed between the two authorities and on such terms, including terms as to the reimbursement of expenditure incurred by the said other authority, as may be so agreed. . . .

[§§ 22–23. Charges for accommodation and management of premises.]

24.—(1) The local authority liable under this Part of this Act to provide residential accommodation for any person shall subject to the following provisions of this Part of this Act be the authority in whose area the person is ordinarily resident.

(2) The local authority liable under this Part of this Act to provide temporary accommodation for any person shall be the authority in whose area the person is.

(3) Where a person in the area of a local authority—

(*a*) is a person with no settled residence, or
(*b*) not being ordinarily resident in the area of the local authority, is in urgent need of residential accommodation under this Part of this Act,

the authority shall have the like duty to provide residential accommodation for him as if he were ordinarily resident in their area. . . .

25.—(1) Where the Board are satisfied that a person in the area of a local authority is in urgent need of accommodation under this Part of this Act, the Board may require the local authority to provide such accommodation for him. . . .

(3) Where a local authority are aggrieved by any requirement made by the Board under subsection (1) of this section, the authority may, but without prejudice to their duty to comply with the requirement in the meanwhile, appeal to the Appeal Tribunal, and on any such appeal the Tribunal may cancel or confirm the requirement of the Board.

[§ 26. Premises maintained by voluntary organisations.]
[§ 27. Investigation of applicants' resources.]

28.—(1) Subject to the provisions of this section, the Minister shall make annual contributions to local authorities in respect of premises provided by them for the purposes of the foregoing provisions of this Part of this Act, being premises provided in accordance with proposals approved by the Minister and used in accordance with any conditions subject to which the proposals were approved. . . .

[§ 29. Welfare arrangements for blind, deaf, dumb and crippled persons, etc.]

[§§ 30–31. Voluntary organisations for the disabled, and old people's organisations.]

[§ 32. Financial adjustments between local authorities.]

[§ 33. Definition of local authorities.]

34.—(1) The following provisions of this section shall have effect as to schemes made under section twenty-one or twenty-nine of this Act.

(2) Subject to the provisions of this section, any such scheme shall be made by the local authority and submitted to the Minister, and shall come into force when approved by him.

(3) Not later than the date on which any such scheme is submitted to the Minister by the council of a county, that council shall send a copy of the scheme—

(a) in the case of London to the Common Council of the City of London and to the council of each metropolitan borough;

(b) in the case of any other county, to the council of each county district in the county;

and the Minister before approving the scheme shall take into consideration any representations by any such council as is referred to in paragraph (a) or (b) of this subsection made with respect to the scheme within one month from the date on which it was submitted to the Minister.

(4) The Minister may approve any such scheme submitted to him either in the form in which it is submitted or with such modifications as he thinks fit.

(5) Any scheme under either of the said sections may be varied or revoked by a subsequent scheme thereunder, and the provisions of the three last foregoing subsections shall apply to such a varying or revoking scheme.

(6) Where in the case of any local authority no scheme is for the time being in force for the exercise of their functions under section twenty-one of this Act, or for the exercise of any powers under section twenty-nine of this Act which the authority are under a duty to exercise, the Minister may require the authority, within such time as he may specify, to submit such a scheme to him for his approval, and if the authority—

(*a*) fail to comply with the requirement, or
(*b*) submit a scheme which appears to the Minister not proper to be
approved by him either as submitted or with modifications,

the Minister may himself make a scheme for the exercise of the said
functions or powers by the local authority.

(7) Where it appears to the Minister that by reason of a change of
circumstances it is expedient that any scheme for the exercise by a
local authority of their functions under section twenty-one or twenty-
nine of this Act should be varied, the Minister may require the
authority, within such time as he may specify, to submit to him for
his approval a scheme for varying the first-mentioned scheme in such
respects as may be specified in the requirement, and if the local
authority fail to comply with the requirement the Minister may
himself make the varying scheme.

(8) This section shall have effect in its application to Scotland as if
for subsection (3) the following subsection were substituted:

"(3) Not later than the date on which any scheme made under section
twenty-one of this Act is submitted to the Minister by the council of
a county, the council shall send a copy of the scheme to the town
council of each small burgh in the county and the Minister before
approving the scheme shall take into consideration any representations by any such town council made with respect to the scheme
within one month from the date on which it was submitted to the
Minister."

35.—(1) For the purposes of this Part of this Act the expression
"the Minister" means the Minister of Health as respects England and
Wales, and the Secretary of State as respects Scotland.

(2) Subject to the provisions of schemes under this Part of this Act,
local authorities shall exercise their functions under this Part of this
Act (including any discretion conferred on them thereunder) under
the general guidance of the Minister, and in accordance with the
provisions of any regulations of the Minister made for the purposes of
this sub-section.

(3) Without prejudice to the generality of the last foregoing subsection, regulations thereunder—

(*a*) may provide for conferring on officers of the Minister authorised
under the regulations such powers of inspection as may be prescribed in relation to the exercise of functions under this Part of
this Act by or by arrangement with or on behalf of local authorities;
(*b*) may prescribe requirements as to the provision to be made in
rules for the conduct of, and preservation of order in, premises in
which accommodation is provided under this Part of this Act by
local authorities;

(*c*) may make provision with respect to the qualifications of officers employed by local authorities for the purposes of this Part of this Act or by voluntary organisations acting under arrangements with or on behalf of local authorities for those purposes.

36.—(1) Where the Minister is of opinion, whether on representations made to him or otherwise, that a local authority have failed to discharge any of their functions under this Part of this Act, or have in the discharge thereof failed to comply with any regulations relating thereto, he may after such inquiry as he may think fit make an order declaring the authority to be in default.

(2) An order under the last foregoing subsection shall direct the authority, for the purpose of remedying the default, to discharge such of their functions, in such manner and within such time or times, as may be specified in the order; and if the authority fail to comply with any direction given under this subsection within the time specified in the order, then without prejudice to any other means of enforcing the order the Minister may make an order transferring to himself such of the functions of the authority as he thinks fit.

(3) Any expenses certified by the Minister to have been incurred by him in discharging functions transferred to him under this section shall on demand be paid to him by the authority from which the functions were transferred.

(4) An authority shall have the like power of raising money required for paying expenses certified by the Minister as aforesaid as they have of raising money for paying expenses incurred directly by them, and the payment of any expenses certified as aforesaid shall, to such extent as may be sanctioned by the Minister, be a purpose for which the authority may borrow money in accordance with the statutory provisions relating to borrowing by that authority.

(5) An order under this section may contain such incidental or supplemental provisions as appear to the Minister to be necessary or expedient, including provision for the transfer to the Minister of property and liabilities of the authority in default.

(6) Where any such order is varied or revoked by a subsequent order, the revoking order or a subsequent order may make provision for the re-transfer to the authority in default of any property or liabilities transferred from that authority to the Minister under the first-mentioned order and for the transfer to that authority of any property or liabilities acquired or incurred by the Minister in discharging any of the functions transferred to him.

[Part IV (General and Supplementary) and seven schedules omitted.]

REPRESENTATION OF THE PEOPLE ACT, 1948
11 and 12 Geo. 6, c. 65

PART I

Parliamentary Franchise and Its Exercise

Parliamentary Franchise and Distribution of Seats

1.—(1) Subject to any Order in Council hereafter made under the House of Commons (Redistribution of Seats) Act, 1944, there shall for the purpose of parliamentary elections be the county and borough constituencies, each returning a single member, which are described in the First Schedule to this Act, and no other constituencies.[1]

(2) The persons entitled to vote as electors at a parliamentary election in any constituency shall be those resident there on the qualifying date who, on that date and on the date of the poll, are British subjects of full age and not subject to any legal incapacity to vote:

Provided that a person shall not be entitled to vote as an elector in any constituency unless registered there in the register of parliamentary electors to be used at the election nor, at a general election, to vote as an elector in more than one constituency.

(3) The qualifying date for parliamentary elections shall be determined by reference to the date fixed for the poll as follows:—

(*a*) in Great Britain—

(i) where the date fixed for the poll is between the fifteenth day of March and the second day of October in any year, the qualifying date shall be, in England and Wales, the twentieth day of the preceding November and, in Scotland, the first day of the preceding December;

(ii) where the date fixed for the poll is between the first day of October in any year and the sixteenth day of the following March, the qualifying date shall in all parts of Great Britain be the fifteenth day of the preceding June;

(*b*) in Northern Ireland (subject to the following provisions of this Act)—

(i) where the date fixed for the poll is between the first day of April and the second day of October in any year, the qualifying date shall be the thirty-first day of October in the preceding year;

[1] No university constituencies are included.

(ii) where the date fixed for the poll is between the first day of October in any year and the second day of the following April, the qualifying date shall be the thirtieth day of the preceding April.

[§ 2. Questions of residence to be determined according to the general principles of the Representation of the People Act, 1918.]

[§ 3. Amendments to the House of Commons (Redistribution of Seats) Acts of 1944 and 1947, and to the Representation of the People Act, 1945.]

[§ 4. Electoral registration officers.]

[§ 5. Duty of registration officers to prepare a spring and autumn register each year.]

6.—(1) The following persons shall have a service qualification for the purpose of this Act, namely,—

(a) any person who is a member of the forces;

(b) any person who is employed in the service of the Crown in a post outside the United Kingdom of any prescribed class or description;

(c) any woman who is the wife of a person having a service qualification and is residing outside the United Kingdom to be with her husband. . . .

(2) A service declaration shall be made only by a person who has a service qualification or, subject to any prescribed conditions, by a person about to leave the United Kingdom in such circumstances as to acquire a service qualification.

(3) A service declaration may be made by such a person notwithstanding the fact that by reason of his age he is not yet entitled to be registered or to vote. . . .

(5) A person whose service declaration is in force on the qualifying date—

(a) shall be treated for the purposes of registration as resident at the address specified in the declaration. . . .

[§ 7. Polling districts and polling places.]

8.—(1) All persons voting as electors at a parliamentary election shall do so in person at the polling station allotted to them under the Ballot Act, 1872, except in so far as this section makes exceptions for—

(a) those registered as service voters;

(b) those unable or likely to be unable to go in person to the polling station for one of the following reasons:—

(i) the general nature of the occupation, service or employment of the person in question;

(ii) that person's service as a member of any of His Majesty's reserve or auxiliary forces;

(iii) the particular circumstances of that person's employment on the date of the poll either as a constable or, for a purpose connected with the election, by the returning officer;

(iv) at a general election, the candidature in some other constituency of that person or that person's wife or husband;

(v) at a general election, the fact that that person is acting as returning officer for some other constituency;

(vi) at a general election, the particular circumstances of that person's employment on the date of the poll by the returning officer for some other constituency for a purpose connected with the election in that constituency;

(*c*) those unable or likely to be unable, by reason either of blindness or any other physical incapacity, to go in person to the polling station or, if able to go, to vote unaided;

(*d*) those unable or likely to be unable to go in person from their qualifying address to the polling station without making a journey by air or sea;

(*e*) those no longer residing at their qualifying address.

(2) A person registered as a service voter may vote by proxy unless either—

(*a*) he is entitled in pursuance of an application made under subsection (4) of this section to vote by post; or

(*b*) he applies for a ballot paper to vote in person before a ballot paper has been issued for him to vote by proxy;

but (where there is in force an appointment of a proxy to vote for him) shall not be entitled to vote in person unless he does so apply.

(3) A person not registered as a service voter if unable or likely to be unable to go in person to the polling station by reason either—

(*a*) of the general nature of his occupation, service or employment; or

(*b*) of his service as a member of any of His Majesty's reserve or auxiliary forces;

may vote by proxy if he applies to be treated as an absent voter and is likely to be at sea or out of the United Kingdom on the date of the poll.

(4) Any of the persons mentioned in paragraphs (*a*) to (*e*) of subsection (1) of this section may vote by post if he applies to be treated as an absent voter and furnishes an address in the United Kingdom to which a ballot paper is to be sent for the purpose:

Provided that—

(*a*) a person shall not be entitled to vote by post if he is not registered as a service voter and there is in force an appointment of a proxy to vote for him; and (*b*) a person shall not be entitled to vote by post on the ground that he no longer resides at his qualifying address if at the time of his application he resides at an address in the same area; and

(*c*) a person registered as a service voter shall not be entitled to vote by post on any ground other than his being so registered.

(5) At an election for which a person's application to be treated as an absent voter is allowed, he shall not be entitled to vote in person. . . .

[§ 9. Applications to be treated as an absent voter to be made to the registration officer.

[§§ 10–11. Voting by proxy.]

[§ 12. Timetable and procedure to be as laid down in the schedules to this Act.]

[§ 13. Register to be conclusive on residence, etc.]

14.—(1) Where, after the counting of the votes by the returning officer (including any re-count) is completed, an equality of votes is found to exist between any candidates at a parliamentary election in any constituency, and the addition of a vote would entitle any of those candidates to be declared elected, the returning officer shall not be entitled to a casting vote but shall forthwith decide between those candidates by lot, and proceed as if the candidate on whom the lot falls had received an additional vote. . . .

[§ 15. Deposits.]

[§§ 16–18. Returning officers and their duties.]

[§§ 19–20. Infringements of secrecy and tampering with postal votes by those present at the counting of votes.]

PART II

General Provisions as to Local Government Franchise and Its Exercise

Local Government Franchise

21.—(1) The persons entitled to vote as electors at a local government election in any electoral area shall be those who—

(*a*) on the qualifying date either—

    (i) are resident in the area; or

    (ii) under the following provisions of this section have a non-resident qualification therein; and

(*b*) are in either case on that date and on the date of the poll, British subjects of full age and not subject to any legal incapacity to vote:

Provided that a person shall not be entitled to vote as an elector in any electoral area, unless registered there in the register of local government electors to be used at the election nor, at an ordinary election for any local government area which is not a single electoral area, to vote as an elector in more than one electoral area.

(2) In England and Wales, a person shall be deemed for the purposes of this section to have a non-resident qualification in an area if he is occupying as owner or tenant any rateable land or premises therein of the yearly value of not less than ten pounds.

(3) In Scotland, a person shall be deemed to have a non-resident qualification in an area if he is the owner, or occupier as tenant, of any lands and heritages within the area which are of the yearly value of not less than ten pounds and in respect of which rates are payable.

(4) The qualifying date for a local government election shall be determined by reference to the date fixed for the poll in the same way as if it were a parliamentary election.

[§ 22. Definitions of residence, occupation, etc.]

23.—(1) It shall be the duty of a registration officer to prepare for the local government areas or parts of local government areas included in the area for which he acts a register of local government electors whenever he prepares a register of parliamentary electors.

(2) The two registers shall so far as practicable be combined, the names of persons registered only as local government electors being marked to indicate that fact.

(3) The elections for which any register of local government electors is to be used shall be determined by reference to the date fixed for the poll in the same way as in the case of the register of parliamentary electors.

(4) Subject to any enactment imposing any disqualification for registration as a local government elector, all persons who may be entitled to vote as electors at elections for which any register is to be used shall be entitled to be registered therein:
Provided that—

(a) a person shall not be entitled to be registered more than once in any local government area; and

(b) a person who on the qualifying date has a service qualification shall not be entitled to be registered as resident in any local government area, except in pursuance of a service declaration such as is mentioned in the next following subsection and in force on that date.

(5) The service declaration in pursuance of which a person having a service qualification may be registered as a local government elector shall—

(a) except in the case of a person who is as a peer subject to a legal incapacity to vote at parliamentary elections, be the service declaration (if any) made by him for the purpose of parliamentary elections; and

(b) in the case of such a person as aforesaid, be a declaration marked
to show that it is available for local government elections only, but
in all other respects the same as other service declarations.

(6) A person entitled as a resident to be registered as a local government elector in any local government area shall not be entitled to be
so registered as a non-resident.

(7) Subsections (3) and (5) of section five and section six of this Act
shall apply for the purposes of this Part thereof as they apply for the
purposes of Part I thereof.

[§§ 24–27. Place and manner of voting.]
[§ 28. Amendments to local elections rules, to bring them into conformity
with those for parliamentary elections.]
[§ 29. Effects of the register, etc.]
[§ 30. Tampering with postal votes and breaches of duty by electoral
officers.]

PART III

Corrupt and Illegal Practices and Other Provisions as to Election Campaign

Parliamentary Elections

32.—(1) Parts III and IV of the First Schedule to the parliamentary
corrupt practices Act (which limit the amount of election expenses)
shall cease to have effect, and for any reference in that Act to the
maximum amount specified in the said Part IV (which deals with the
aggregate amount of the permitted expenses) there shall be substituted
a reference to the following maximum amount, namely—

(a) in relation to an election in a county constituency, four hundred
and fifty pounds together with an additional twopence for each
entry in the register of parliamentary electors to be used at the
election;

(b) in relation to an election in a borough constituency, four hundred
and fifty pounds together with an additional penny halfpenny for
each such entry as aforesaid:

Provided that, if the said register is not published before the day of
publication of the notice of election, then for any reference in this subsection to an entry in the register there shall be substituted a reference
to an entry in the electors lists therefor as first published which gives
the name of a person appearing from those lists to be entitled to be
registered.

(2) The said maximum amount shall not be required to cover the
candidate's personal expenses as defined in the said Act, but shall
cover the whole of any fee paid to the candidate's election agent. . . .

(6) In Northern Ireland paragraphs (a) and (b) of subsection (1)
and subsection (2) of this section shall not apply and—

(*a*) the maximum amount referred to in the said subsection (1) shall (subject to the proviso to that subsection) be the same as at the passing of this Act, namely, twopence for each entry in the register of parliamentary electors to be used at the election; and

(*b*) the said maximum amount shall not be required to cover either the candidate's personal expenses as defined in the said Act or (to an amount not exceeding in the case of an election in a county constituency seventy-five pounds and in the case of an election in a borough constituency fifty pounds) the fee, if any, paid to his election agent.

(7) This section shall apply for the purposes of the first general election after the passing of this Act and any subsequent election.

33.—(1) Subject to the provisions of this section, a person shall not, with a view to supporting or opposing the candidature of any individual as against any other or others at a parliamentary election, either let, lend or employ, or hire, borrow or use, any motor vehicle for the purpose of the conveyance of electors or their proxies to or from the poll, and a person knowingly acting in contravention of this subsection shall be guilty of an illegal practice within the meaning of the parliamentary corrupt practices Act:

Provided that—

(*a*) the court before whom a person is convicted under this subsection may, if they think it just in the special circumstances of the case, mitigate or entirely remit any incapacity imposed by section ten of the said Act; and

(*b*) a candidate shall not be liable, nor shall his election be avoided, for an illegal practice under this subsection committed without his consent or connivance by an agent other than his election agent.

(2) Where it is shown—

(*a*) that a motor vehicle was employed for the purpose aforesaid; and

(*b*) that at the time when it was so employed there was to the knowledge of any person employing or using it for that purpose displayed on it or on a trailer drawn by it any placard, colours or other thing indicating a preference for or against any candidate at the election;

it shall be presumed until the contrary is shown that that person was so employing or using it with a view to supporting or opposing the candidature of some individual as against some other or others.

(3) Nothing in this section shall—

(*a*) render unlawful anything made lawful by subsection (3) of section fourteen of the parliamentary corrupt practices Act (which relates to the use of vehicles by electors at their joint cost); or

(*b*) prevent any person employing a motor vehicle for the purpose of conveying to or from the poll himself or any member of the same household, or borrowing a motor vehicle from a member of the same household to be employed for that purpose; or

(c) prevent a candidate at an election or some person on his behalf employing a motor vehicle for the purpose of conveying any person to or from the poll, if the conditions hereafter mentioned in this section are complied with, or borrowing a motor vehicle to be employed for that purpose from any person; or

(d) prevent a person lending or using a motor vehicle in a case in which it is lawfully borrowed or employed by virtue of either of of the last two foregoing paragraphs.

(4) The conditions under which a motor vehicle may be employed under the said paragraph (c) by or on behalf of a candidate are the following:—

(a) the motor vehicle shall be registered in the prescribed manner with the returning officer, and there shall be prominently displayed thereon a placard indicating that it is so registered;

(b) the number of motor vehicles so employed shall not exceed in a county constituency one for every fifteen hundred electors or in a borough constituency one for every twenty-five hundred electors. . . .

[§ 34. Free postage for candidate's electoral address.]

[§ 35. Candidates to have the right to use certain schools and halls for election meetings.]

[§ 36. Use of committee rooms in schools.]

37.—(1) No person shall, with intent to influence persons to give or refrain from giving their votes at a parliamentary election, use, or aid, abet, counsel, or procure the use of, any wireless transmitting station outside the United Kingdom for the transmission of any matter having reference to the election otherwise than in pursuance of arrangements made with the British Broadcasting Corporation for it to be received and transmitted by that Corporation.

(2) No person shall for the purpose of promoting or procuring the election of any candidate at a parliamentary election issue any poll card or document so closely resembling an official poll card as to be calculated to deceive.

(3) Any offence under this section shall be an illegal practice within the meaning of the parliamentary corrupt practices Act:

Provided that the court before whom a person is convicted of an offence under this section may, if they think it just in the special circumstances of the case, mitigate or entirely remit any incapacity imposed by section ten of that Act.

(4) Where any act or omission of an association or body of persons, corporate or unincorporated, is an illegal practice under this section,

any person who at the time of the act or omission was a director, general manager, secretary or other similar officer of the association or body, or was purporting to act in any such capacity, shall be deemed to be guilty of the illegal practice, unless he proves that the act or omission took place without his consent or connivance and that he exercised all such diligence to prevent the commission of the illegal practice as he ought to have exercised having regard to the nature of his functions in that capacity and to all the circumstances.

[§§ 38–40. Extensions and amendments to local corrupt practices Act.]
[§ 41. Candidates not liable for rates on premises used for election meetings.]

42.—(1) No expenses shall, with a view to promoting or procuring the election of a candidate at a parliamentary or local government election, be incurred by any person other than the candidate, his election agent and persons authorised in writing by the election agent on account—

(*a*) of holding public meetings or organising any public display; or
(*b*) of issuing advertisements, circulars or publications; or
(*c*) of otherwise presenting to the electors the candidate or his views or the extent or nature of his backing or disparaging another candidate:

Provided that paragraph (*c*) of this subsection shall not—

(i) restrict the publication of any matter relating to the election in a newspaper or other periodical; or
(ii) apply to any expenses not exceeding in the aggregate the sum of ten shillings which may be incurred by an individual and are not incurred in pursuance of a plan suggested by or concerted with others, or to expenses incurred by any person in travelling or in living away from home or similar personal expenses. . . .

[§§ 43–56. Miscellaneous amendments to election expenses; penalties for corruption; powers of the courts to restrain false statements; periods of incapacity for corrupt and illegal practices, etc.]
[Parts IV and V (§§ 57–65) contain special provisions for local government elections in England and Wales, and Scotland.]
[Part VI (§§ 66–80) contains supplemental provisions as to registration, etc. Short title in § 81. Thirteen schedules.]

GAS ACT, 1948
11 and 12 Geo. 6, c. 67

Part I

Area Gas Boards and the Gas Council

1.—(1) There shall be established Boards . . . in this Act referred to as "Area Boards", for the areas which are described in general terms in [the first Schedule]. . . .

(2) Every Area Board shall have power to carry on all such activities as it may appear to the Board to be requisite, advantageous or convenient for them to carry on for or in connection with the discharge of their duties. . . .

2.—(1) There shall be established a Council, to be known as the Gas Council, and it shall be the duty of that Council—

(a) to advise the Minister on questions affecting the gas industry and matters relating thereto; and
(b) to promote and assist the efficient exercise and performance by Area Boards of their functions.

(2) The Gas Council shall have power, if so authorised by all the Area Boards or a group of Area Boards, to perform services for, or act on behalf of, the Boards concerned in relation to matters of common interest to those Boards. . . .

[§ 3. Research.]
[§ 4. Training and education.]
[§ 5. Constitution of Area Boards and the Gas Council.]
[§ 6. Minister's power to define and vary areas for which Boards are established.]

7.—(1) The Minister may give to Area Boards generally or to a particular Area Board or to the Gas Council such directions of a general character as to the exercise and performance . . . of their functions as appear to the Minister to be requisite in the national interest, and they shall give effect to any such directions:
Provided that—

(a) before giving any such direction, the Minister shall consult with the Gas Council; and
(b) before giving any such direction to a particular Area Board, the Minister shall consult with that Board. . . .

9.—(1) A Council, to be known as a Gas Consultative Council, shall . . . be established for the purposes mentioned in this section for the area of every Area Board.

(2) A Gas Consultative Council shall consist of a chairman appointed by the Minister and not less than twenty nor more than thirty other members appointed by the Minister. . . .

(4) The Gas Consultative Council for each area shall be charged with the duties—

(*a*) of considering any matter affecting the supply of gas in the area . . .

(*b*) of considering and reporting to the Area Board on any such matter which may be referred to them by that Board. . . .

10.—(1) Every Area Board and the Gas Council shall, as soon as possible after the end of each financial year, make to the Minister a report on the exercise and performance by them of their functions during that year and on their policy and programmes, and every Area Board shall, as soon as their report has been made to the Minister, send a copy thereof to the Gas Council.

(2) Every such report of any Area Board or of the Gas Council . . . shall set out any direction given by the Minister to the Board or Council during that year unless the Minister has notified the Board or Council of his opinion that it is against the interests of national security to do so. . . .

(5) The Minister shall lay before each House of Parliament a copy of the report made for each financial year by each Area Board and the Gas Council, and shall at the same time lay before each House of Parliament a report with respect to the exercise of his functions during that year under this Act except as regards matters which in his opinion it is against the interests of national security to disclose.

[§§ 11–77 and four Schedules omitted.]

PARLIAMENT ACT, 1949
12, 13 and 14 Geo. 6, c. 103

An Act to amend the Parliament Act, 1911.

[*16th December 1949.*]

1. The Parliament Act, 1911, shall have effect, and shall be deemed to have had effect from the beginning of the session in which the Bill for this Act originated (save as regards that Bill itself), as if—

(*a*) there had been substituted in subsections (1) and (4) of section two thereof, for the words "in three successive sessions", "for the third time", "in the third of those sessions", "in the third session", and "in the second or third session" respectively, the words "in two successive sessions", "for the second time", "in the second of those sessions", "in the second session", and "in the second session" respectively; and (*b*) there had been substituted in subsection (1) of the said section two, for the words "two years have elapsed" the words "one year has elapsed":

Provided that, if a Bill has been rejected for the second time by the House of Lords before the signification of the Royal Assent to the Bill for this Act, whether such rejection was in the same session as that in which the Royal Assent to the Bill for this Act was signified or in an earlier session, the requirement of the said section two that a Bill is to be presented to His Majesty on its rejection for the second time by the House of Lords shall have effect in relation to the Bill rejected as a requirement that it is to be presented to His Majesty as soon as the Royal Assent to the Bill for this Act has been signified, and, notwithstanding that such rejection was in an earlier session, the Royal Assent to the Bill rejected may be signified in the session in which the Royal Assent to the Bill for this Act was signified.

2.—(1) This Act may be cited as the Parliament Act, 1949.

(2) This Act and the Parliament Act, 1911, shall be construed as one and may be cited together as the Parliament Acts, 1911 and 1949, and accordingly subsection (1) of section four of the Parliament Act, 1911 (which specifies the words of enactment to be inserted in a Bill presented to His Majesty under that Act) shall have effect with the substitution of the words "the Parliament Acts, 1911 and 1949" for the words "the Parliament Act, 1911."

REGENCY ACT, 1953
2 Eliz. 2, c. 1

Whereas Your Majesty, by Your Majesty's Royal Message to both Houses of Parliament, has been pleased to recommend that Parliament should consider the expediency of providing that His Royal Highness the Duke of Edinburgh should be the Regent if a child of Your Majesty and His Royal Highness accedes to the Throne while under the age of eighteen years or if a Regency becomes necessary during the lifetime of Your Majesty while there is no child or grandchild of Your Majesty and His Royal Highness who can be the Regent, and also the expediency of amending the law so that the heir apparent or heir presumptive to the Throne should be capable of being Regent if he or she has attained the age of eighteen years:

And whereas Your Majesty by the same Message recommended that Parliament should consider the amendment of the Regency Acts, 1937 and 1943, so as to add Her Majesty Queen Elizabeth the Queen

Mother to the persons to whom, as Counsellors of State, royal functions can be delegated:

Now, therefore, we, Your Majesty's most dutiful and loyal subjects, the Lords Spiritual and Temporal, and Commons, in this present Parliament assembled, do most humbly beseech Your Majesty that it be enacted, and be it enacted by the Queen's Most Excellent Majesty, by and with the advice and consent of the Lords Spiritual and Temporal, and Commons, in this present Parliament assembled, and by the authority of the same, as follows:

1.—(1) If a Regency becomes necessary under the Regency Act, 1937, on the succession to the Crown of a child of Her Majesty and His Royal Highness the Duke of Edinburgh while under the age of eighteen years, His Royal Highness, if living, shall be the Regent.

(2) If a Regency becomes necessary under the Regency Act, 1937, during the reign of Her present Majesty, His Royal Highness the Duke of Edinburgh, if living, shall be the Regent unless, or (as the case may be) until, there is a child or grandchild of Her Majesty and His Royal Highness who can under the provisions of the said Act be the Regent.

(3) The preceding provisions of this section shall have effect subject to—

(*a*) subsection (2) of section three of the Regency Act, 1937[1] (which enumerates the disqualifications for becoming or being Regent), and

(*b*) subsection (5) of that section (which provides for the case where the Regent is incapacitated by infirmity for performing the royal functions or is not available for the performance of those functions),

but, save as aforesaid, that section shall have effect subject to the preceding provisions of this section.

(4) Where His Royal Highness the Duke of Edinburgh is Regent by virtue of this section, section six of the Regency Act, 1937 (which relates to the appointment of Counsellors of State) shall have effect as if the following provision were substituted for subsection (4) thereof:

"(4) The provisions of this section shall apply in relation to a Regent with the substitution for references to the Sovereign of references to the Regent and the omission, in subsection (2) thereof, of the reference to the wife or husband of the Sovereign."

2. The heir apparent or heir presumptive to the Throne shall be deemed for all the purposes of the Regency Act, 1937, to be of full age if he or she has attained the age of eighteen years.

---

[1] "(2). A person shall be disqualified from becoming or being Regent, if he is not a British subject of full age and domiciled in some part of the United Kingdom, or is a person who would, under section two of the Act of Settlement, be incapable of inheriting, possessing, and enjoying the Crown; and section three of the Act of Settlement shall apply in the case of a Regent as it applies in the case of a Sovereign."

3. Her Majesty Queen Elizabeth the Queen Mother shall be added to the persons whom subsection (2) of section six of the Regency Act, 1937 (as set out in section one of the Regency Act, 1943)[1] requires, subject as therein mentioned, to be the Counsellors of State for the purposes of any delegation of royal functions under that section, and accordingly during her life that section shall have effect as if a reference to her were inserted in subsection (2) thereof next after the reference to the wife or husband of the Sovereign.

4.—(1) This Act may be cited as the Regency Act, 1953, and shall be construed as one with the Regency Acts, 1937 and 1943, and those Acts and this Act may be cited together as the Regency Acts, 1937 to 1953.

(2) In subsection (2A) of section six of the Regency Act, 1937 (set out in section one of the Regency Act, 1943) the words "The heir apparent or heir presumptive to the Throne if not under the age of eighteen years shall not be disqualified from being a Counsellor of State by reason only of his not being of full age, but save as aforesaid" (being words rendered unnecessary by section two of this Act) are hereby repealed.

[1] " . . . the Counsellors of State shall be the wife or husband of the Sovereign (if the Sovereign is married), and the four persons who, excluding any person disqualified under this section, are next in the line of succession to the Crown, or if the number of such persons next in the line of succession is less than four, then all such persons . . ."

Parliament

REFORM OF THE SECOND CHAMBER, 1918

Letter from Viscount Bryce to the Prime Minister, reporting the conclusions of the Conference on the Reform of the Second Chamber (Cd. 9038; 1918)

FUNCTIONS APPROPRIATE TO A SECOND CHAMBER

6. (1) The examination and revision of Bills brought from the House of Commons, a function which has become more needed since, on many occasions, during the last 30 years, the House of Commons has been obliged to act under special rules limiting debate.

(2) The initiation of Bills dealing with subjects of a comparatively non-controversial character which may have an easier passage through the House of Commons if they have been fully discussed and put into a well-considered shape before being submitted to it.

(3) The interposition of so much delay (and no more) in the passing of a Bill into law as may be needed to enable the opinion of the nation to be adequately expressed upon it. This would be specially needed as regards Bills which affect the fundamentals of the Constitution or introduce new principles of legislation, or which raise issues whereon the opinion of the country may appear to be almost equally divided.

(4) Full and free discussion of large and important questions, such as those of foreign policy, at moments when the House of Commons may happen to be so much occupied that it cannot find sufficient time for them. Such discussions may often be all the more useful if conducted in an Assembly whose debates and divisions do not involve the fate of the Executive Government.

ELEMENTS THAT OUGHT TO FIND A PLACE IN THE SECOND CHAMBER

7. (1) Persons of experience in various forms of public work, such as judicial work, Local Government work, Civil Service work, Parliamentary work; persons possessing special knowledge of important departments of the national life, such as Agriculture, Commerce, Industry, Finance, Education, Naval and Military Affairs; and persons who possess a like knowledge of what are called Imperial Questions such as foreign affairs and matters affecting the Over-Seas Dominions.

(2) Persons who, while likely to serve efficiently in a Second Chamber, may not have the physical vigour needed to bear the increasing strain which candidacy for a seat in the House of Commons, and service in it involve.

(3) A certain proportion of persons who are not extreme partizans, but of a cast of mind which enables them to judge political questions with calmness and comparative freedom from prejudice or bias. . . .

POSITION WHICH THE SECOND CHAMBER OUGHT TO HOLD . . .

8. It was agreed that a Second Chamber ought not to have equal
powers with the House of Commons, nor aim at becoming a rival of
that assembly. In particular, it should not have the power of making
or unmaking Ministeries [*sic*], or enjoy equal rights in dealing with
finance. . . .

All precautions that could be taken ought to be taken to secure
that in a Reformed Second Chamber no one set of political opinions
should be likely to have a marked and permanent predominance, and
that the Chamber should be so composed as not to incur the charge of
habitually acting under the influence of party motives. . . .

It should . . . endeavour to enlighten and influence the people
through its debates, and be recognised by the people as qualified,
when a proper occasion arose, to require the reconsideration of
important measures on which their opinion had not been fully ascertained.

COMPOSITION OF THE SECOND CHAMBER

10. The principle of endeavouring to preserve some real measure of
continuity between the House of Lords and the new Second Chamber,
a principle accepted by all, though some members attached more
importance to it than did others, suggested that a certain portion of
the Chamber should be taken from the existing peerage, but the other
principle that three important requisites for the strength of the Chamber would be found in its having popular authority behind it, in its
opening to the whole of His Majesty's subjects free and equal access
to the Chamber, and in its being made responsive to the thoughts and
sentiments of the people, also prescribed that the large majority of the
members should be so chosen as to enjoy that popular authority. . . .

11. The Conference rejected the idea of having a chamber elected
on the basis of a property qualification . . . [and] . . . proceeded to
examine five methods that might be adopted for constituting that
popular element in the Chamber which it had been agreed to make
predominant.

[The methods were:

(i) *Nomination by the Crown.* It was thought unlikely that the country would
favour this.

(ii) *Direct Election.* This was rejected, principally because "it was forcibly
urged that a Chamber elected on the same franchise . . . would inevitably
become a rival of the House of Commons, and would, because it had an equal
'mandate' from the people, be likely to claim equal financial powers, and tend
to fall into conflict with that principle of the Constitution which assigns to the
House of Commons the function of making and unmaking Administrations."

(iii) *Election by Local Authorities.* It was objected that this method "would
certainly introduce party politics into the elections of those County Councils

and Borough Councils which had hitherto been conducted on non-party lines . . ."

(iv) *Selection by a Joint Standing Committee of Both Houses.* It was felt that a "broader basis" of election was required.

(v) *Election by the House of Commons.* The majority of the Conference recommended that the Second Chamber should consist of 327 persons, of whom 246 should be elected by members of the House of Commons (grouped into territorial areas), and the remaining 81 (to be chosen at first from the existing peerage) by a Joint Standing Committee of both Houses. The tenure of seats would be of 12 years, and one-third of the members would retire every four years.]

Legislative Functions of the Second Chamber

43. . . . It has always been understood in this country . . . that the Second Chamber should be entitled to full power in the sphere of such legislation as is not of a financial character. . . .

45. It is recognised on all hands that Bills of a purely financial nature belong to the House of Commons alone and ought not to be rejected or amended by the Second Chamber.

But what is a purely financial Bill?

46. . . . The Conference spent many hours in trying to find such a definition, but without success. . . . But an examination of the cases of doubt which had arisen in this country and elsewhere, showed that most, perhaps nearly all of them, could have been disposed of after a not very protracted discussion round a table by a dozen practical fair-minded men; and the Conference was thus led to believe that the best method of treating these doubtful and disputable Bills would be to refer them to a small carefully selected Joint Standing Committee of both Houses of Parliament, making its decision final. . . .

[There should, therefore, be a Finance Committee, of not more than seven members from each House, to which either House might refer controversial financial Bills. Those Bills, or parts of Bills, which the committee declared to be non-financial might be handled in the normal way by the Second Chamber.]

Adjustment of Differences between the two Houses

[Differences should be settled at a Free Conference of not more than sixty members drawn from both Houses.]

49. . . . If and when agreement is reached by the Free Conference its terms would be reported to both Houses. Each House would then consider them and accept them or reject them. . . . If, however, the Bill (as reported by the Free Conference) was accepted by one House but rejected by the other, some further method of effecting an adjustment would be required. . . .

52. . . . Three such methods were put forward for consideration. . . .

53. The first was that the House which accepted the Bill as reported by the Free Conference should have the right of referring it to a

Parliament

Joint Sitting of both Houses. . . . [This] finally failed to command general assent.

54. A second plan was that of referring the matters in controversy between the Houses to the country by means of a Referendum or popular vote of all the registered electors. . . .

55. The majority of the Conference, however, did not approve this plan on the ground (among others) that the use of the Referendum once introduced could not be confined to the cases for which it was in this instance proposed, that it might tend to lower the authority and dignity of Parliament, and that it was unsuited to the conditions of a large country, and especially of the United Kingdom, for different parts of which different legislation is sometimes required.

56. . . . [A] method of adjustment . . . was at last discovered by returning to and carrying further that mode of proceeding by Free Conference. . . .

. . . This step would be to send the Bill back to the Free Conference, which would take up the matter again in the Session next following that in which the Bill originated. If the Free Conference should then, after further consideration, again report the Bill to the Houses in the same form in which it had been previously reported, the Houses would again consider the Bill.

If they both agreed to it, it would pass; if they both disagreed to it, or if the House of Commons alone disagreed, it would lapse. If, however, the House of Commons alone agreed to the Bill, and it had been reported by the Free Conference by a majority of not less than three of the members present and voting, it would be submitted for the Royal Assent.

Should the Free Conference however fail to agree to report the Bill again in the same form, or if the majority by which it agreed to report it should be less than three the Bill would lapse, unless of course it was accepted by both Houses as reported.

61. . . . We had to reconcile the sentiment of attachment to a venerable institution with the needs of new social conditions and the demands of new phases of thought. There were two principles on which a Second Chamber might be constructed. One was that of filling a House with the largest available number of capable and experienced men whose presence would win for it that kind of authority which comes from personal eminence. The other principle was that of creating a Chamber which should be most quickly responsive and most fully responsible to public opinion, drawing its strength from the fact that it had been popularly elected. It was impossible to give full scope and application to either of these principles and to secure in ample measure the benefit of either source of strength without losing some of the merits to be expected from the other. We had, therefore, to find means whereby to combine as many as possible of the advantages

with as few as possible of the defects of either course, and we had to remember that a plan which philosophers might approve would not necessarily find like favour with the bodies by whose will it would have to pass into law. So, too, when the powers of the Second Chamber had to be defined, similar perplexities arose. It was generally agreed that a Second Chamber would be of little use unless it were strong enough to differ from the House of Commons when a proper occasion arose—a proper occasion being one in which there was reason to believe that some decision of the Commons did not express the full and deliberate will of the people. But it was also agreed that the Second Chamber ought not to be so strongly entrenched as to dispose it to engage in frequent contests with the House of Commons, so as to embarrass the Executive and clog the wheels of legislation. It thus became necessary to steer a middle course between these extremes. . . .

THE DISSOLUTION OF PARLIAMENT, 1923

From a speech by Mr. H. H. Asquith at the National Liberal Club on 18 December 1923

MR. ASQUITH: . . . And now let me say here, by way of parenthesis, there seems to be a good deal of confusion in the public mind on the subject of the power of dissolution. I may claim to speak, I won't say with authority, but with some experience on this matter, for I am the only person now living who has felt it his duty to advise the Crown to dissolve Parliament twice in a single year—the year 1910. . . . I need hardly tell you there is absolutely no analogy between that case and the circumstances of the present time.

The dissolution of Parliament is in this country one of the prerogatives of the Crown. It is not a mere feudal survival, but it is part, and I think a useful part, of our constitutional system, for which there is no counterpart in any other country. . . . It does not mean that the Crown should act arbitrarily and without the advice of responsible Ministers, but it does mean that the Crown is not bound to take the advice of a particular Minister to put its subjects to the tumult and turmoil of a series of General Elections so long as it can find other Ministers who are prepared to give it a trial. The notion that a Minister—a Minister who cannot command a majority in the House of Commons, but who is in a minority of 31 per cent.—the notion that a Minister in those circumstances is invested with the right to demand a dissolution is as subversive of constitutional usage as it would, in my opinion, be pernicious to the general and paramount interests of the nation at large. . . .

LEGISLATION AND PARLIAMENTARY TIME, 1930

House of Commons Debates, 18 February 1930; Official Report, cc. 1226–7

COLONEL ASHLEY: . . . I am naturally anxious that the [Road Traffic] Bill should receive a favourable reception, because . . . I had certainly a substantial share in the fashioning of the Bill. In 1927 I circulated, for criticism and suggestion, a draft Traffic Bill to all local authorities and organisations of people who were legitimately interested. That Bill was not founded on my personal opinion, but on the reports of two Departmental Committees. It was not, if I may say so, a Government Bill. It was not an official Bill in the sense that we did not tie ourselves down to any of the details, and it was circulated solely for the purposes of gathering criticisms and remarks, so as to enable us to ascertain the real views of the people concerned. . . .

. . . This Bill is long overdue, and I make a present of that remark to any hon. Member opposite who may wish to ask me why I did not introduce it when I had the honour to occupy the position of Minister of Transport. But the reason for that is well known. Every Government wishes to pass more legislation than there is time for, and if a Department has had one big Measure allotted to it in the course of a Parliament, it is considered to be lucky. We in the Ministry of Transport had the Electricity Act. Naturally, all the other Ministers make it their business to see that one Department does not get more than one Bill of that importance in order that their own Departments may have opportunities. That is the real explanation of why the Traffic Bill was kept over for two or three years. . . .

THE WORKING OF THE HOUSE OF COMMONS, 1931

Evidence before the Select Committee on Procedure on Public Business (H.C. 161 of 1931)

(A) THE RIGHT HON. J. RAMSAY MACDONALD, M.P., THE PRIME MINISTER, EXAMINED:

Sir Hugh O'Neill

8. Might I ask . . . one question which, perhaps, rather goes to the root of the matter. Do you consider, Prime Minister, that the main function of the procedure of Parliament should be primarily to get things done as quickly as possible, to get things through; of course

that would favour principally the Government; or should it be really aimed principally at favouring careful deliberation and adequate criticism of the different measures that are brought forward?—It is really a combination of both. . . . Standing Orders and Procedure Rules should limit abuses as much as possible, but protect the right of the Opposition to be heard, and to give counsel, and to make its position clear to the country; and, against that, you have to balance up the rights of the Government, which are, in a sentence, to get legislation through after due examination. A Parliamentary machine is rather like a living organism, you have to balance up rights and wrongs.

9. Do you consider the procedure of Parliament unduly handicaps the Government in getting its business through?—On the whole, yes.

10. So any reforms you would suggest would be in the direction of making it easier for the Government to get its business through, and consequently putting more spokes in the wheels of the Opposition, whose object it is to prevent and delay business?—If the business of the Opposition is to delay, then I am perfectly willing to put spokes in their wheel. If the business of the Opposition is to secure adequate examination, I do not propose to put any spokes in their wheel. Members disagree as to where the line between the two is to be drawn.

29. . . .—This fundamental question comes. Really, what is the House of Commons itself? It consists not only of a Government, but of an Opposition, and they have both got functions and rights. The great right of the Opposition is the full discussion of measures proposed by the Government. It is there, I think, that our fundamental weakness lies. There is a doctrine that it is the function of the Opposition to oppose. I have always regarded that as a crime against the State. It is not the function of the Opposition to oppose; it is the function of the Opposition to oppose Second Readings, but once the Second Reading has been accepted, the only function of the Opposition is to improve in its own direction within the scope of the Vote that has been registered, that is, that it should have full liberty to examine on Committee and Report, and then to say its final word of opposition on the Third Reading of the Bill. The Opposition has no right to obstruct in the sense of making Parliament barren or unproductive. . . .

(B) THE RIGHT HON. STANLEY BALDWIN, M.P., EXAMINED:

Mr. Hore-Belisha

237. Do not you think it is impossible for any Parliamentary Assembly to control finance in detail, unless it delegates that function to an expert Committee?—I think, in practice, that is so. . . .

MBG

Mr. Ede

239. . . . Is it not a fact that at the time when the grants were made more or less directly to the King, the Executive was outside the House, whereas today the Executive is in the House, is an integral part of the House, and in a good many Parliaments the Parliament could not continue unless the Executive was constantly there voting for itself?—Yes.

243. We are trying to carry on in the twentieth century a system that is based on a theory when the composition of the House in relation to the Executive was entirely different?—Yes.

244. Is there any remedy for that, that will enable the House to recover control of finance and to examine for necessary economies itself, without the dreadful alternative of having to throw the Government out to do it, and getting a Government that quite possibly it does not want in return?—I quite see what you mean, but all the economies that you are talking about, and all the economies that can be obtained, or that you could hope to obtain, by what you call control of Parliament, are a mere bagatelle compared with the power that the House of Commons has itself of spending money. There, I think, your observation comes in perfectly truly, Mr. Hore-Belisha. It is broad policy that means, I will not use the word "extravagance," but that means expenditure. Over that the House of Commons has complete control, but, of course, that control is whether or no it accepts certain Bills. As you were saying, it means the dismissal of a Government if they do not like to spend money. The amount of subjects to which the control of Parliament, in the way of examining the details of expenditure extends, is really very limited.

(C) The Right Hon. David Lloyd George, M.P., Examined:

Chairman (Mr. Ernest Brown)

350. The Committee would like to know whether you consider there is any justification for the public criticism of the present system of procedure . . .?— . . . I have no doubt at all there is a good deal of criticism of Parliamentary institutions altogether, and I think there is a very great and growing disappointment with Parliament . . . [353] . . . The only real endeavour made in recent years to secure economy has been in consequence of pressure from outside on the Executive. I am referring to the Geddes Committee. There has been no examination by the House of Commons itself of the Estimates . . . That will be my first criticism on the procedure of the House of Commons, and one of the reasons why I think on the whole it is losing a good deal of prestige amongst the masses of the people. . . . My [second] criticism would be that the control of the Executive by the House of Commons is confined to rather perfunctory discussions,

which do not excite any real interest, apart from an element of censure which is conducive to excitement, but does not achieve the real purpose of establishing control over the Executive. . . . [356] . . . The fact of the matter is that the House of Commons has no real effective and continuous control over the actions of the Executive. I noticed that questions were put—I forget whether to Mr. Baldwin or to the Prime Minister—with regard to the setting up of Committees and the analogy of the municipalities was referred to. I think there is a good deal to be said about that. Every municipality in the land has committees which consider every important detail of administration, and report upon it to the council. The general discussions take place there. The examination in detail takes place in the committees which are set up for that purpose. You have a finance committee, a surveyors' committee, a police committee, and a health committee, and there are all kinds of committees. On questions of principle you have a debate in the council chamber, but the close examination takes place by committees where the officials are present and questions can be put to them, and if the committees would like to have any outside opinion, if they think any other opinion would enlighten them upon the topics they are examining, they can send for anybody. But you have no machinery of that kind in the House of Commons, and until you have it the House of Commons will have no effective control over the Executive. . . .

Mr. Hore-Belisha

362. That committee would control the Departmental affairs in regard to administration?—No. I would not like to say that. The control must rest with the Minister because he is responsible to Parliament, and through Parliament to the Crown. The Minister must have the ultimate say, subject to what Parliament says, but it would enable the House of Commons effectively to supervise, and not only that, but to keep itself informed.

363. Do you envisage the Minister being Chairman of such a committee?—No. The Minister is in the House.

364. He is summoned before the committee?—Yes; he comes before the committee.

365. And a Civil Servant might also be summoned?—Certainly. I would suggest that you have power to send for anybody.

366. And no information could be withheld?—Oh, no. . . .

Chairman

909. . . . There has been some difference of opinion as to the comparative merits of the guillotine and the kangaroo, and as to where they ought to be applied, and to what Bills?—I have come to the conclusion that there is a certain type of Bill you can never get through

the House of Commons unless you have a guillotine. If it is a highly controversial Bill, I think it is quite impossible to get it through. . . .

Mr. Hore-Belisha

935. You agree that the guillotine is a device to be resorted to in exceptional circumstances only?—In exceptional circumstances, certainly.

936. Then you disagree with the Prime Minister, who suggested it should be a normal process?—I am not in favour of making it a normal process. You know by the very touch of the thing what Bills are likely to provoke, I do not like to use the word 'obstruction,' but obstructive opposition; not only obstructive opposition, but an opposition which cannot be restrained within the bounds of time.

937. You think every Bill ought to be sent upstairs to a small Committee?—Yes, I have absolutely no doubt about that.

938. Except the major Bills?—Yes. . . . [1034] . . . my suggestion is that you should have many more Committees. You would have Committees, first of all, to deal with administration. You would have Committees to deal with legislation, and then one Member would say: "I am a Member of the Budget Committee or the Finance Committee"; another Member would say: "I am a Member of the Committee which deals with the defence of this country"; and so on. There is no doubt at all that it gives an absolutely new status to a Member, and enables you to give him a blue ribbon without making him a Member of the Administration. . . .

(D) Sir Archibald Sinclair, M.P., Examined:

Captain Bourne

1262. . . . You said that you would like smaller and more numerous Standing Committees?—Yes.

1263. I suppose you realise that there are at the present moment only three decent Committee Rooms in the House? I am putting it as a question that it would be difficult to bring it in at once?—Frankly, I did not quite realise that structural difficulty, but I imagine it could be overcome.

1264. I imagine it could be overcome, but actually if Standing Committees are to sit in private Committee rooms of that sort, there are only two good ones and two bad ones in the House; there are No. 14, No. 10, the Grand Committee Room in Westminster Hall, and No. 12. Those are the only ones which exist, and No. 12 is very small?—Perhaps with smaller Committees it would be possible to put up a partition.

1265. It would necessitate a certain amount of structural alteration of the House. I do not know whether you realised that?—Yes, it would.

(E) THE RIGHT HON. LORD EUSTACE PERCY, M.P., EXAMINED:

Chairman

1886. I think the Committee has received a memorandum which you kindly forwarded. I do not know whether you would prefer to deal with it, or shall we incorporate it in the minutes as it is?—Just as you wish. The memorandum is as follows:

"1. Proposals for reforming the procedure of the House of Commons usually fail because their purpose is not defined. By demanding that it should be more businesslike without defining what its business is, reformers often get no further than proposals which would make it look more businesslike, without really enabling it to do more business.

"2. The proper business of the House of Commons may be defined roughly as follows: to focus public attention on the important issues of the day, to grant taxation limited to the immediate needs of the Executive, to appropriate the public revenues to particular services, to press the Executive (in return for the taxes granted) for the redress of popular grievances, and to grant the Executive such additional legal powers as may be necessary for the efficient conduct of public administration.

"The critic may object that this definition is an old-fashioned one. The reply to that objection is that, whether we like it or not, the House of Commons has never succeeded in extending its effective action much beyond the field where it had established itself two hundred years ago, after it had asserted its legitimate rights against the Crown. It does not, and cannot, itself govern the country, and many of its present defects probably arise from the recent 'democratic' tendency to convert it into a sovereign parliamentary assembly on the Continental model, governing the country through a committee of ministers. In our constitutional practice, the distinction between Executive and Legislature is, in essence, more clearly drawn than in the written constitutions of countries which have nominally adopted the principle of the 'separation of powers.' The King's Ministers are responsible to Parliament, but they are responsible for the discharge of duties which Parliament is radically unfitted to discharge for itself. It is not even the business of the House of Commons to 'control' the King's Ministers, if by that is meant to control the detail of their administration or even of their expenditure. It controls Ministers most effectively by forming a broad general opinion as to their personal reliability and treating them accordingly, but it never has been, and never will be, able to offer them authoritative guidance in the efficient and economical management of their departments. . . .

"5. We now come to the more difficult questions of the duties of the House in regard to taxation and legislation. In considering these questions, we must at the outset face the really serious charge which can be levelled against the House. It is not that on really far-reaching and contentious Bills we prolong debate and hamper the Government. . . . The serious charge is that we obstruct non-contentious legislation in order that there may be less time for the passage of contentious legislation. There can be no improvement in Parliamentary procedure unless this practice is abandoned. But we must also face the fact that this practice will not be, and perhaps ought not to be, abandoned unless at the same time some limit is placed on the time available for contentious legislation. Obstructive tactics largely arise from uncertainty as to the allocation of Parliamentary time during a Session; the early months of every Session are a kind of gamble on time, and a keen Opposition often deprives the Government of more time than, even in its own view, is good for the conduct of necessary business, while a busy Government often wastes the time of the House by introducing more legislation than it could pass even if the Opposition abstained from all obstruction.

"6. The only remedy for this is to fix the length of Parliamentary Sessions and, to some extent, to allocate time to fixed objects during each Session. . . ."

(F) The Right Hon. Sir Herbert Samuel, M.P., Examined:

Chairman

2531. You were, I believe, the Chairman of the Select Committee on National Expenditure in 1917–1918?—Yes.

2533. . . .—The reference to that Committee covered partly the same ground as the reference to your present Committee. We had among other things to consider the procedure of this House in relation to Supply and Appropriation, so as to secure more effectual control by Parliament over public expenditure. . . . We issued a questionnaire to a large number of authorities on matters of procedure . . . and the consensus of opinion that was shown by the replies . . . was very strongly in favour of the establishment of an Estimates Committee. . . .

Captain Bourne

2536. Would you elaborate a little what you mean by examination of the Estimates by a Committee . . .?—Yes, certainly. Perhaps first I might say the reasons why we made that recommendation. . . . We found that for 25 years on no occasion had the House of Commons ever of its own motion reduced any Estimate presented to it on financial grounds, and I believe that during the years that have elapsed since 1918 the same condition has applied. The law of the Constitution does not allow the House of Commons to increase any of the Estimates that are submitted, and the practice of the Constitution has not in fact allowed the House of Commons on any occasion to reduce an Estimate.

The currents of opinion within the House of Commons may influence the amount of expenditure, but there is no formal direct control over expenditure by the House itself. The Treasury control was in our view not adequate. The Treasury is part of the Executive. If the Minister who wishes to increase expenditure under any head secures the personal assent of the Chancellor of the Exchequer, the Treasury is necessarily silent. . . . A Committee was appointed after the war under the name of the Estimates Committee in 1922, and has been appointed annually ever since. . . . [It] differs in many particulars from what was contemplated by the Committee of 1918. In the first place, we suggested as a matter of fact that there should be two Committees . . . of 15 Members each, which would be able to examine each year a very considerable portion of the whole body of Estimates. That was not done; there is one Committee of 26 Members. And more important than that, we recommended very strongly that there should be a technical adviser attached to the Committee who should be its own officer and whose duty it would be to examine the Estimates or some groups of Estimates each year and report to the Committee upon them. . . . Estimates are very technical things, and it needs an expert to understand them. A mere Committee of the House of Commons of ordinary average Members faced by the great blocks of Estimates that are circulated each year are helpless, and we reported in our view the appointment of such an officer was essential; we used that word. The Comptroller and Auditor General, for reasons which we gave, could not perform in our view those functions as well. We suggested that an Officer of the Treasury would not be adequate. The Treasury, after all, have already passed all the Estimates, and therefore merely to attach an Officer of the Treasury to an Estimates Committee of the House of Commons would be to ask an official of a Department to draw the attention of the Committee to what might be regarded as the failure of his own Department to exercise adequate control; in addition to which the Treasury is merely a branch of the Executive. . . . No officer was in fact attached to the Committee at all until 1926, and then it was an Officer of the Treasury. . . . That is the main reason in my view why the Estimates Committee has not been as effective as we anticipated in 1918 that such a body might be.

Then there is the second point. We recommended very strongly that there should be an opportunity for discussion in the House of Commons itself of any particular recommendations made by an Estimates Committee. . . .

Chairman

2537. May I ask in what form the Committee proposed that this opportunity should present itself to the House?—We suggested that some of the Supply days . . . should be allocated. . . . And, further, we ventured to make a strong recommendation that discussions and divisions on reports of the Estimates Committee should not be regarded as questions of confidence in the Government of the day. . . . [2538] . . . The Estimates Committee, we suggested, should not deal with questions of policy. Of course, it is very difficult to draw any line, and on some particular occasion the Government might regard a particular economy as trenching upon policy. Then we reported in these words: "That limitation should exclude from their recommendations any proposals which, if carried against the Government, could properly entail either their resignation or a dissolution of Parliament."

Sir Basil Peto

2539. If I might just interrupt, would not that militate against any successful check being put upon expenditure by such a Committee if the proposal was of a major character of any size at all?—I do not know about any size at all. You ought not to apply questions of the rule with regard to policy too rigidly. I should say it was a question of policy whether you should have two more battleships or not, but it would not be a question of policy what should be the scale of pay of a particular class of employees.

Mr. Ede

2540. You would not convince Mr. W. J. Brown of that?—No. . . . [2541] . . . You cannot, I think, give any definition of what is policy and what is not.

2542. And in the same way can one give a definition of what is confidence and what is not? Can anybody do that except the Government?—I think that in the last resort that is so, but all that I am pleading for is that there should be a change in the convention, which used to regard everything as a vote of confidence. . . .

(G) SIR MALCOLM RAMSAY, THE COMPTROLLER AND AUDITOR-GENERAL, EXAMINED:

Chairman

3686. The Committee is much obliged to you . . . for your very full Memorandum.—The Memorandum was as follows:

" . . . 2. The present system has, I believe, been generally criticised on the ground of its ineffectiveness in controlling the Executive, especially as regards expenditure. Such criticism is, in my opinion, to a large extent misdirected as proceeding from an imperfect appreciation of the functions of Parliament: of what it can and ought to do. . . .

" 3. . . . If on the other hand 'Ineffectiveness in controlling the Executive' is used merely in a general sense, then I should say that during the past 30 years, and specially since the outbreak of the European War, Parliament has allowed the Executive a freer hand in financial matters.

"4. This result is due not so much to defects in the financial procedure, which still allows the House opportunity in plenty of financial criticism, but to other causes. On the one hand, there is the enormous growth both in volume and complexity of expenditure, and the financial and economic difficulties arising out of the War: on the other, there has been a change in the attitude of Members at large. . . .

"5. The following examples may illustrate my meaning:

(*a*) *Borrowing.* Before 1914 H.M. Government could not issue a public loan or borrow money (apart from purely temporary advances) except on the authority of a resolution passed in Committee of Ways and Means . . . which was the foundation of a Bill giving specific authority for the amount and nature of the issue. But these limitations were swept away by the War: and now under the provisions of the War Loan Acts, 1916 and 1919, and the Finance Act, 1921 (s. 47), the Treasury has a general power, until Parliament otherwise determines, of replacing any securities issued during the War. . . .

"(*b*) The institution of *separate Funds*, such as the Road Fund (fed by assigned taxes), the Development Fund, the Forestry Fund and the Empire Marketing Fund (all three fed by Grants in Aid), has probably tended to emancipate the Executive from control or at any rate to curtail the opportunity of informed criticism in Parliament. . . .

"(*c*) A growing proportion of the public expenditure has taken the form of *block grants*, e.g. the grant for Scottish Education (which is in a fixed ratio to the expenditure of England and Wales) or the grants towards police expenditure and health services (a fixed proportion of the expenditure of Local Authorities).

"6. *Functions of the Comptroller and Auditor-General.* The Public Accounts Committee differs radically from the Estimates Committee in that attached to it is a special officer, uncontrollable by the Executive, responsible directly to Parliament, and removable only on a Resolution of both Houses, who—and this is most important—is assisted by an examining staff of some 230 persons, of whom all but 40 are actually quartered in the premises of the Departments whose accounts are audited, and of whom all are engaged continuously throughout the year in examining the public accounts and have direct access to the books and other departmental records. . . .

"7. *Functions of the Public Accounts Committee.* The Committee itself has a purely general reference: 'to examine the accounts' and while it takes as its text the reports of the Comptroller and Auditor-General, it is at liberty to and does explore the field of economy.

"Unlike the Estimates Committee, it is not expressly excluded from making recommendations involving questions of policy, but it ventures warily into that domain. 'Policy' is a vague term, and doubtless different Committees would adopt a different definition. But probably most Members would agree that while the Committee would be very ill-advised to attempt to criticise major decisions of policy which have already been decided by Parliament as a whole, . . . it is not debarred from referring to minor matters of policy or calling attention to certain aspects of policy, particularly such as might not be familiar to the House. Thus, it would seem not improper for the Committee to point out that some particular policy has proved more expensive than was anticipated or to ask whether a particular object cannot be attained by some alternative and cheaper method. . . .

"9. . . . Its influence is not only *direct*. . . . [10] It is also *indirect*, but not less valuable though incalculable and unseen. It is still true, as Mr. Gibson Bowles said in 1903, that 'there is ground for believing that the spending Departments stand more in awe of the Public Accounts Committee than of the House itself, probably because there is less chance of escaping its close scrutiny.'

"The mere fact that the Committee exists, and that the Comptroller and Auditor General can invoke its assistance, fortifies the Accounting Officers against temptation to stray from the path of economy or of financial regularity: further, it enables the Comptroller and Auditor-General to dispose at once, and in his stride, of many matters of which Parliament never hears. . . .

"16. The *Estimates Committee* has, I am afraid, failed to realise the expectations of those who advocated its establishment. . . . This result . . . is not due to any shortcoming on the part of the Committee, but to the difficulties (foreseen by many experts) which are inherent in any attempt to institute detailed examination and control by the House of Commons without offence to the cardinal doctrine of Cabinet and Ministerial responsibility.

"17. Chief of these is the extent, imperfectly realised, to which policy covers expenditure. All the big money lies in policy, as is shown by the following analysis of the Estimates for 1931 taken from the Budget Statement, H.C. 90.

Taking the various categories there shown in Table VI, we find:

		£
1. Grant Services account for .	. . .	149,339,000
2. Pensions and Insurance account for	. .	150,192,000
3. Defence accounts for .	. . .	111,412,000
4. Tax Collection accounts for.	. . .	11,516,000
5. Debt Interest and Management account for .	.	302,950,000
6. All other services account for	. . .	25,907,000
Total ordinary expenditure	. . .	£751,316,000

"Items 1, 2, and 5 are determined almost entirely by policy. Nearly all of item 3, again, is policy, and of the remaining items, 4 and 6 (which amount to £37,423,000 or less than 5 per cent. of the whole ordinary expenditure), a great deal consists of salaries (which again are matters of policy) fixed by the Government on the recommendations of Royal Commissions, or as the result of agreements arrived at with Staff Associations, or of decisions given by arbitration and other courts. . . ."

"22. (1) If expenditure, including the policy of expenditure, is to be reviewed in detail by a Committee or Committees of the House a revolutionary change must be made in procedure and indeed in the constitution. . . ."

Chairman

3765. The Public Accounts Committee have, on occasion, called Ministers of the Crown in front of them, and questioned them on matters of policy, have they not?—That is so, yes.

3766. But it is very infrequent, is it not?—Very rare. We have had two instances in my experience; we had the Secretary of State for Air down once, and the Secretary of State for War.

(H) Sir William Graham-Harrison, Parliamentary Counsel to the Treasury, Examined:

Mr. Ede

4422. If the House increased the number of Standing Committees upstairs so that there might be additional Bills in front of Committees at the same time, it would probably involve an increase in your Department to cope with the work involved, would it not?—It would mean, I imagine, that a good many more Bills would get through altogether, would it not?

4423. Presumably that would be the object of doing it, of having more Bills simultaneously considered in Committee?—I do not think we can turn out much more than we are doing now, with our present staff. I should like to say that nothing is more difficult in the world than to get people to come to my office. It is highly specialised and is extremely unpopular.

Mr. Malone

4424. Why is that?—Because it is slavery.

Chairman

4425. It is a blind alley?—Perhaps you do not know how one has to work. One begins at 10 to half-past, and one cannot make a single engagement for the evenings of Monday, Tuesday, Wednesday and Thursday. I have to work on Friday, and the only time I get for

thinking about anything without interruption is Saturday. I have to
work on Sunday too through the session.

Mr. Leach

4426. What is your recruiting method?—One talks to one's friends
down at the Temple and Lincoln's Inn and sees if they have anyone
who is at all likely . . . I have had enormous difficulty in getting anybody who is competent. I have a very good staff now, but it was very
difficult to get them, and I could not get them at all until I told the
Treasury that I must have more money to pay them. . . .

4428. Have you drawn any men out of private practice?—Yes, a few.
I have two men from quite large practices. I do not think they like it very
much now they have come.

Mr. Ede

4429. As far as I can gather from your description of it the life is
very much like the life of a Member of Parliament, except there is no
publicity for it?—I think perhaps we get abused more than you do.

A MEMBER AND HIS TRADE UNION, 1931

House of Commons Debates, 8 September 1931; Official Report, cc. 5–6

MR. SPEAKER: I have to inform the House that I have received a
letter from the hon. Member for the Newton Division of Lancaster
(Sir Robert Young) announcing his resignation of the office of Chairman of Ways and Means. The letter is as follows:

"DEAR MR. SPEAKER,

"It is my duty to inform the House of Commons through you
that a situation has arisen which makes it necessary for me to resign
the position of Chairman of Ways and Means.

"On 26th August, as a result of the changed political situation, I
wrote a letter to my constituency and said:

" 'The Chairman of Ways and Means is appointed for the duration of
Parliament. It is, however, a Party nomination but subject to the approval of
the House of Commons. I was appointed by unanimous consent. Nevertheless
should the Prime Minister on the one hand, or the Labour party on the other
side, think I should resign I shall certainly do so.'

"I sent a copy of the letter to the Prime Minister, the Leader of the
Opposition, and to the executive of the Amalgamated Engineering
Union. The Prime Minister did not ask me to resign. My trade union
executive, however, expressed the opinion that I should tender my
resignation. . . ."

ALLOCATION OF TIME, 1935

House of Commons Debates, 11 February 1935; Official Report, cc. 1710–11.

THE LORD PRESIDENT OF THE COUNCIL (MR. STANLEY BALDWIN): . . . I desire to inform the House of an agreement which has been reached with regard to the time to be devoted to the Committee stage of [the Government of India] Bill, and . . . I think this agreement redounds immensely to the credit and the common sense and the responsible sense of the House. I am grateful to all sections of the Opposition for having joined in it. . . .

The agreement is this. The Government propose to allocate 30 days for the Committee stage of the Government of India Bill, and 26 of those days will be apportioned by a time-table Resolution, so that the House may have a definite programme, while the remaining four days will be reserved and drawn upon if it should be found that any particular apportionment is inadequate. I think that a very wise and sensible provision. It will enable great matters of principle to be debated at length and I think will constitute a useful precedent which might well be followed in the future. If this proposal can be worked with good will, the elasticity of such an arrangement will undoubtedly lead to the convenience of Members. I am pleased to be able to inform the House that the Chief Whip has secured a large measure of agreement with regard to the arrangement of the time-table. It is proposed that an informal committee representing all parties and all sections shall meet and draw up a time-table for the 26 days in the most convenient form, and the Chairman of Ways and Means has kindly consented to take the chair of that Committee. . . .

PROCEDURE ON MONEY RESOLUTIONS, 1937-8

House of Commons Debates, 9 November 1937; Official Report, cc. 1593–6

MR. LAMBERT asked the Prime Minister what action the Government propose to take with regard to the report of the Committee on Money Resolutions?

THE PRIME MINISTER (MR. NEVILLE CHAMBERLAIN): . . . The Select Committee in their report make two main recommendations which may be summarised shortly as follow:

First, the passing of a declaratory resolution by the House to be enforced by the authority of the Chair indicating certain general lines upon which Financial Resolutions should be drawn.

Secondly, the alteration of Standing Orders so as to allow the

Second Reading of Money Bills (other than those originating in Committee of Ways and Means) to be taken before consideration of the relevant Financial Resolutions in Committee.

The Government, for their part, are prepared to accept in substance the second recommendation, as enabling hon. Members to express their views on the detailed provisions of the Bill at an early stage, and as meeting the criticism that the House should not be required to examine and discuss the terms of the financial provisions as set out in the Financial Resolution before being fully informed of the Government's intentions as detailed in the clauses of the Bill. . . .

While appreciating the considerations upon which the resolution included in the first recommendation is founded, the Government cannot feel that the directions set out therein are compatible with the fundamental principle embodied in Standing Order No. 63, namely, that of the Crown's initiative in regard to expenditure, a principle the wisdom of which the Committee recognised. . . .

Although unable to subscribe to the proposed declaratory resolution, His Majesty's Government . . . welcome the opportunity of declaring that it is their definite intention to secure that Financial Resolutions in respect of Bills shall be so framed as not to restrict the scope within which the Committee on the Bills may consider amendments further than is necessary to enable His Majesty's Government to discharge their responsibilities in regard to public expenditure and to leave to the Committee the utmost freedom for discussion and amendment of details which is compatible with the discharge of those responsibilities.

Accordingly, written instructions are being given to Departments and to the Parliamentary Counsel's Office drawing attention to the Report of the Select Committee on Procedure relating to Money Resolutions and to the statement which I am now making and requiring that in future the terms of any Financial Resolution, for the drafting of which they are responsible, shall not be so drawn as to involve undue restrictions and that this declaration shall be complied with. The House may wish to hear the actual terms of the instructions. They are as follow:

"SIR,

"Financial Resolutions

"I am directed by the Lords Commissioners of His Majesty's Treasury to invite your attention to the Report of the Select Committee on Procedure relating to Money Resolutions (H.C. 149 of 1937) and to the reply given by the Prime Minister in the House of Commons on 9 November 1937, and in particular to the declaration that it is the definite intention of His Majesty's Government to secure that financial resolutions in respect of Bills shall be so framed as not to restrict the scope within which the Committee on the Bills may consider amendments further than is necessary to enable the Government to discharge their responsibilities in regard to public expenditure and to leave to the Committee the utmost freedom for discussion and amendment of details which is compatible with the discharge of those responsibilities.

"I am further to request that the necessary steps be taken to acquaint all those concerned with the requirement that the terms of any Financial Resolution, in the drafting of which they are concerned, shall not be so drawn as to involve undue restrictions and that the Government's declaration shall be complied with in all cases.

"I am, etc."

House of Commons Debates, 1 February 1938; Official Report, c. 105
Ordered:

"That a Bill (other than a Bill which is required to originate in Committee of Ways and Means) the main object of which is the creation of a public charge may either be presented, or brought in upon an Order of the House, by a Minister of the Crown, and, in the case of a Bill so presented or brought in, the creation of the charge shall not require to be authorised by a Committee of the whole House until the Bill has been read a Second time, and that after the charge has been so authorised the Bill shall be proceeded with in the same manner as a Bill which involves a charge that is subsidiary to its main purpose."

Ordered:

"That this Order be a Standing Order of the House."

[The Prime Minister.]

DELEGATED LEGISLATION

(A)

House of Commons Debates, 27 January 1937; Official Report, cc. 1026 sqq.

MR. DINGLE FOOT: I beg to move,

"That in the opinion of this House, the power of the Executive has increased, is increasing, and ought to be diminished."

. . . There are two aspects of this subject to which I want to call the attention of the House. The first is the continuous encroachment of the Executive at the expense of the House of Commons, with the result that this House becomes more and more subservient to the Government of the day. The second is the attempt that has been deliberately made in Statute after Statute in recent years to invest Government Departments with completely arbitrary powers. Hon. Members will not be surprised if I have occasion to quote the words of the Lord Chief Justice . . . which he wrote in his book published eight years ago:[1]

[1] Lord Hewart of Bury, *The New Despotism* (London, 1929).

"The old despotism, which was defeated, offered Parliament a challenge. The new despotism, which is not yet defeated, gives Parliament an anaesthetic. The strategy is different, but the goal is the same. It is to subordinate Parliament, to evade the courts, and to render the will or caprice of the Executive unfettered and supreme."

. . . I know that it is inevitable in these days that we in Parliament should delegate a good deal of authority to bodies outside, and I know that we have to give Government Departments considerable power to issue Orders, Rules and Regulations; but the feature of almost all Regulations, even when they come under the review of this House and require affirmative Resolutions, is that they cannot be amended. We cannot do more than either accept or reject them as a whole. . . .

[*The House was counted out.*]

(B)

House of Commons Debates, 17 May 1944; Official Report, cc. 202 sqq.

Mr. Molson: I beg to move,

"That this House would welcome the setting up of a Select Committee . . . to carry on a continuous examination of all Statutory Rules and Orders and other instruments of delegated legislation presented to Parliament. . . ."

There are a number of reasons why delegated legislation is not only desirable but necessary. In the first place, it economises the time of the Legislature. . . .

In the second place, delegated legislation is flexible. It can limit the application of legislation by time, location, ownership, age or otherwise, and all these limitations are able to be changed at short notice. . . .

In the third place, the value of delegated legislation is that, in a sudden emergency, it enables the Legislature to dispense with long deliberation and to arm the Executive with the special powers that are needed. . . .

In the fourth place, where a Legislature is forced to influence the economic life of the country by physical measures, powers of this kind are almost inevitable. When we are using duties, quotas, licences, bounties and various other expedients, it is obvious that some power has to be given either to the Treasury or the Tariff Advisory Committee to give effect to the policy of Parliament. . . .

Among those who have given special attention to the matter of delegated legislation there are many who think that we should rely upon the courts to protect the people's liberty. I venture to think that that is an error. The courts are only suited for the purpose of determining what is legal and what is illegal. What we are primarily concerned about are Orders and Regulations issued by the Executive which are perfectly lucid and legal but which are bureaucratic, vexatious, embarrassing and harassing to the subject. Whether or not this House should approve an Order of that kind is a political decision which only a Legislature is competent to make. . . .

Mr. SILVERMAN: There has been so far throughout the Debate a considerable amount of agreement. Certain principles appear not to be controversial at all. One is that the delegation to Ministers of Parliament's sovereign right to make laws is to that extent an infringement and an abrogation of the functions of Parliament. The second thing that appears to be agreed is that, even though that be conceded, it is inevitable in our complicated world that, if this House is to function at all, such delegation shall be made. . . . The third . . . is that it remains necessary, and becomes more and more necessary, that the House should apply some kind of selective principle. While it agrees that some part of its sovereign authority to make law must be handed over to Ministers, we must, in order that we may retain our control of the laws of the country, retain our own responsibility for what is done. We may delegate the act, but we cannot delegate the responsibility for the act. . . .

. . . What are the conditions on which judicial functions can be exercised? The first is that the tribunal, the judge, shall have no interest whatever in the result of the case he is trying. The second is that he shall be answerable to nobody for what he does. . . . He has to be free from criticism or penalty for what he does, and he has to be uninfluenced, in his judicial determination of a question before him, by the consequences of what he does. It is not for the court to say: "We will not do justice in this case because the consequences go far beyond the importance of the case." He has to do justice in the case before him, though the Heavens fall. Unless those three conditions are satisfied, judicial functions cannot be exercised at all.

. . . Those conditions, which are vital to the exercise of judicial functions, are the antithesis of the principles on which we work in this House. . . .

. . . I say that, inevitably, when the House is concerned to consider whether the Minister is right or wrong in the exercise of his functions under the Regulations, it may have to consider at one and the same time two distinct questions. One is: "Does the House wish the Government to fall?" The other is: "Was the particular exercise right or wrong?" . . .

THE SECRETARY OF STATE FOR THE HOME DEPARTMENT (MR. HERBERT MORRISON): . . . [The] terms of reference must be such that the Committee does not try to do the work of the courts of law. It is not for the Committee to decide—indeed, it is not for Parliament to decide what is the proper, legal interpretation of a Statute, or whether Regulations are within the legal terms of the Statute. That is for the courts, and it is constitutionally of the greatest importance that the independence and freedom from Parliamentary interference of the courts, even to the extent of Parliament not trying to interpret the law, should be guarded. . . .

[Motion, by leave, withdrawn.]

(C)

House of Commons Debates, 21 June 1944: Official Report, cc. 310–11
Ordered:

"That a Select Committee be appointed to consider every Statutory Rule or Order (including any Provisional Rule made under Section 2 of the Rules Publication Act, 1893) laid or laid in draft before the House, being a Rule, Order, or Draft upon which proceedings may be taken in either House in pursuance of any Act of Parliament, with a view to determining whether the special attention of the House should be drawn to it on any of the following grounds:

"(i) that it imposes a charge on the public revenues or contains provisions requiring payment to be made to the Exchequer or any Government Department or to any local or public authority in consideration of any licence or consent, or of any services to be rendered, or prescribes the amount of any such charge or payments:

"(ii) that it is made in pursuance of an enactment containing specific provisions excluding it from challenge in the courts, either at all times or after the expiration of a specified period:

"(iii) that it appears to make some unusual or unexpected use of the powers conferred by the Statute under which it is made:

"(iv) that there appears to have been unjustifiable delay in the publication of it:

"(v) that for any special reason, its form or purport calls for elucidation."

Ordered:

"That the Committee shall have the assistance of the Counsel to Mr. Speaker."

Ordered:

"That the Committee have power to sit notwithstanding any Adjournment of the House, and to report from time to time."

Ordered:

"That the Committee have power to require any Government Department concerned to submit a memorandum explaining any Rule, Order, or Draft which may be under their consideration or to

depute a representative to appear before them as a Witness for the
purpose of explaining any such Rule, Order, or Draft."

Ordered:

"That it be an Instruction to the Committee that before reporting
that the special attention of the House should be drawn to any Rule,
Order, or Draft the Committee do afford to any Government Department concerned therewith an opportunity of furnishing orally or in
writing such explanations as the Department think fit."

[*Mr. Herbert Morrison.*]

(D)

*Special Report from the Select Committee on Statutory Instruments (H.C. 125
of 1950)*

[Select Committee appointed to consider every Statutory Instrument laid
or laid in draft before the House, being an Instrument or Draft of an Instrument upon which proceedings may be or might have been taken in either
House in pursuance of any Act of Parliament, with a view to determining
whether the special attention of the House should be drawn to it on any of
the following grounds:

(i) that it imposes a charge on the public revenues or contains provisions
requiring payments to be made to the Exchequer or any Government Department or to any local or public authority in consideration of any licence or
consent, or of any services to be rendered, or prescribes the amount of any
such charge or payments;

(ii) that it is made in pursuance of an enactment containing specific provisions excluding it from challenge in the courts, either at all times or after the
expiration of a specified period;

(iii) that it appears to make some unusual or unexpected use of the powers
conferred by the Statute under which it is made;

(iv) that it purports to have retrospective effect where the parent Statute
confers no express authority so to provide;

(v) that there appears to have been unjustified delay in the publication or
in the laying of it before Parliament;

(vi) that there appears to have been unjustifiable delay in sending a notification to Mr. Speaker under the proviso to subsection (1) of section four to
the Statutory Instruments Act, 1946, where an Instrument has come into
operation before it has been laid before Parliament;

(vii) that for any special reason its form or purport calls for elucidation.]

1. Your Committee have examined 682 Statutory Instruments and
Drafts of Instruments since the beginning of the Session and have
drawn the attention of the House to seven. Of the 682 Instruments
examined, 325 arose out of Emergency legislation, i.e. were presented
under the Supplies and Services (Transitional Powers) Act, 1945, as
extended by the Supplies and Services (Extended Purposes) Act,
1947, the Emergency Laws (Transitional Provisions) Act, 1946, or the

Goods and Services (Price Control) Acts, 1939 and 1941. Of the seven Instruments brought to the special attention of the house, one was reported under the fifth head of the Committee's Order of Reference (unjustifiable delay in laying before Parliament) and six under the seventh (need for elucidation). . . .

(E)

Report from the Select Committee on Delegated Legislation; 27 October, 1953.
(H.C. 310 of 1953)

1. Your Committee were appointed by a resolution of this House on the 18th of December, 1952, to consider in what respects the existing procedures, by which the control of this House over delegated legislation is exercised, need to be improved or supplemented and by what means this can best be achieved. . . .

4. Your Committee have been asked, in the first place, to consider the existing procedures by which the control of this House over *delegated legislation* is exercised.

5. The power to legislate, when delegated by Parliament, differs from Parliament's own power to legislate: Parliament is supreme and the power of the Queen in Parliament to legislate is unlimited. On the other hand, the power of legislation granted by Parliament to another body or persons is limited by the exact extent of the delegated power so granted; the purported exercise of power beyond the extent so granted will be *ultra vires* and ineffective.

6. The legality of an Act of Parliament cannot be challenged in or by the Courts of Law, but the question whether subordinate legislation is within the power delegated by Parliament can be and is challenged in and by the Courts of Law.

7. Frequently, subordinate legislation is issued in the form of an Order in Council, that is an Order expressed to be made by Her Majesty by and with the advice of Her Privy Council and signed by the Clerk of the Council.

But not every instrument so issued is an enactment of subordinate legislation under a power delegated by Act of Parliament.

Orders in Council are of two kinds and they differ fundamentally in constitutional principle. The two kinds are:

(a) those made in virtue of the Royal Prerogative, and
(b) those which are authorised by Act of Parliament.

The Royal Prerogative is that which remains of the original sovereign power of the Crown to legislate without the authority of Parliament, e.g. power to declare a rigid blockade of enemy territory in time of war. This power is in no sense delegated and Orders in Council issued in exercise of this power are not subordinate; they are original legislation. Your Committee are not concerned with them in this report. Your Committee have to consider (*inter alia*) those Orders in Council made under the authority of an Act of Parliament. . . .

20. The figures for 1952 were:

Acts of Parliament, 64; one volume of 1,437 pages (including, as it happened, over 900 pages of merely consolidating statutes); Public Instruments; registered, 1,029—3 volumes of 3,980 pages; Local Instruments, registered, 1,283—not published collectively. . . .

24. One classification of the instruments of delegated legislation is into:

(*a*) Those which are required by the enabling Act to be laid before Parliament;

(*b*) Those which are not so required by the enabling Act.

25. The requirement to lay before Parliament first occurred in the Acts of the 1830's, but it was not regularly insisted upon until a long way into the 19th century. The requirement and the nature and extent and timing of it are matters entirely governed by Parliament in passing the enabling Bill empowering the making of the particular instrument. . . .

28. Figures are available of the annual totals of Statutory rules and orders or Statutory instruments registered since the beginning of 1894. From the first, as already stated, the register discriminated between those which were General and those which were Local. Local ones deal with such matters as Local Authorities' powers, fishery districts, traffic orders about built-up areas, or one way streets, burial grounds, diseases of animals, water supply, land drainage, wild bird protection and so on. With certain exceptions, referred to below in paragraph 31, Parliament has not thought it worth while to exercise any special control over, or even to require information about, instruments of merely local application. . . .

29. . . . The annual combined total of all instruments, general and local, has never exceeded 3,000; the annual total of general instruments has never exceeded 2,000. But to estimate the total of all instruments in operation to-day would be mere guesswork . . .

31. Sir Cecil Carr[1] estimated that out of 377 draft or final instruments which came before the Scrutiny Committee (hereafter referred to) this year only 79 could be described as local in character. They were made up as follows: 37 sets of London Traffic Regulations; 14 orders restoring rights of way suspended under War Regulations; 6 re-arranging boundaries of constituencies; 6 Scottish hydro-electric schemes; 3 amending Local Acts; 3 bringing into force in specified areas the statutory provisions for special designations of milk; 2 dealing

---

[1] Counsel to Mr. Speaker.

with open spaces in London; 5 relating to Local Courts; 2 altering
statutory areas for gas and electricity; 1 relating to levy of expenses
in a fisheries district.

32. The decision whether power shall be granted to a subordinate
authority to legislate is made by the Queen in Parliament, and the
decision also provides the conditions under which that authority shall
be exercised. The decision is contained in the enabling Act.

33. We asked for information from 22 Departments on two points,
namely:

(1) the procedure followed in the Department in connection with
drafting a clause in a Bill giving power to make regulations, and,

(2) the procedure followed in the Department in making the
regulations. . . .

36. In broad outline, the methods followed in all the Departments
are the same.

37. The procedure in connection with the preparation of a bill is
as follows:

(1) All important matters of policy and principle are dealt with
directly in the Bill itself and the general practice is to limit regulation-
making powers to:

(*a*) matters too detailed, e.g. procedural points or technical issues;

(*b*) matters in which elasticity is desirable to enable alterations to
be made in the light of changed circumstances;

(*c*) matters in which new Statutory powers are being created and
in which the line of future developments cannot be fully foreseen.

(2) The Minister throughout is responsible. He settles the general
line of the proposed legislation. The Clause giving power to make
regulations is carefully considered from the outset and the Minister
decides its form and the extent of the powers which he will recommend
to Parliament.

38. Then with regard to the instrument, made in pursuance of the
power given by the enabling Act, the practice is to follow the instructions of the Minister. Wherever practicable, outside interests which
may be affected (e.g. local authorities, trade interests, professional
organisations and so on), are consulted informally. The document is
then drafted by the Legal Staff of the Department. In some Departments there is a regular Committee of senior officials of the Department
who go through all draft instruments in detail and report thereon to
the Minister before he signifies his final approval.

39. All regulations which are subject to Parliamentary procedure
and all other regulations of importance are signed by the Secretary of
State or other Minister responsible. In minor cases such as those
relating to purely local matters, the instrument may be signed on behalf

of the Minister, provided, even in the those cases, that the approval of the Minister has first been obtained.

40. In certain cases subordinate legislation is submitted for approval to the Legislation Committee of the Cabinet whose terms of reference leave it to the discretion of the Minister concerned to decide whether a particular instrument should be submitted in draft to the Committee. The Committee must, however, have an opportunity of examining:

(*a*) all Orders in Council under emergency or transitional legislation.

(*b*) all statutory instruments likely to affect a large number of Departments whose interests cannot conveniently be ascertained by direct consultation.

(*c*) all statutory instruments likely to give rise to criticism by the Scrutiny Committee hereinafter referred to.

(*d*) all statutory instruments involving any departure from precedent, e.g. in the type of penalties imposed, in the procedure relating to such matters as appeals, or in encroachments on the liberty of the subject.

The Legislation Committee is presided over by a Senior Cabinet Minister and normally includes the Lord Chancellor, the Leaders of the two Houses, and Law Officers and the Chief Whip. The Department concerned with the proposed instrument prepares and sends to the Committee a memorandum explaining why the Order is required and the Minister has to obtain the approval of his colleagues. . . .

46. . . . In 1944 a sessional Committee of the House was established. It has been continued in all subsequent sessions. It is now known as the Select Committee on Statutory Instruments but it is usually and in this Report referred to as the "Scrutiny Committee."

47. The Scrutiny Committee consists of eleven members. The quorum is three. The practice is to appoint a member of the Opposition as Chairman and this seems to be in process of becoming a convention. It usually meets fortnightly, and, in special circumstances, more often. . . .

48. The Scrutiny Committee cannot consider or report on the merits or policy of any of the instruments. In drawing the attention of the House to an instrument, it gives no detailed reasons, but merely refers to the heading under which it reports. Before, however, it reports, it must and does hear what the Department concerned with the instrument has to say. The Department's answer is annexed to the report and usually indicates the Committee's point. In several sessions the Committee has submitted a Special Report containing general comments on possible improvements in departmental practice. Treasury circulars have directed the attention of Departments to these Special Reports.

49. There are two matters in connection with the Scrutiny Committee to which attention should be directed, namely:

(*a*) Owing to the delay in setting up the Committee at the beginning of a Session, the time-limit for moving an address against some instruments may expire before the Committee examines them. That, in fact, happened this Session. This defect could be mitigated, if not overcome, by making it a permanent Standing Committee instead of one appointed each Session.

(*b*) The time-lag caused by obtaining and considering the Department's answer has the consequence that the Committee's report sometimes reaches the House too late to be effective.

50. From its inception towards the end of 1944 down to the end of last year, the Scrutiny Committee had seen some 6,900 instruments, namely all that are subject to either the affirmative or negative procedure of the House. It drew the attention of the House to 93 of these.

51. Sir Cecil Carr, who attends and advises the Scrutiny Committee, made this comment on all officially registered instruments and those which come before the Committee.

"The total of nearly 7,000 instruments examined may be compared with the total of approximately 19,400 instruments officially registered in the same period. Probably some 10,250 of this gross total were public instruments. If so, and if generalisation is pardonable on figures so imprecise, it seems that not quite 70 per cent. of the general instruments come within the purview of Parliament as either requiring affirmative approval or exposed to the negative procedure. Anyone who cares to study the contents of the annual volumes of statutory instruments will probably be satisfied that much of the text is of a routine or administrative character involving no great issues of liberty or public rights."

52. The nature of a Statutory Instrument, the requirement of publication and the standard machinery of parliamentary control are prescribed in the Statutory Instruments Act, 1946 (brought into force on January 1st, 1948), and the Statutory Instruments Regulations, 1947, made thereunder. . . .

Parliamentary Control

64. As stated in paragraphs 32 to 38, the Minister introducing a Bill is responsible for the decision to propose to Parliament that a clause be included in the Bill empowering the making of statutory instruments embodying some legislation. The Minister proposes, but Parliament itself decides in each enabling Act.

(*a*) whether power shall be delegated to make subordinate legislation.

(*b*) to whom the power shall be delegated.

See p. 97

(*c*) the extent of the power.

(*d*) the form in which it shall be exercised,

(*e*) whether the instrument whereby the power is exercised shall or shall not be laid before Parliament.

(*f*) whether the instrument shall be subject to an affirmative or a negative resolution or neither.

65. Parliament has dealt in various ways with instruments embodying delegated legislation which have to be laid before it:

(*a*) Laying without further provision for control;

(*b*) Laying with deferred operation;

(*c*) Laying with immediate effect but subject to annulment;

(*d*) Laying in draft but subject to resolution that no further proceedings be taken;

(*e*) Laying in draft and requiring affirmative resolution;

(*f*) Laying with operation deferred until approval given by affirmative resolution;

(*g*) Laying with immediate effect but requiring affirmative resolution as a condition of continuance.

The most usual are (*c*) laying with immediate effect but subject to annulment and (*e*) laying in draft and requiring affirmative resolution. . . .

77. In his memorandum Sir Frederic Metcalfe, the Clerk of the House, produced an analysis of the time taken by the House in considering statutory instruments.

In session 1951–52 the total time taken in the House on Affirmative Resolutions was $14\frac{1}{2}$ hours and on motions under the negative procedure was just over 25 hours. In the session 1952 to the 5th February, 1953, the total time taken on Affirmative Resolutions was 18 hours 8 minutes and on the Negative procedure 9 hours. Motions under the negative procedure are hereafter referred to as "prayers", a term derived from the words "An Humble Address, praying"—which occur in the form of the motion.

78. As the Minister concerned wants the instrument awaiting the affirmative resolution to become effective, the Government, as has been stated, find the time for the resolution to be brought forward and, if the House so requires, debated. Although affirmative resolutions, like prayers, are business exempted from Standing Order as to time of adjournment, the necessary time is, on occasions, found before the usual hour of adjournment. Sir Frederic Metcalfe has supplied a summary and an analysis of the time taken before and after 10 p.m. in the sessions from 1947 to 1952. The figures show that the number of resolutions and the time taken thereby is slightly greater after than before 10 p.m.

79. The prayer to annul a statutory instrument is put down by a Member. Any Member may put it down and he may or may not be supported by other Members. The Member putting down the prayer must seek an opportunity upon which to move the prayer. That opportunity will not occur until Government business is disposed of and this normally means that the opportunity will not occur until after 10 p.m.

The Member moving the prayer must try to ensure that there is a quorum of Members (namely 40) present. Moreover, the Government must also be prepared to require the attendance of their supporters in case there is a division. The Government can move the adjournment of the House immediately before a prayer. This power could be so exercised as to prevent discussion of the motion or the annulment of the instrument within the statutory period. In practice, only occasional use of the power has been made. It could, however, be effective and practicable against obstruction. A prayer may be put down against every single statutory instrument and an opportunity sought to move it. If that were done then the whole business of the House would soon be brought to a complete standstill.

80. As it is, the House may sit on for a considerable time each night after its normal hour of rising. It has sat on many occasions into the small hours of the morning of the next day and even through the night.

81. The question has thus arisen not only as to the convenience of Members, and the time available for the proper discharge of the ordinary business of the House, but also whether, by the method and time now available and the advantage that may be taken of it by a Member or a group of Members, the House is fully aware of the matters that may arise on a statutory instrument and so exercise that control which is necessary and desirable. . . .

107. Your Committee therefore recommend:

(1) That, with regard to Statutory Instruments which are subject to the Negative Prayer, the procedure shall continue as at present, except that if a prayer is under discussion at 11.30 p.m. the Speaker shall at that hour put the question to the House, unless he shall be of opinion that:

(*a*) owing to the lateness of the time of starting the discussion on the prayer, or

(*b*) owing to the importance of the issues raised by the Statutory Instrument,

the time for debate has not been adequate, the debate shall be adjourned to the next ordinary sitting day of the House (other than a Friday) when it shall be resumed at the end of Government business for that day and it shall be subject to the same procedure as on the first day;

(2) That the Prayer for the annulment of a Statutory Instrument should set out the reasons for such annulment;

(3) That the Scrutiny Committee should not be made into a Standing Committee but its appointment at the beginning of each Session should be treated as a matter of urgency.

(4) That the Scrutiny Committee should include with its Report to the House any letter from it to a Government Department in which the point in issue on a Statutory Instrument, and the reason for inviting a Departmental Memorandum, are indicated, and the Committee should, as now, include also the reply of the Department.

(5) That the period of 40 days shall commence from the day when the Statutory Instrument is available to Members in the Vote Office and that the date when it is so available be placed thereon; but that where the Scrutiny Committee in their Report draw the particular attention of the House to a Statutory Instrument, then the time shall be 10 days from the date when the Report of that Committee is made or the statutory 40 days, whichever time is the longer;

(6) That at the head of a Statutory Instrument there shall be printed a note stating whether it is subject to the Affirmative or to the Negative procedure or whether it is exempt from both processes;

(7) That the recommendations made by the Donoughmore Committee in paragraph 15, page 64, of their Report be endorsed, namely, that the expressions "regulation, rule, order" should not be used indiscriminately to describe the Instruments by which the law-making power conferred on Ministers by Parliament is exercised.

THE LEADER OF THE OPPOSITION, 1937

(A)

House of Commons Debates, 9 December 1937; Official Report, cc. 564–5

MR. LIDDALL asked the Prime Minister whether he will give an early date for the discussion of the motion standing in the name of the hon. Member for Lincoln?

["That in view of the fact that at Madrid on 6 December 1937, notwithstanding he had, before leaving this country, given an undertaking not to take part in any activities liable to be interpreted as inconsistent with His Majesty's Government's policy of non-intervention, the Leader of His Majesty's official Opposition (Mr. Clement Attlee) stated publicly, 'When we return to London, administered by Socialists and workers, we shall convene a public meeting to inform the people about the facts of the situation and unbeaten invincible Republican Spain', this House declares that the Right Honourable Gentleman the Member for Limehouse is guilty of a breach of faith and is unfit to again be granted a visa to Spain."]

(B)

House of Commons Debates, 13 December 1937; Official Report, cc. 821-4

MR. ATTLEE: Mr. Speaker, I desire, with your permission to make a personal statement. . . .

The basis of the charge [in Mr. Liddall's motion] appears to be that because at a luncheon party given in my honour by the Commander-in-Chief of the Spanish Army, in response to a speech of welcome, I expressed my sympathy with the Spanish Government and my intention of informing the people of this country of the facts of the situation, I had thereby violated an undertaking given before my departure from this country. . . . Before proceeding to Spain I signed an undertaking in the following terms:

"I undertake that nothing shall take place in the course of my visit that could be considered as implying any intervention by me on behalf of either side of the present dispute in Spain."

This is the common form signed by all persons proceeding from this country to any part of Spanish territory. It applies to business men, journalists and relief workers. It is exacted from British subjects by His Majesty's Government in pursuance of the policy of non-intervention. . . .

The assumption underlying the Motion . . . is that the signing of this undertaking imposes upon the signatory the duty of refraining, while in Spain, from expressing any opinion in favour either of the Government of Spain or of the rebels. I cannot possibly accept such an interpretation. If such were the meaning of this undertaking it would be one which no British Government ought to impose and which no Member of Parliament who had regard to the rights and privileges of Members could possibly accept. It would mean that a Member of Parliament, of any party, must not express his own opinions, but must reflect the policy of the Government; that he may go to Spain, but only in a muzzle. I do not believe for one moment that this was the purpose aimed at in exacting the undertaking. If I had thought this to be the meaning of the undertaking, I would never have signed it, for I could not have implemented it.

Obviously, a Member of Parliament, especially the leader of a party, is bound, in the course of conversation, or on occasions of more formality, such as the exchange of courtesies, to express opinions on the merits of the contest in Spain. . . .

It cannot be too strongly emphasised that a private Member of Parliament does not by his words or actions involve the British Government, but that he is a free man with the right of freely expressing his opinions. In his Motion, the hon. Member for Lincoln has specifically referred to me as "the Leader of His Majesty's Official Opposition," and seems to imply that this places me in a special category. The Leader of the Opposition is a private Member. He owes no allegiance to the Government. No action of his can in any way implicate the Government. He is responsible only to his constituents and to the Members from whom he derives his position. He is, I think, under a special obligation to defend the rights and privileges of private Members, particularly the right of every Member to express his opinion freely on all matters of public policy. I make no excuse or apology for anything said or done by me in the course of my visit to Spain. The particular words of which the hon. Member for Lincoln complains are inaccurately reported, but I make no attempt to shield myself by alleging misrepresentation. I did state my sympathy for the Spanish people and the Spanish Government, and I did state the intention of the party which I have the honour to lead to do their utmost in every legitimate way to assist them in their struggle. I claim that, as a Member of this House, I have every right to do so. I utterly repudiate the suggestion that in doing so I have broken any pledge.

THE PRIME MINISTER (MR. NEVILLE CHAMBERLAIN): I rise only to say this. . . . I hope the House will now accept this statement, and take what seems to me the right and most dignified course—namely, to let it rest there.

THE DISSOLUTION OF PARLIAMENT, 1944

House of Commons Debates, 29 March 1944; Official Report, c. 1516

MR. PRICE: . . . [It] is impossible to say that, because this House has on this occasion voted against the Government [in amending the Education Bill, to provide equal payment for men and women teachers], therefore there is no confidence in the Government. . . . [The] Prime Minister . . . is claiming for the Executive now to dissolve Parliament and go to the country——

THE PRIME MINISTER (MR. CHURCHILL): I never said anything of the sort. I must make it absolutely clear that it does not rest with any Prime Minister to dissolve Parliament. The utmost he can do is to tender advice to the Crown.

MR. PRICE: That, of course, is the law, but in actual fact the advice comes from the Prime Minister.

THE PRIME MINISTER: This is one of the exceptional occasions when the Prerogative of the Crown comes into play and where in doubtful circumstances the Crown would refer to other advisers. It has been done on several occasions. I must make it absolutely clear that it does not rest with the Government of the day. It would be most improper on my part to use any language which suggested that I have the power to make such a decision.

COMMITTEES OF THE HOUSE OF COMMONS, 1945

Proceedings before the Select Committee on Procedure, 1945–6

THE RIGHT HON. HERBERT MORRISON, M.P., LORD PRESIDENT OF
THE COUNCIL, EXAMINED:

Mr. Messer

134. As is known by those who have had any experience of Committees, a lot of time has been wasted sometimes owing to the inability to get a quorum. Of course we understand that it is the Government's job to ensure its quorum, but does Mr. Morrison think it would be an improvement if the Selection Committee selected smaller Committees as permanent Committees, with a number of added people who would have specialised knowledge and that the quorum should be reduced?— On the face of it, I am sympathetic to the point that Mr. Messer puts. There are some complications about it. My whole bias would be in favour of smaller Committees sitting round a horseshoe table and arguing out in a friendly and objective way the details of a Bill. The question is whether they would argue them out in a friendly and co-operative way, and whether they would act in the horseshoe spirit, which is rather contrary to the general Parliamentary tradition on the handling of Bills on Committee stage. If they could do it in the right spirit, in the spirit that would be conducive to that end, there is a lot to be said for a smaller Committee, but I doubt whether it fits into our Parliamentary traditions that they will do so. The trouble about a small Committee is, to be perfectly frank, that it reduces the Government's majority, and if the Government's majority is reduced too much, whatever Government it may be, irrespective of Party, then the risk tends to increase unless it has got absolutely iron reliability on the part of its own members, which it has not always got in a Committee. . . .

Now, as to the matter of specialisation of members, I think that the principle which now obtains, whereby there is a Committee A, B, C, and so on, with a number of members on it to which a number of members are added who want to go on, or are supposed to have special knowledge and probably very often have special knowledge about it, is right. But I would not myself favour the principle that you tried to turn the Standing Committees into specialists on a Bill. I think a lot of longhaired planners on a Town Planning Bill, all of them long-haired, would be a dreadful thing. A substantial body of common-sense citizens would be a good thing. I think a body of 100 per cent. educationists on an Education Bill would be a dreadful thing, or a body of doctors on a Health Bill. The great quality of Parliament is the quality of sense, of average intelligence examining into these matters, being a sort of Jury, and I do not favour the specialist committee too much; but a specialist element on a Committee is a good thing. . . .

136. You do spend a lot of time in Committee, and when you get to the end of a Session, and you are not able to complete it, it means that the whole of that time has been wasted. Is there not some argument in favour of carrying on to the next Session?—There is. I am in two minds about it. It is an awful thing if the House and the Committees have considered a Bill at some length and then the prorogation comes and off it goes. It is a very sad event, and it is a shocking waste of Parliamentary time. On the other hand, as with most things about Parliamentary procedure, there are two angles to it. If the Government knows that it can carry on it may be less forthcoming in coming to a compromise with the Opposition and its critics; it may be more obstinate and more pigheaded; there is that against it. The other thing is that the Opposition is in a dilemma, too. If it proceeds to block or obstruct a Bill towards the end of a Session, which it knows to be popular, it may think twice about it, if it means the death of the Bill. It may think more about it if the Bill is unpopular, or it believes it is unpopular. Therefore, it is a two-edged sword; it cuts both ways. In my present mood (I reserve the right to change my opinion), I should say that taking the balance of things, on the whole it is a good thing that both the Government and the Opposition should know that if they do not get their business finished by a certain date then something sad is going to happen. It is a good incentive to both sides, and whilst I want guillotines and closures, and whatnot within reason, I think it is a good thing to reserve the element of excitement, adventure, and even gamble, about Parliament, in some respects, because it keeps us all alive . . . .

PARLIAMENTARY CONTROL OF NATIONALISED INDUSTRIES

(A)

House of Commons Official Report; Standing Committees, 1496–47, Vol. II, cc. 1500 sqq.

Transport Bill; Standing Committee B; 25 February 1947

SIR DAVID MAXWELL FYFE: . . . the Minister is taking extremely wide and unnecessary powers. It will be observed that . . . he—

may, after consultation with the Commission—

and, of course, consultation with the Commission ties him to nothing, but merely means that there must be a discussion between his officials and the officials of the Commission—

... give to the Commission directions of a general character as to the exercise and performance by the Commission of their functions . . .

That, again, would be very wide in itself; but there are the additional words:

... in relation to matters which appear to him to affect the national interest. . . .

We have heard from the learned Attorney-General that when such words as "appear to him" are inserted in a Clause, the effect is to leave it entirely to the Minister, without check or control of any kind, and to make the test an entirely subjective one. Therefore, it appears to us that it is equivalent to saying he may give directions of a general character on any matter on which he chooses. . . .

MR. BARNES: . . . There is a definite constitutional change in the legislation we are introducing in this Parliament with regard to public corporations from what prevailed in similar types of corporations before the war. For instance, in the legislation which created bodies like the London Passenger Transport Board or the Electricity Commissioners, you do not find within the provisions of those Acts of Parliament the powers which the Minister is given in . . . this Bill, but then it was not contemplated by the Government of the day that they should be part of the economic organisation of the State to secure, or to give their contribution towards, a policy of full employment. . . .

(B)

House of Commons Official Report; Standing Committees, 1946–47, Vol. IV, cc. 633 sqq.

Electricity Bill; Standing Committee E; 13 March 1947

MR. R. S. HUDSON: . . . I think it would be for the general convenience of the Committee if I asked the Minister if he could give us a short description of how he visualises the development of his relations . . . with the Central [Electrical] Authority. For example, we would like to know of the extent to which he visualises the Central Authority will be under his control, and to what extent can Parliament hold the Minister responsible for the actions of the Central Authority. . . .

THE MINISTER OF FUEL AND POWER (MR. EMMANUEL SHINWELL): . . . To begin with, we are following the precedent created in 1938 by the then Conservative Government, when the Board of Trade was empowered to give to the Coal Commission general directions as to the exercise of their functions in a certain part of the Coal Act. The powers so vested in the Board of Trade were to be exercised without consultation. We have gone further . . .; we have said that the Minister may exercise his power of general direction after consultation with the Central Authority. The procedure we propose to adopt is provided for in the Coal Industry Nationalisation Act; it is also in the Civil Aviation Act. . . .

[The] National Coal Board was appointed by the Minister (that is, by myself), and . . . he took no responsibility for appointments to be made by them. There was no provision in the Coal Industry Nation-alisation Act for the setting up of Divisional Boards or Area Boards. . . . That was left entirely to the discretion of the National Coal Board; they were to create the organisation appropriate to the proper con-duct of the industry. Therefore, when questions were addressed to me in the House on the administrative activities of the National Coal Board I naturally declined to give an answer, because upon these matters I did not enter into consultation with the National Coal Board. . . .

With regard to our purpose in seeking this power of general direc-tion, I will endeavour to give three reasons which apply so far as electricity supply is concerned. . . . It is [not] desirable that in the provision of huge structures like generating stations, strategical interest should be ignored. . . .

Regarding the provision of electricity supply, it is . . . part of the Government's economic policy to provide for development in what were previously regarded as depressed or special areas. . . . It may, therefore, be necessary for the Minister to exercise a power of direction and to indicate to the Central Authority that it is desirable to provide electricity supplies in a particular area in order to fit in with the Government's economic policy.

There is also the question of research. . . . [It] is desirable that the Government should be able to give some indication of a new departure breaking into new fields of study and research, and to ask for investiga-tion into matters of this sort. . . .

(C)

House of Commons Debates, 4 December 1947; Official Report, cc. 565 sqq.

MR. HERBERT MORRISON: In the light of experience so far gained, the Government have reviewed the question of replies to Parliamentary inquiries about the work of socialised industries. . . .

Under recent legislation, boards have been set up to run socialised industries on business lines on behalf of the community; and Ministers are not responsible for their day-to-day administration. A large degree of independence for the boards in matters of current administration is vital to their efficiency as commercial undertakings. A Minister is responsible to Parliament for action which he may take in relation to a board, or action coming within his statutory powers which he has not taken. This is the principle that determines generally the matters on which a Question may be put down for answer by a Minister in the House of Commons. Thus, the Minister would be answerable for any directions he gave in the national interest, and for the action which he took on proposals which a board was required by Statute to lay before him.

It would be contrary to this principle, and to the clearly expressed intention of Parliament in the governing legislation, if Ministers were to give, in replies in Parliament or in letters, information about day-to-day matters. Undue intervention by the Minister would tend to impair the board's commercial freedom of action. The boards of socialised industries are under an obligation to submit annual reports and accounts which are to be laid before Parliament. In the Government's view, it is right that Parliament should from time to time review the work of the boards, on the basis of the reports and accounts presented to Parliament. . . .

(D)

House of Commons Debates, 7 June 1948; Official Report, cc. 1635 sqq.

MR. SPEAKER (COLONEL CLIFTON BROWN): . . . I am now in a position to state the conclusions I have reached after careful consideration of the difficulties which have recently arisen with regard to Questions dealing with the nationalised industries.

. . . Questions addressed to Ministers should relate to the public affairs with which they are officially connected, to proceedings pending in Parliament or to matters of administration for which they are responsible. Rule 26 . . . excludes Questions repeating in substance Questions already answered or to which an answer has been refused. . . .

. . . The Government, in their desire not to interfere in the day to day activities of the Boards of nationalised industries, have by what might be termed a "self-denying ordinance" refused to answer many Questions on subjects which, by a strict interpretation of the statutes, might be held to fall within their responsibility. They are fully entitled to do so—that is a matter for their discretion. But such a refusal brings into action Rule 26 . . . and prevents the admission to the Question Paper of all future Questions dealing with the class of matters dealt with by the Question to which an answer was refused.

I have come to the conclusion that in the case of an entirely novel branch of the administration, such as that relating to the nationalised industries, the strict application of this Rule might operate more harshly than either Ministers or Members generally would wish. I am, therefore, prepared to make a suggestion which I hope will recommend itself to the House, for the power of dispensing with its recognised rules belongs to the House alone and not to me.

I propose to leave the Rule which excludes Questions on matters outside Ministerial responsibility unchanged. But I am prepared, if it is generally approved, to exercise my discretion to direct the acceptance of Questions asking for a statement to be made on matters about which information has been previously refused, provided that, in my opinion, the matters are of sufficient public importance to justify this concession. . . .

. . . of course, it by no means follows that Ministers will be bound to answer any Question which I have allowed as being of "public importance"; that is their affair. . . .

(E)

House of Commons Debates, 25 October 1950; Official Report, cc. 2795 sqq.

THE LORD PRESIDENT OF THE COUNCIL (MR. HERBERT MORRISON): I beg to move,

That this House notes the steps which have been taken to give effect to the responsibility to the community (including consumers and workpeople) of the socialised industries, and will welcome any further measures to increase their public accountability, consistently with the duty of the Boards to manage the industries with maximum efficiency in the public interest.

. . . In the first place, it is desirable that the House should try to make up its mind as to the basis upon which it desires these commercial undertakings to be run. It is a perfectly fair case for argument whether a publicly-owned industry should be vested in a Minister and allocated to ordinary State departmental management.

MR. OLIVER LYTTELTON: Like the Post Office.

MR. MORRISON: Like the Post Office. . . . For example, it is arguable whether gas and electricity could not have been adequately managed directly by the Minister of Fuel and Power rather than being placed under a public corporation, or what now amounts to a series of public corporations because of the area boards. . . .

. . . it is often urged that when it comes to the sheer business of commercial matters the machinery of a State Department necessarily works slower than that of an ordinary commercial concern. There is truth in that, not because of any inherent incompetence in the Civil Service or of State administration, but precisely because Ministers are absolutely responsible to Parliament for everything that happens in their Departments. And that is right; that is as it should be.

But the consequence necessarily is that when civil servants are doing things, either with the specific authority of a Minister or in accordance with the policy he is presumed to have approved, and probably has, or in ordinary day-to-day affairs where policy does not arise, there is in the minds of the civil servants inevitably the consideration: Is there likely to be a Parliamentary argument about this? Is there likely to be criticism in the Press? Is the Minister likely to find himself in disagreement with his colleagues in the Government? Or is there likely to be in any form bother and trouble about it?

Consequently, the Civil Service machine, with minutes going to and fro, must inevitably be cautious and careful because of the possibility of Parliamentary trouble, trouble with the public, criticism in the Press, and so on. One does not want to discourage this too much, because a healthy respect for Parliament by the civil servants in the State Departments is a good thing. . . . It is an inevitable consequence that because the State Department realises the responsibility of the Minister to Parliament, and has the instinct that it must try to keep its Minister out of trouble, we get caution, checking and counter-checking in a way that is not in accordance with commercial practice or with the speed of decision which is desirable in business undertakings.

. . . When we set up a public corporation, what are we trying to do? We are trying to get the best of both worlds. After all, that is half the art of politics, of Parliament and of public administration. . . .

We are trying to do this: First, we have a public concern . . . in which is invested the public ownership of certain economic undertakings, and there are channels of accountability, of Parliamentary argument and of discussion. Secondly, we try to graft on to that basis a commercial or business management capable of acting with speed, capable of rapid decisions, and a business concern which is in a situation whereby it can make mistakes from time to time without causing an immediate Parliamentary crisis or furore, or great criticism or embarrassment for the Minister.

. . . if we have a public corporation, in order to get the advantages of commercial management and in order to free it from other meticulous Parliamentary and political control, the House must take it that, in those circumstances, the details of Parliamentary questions and the details of Ministerial management, supervision and control have to be foregone. . . .

Suppose we accept the "whole-hog" doctrine that a Minister has to be answerable to Parliament for everything a board does, and that members of boards must be liable to be summoned before a Select Committee for annual examinations at some length. The inevitable consequence follows that there will develop in the minds of the members of the boards, their officers and their commercial employees the same sort of spirit as in the Civil Service—that they will look over their shoulder and be exceedingly careful, because they may be pulled up by a Parliamentary question or by a Select Committee of the House of Commons. We shall have evolving within the management of these boards the same spirit that we have in the Civil Service, something that is quite good in its own sphere but that would not be good in the case of these boards. . . .

I come now to the suggestion, which has been made in more than one quarter, that a Select Committee or Select Committees should be set up to examine the publicly-owned industries from year to year and report to the House on their conduct. Members who have made this suggestion have realised that it would be necessary to provide the Select Committee with an official, who would presumably need a staff, so that the Committee could get adequate and competent advice, giving them the raw material on the basis of which appropriate questions could be put.

The suggestion has been made for the appointment of an official, something like the Comptroller and Auditor-General, but perhaps with special commercial and business experience, to advise the Committee in the same way as the Comptroller and Auditor-General advises the Estimates Committee [*sic*] and the Public Accounts Committee. That is an idea and a possibility, but we are rather against it for the reasons I have already indicated. It would take up a good deal of the time of the chairman and the other members of the board and their principal officers. It would take them away from their business and it would tend to make them nervous throughout the year about appearing before the Select Committee. . . .

That is not to say there should not be periodical reviews of these great economic undertakings, which are of such great importance to the nation. We are disposed to think that we might here follow—and I have the agreement of the chairmen of the boards to this course— the procedure which has been adopted in connection with the periodical inquiry into the British Broadcasting Corporation. They are inquiries by citizens who hear evidence from other people, pay visits, and make a report, which, in due course, is available to Parliament and the public.

. . . It must not be too often. I think that something in the nature of a seven-year period would be about right for the public corporations. If they are held too often, there is the disadvantage that the men running them would get nervous and be looking over their shoulder. I think about seven years would be right. It would be right to include a limited number of Members of Parliament as was done in the case of the B.B.C. Inquiry. It would be a valuable element and would give an association with the Parliamentary institution without the disadvantages of the Select Committee.

We have discussed this with the chairmen of the boards and they are agreeable in principle to this being done. I am happy to say there is agreement about it. The object would be to conduct an examination not so much of a technical character but broadly, and to make recommendations on policy and structure. This is really a move forward in the matter of public accountability of a character that would not interfere with the commercial efficiency of the boards. . . .

SIR RALPH GLYN: . . . The point of this Debate, surely, is whether Parliament is willing to surrender its control over expenditure. . . . [There] are certain public industries which are maintained by a subsidy from Parliament. The air services are public, nationalised bodies and are dependent on subsidies. Transport is not; it is to be organised in such a way as to operate independently. All the nationalised bodies, however, if they want to raise funds, have power under the Acts which were passed by this House to go to the Treasury and get a guarantee before they make an issue—that is, public money. I was rather distressed when the Lord President, of all people, seemed to ignore the chief duty of the House of Commons as the guardian of public expenditure. If we do not carry out that duty, we give up one of our main functions. . . .

MR. OLIVER LYTTELTON: . . . First of all, let us look at Parliamentary control. The plain fact is that the structure of government, considering the way it has arisen and the duties and responsibilities of this House, cannot be satisfactorily geared to a corporation engaged in day-to-day business. . . .

Secondly, where a public monopoly is operated with all the force of authority of this House and of Ministers who are responsible to this House, there can be no satisfactory protection for the consumer. . . . The third point is that when we come to administrative efficiency we must find that decentralisation . . . is entirely the opposite of the theory of nationalisation. Decentralisation means giving autonomy, or very nearly, to local bodies, whether local authorities or local boards. . . .

. . . I turn, first, to the matter of accountability. . . . If the day-to-day administrative details are to be the subject of day-to-day questioning across the Floor of this House, then I give my opinion, for what it is worth, that administration will become practically impossible. Apart from the time that would be spent in answering questions upon administrative detail, there is also the psychology which is built up.

All of us who have been Ministers, and many of us who have not, are aware of the splash with which a Parliamentary Question falls into the Ministerial pool, and how the Civil Service is engaged upon trying to prevent the ripples from spreading. These Questions arrive in a Government office rather as the broker's man or a bailiff arrives in the house of the debtor. . . . The whole technique of the Civil Service is at the disposal of the Minister to try to prevent the hon. Member who has put the Question on the Order Paper from finding out what is really going on, covering up the mistakes. At long last, if a concession has to be made to an intrusive Member, the Civil Service very rightly tries to localise the effect and to prevent the concession from becoming a precedent.

This psychology has many disadvantages in the ordinary administration of Acts of Parliament, but it would be quite fatal—and I think the Lord President agrees with me on this—if it were applied to national boards in day-to-day industry. It would act as a brake to the whole effort. If hon. Members ask the Minister of Transport why the cod on the 6.30 from Waterloo once again tastes like cold, damp cotton-wool, the task of the right hon. Gentleman, which is clearly far beyond his or anybody else's powers already, would become quite impossible. I think this is common ground, but, on the other hand, and speaking more seriously, vast sums of public money have been invested in these industries. The idea of a Minister disclaiming responsibility for this investment is repugnant to the ideas of Parliamentary control of expenditure and cuts across the control of the purse which, both actually and historically, is the first sanction in the hands of this House. . . .

I find the subject a difficult one and I can do no more than suggest some steps towards a solution. I believe that Ministers have to accept responsibility for much more questioning upon these national boards and that they have to exercise the right, which they have, of not answering the questions if, in their judgment, these apply to trivial administrative details. The House of Commons will be an extremely good judge of whether this refusal is being used in the public interest . . . or as a cloak to conceal administrative incompetence. . . .

(F)

Report from the Select Committee on Nationalised Industries (H.C. 332 of 1952)

2. Your Committee have decided to concentrate in their First Report upon Questions to Ministers. . . .

6. In general, Questions must be confined to matters for which the appropriate minister is responsible. In the case of the Nationalised Industries, a large amount of responsibility has been vested in the Board. The list of duties for which the Minister is still responsible, and on which he may therefore by the practice of the House be questioned, is usually set out in a definite Section in each Statute. The duties vary slightly from one industry to another, but very roughly may be classified as:

(a) giving to the Board directions of a general character as to the exercise and performance by the Board of their functions in relation to matters appearing to the Minister to affect the national interest;
(b) procuring information on any point from the Board;
(c) a number of specific duties in connexion with the appointments, salaries and conditions of service of members of Boards; programmes of research and development, and of education and

training; borrowing by Boards; forms of accounts and audits; annual reports; pensions schemes and compensation for displacement; and the appointment of Consumers' Councils, their organisation and operation. . . .

14. Your Committee are aware of a strong desire in some quarters to make the Nationalised Industries as generally subject to Parliamentary Questions as the Post Office and all the other Civil Departments. Certain points, however, must be borne in mind in considering the advantages and disadvantages of such a policy.

15. The public corporations which control the Nationalised Industries were constituted on different lines from the usual civil departments. The public corporations were established as independent entities, with statutory obligations to meet their expenditure by their own revenue. Their activities involve commercial transactions on a large scale, and it is desirable that they should not be unduly hampered by external interference. On the other hand, it is urged that the nation has become the owners of the enormous assets involved in those industries, and it is widely felt that there should be means of enquiry and criticism. . . .

17. The basic feature of the Parliamentary Question is that it is answered by the Minister ultimately responsible for the decisions about which he is questioned. Under their existing constitution, the Nationalised Industries are not subject to any direct control by Ministers in individual matters of detail. Your Committee therefore feel that without altering the terms of the statutes under which the public corporations are constituted, which they are not empowered to recommend, Questions on matters of detail in the Nationalised Industries are inappropriate.

18. On the other hand, Your Committee are convinced that the present method of placing the onus of determining in the first place whether a Question which is not obviously ruled out under paragraph 17 above should be placed upon the Order Paper should not rest upon the Clerks at the Table. Where the identical Question, or the same Question in slightly different terms, has been previously asked, the Clerks at the Table are clearly obliged to refuse it. But in the case of questions which are not obviously matters of repetition or matters of detailed administration the questions should be allowed to appear on the Order Paper and the Minister would have to answer or refuse to answer on the floor of the House. . . .

(G)

Report from the Select Committee on Nationalised Industries (H.C. 235 of 1953)

2. Our terms of reference direct us to consider the present methods by which the House of Commons is informed of the affairs of the

Nationalised Industries, and to report what changes, having regard to the provisions laid down by Parliament in the relevant statutes, might be desirable in those methods. The present methods . . . of obtaining information . . . comprise the following:

(1) *Debate on Motions*

(*a*) Motions specifically concerning one or more of the industries, either moved by a Minister or by some other Member when the Government have given time for the debate;

(*b*) "Ballot Motions" in Private Members' time;

(*c*) Debate on the Address in reply to the King's Speech;

(*d*) The daily half-hour adjournment at the close of the sitting;

(*e*) Adjournment Motions moved by a Minister for the purpose of debating a particular subject.

(2) *Debate in Committee of Supply* or on an amendment to the question "That Mr. Speaker do now leave the Chair" (under Standing Order No. 17 (2) for Committee of Supply).

(3) *Debate on Bills* whether Public or Private dealing with one or more of the industries.

(4) *Debate on Motions to approve or annul Orders* or other Statutory Instruments made by Ministers under the various nationalisation Acts.

(5) *The annual reports and accounts* of the various Boards and Commissions, which are laid before Parliament.

(6) *Questions to Ministers.* . . .

3. There is, however, no doubt that there is a general desire for information about the Nationalised Industries. The Nationalised Industries publish voluminous reports, but these do not completely meet the needs of Parliament or the public, partly owing to their sheer volume and complexity, and partly because information is not necessarily available on the matters on which it is required or when it is required. . . .

5. A matter which also weighed in our minds was that the Nationalised Industries had insufficient opportunity of presenting their case to Parliament and the public, and were exposed to public pressure in various ways and much irresponsible criticism. That there was this difficulty was confirmed by Lord Hurcomb,[1] who said, "One of the very greatest handicaps under which anyone in my position suffers is that he gets no opportunity of stating his own case or of explaining what are his difficulties direct to Members of Parliament." . . . "It has been borne on me, if I may say so, without causing offence in any quarter, . . . that a great many misapprehensions do exist, and perhaps decisions are taken on some supposition of fact which is not correct." . . .

---

[1] Chairman of the British Transport Commission.

7. The arguments in favour of the proposal to set up a Committee [to inform Parliament of the affairs of these industries] were briefly summarised in the evidence given by Mr. Molson, speaking for himself, . . . in the following words:

In the past the House of Commons has always found it convenient, when confronted with a special problem, to appoint a committee. I think the reasons for this are threefold. First, in order that a few Members of Parliament may give intensive study to the problem; secondly, that there may be inter-rogation of witnesses and investigation of papers and maps; thirdly, in order that in the seclusion of a committee room there may be comparative freedom from political prejudice. . . . I believe that the committee which I am advocat-ing should elucidate what I might call deep problems of policy. I am sure it is important to avoid day-to-day interference with detail, but there is I think a great need that from time to time Parliament should have an oppor-tunity of taking stock.

8. The possibility of setting up a Committee was put to Lord Hurcomb and Sir Edward Bridges,[1] and additional arguments for the proposal were given by them. . . . Lord Hurcomb said:

The sort of Committee that it seems to me would do much to satisfy the very legitimate demand of Parliament for a greater knowledge than can be got in debate about the affairs of one of these great corporations, would be something in the nature of a standing committee, so that there would be continuity of *personnel*—a group of members who took a special and continuing interest in a particular activity, not merely because it was nationalised, but more from the actual interest that the Committee has in the subject.

He went on to say that—

A Committee of this sort would, or ought to mean, on that aspect, as these matters get further away from the highly controversial, that a large number of Members of Parliament would have an opportunity of satisfying themselves and conveying, not by way of attack and of public speech, but by way of suggestion to the organisation, the points where they thought something might be going wrong, or at any rate, would be worth looking into. That would be of great value.

9. It was strongly represented to us that the proposal to set up a permanent Committee of enquiry . . . was not only contrary to the spirit and intention of the Acts under which the industries were nation-alised, but an innovation in and hostile to the general pattern of the British constitution. As Lord Reith[2] said:

I should have thought the appointment of a select committee, *ad hoc*, on a Nationalised Industry was in effect a negation of what Parliament deliberately did in setting it up. Parliament passed a sort of self-denying ordinance taking from itself the right of direct interference, as with Government Departments.

---

[1] Permanent Secretary to the Treasury.
[2] Chairman of the Colonial Development Corporation.

Unless there is to be a revision of attitude, I would have thought it was contrary to the principle of what was done that you should set up a committee whether of one House or both. . . . It would seem a sort of institutionalisation of the Parliamentary Question, the very thing Parliament denied itself. . . .

10. The same argument was enlarged by Mr. Herbert Morrison. Later . . . he adduced a more fundamental objection. When he was asked "Really, your objection to the Select Committee is not only to its possible ineffectiveness, but also that it is not perhaps the function of Parliament to intervene on the efficiency side to the extent which is envisaged by a select committee going into it?" he answered, "I would die for Parliament—I have an enormous admiration for it—but I do not think it is the kind of body to which you could entrust this to the point of alteration of the actual management of a complex industrial concern."

11. Another argument against the proposal was that a Committee would raise the whole question of the responsibility for managing and directing the operations of the public corporations. If a Select Committee were constantly enquiring into the policy and operations of the corporation, it would necessarily cause uncertainty in the industry as to where the ultimate decisions lay; and this might possibly make accountability less rather than more secure. As Lord Reith said, when the proposal was put to him, "For whom would the public corporation be working, putting it quite straightly?" And he indicated that a select committee which might start as a friendly communicative body might end by investigating and controlling.

12. The main argument, however, which has been advanced against the proposal is that it would impede the working of the Nationalised Industries and destroy initiative in them. . . . Witnesses were apprehensive of a committee if its functions included enquiries into wide decisions of policy. . . . Witnesses expressed themselves even more strongly over the possibility that the Committee might investigate the detailed management of the industries. Lord Reith even spoke of it as a terrifying prospect. . . .

14. The basic argument for the establishment of a Committee to be a liaison between the nationalised industries and Parliament and elicit such information as is necessary on behalf of the House of Commons is that such a Committee is the only practical means of performing those functions. Last session we investigated the possibility of extending the sphere of the Parliamentary Question, and reported that it was inadvisable. Apart from this the number of ways by which the House of Commons can, on its own initiative, obtain information is limited. There is debate, the various forms of which we have already set out, but which has not fully satisfied members and sometimes has not occurred sufficiently frequently or sufficiently soon after the issue of Reports; there is the procedure of moving for returns, which is not

frequently used or altogether appropriate. There remains only the Committee, a body appointed by the House to obtain information for it.

15. We have therefore decided that we must either accept the objections, and thus abandon all possibility of dealing with the present situation; or, despite the difficulties make—with due safeguards—provision for such an enlargement of the field of parliamentary accountability as will provide the House of Commons with the information which it rightly requires without, in obtaining that information, interfering with or jeopardising the efficiency of the Nationalised Industries. A Committee appears to be the most appropriate means by which this can be done. It is essential that the Committee which we are recommending will, when appointed, set up a tradition of conduct which will result in its being regarded by the Board not as an enemy, or a critic, but as a confidant, and a protection against irresponsible pressure, as well as a guardian of the public interest. . . .

16. . . . The arguments in favour of a Joint Committee [of both Houses of Parliament] . . . are that the House of Lords has a great number of members with business and other experience available for the work; that in general the peers are less encumbered with the pressing distractions of everyday work; that the members of the other House are less dedicated to party allegiance; that their membership of their House would give the committee the element of continuity which it would need; and that if a Committee were appointed of one House alone, the other House might possibly set up another Committee with unfortunate results.

17. We feel, however, that some of the work of the proposed Committee must be of a financial nature, and would be more fittingly done by a Committee of the House of Commons. Nationalisation arose as an act of policy and, for certain industries and services, has been carried into law on the initiative of the representatives of the people in the House of Commons. It can be said that the general public are now the owners of the Nationalised Industries. It seems entirely appropriate to us, therefore, that any Parliamentary Committee set up to examine, and obtain information about, these industries at this stage of their development should be an exclusively House of Commons Committee. . . . On balance therefore we decided with some regrets against the proposal of a Joint Committee.

18. . . . the proposed Committee . . . should, we considered, take over the right which the Committee of Public Accounts at present has to examine the accounts of the Nationalised Industries, and which that Committee is unable at present fully to exercise. . . .

20. . . . the Committee should, in our opinion, be empowered to extend its enquiries more widely than those which the Committee of Public Accounts makes into the Government Departments. It should

have a regard, not merely to present and past financial probity and stability, but to future plans and programmes.

21. . . . . we consider that the Committee should have power to get information as to the policy of the corporations. It would have no need to investigate any decision which is the result of a direction from the responsible Minister, and for which he is accountable to Parliament. Again, any matters which are normally decided by collective bargaining arrangements should be avoided. . . .

28. In considering a model for the organisation of the Committee, we had in mind the Committee of Public Accounts. . . . That the Committee of Public Accounts should . . . have proved more successful than the Select Committee on Estimates is undoubtedly due to the work of the Comptroller and Auditor-General and his staff. . . . It was clear to us that the proposed new Committee would need the assistance of a similar permanent official. . . . It was, however, realised that as the proposed Committee would have to deal more with contemporary and future matters than is the case of the work of the Committee of Public Accounts, the permanent official would have a different approach from the Comptroller and Auditor-General. . . .

33. It was . . . suggested that the permanent officer of the Committee should be an officer from a central department of State, perhaps the Treasury. After consideration, however, we feel that the permanent officer of the Committee, once appointed, should be a servant of the House of Commons, and not of the Government or any of the corporations, and not removable except by an address from each House of Parliament.

34. We have come to the conclusion that the staff of the proposed committee should be as follows: There would necessarily be a Clerk to the Committee supplied from the staff of the Clerk of the House in the normal way. Then there would be a permanent official of a status roughly equivalent to the Comptroller and Auditor-General or Mr. Speaker's Counsel. He would work with the assistance of at least one professional accountant, and such other staff as the Committee may deem useful, and would examine the reports and accounts of the Nationalised Industries in order to direct the Committee's attention to matters requiring examination. If the Committee so desired, the Minister in charge of the Department responsible for the general oversight of the industry whose affairs were under review should be invited to send a senior official to assist the Committee in the examination of evidence. . . .

THE WORKING OF THE HOUSE OF COMMONS, 1946

Third Report from the Select Committee on Procedure (*H.C. 189 of 1946*)

I.—INTRODUCTION

1. When Your Committee were appointed in August, 1945, they were instructed to report as soon as possible upon a scheme for the acceleration of proceedings on public bills. . . . In the course of this inquiry, the Clerk of the House [Sir Gilbert Campion] was invited and undertook to prepare a comprehensive scheme for the reform of parliamentary procedure. . . .

3. The last comprehensive inquiry into the procedure of the House was made in 1931–32 by a Select Committee under the chairmanship of Mr. Ernest Brown. The problem facing that Committee was how to adapt procedure to the growing pressure of business, a problem which, as they recognised, was by no means new and presents itself "in almost every elective assembly in countries where modern views as to the powers and duties of the State are finding expression." The problem facing Your Committee is fundamentally the same—in the course of the intervening fifteen years it has only become more acute. But the atmosphere in which Your Committee approach their task is entirely different from that in which the former Committee found themselves. The country was then undergoing a time of severe economic stress, of industrial depression and widespread unemployment, and there was a tendency to criticise all the institutions of government, including Parliament itself. Correspondingly, many of the remedies proposed to that Committee were of a kind which would have fundamentally changed the whole character and function of Parliament. Your Committee have been appointed at a time when the country has recently emerged from a war in which parliamentary activity was maintained and contributed in large measure to its successful prosecution. Consequently there is not at the present time any strong or widespread desire for changes in the essential character of the institution. Indeed, the prestige of Parliament has probably never stood higher.

4. With these considerations in mind, Your Committee do not feel that they are called upon to consider or recommend any proposal to alter the essential character of the House of Commons. But past success affords no ground for complacency about the present, still less about the future, and, as Sir Gilbert Campion remarks, parliamentary procedure tends always to be a little out of date. The danger to parliamentary government in this country at the present time is less likely to arise from lack of confidence in it than from the overwhelming

burden which the growth of Governmental activity places upon it. This burden has become greater, not less, with the arrival of peace, and it seems probable that it may increase. It is therefore a matter for constant vigilance to ensure that the machinery is continuously adapted and strengthened to bear the new burdens put upon it. . . .

5. The problem therefore is how to adapt the procedure of the House to enable it to perform efficiently all its functions in relation to present and prospective governmental activity. The Clerk of the House accordingly devotes the first part of his memorandum to an analysis of parliamentary time from the point of view of the various functions which the House of Commons is called upon to perform. He adopts a fourfold classification: representation of popular opinion, control of finance, formulation and control of policy, and legislation. Dismissing representation from his calculations, because it has no special form of procedure allocated to it, he proceeds to analyse the amount of time spent on these functions. . . . This analysis shows that in the last 40 years (excluding the war years), the overall length of the Session has not varied much, and that the distribution of time between the various functions has remained remarkably steady. Legislation, as might be expected, has occupied the largest amount of time, slightly under half on an average. Control of policy and administration is found to occupy a relatively high proportion, roughly 40 per cent., and is the most constant element of all. Control of finance occupies the least time, about 10 per cent. of the session.

II.—LEGISLATION

6. . . . legislation takes up more of the time of the House than either of the other two main functions. Over the last 40 years it has on the average occupied not quite half the total time available, and the proportion has remained remarkably constant during the period. In the first part of the period, 1906–13, when the average length of the session was 149 days, 75·7 days were spent on legislation; in the second part of the period, 1919–29, when sessions tended to be shorter (139·9 days on the average) the amount of time spent on legislation fell proportionally to 62·8 days; and in the last part of the period, 1929–38, when sessions became longer again (157·7 days on the average), the average time spent on legislation rose to 79·7 days.

7. Although the *proportion* of the session spent on legislation remained constant, . . . the volume of legislation per session rose steadily throughout the whole period. In the first part of the period, the average number of pages in the sessional volume of the statute book was 355; in the second part of the period, in spite of shorter sessions and fewer days spent on legislation, an average of 641·8 pages of statutes were

passed per session; and in the last part of the period the average rose
to 995 pages. In other words, the speed of legislation has increased
from 4·9 pages per legislation day to 13·5 pages. Thus the volume of
legislation increased nearly $2\frac{3}{4}$ times, and this result was possible
without increasing the number of days spent on legislation because the
speed of legislating increased in the same proportion.

8. Various causes may have contributed to this result, but so far as
procedure is concerned the saving of time has been brought about by
extending the use of standing committees and by intensifying such
methods of curtailing debate as selection of amendments, the allocation of time (the "guillotine"), and the closure, though the last-named
was used sparingly in the last part of the period.

9. . . . Sir Gilbert Campion infers that it is hardly possible to save
any more of the time of the House by any of the existing methods, and,
if more time is to be saved, some radical reform of procedure is
necessary. . . .

10. The solution Sir Gilbert Campion proposes is that the House
should delegate the detailed consideration of bills at the report stage
to committees. . . . Apart from the Scottish Standing Committee,
there would be two large standing committees consisting of 75 to 100
Members. Each of the three standing committees would be divided
into three sub-committees of 25 Members each. The committee stage
of bills referred to a standing committee would be taken, not by the
standing committee itself, but by one of its sub-committees, reinforced
by the addition of 15 Members in respect of each bill. The sub-
committee, having considered a bill in the usual way, would report
it, not to the House, but to its parent standing committee, which
would consider the bill in the same way as the House does at the report
stage. At this stage, any Member who had given notice of an amendment to a bill committed to a standing committee, might, although
not a member of that standing committee, attend and move such
amendment and take part in debate upon it, without, however, the
right to vote. The standing committee would then report the bill to
the House, which could, if it wished, recommit it to the standing committee, but could not amend the bill itself. The bill could, however,
be debated as a whole on the motion for its consideration, and when
this was agreed to, would stand for third reading. . . .

11. . . . The main objection in Your Committee's view is to the
principle of the scheme. The removal of the report stage of bills from
the floor of the House would be, in the words of Mr. Speaker, "a
drastic interference with the rights of private Members", and would
also adversely affect any smaller parties who could not receive adequate
representation on the committees and sub-committees; and the suggestion . . . that a Member who was not a member of a standing committee could move amendments without the right to vote, is entirely

contrary to the traditional practice of the House. There would also be the practical difficulty that a serious bottle-neck might occur in a standing committee when a number of bills were coming forward for consideration by the main committee at the same time as its members were engaged upon the committee stage of other bills in the sub-committees. For these reasons Your Committee are unable to recommend the proposal to the House. . . .

III.—CONTROL OF POLICY AND ADMINISTRATION

24. Control of policy and administration occupies on an average about 40 per cent. of the time of the House—an allocation which on the face of it appears adequate. But the classification is misleading. The line between policy and administration may be difficult to draw, and it is not possible to distinguish forms of procedure which are used for the specific control of one or the other. Nevertheless the control of policy and the control of administration are two broadly distinct functions, and if the several forms of procedure which together fall under this head are examined, it will be seen that by far the greater part of them is used for the discussion of questions of broad policy rather than of administrative detail. Thus the Debate on the King's speech (5·8 days per session) is used to discuss the broad outlines of the Government programme. Adjournment motions (5·9 days) lend themselves to discussion of administrative points, but are often used for raising questions of policy; and substantive motions (14·2 days) are used to raise larger subjects. Above all, the business of Supply, which accounts for the largest amount of time under this head (32·3 days), has in recent years tended more and more to provide opportunities for debates on policy. The debates on the various stages of the Consolidated Fund Bills tend to be taken up with full-day discussions on general policy rather than with details of administration. The Estimates themselves, which in theory provide the occasion *par excellence* for the raising of grievances against administration, have of late years tended to be used for the discussion of major issues of policy. An analysis of the Departments selected for discussion on Supply days bears out this impression. Out of 202 days allotted to Supply in ten sessions in the period 1921 to 1937–38, 24¼ were used for the discussion of the Defence Services, 21½ for Scottish Departments, 20 for the Foreign Office and 16½ for the Ministry of Labour. If it be admitted that the debates on the 21½ days spent on Scottish Departments may have been largely administrative in character, it is fair to assume that the larger part of the time ostensibly given to the discussion of the Fighting Services, the Foreign Office and the Ministry of Labour, was actually used to discuss national issues of defence, foreign policy and economic problems.

In fine, the amount of time devoted to really administrative points, so far from tending to increase with the growth of administrative activity, has greatly diminished.

25. While the time spent on discussing administrative detail in the House has decreased, the field of administration itself has steadily increased. Much modern legislation is of an administrative character. Moreover, an increasing number of statutes confer upon a Minister or some other authority power to legislate upon matters of administrative detail. How great this field of administrative activity has grown is indicated by the fact that Statutory Rules and Orders . . . exceed in volume the annual output of statutes. Leaving out of account the war years as exceptional, the number of Statutory Rules and Orders registered in 1937 was 1,231, in 1938, 1,661, and in 1945, 1,706.

26. The form of parliamentary control applicable to a Statutory Instrument is laid down by the Act under which it is made. For the great majority of Instruments, the governing Act provides no parliamentary control at all. In the year 1944, 291 Instruments, out of a total of 1,483 registered, were subject or liable to parliamentary proceedings.

27. Parliamentary control, where it is provided, broadly stated, may take one of two forms. Either the Instrument has to be confirmed by a resolution of both Houses (sometimes by the House of Commons alone); or the Instrument remains in force unless a motion to annul it is carried by either House within a period prescribed by the Act. In either case the proceedings are exempted business and are usually taken at the end of the day.

28. Thus, apart from the relatively few Instruments which require an affirmative resolution, only those in which a Member may discover cause for objection are discussed in the House. Until 1944, there was no provision for systematically scrutinising Instruments. In that year the Select Committee on Statutory Rules and Orders, etc., was set up. . . .

29. . . . . the opportunities for discussing delegated legislation in the House are extremely limited and not altogether satisfactory. On an average the actual time so spent has amounted to the equivalent of 1·6 days per session. In view of this fact and in view of the impossibility of finding much more time for the discussion of Statutory Instruments in the House, Sir Gilbert Campion suggests that part of the task of supervising this form of administrative activity might suitably be entrusted to a select committee. He suggests that the existing Select Committee on Statutory Rules and Orders, etc., might be empowered to consider and report on any Statutory Instrument in force from the point of view of its efficiency as a means of carrying out the purposes named by the governing Act. Such a Committee would be precluded by its terms of reference from criticising the policy of the Act under

which the Instrument was made. Its task would be to inform itself of the various practical considerations which the responsible Departmental officers had in mind in framing the Instrument and on the basis of this information to consider whether the Instrument was well designed for its purpose and whether the method chosen was the least injurious to the rights of the citizen. . . .

30. Sir Gilbert Campion's proposal would go some way to supplement the inadequate and unsatisfactory opportunities which the House at present possesses for exercising its control over one aspect of administration. Your Committee consider, however, that the delegation of legislative power raises issues beyond the scope of the present investigation. . . .

IV.—CONTROL OF FINANCE

31. Control of finance occupies on an average about 10 per cent. of the time of the House. The explanation of this relatively small allocation of time to a subject of such magnitude and importance is that of the two financial functions which fall under this head, the imposition of taxation and the control of expenditure, the latter has to a large account passed from the House itself to the Committee of Public Accounts and the Select Committee on Estimates. Thus the fifteen days a session which on an average the House has devoted to financial control represent only its taxing function and include nothing for control of expenditure.

(1) *Control of Taxation*

32. The procedure of the House which is concerned with the authorisation of taxation consists of the various stages of the Finance Bill and the Ways and Means resolutions upon which it is founded.

33. The suggestion was made by the representatives of the Government that a small amount of time might be saved by shortening the proceedings on the Budget Resolutions and the Finance Bill. It was said that the present procedure involves duplication at two points: that the committee stage of the Budget Resolutions is duplicated in the second reading of the Finance Bill, and the report stage of the Resolutions in the committee stage of the Finance Bill. It was therefore proposed that at the report stage of the Budget Resolutions the question should be put without amendment or debate, points of detail being left for discussion at the committee stage of the Finance Bill.

34. The duplication involved in the present procedure is more apparent than real. The clauses of the Finance Bill do not by any means repeat the phraseology of the Budget Resolutions nor is the debate necessarily similar in character. It is true that the same points may be raised on the committee stage of the Bill as on the report stage of the resolutions, but the earlier stage is more suited, and is in fact

largely used, for a more general financial discussion, while the later stage is the appropriate stage for considering in detail the Chancellor's taxation proposals and, in particular, the "machinery" clauses which have no counterpart in the resolutions. Moreover, there is a certain practical convenience in the present arrangement. The debate on the resolutions follows closely on the Chancellor's announcement of his proposals and the House has only time to form general conclusions. Moreover, they have all to be passed without prior notice in Committee of Ways and Means on Budget Day, so that the report stage is the first opportunity on which Members can express their opinion by vote on each separate proposal. The interval between the debate on the resolutions and the Committee stage of the Bill provides an opportunity alike for the Government and the House to consider in closer detail the implications of the Chancellor's proposals, before they are finally embodied in the clauses of the Bill.

35. But perhaps the aspect of the matter which weighs most strongly with Your Committee in examining this proposal is the broad question of the amount of time devoted to control of taxation. Fifteen days, approximately 10 per cent. of the session, does not seem to Your Committee to be an excessive amont of time to devote to so important a subject. It may be that some of this time is wasted on repetitive arguments, but, if so, that is less a criticism of the procedure than of the use made of it by the House. Curtailment of the time devoted to this subject is not the remedy; it might be said with equal force that it would also limit the opportunities for raising new points. Your Committee do not feel that they can recommend to the House a proposal which, besides having certain practical inconveniences, would still further curtail the opportunities of Members for taking part in one of the most important debates of the year

(2) *Control of Expenditure*

36. The passing of Estimates in the Committee of Supply is the formal procedure by which the expenditure of Departments is authorised, but, as is well known, this procedure has almost ceased to serve the purpose of financial scrutiny, and is used almost exclusively for the criticism of policy and administration. The origin of this development is to be found in the ancient claim of the Commons to refuse grant of supply until their grievances had been redressed, a right which has in the course of time come to be exercised within the Committee of Supply itself. But the consequent change in the function of the Committee of Supply is also a practical justification, which cannot be expressed better than in the words of the Select Committee of 1931–32:

The Committee of Supply is a Committee of 615 Members. They cannot, therefore, effectively consider the details of finance. The time at their disposal is strictly limited. They cannot examine witnesses; they have no information before them but the bulky volumes of the Estimates, the answers of a Minister to questions addressed to him in debate, and such casual facts as some indefatigable private Members may be in a position to impart. A body so large, so limited in its time, and so ill-equipped for inquiry would be a very imperfect instrument for the control of expenditure even if the discussions were devoted entirely to that end. But these discussions afford during twenty days practically the only opportunity in the course of the year for the debate of grievances and of many questions of policy. In the competition for time such matters usually take precedence, and questions of finance, especially those affecting the whole field, are crowded out.

37. As a consequence of this change in the predominant functions of the Committee of Supply, the House of Commons has perforce devised other means outside the House itself for the detailed examination of expenditure. At the present time financial criticism and control are exercised by two bodies, the Committee of Public Accounts and the Select Committee on Estimates. It will perhaps assist the understanding of the present position, if the origin of these two Committees is briefly recalled.

The Committee of Public Accounts

38. In the eighteenth century there was no uniform system of public accounts, still less was there any method for bringing them regularly under parliamentary scrutiny. It was not until 1831 that the first "Appropriation Accounts," showing the actual expenditure of the Navy and Victualling Boards under each head, were introduced. This system of Appropriation Accounts was extended to the War and Ordnance Offices in 1856. In 1857 a Select Committee recommended that the system should be extended to the Civil and Revenue Departments and that the whole of the resulting accounts should be "annually submitted to the revision of a Committee of the House of Commons to be nominated by Mr. Speaker." Four years later the Standing Order (now No. 74) was passed, which instituted the Committee of Public Accounts, but the remaining recommendations of the Committee were not implemented until 1866, when the Exchequer and Audit Act was passed. As a result of this Act a complete reorganisation of the system of preparing accounts for audit was made, and in 1869 the first complete accounts of the whole public service were laid before Parliament.

39. The Exchequer and Audit Act also instituted the Office of Comptroller and Auditor-General. This officer is appointed by Letters Patent but is responsible to the House of Commons alone. His officers conduct a continuous examination of the expenditure of Departments and his comments arising from this examination are embodied in reports which are made annually to the House of Commons and considered, along with the Appropriation Accounts to which they relate,

by the Committee of Public Accounts. In the light of these Reports and their own investigations the Committee in turn report their observations to the House. These reports are considered by the Treasury, in order that effect may be given to the recommendations which they contain, and the Treasury's decisions are contained in a Minute which is communicated to the Committee.

40. The establishment of the Committee of Public Accounts and the institution of the office of Comptroller and Auditor General are thus seen as parts of a great scheme of reform whereby the House of Commons secured an effective machine for ensuring that the money which it had voted was spent on the objects for which it was intended. This system has remained unaltered to this day.

The Select Committee on Estimates

41. Select Committees on Estimates, and their war-time equivalent, the Select Committees on National Expenditure, have only been regularly appointed since 1912, but their prototypes are to be found at a much earlier date. For the function which they perform, that of controlling expenditure, was one which in the 19th century the House of Commons frequently though sporadically entrusted to Select Committees under other names. Thus, for example, there were Select Committees on Army Expenditure, Navy Expenditure, Expenditure for Miscellaneous Services, Expenditure and Management of Woods and Forests (including the Department of Works and Buildings) in 1848, and in both the years 1849 and 1850 Select Committees on Army and Ordnance Expenditure were appointed. These Committees performed functions precisely similar to those entrusted to the modern Estimates Committees as their terms of reference indicate: "to inquire into the Expenditure on . . . and to report their observations to the House." Their Reports also show that the basis of these inquiries were the Estimates presented to Parliament. When therefore for the first time in 1912 a Committee was appointed with the task of examining *all* the Estimates (or rather such of them as it should think fit) the innovation was one of name rather than of substance. The House had merely substituted a more systematic method for the control of expenditure for the sporadic and piecemeal expedients of the 19th century.

Proposed Public Expenditure Committee

42. The foregoing account of the different origins of the Public Accounts Committee and the Estimates Committee indicates the difference in their functions. The Public Accounts Committee is primarily an instrument to ensure financial regularity in the Accounts, the function of the Estimates Committee is to criticise expenditure on the basis not of regularity but of economy and sound business principle.

Sir Gilbert Campion suggests that these two functions could with advantage be combined in the work of a single committee, to be called the Public Expenditure Committee. On the face of it, the difference in function would appear to be a strong objection to this course. But, although in principle the functions of the two Committees are distinct, their subject matter is in fact the same. The public Accounts Committee works on the Appropriation Accounts and the Estimates Committee works on the Estimates, but the sums which appear this year as estimates of expenditure will eventually become items in the corresponding Appropriation Accounts. The difference is one of time rather than of subject matter or method. The actual practice of the two Committees bears out this view. The Public Accounts Committee, though it is formally charged only with the examination of expenditure appearing in the Appropriation Accounts, frequently carries its investigations beyond the year of account into the immediately past financial year and even into the current year. This practice, though not formally covered by the terms of reference of the Committee, is recognised by the House as legitimate. The Comptroller and Auditor General was explicit on this point. "It is very often the fact," he said, "that the Public Accounts Committee is considering, in 1946, expenditure which was almost a token sum in 1944, and did not really commence effectively until 1945 or perhaps even until 1945 is some way advanced. . . ." Similarly, it would be easy to show that the Estimates Committee frequently carries its investigations into expenditure back into the last financial year and even into the year before that—the year of account which is the primary responsibility of the Public Accounts Committee. And indeed it is inevitable that both Committees should stray beyond the financial year with which they are primarily concerned. Criticism of expenditure would be almost impossible if it were strictly confined to the sums which happen to be brought to account or to appear in the Estimates of a single year. This is specially true of long-term schemes and projects involving expenditure over a period of years. Common sense requires, and the House acknowledges the necessity, that both Committees should carry their inquiries outside the financial year which the order of the House refers to them.

43. For these reasons Your Committee consider that the functions of the Committee of Public Accounts and the Estimates Committee would be better performed by a single Committee. Such a Committee would have no powers beyond those possessed by the separate committees now, and there would be no change in the position or duties of the Comptroller and Auditor General either in relation to the Department or the Committee. The advantage of combining both functions in a single Committee working through sub-committees is twofold. First, the knowledge and experience gained by examination of the Accounts would be brought to bear upon the examination of

current expenditure, and *vice versa*. Secondly, a single committee with
sub-committees provides a method for co-ordinating the whole work
of the examination of expenditure, for which neither overlapping
membership nor any other method of liaison is a satisfactory substitute.
The result would be a strengthening of parliamentary control of
expenditure and it might be that fewer Members would be needed for
this work. . . .

THE HOUSE OF LORDS IN SEPARATE SESSION, 1947

House of Lords Debates, 13 August 1947; Official Report, cc. 1396 sqq.

LORD AMMON: My Lords, I beg to move that this House do now
adjourn until Tuesday, October 14. . . .

THE MARQUESS OF SALISBURY: My Lords, I beg to move as an
Amendment to the Motion, to leave out the words "Tuesday, October
14" and insert "Tuesday, September 9." In moving this Amendment
I can assure the Government, if they need such an assurance, that we,
on this side of the House, are not acting in any Party spirit or with the
mere object of causing any embarrassment to the Government. We
have, I think it will be agreed in all parts of the House, taken a moderate and, I hope, a statesmanlike attitude towards the Supplies and
Services (Extended Purposes) Act. Although we have protested against
the extent of the powers which are given to the Government,
especially under Section 1 (1) (*c*), we have been at pains not to give
any legitimate grounds for any charge that we have made it impossible
for the Government to use what means they feel desirable to tackle
this crisis with which the country is faced.

But there is no doubt that the introduction of this legislation, with
the very wide powers which it confers, and at a time when Parliament
is separating for the summer Recess for over two months, has exposed
what I may perhaps describe as rather a serious defect in the constitutional machinery of this country, which I think it is for Parliament
as far as they can to try to remedy. In the old days, of course, practically all legislation was by Act of Parliament, and Parliament went
through every word of every clause of that legislation. In such circumstances there was fully effective protection for the community. But
within recent years (and I am not referring merely to the period
during which the present Government have been in power) there has
been a new development—namely the growth of delegated legislation.
As your Lordships know very well, blanket powers are given to Ministers to make Orders within the limitations of the main Acts and as
soon as they are made those Orders come into active operation. It is

quite true that under the Constitution they must be laid before Parliament, and, as your Lordships know, either House can pray against them.

That is, of course, some protection when Parliament is sitting, but if Parliament is not sitting Orders may become operative weeks, or even months, before Parliament can consider them. I should think it would be generally agreed by noble Lords in every part of the House, whatever they may feel about this measure which we have so lately been considering, that that is not an entirely satisfactory situation. Indeed, it is a very unsatisfactory situation. It is to meet this new difficulty that we are proposing that, if necessary, this House, at any rate, should meet at convenient intervals during the Recess to examine such Orders.

No doubt the noble and learned Viscount, the Lord Chancellor, would point out, if I did not, that in these circumstances this House cannot pray against Orders, because Orders have to be laid before Parliament; and if only one House happens to be in Session they clearly cannot be so laid. In those conditions all the House can do is to examine and discuss them when they come out. That would be, or it might be, a useful function for us to perform. An earlier meeting of this kind, under the existing rather anxious conditions, might have this additional advantage: It might well give opportunity, if such were required, for general discussion of developments in the economic situation since the House last sat. . . .

THE LORD CHANCELLOR (VISCOUNT JOWITT): My Lords, your Lordships on these Benches are really becoming very revolutionary. I and my Party are old-fashioned Constitutionalists in this matter and I am bound to point out that, so far as I know, this has never been done before. . . .

The constitutional position is quite plain. It is for each House . . . to exercise its right to adjourn itself independently of the Crown (which means the Government of the day) and of the other House . . . [On] August 10, 1914, . . . this House resolved that—

whenever during the present Session of Parliament this House stands adjourned for more than two days and it appears to the satisfaction of the Lord Chancellor that the public interest requires that the House should meet at any earlier time during such adjournment, the Lord Chancellor may give notice to the Peers that he is so satisfied and thereupon the House shall meet at the time stated in such Notice and transact business as if it had been duly adjourned to that time.

Since that date alterations have been made in that Motion. The Chairman of Committees in the House of Lords is now frequently included, together with the Lord Chancellor, and since 1931 the Motion has been so made that the Lord Chancellor or the Chairman of Committees cannot act save after consultation with the Government. In its more modern form, in practice I understand it means that this is done with the approval of the Government. But I would point out that under the 1914 Resolution it was left to the Lord Chancellor to act independently and call your Lordships back if, and only if, in his or their opinion there was some case for so doing. . . .

On Question, Amendment agreed to.

Motion, as amended, agreed to, and ordered accordingly.

House of Lords Debates, 9 September 1947; Official Report, cc. 1409 sqq.

THE FIRST LORD OF THE ADMIRALTY (VISCOUNT HALL): . . . Now, without any further preamble, I propose to tell the House that His Majesty's Government cannot agree that it is proper for the present occasion to be used for a general debate upon the state of the nation or, indeed, as an opportunity for eliciting any new statement of Government policy. In our view, whatever may be the constitutional right of your Lordships to meet as and when you please, it would certainly not be constitutional for His Majesty's Government to regard a meeting of this House alone, in the middle of the Parliamentary Recess, as a meeting of Parliament for the making of an important announcement of Government policy. Indeed, your Lordships yourselves would object, and very rightly so, if His Majesty's Government summoned only members of another place for the same purpose while they left your Lordships still inoperative and in adjournment. And yet, though I need hardly remind your Lordships that the other place is the Chamber of the popularly-elected representatives of the country, you are asking us to treat them as of no account——

NOBLE LORDS: No.

VISCOUNT HALL: —and to give your Lordships information upon Government policy while we deny it to another place. Neither this Government nor any other . . . can have one policy in regard to the sittings of another place during the Recess and another policy for your Lordships' House. We could not refuse to meet another place until October 20 and at the same time be willing to meet your Lordships this afternoon for a general debate on the economic situation. . . .

I should say to your Lordships that it is not the Government's intention that any speech other than the speech I am making at the present time shall be made from this Bench during to-day's proceedings. . . .

THE MARQUESS OF SALISBURY: . . . it is clear that the Government are unwilling to make a statement. . . . Nor does it appear that there is anything important to be discussed arising from the Supplies and Services Act. Many people will find this a little surprising. The Bill was hustled through Parliament with feverish haste before the House rose in August. We were told that it was urgent and vital that the Government should have the very widest powers immediately; and there were fears raised that there would be very far-reaching action indeed. But there is one thing, I think, that never occurred to any of us, and that is that no important Orders at all would be made. That, however, appears to be the position. All we can do is to take note of it. . . .

PARLIAMENTARY PRIVILEGE AND PARTY MEETINGS, 1947

Report from the Committee of Privileges (H.C. 138 of 1947)

[In April 1947, at a time when several London newspapers were reporting, in some detail, accounts of private meetings of the Parliamentary Labour Party, Mr. Garry Allighan, M.P., wrote an article alleging that this news "leaked" to the Press through Members of Parliament, who disclosed confidential information for a fee, in unguarded talk when under the influence of liquor, or in return for favourable publicity. In the course of the proceedings of the Committee of Privileges, it was disclosed that Mr. Allighan had supplied information about private party meetings to an evening newspaper. The Committee considered that he had been "guilty of an aggravated contempt of the House of which he is a Member and of a gross breach of privilege"; he was later expelled from the House of Commons.]

14. On any view this is a case of great seriousness. It is also one of much difficulty from the point of view of the law and custom of Parliament. . . . Your Committee are very mindful of the fact that Parliament has no right to extend its privileges beyond those to which recognition has already been accorded and they believe that it would be contrary to the interest both of Parliament and of the public so to do. On the other hand, the absence of an exact precedent does not in itself show that a particular matter does not come within some recognised principle of Parliamentary privilege.

15. Moreover, it is to be remembered that the right to punish for contempt is by no means restricted to the case where some actual privilege has been infringed. The two matters are distinct.

16. Whether or not the matter has by analogy some relation to the privilege that Members are entitled to be free from molestation, it has long been recognised that the publication of imputations reflecting on the dignity of the House or of any Member in his capacity as such is punishable as a contempt of Parliament. It is true that the imputation upon a Member to come within this principle must relate to something which he has done as such, that is to say incidentally to and as part of his service to Parliament. Thus in an extreme case concerning *The*

Times in 1887,[1] an allegation that certain Members "draw their living . . . from the steady perpetration of crimes for which civilisation demands the gallows" was held not to constitute a contempt in that it did not refer to the action of the Members concerned in the discharge of their duties as such. Reflections upon Members, however, even where individuals are not named, may be so framed as to bring into disrepute the body to which they belong, and such reflections have therefore been treated as equivalent to reflections on the House itself. It is for the House to decide whether any particular publication constitutes such an affront to the dignity of the House or its Members in that capacity as amounts to contempt of Parliament.

17. In modern times the practice of holding private meetings in the precincts of the Palace of Westminster of different parties has become well established and, in the view of Your Committee, it must now be taken to form a normal and everyday incident of parliamentary procedure, without which the business of Parliament could not conveniently be conducted. Thus, meetings held within the precincts of the Palace of Westminster during the parliamentary session are normally attended only by Members as such, and the information which is given at such meetings is, in Your Committee's view, given to those attending them in their capacity as Members. Your Committee therefore conclude on this matter that attendance of Members at a private party meeting held in the precincts of the Palace of Westminster during the parliamentary session, to discuss parliamentary matters connected with the current or future proceedings of Parliament, is attendance in their capacity of Members of Parliament. It does not, of course, follow that this conclusion attracts to such meetings all the privileges which are attached to the transactions of Parliament as a whole.

18. It follows that an unfounded imputation in regard to such meetings involves an affront to the House as such. Your Committee consider that an unjustified allegation that Members regularly betray the confidence of private party meetings either for payment or whilst their discretion has been undermined by drink is a serious contempt.

19. Where, as here, the contempt alleged is the making of such a charge against Members, proof that the charge was true would not, in Your Committee's view, of necessity provide a defence. If the publication were intended to bring to light matters that were true so that an end might be put to them, then, however discreditable the facts, Your Committee consider that such a publication, for such a high purpose, would constitute a defence. It was not suggested the article in question here was published with any such object.

20. Whether the actual betrayal of information about a private meeting of Members held in a Committee Room of the House or its publication in the Press constitutes a distinct breach of privilege is a

---

[1] *Parl. Deb.* (1887), 311, c. 286.

separate and more difficult matter. Although the publication of reports of debates is technically a breach of privilege . . . this rule is not now enforced in the case of *bona-fide* reports. It would, it is true, be different if the House had resolved to sit in secret session; and if a Committee had resolved to transact its proceedings behind closed doors, this decision, although it does not exclude the right of other Members of the House to attend, would no doubt result in any publication of what had taken place constituting a contempt. If the true basis of this latter rule is not that the publication involves a breach of confidence but that it involves a premature disclosure before the Committee has reported to the House, it would be difficult to draw any analogy with the private party meeting, since in the latter case no report to the House is involved and no question of premature disclosure. On the other hand, it appears to be clear that the orders against publication of debates can be enforced where the publication is made in bad taste. Where a Member publishes confidential information to a newspaper for reward, or where a newspaper pays a Member for betraying confidential information which it proceeds to publish, it could hardly be said that either publication had been made in good faith. It is arguable, therefore, that the publication of confidential information given for or obtained by payment, about the transactions at a private party meeting, could by analogy be treated as a breach of the rule against publication of Parliamentary proceedings. In Your Committee's view, however, this would be straining the rule, and this they are not inclined to do. They content themselves with observing that publication of information about secret meetings of his party by a Member clearly involves a gross breach of confidence but is not in itself a breach of privilege.

21. This, however, does not dispose of the matter. It is clearly a breach of privilege to offer a bribe or payment to a Member in order to influence him in his conduct as a Member. An obvious case would be to vote in a particular way. It would be unobjectionable to persuade a Member to exercise his vote in a particular way: it is the element of payment which gives rise to the offence. Once it is conceded, as Your Committee think it must be, that the information which Members obtain at private party meetings held as aforesaid is obtained by them in their capacity as such, it seems to Your Committee to follow that if they sell such information, or others buy it, the transaction is still with a Member as such and the payment relates to the Member's conduct in his capacity as a Member. The information has come to him confidentially as a Member; it is only as a Member that he can part with it. In Your Committee's view, therefore, the making of a payment in order that a Member should specially note what took place at the meeting and should disclose information about it, or the acceptance of such a payment, constitutes a transaction in the nature of

bribery of a Member in regard to what is part of his work in Parliament and is a breach of the privileges of this House. . . .

26. Your Committee are glad to know that editors and journalists generally share their view that, quite apart from any question of privilege, transactions between newspapers and Members of the House whereby the latter disclose confidential information in return for payment by the former are discreditable to both parties and quite out of accord with the best standards of journalism.

POWERS OF THE HOUSE OF LORDS, 1948

House of Lords Debates, 27 January 1948; Official Report, cc. 629 sqq.

Parliament Bill: Order of the Day for the Second Reading read

THE LORD PRIVY SEAL (VISCOUNT ADDISON): . . . The fact is that under the Parliament Act as it stands, if your Lordships' House were so minded, the last two years' work of a Government in the House of Commons, supported by a Labour or a Liberal majority, as the case may be, might be largely sterilised. . . .

Subject to certain adequate safeguards, however, there is nothing in the function of delay which means that that power shall be so used as to sterilise the last two years of the activities of an anti-Conservative Government. There is nothing in that which involves a claim that this House shall decide whether an act of the House of Commons is or is not in accordance with the mandate of the people. There is nothing in that function of delay which confers upon this House the power to determine what shall be the issues at a General Election. I am now going to confess frankly some of the causes of uneasiness which led to this Bill. Many a time in this House . . . I have had to listen to the question whether this or that proposal of the Government was in accordance with the mandate of the people, or words to that effect. I want to say a word on this "mandate" claim, with complete frankness. . . .

The claim to decide whether a subject is or is not in accordance with the mandate of the people contains this implication that, if this House is of opinion that it is not in the mandate, this House is at liberty to reject it; that is the deliberate and obvious implication. We challenge that implication from the very start. We claim that it is for the elected representatives of the people to decide whether an issue is or is not to be the subject of Parliamentary activity. . . .

. . . There is the point of difference. We do not accept, and we do not intend to accept, that this House, entirely unrepresentative, shall be the final arbiter as to what is and what is not the opinion of the people. There is the point of actual difference, and there can be no compromise on that. In our view, it must be the elected Chamber that has finally to decide these issues.

Let us examine this from another aspect. Of necessity in the life of any Parliament, a large number of issues must arise which were not foreseen or which were not in anybody's mind at the time of the Election. . . . But that does not in any way invalidate the claim or right of the representative House to introduce measures on these matters. There is no question of mandate at all. . . .

THE MARQUESS OF SALISBURY: . . . The effect of this Bill is really to truncate the powers of this House in such a way as to reduce it, as a balancing factor in the Constitution, to a mere farce. Such a truncation of powers . . . would quite definitely lay the country open to all the dangers of single-Chamber Government. . . .

. . . What is essential, if a Parliamentary democracy is to succeed, is that both Parties should know that if a Government, either of the Left or of the Right—because it applies equally to both—with a temporary majority in the House of Commons, were to introduce really extreme measures, there is in existence a Second Chamber able to stop them. If that protection where to be removed, the defeated Party —and, as I say, it applies equally to the Right and the Left—frantic with anxiety, might well begin to flirt with unconstitutional practices. . . .

. . . We on this side of the House ask no more than that issues affecting the welfare of the electorate, where their judgment is unknown or doubtful, should be referred for their consideration, or at least deferred for a short time to enable their views to be found out. That is the whole reason for our stand for an effective Second Chamber. . . . If the present House of Lords is not the right body to exercise this power, let it be amended; but do not remove this essential safeguard against extreme action by the Right or by the Left. . . .

REFORM OF THE HOUSE OF LORDS, 1948

Agreed Statement on the Conclusion of the Conference of Party Leaders, February-April, 1948 (Cmd. 7,380, 1948)

4. At the first Meeting, the Party representatives agreed that discussion should embrace proposals relating to the reform of the Composition of the House of Lords, and proposals relating to the Powers which should be vested in any reformed House. These two subjects, though capable of separate consideration, were to be regarded as

interdependent, and it was recognised that failure to agree either on Composition or on Powers might result in general agreement on the future of the House of Lords not being reached. . . .

7. On this question of Powers considerable discussion took place, but the Conference failed to reach agreement. The views put forward by the respective groups of Party Leaders are set out in the following paragraphs 8 to 10.

8. The representatives of the Government expressed their willingness to see a Second Chamber possessed of proper facilities for debating public affairs and for revising legislation. The procedural arrangements should secure to each House a proper time for the consideration of amendments to Bills proposed by the other; but they should not be such as to enable the Second Chamber to impose its will on the House of Commons and to force the Government to seek a General Election against its own inclination and that of the Commons. The principal organ of democratic government is the House of Commons, which is elected by the People. The danger in modern conditions is that the machinery of democratic government may act too slowly rather than too quickly. Under the Parliament Act, 1911, the procedure enables a House of Lords hostile to the Government of the day to render the legislative programme of the Government ineffective in the fourth and fifth sessions of a quinquennial Parliament. In the result, the will of the Government and of the People could be thwarted by a Second Chamber which, not being elected, is not directly responsible to the People. The Government representatives agreed that it is important that points of dispute between the two Houses should be appreciated by the public, but they considered that the proposals of the Parliament Bill adequately safeguard constitutional rights in this respect, and afford sufficient time for public opinion (which formulates more rapidly in modern conditions than was the case thirty years ago) to understand and pronounce upon a disputed issue.

The Government representatives recognised, however, that under the Parliament Act procedure, as proposed to be amended by the Bill, the Second Chamber might not have a sufficiently long period to consider a disputed measure if, for any reason, the Bill took an exceptionally long time in its passage through the House of Commons. As part of a general agreement over the reform of the House of Lords, they would have been prepared to suggest to the Labour Party that the "period of delay" which, under the Parliament Bill, would be one year from Second Reading in the Commons on the first occasion, should be extended to nine months from Third Reading if, in the case of a particular Bill, the latter period proved to be the longer. The Government representatives could not recommend any further extension inasmuch as the effective legislative use of the fourth session of a quinquennial Parliament would thereby be in jeopardy. It was further argued that the greater the powers given to a Second Chamber, the more might be the necessity for the Prime Minister of the day to attempt to redress an adverse political balance in that Chamber by the creation of additional Peers, and the greater the danger that the Second Chamber might in fact become a rival of the Commons.

9. The Leaders of the Official Opposition find themselves unable to agree to what they regard as the virtual elimination of the suspensory period. They feel that this would be in conflict with the whole intention of the Parliament Act of 1911. They hold that the purpose of the power of delay, which formed an integral part of the Parliament Act procedure, has never been to enable the Second Chamber to thwart the will of the People. It is an essential constitutional safeguard to ensure that, in the event of serious controversy between the two Houses of Parliament, on a measure on which the view of the electorate is doubtful, such a measure shall not pass into law until sufficient time has elapsed to enable the electorate to be properly informed of the issues involved and for public opinion to crystallise and express itself. The "one year's delay" from the Second Reading in the House of Commons proposed in the Parliament Bill now before Parliament is in fact largely illusory. For experience shows that it may take eight months for a Bill to pass through the ordinary processes of Parliament. Such a curtailment of the powers of the Second Chamber as is involved in the Government proposals would, in the view of the Opposition, represent a formidable step towards Single Chamber Government, with all the risks entailed. And this is an especial danger in a country like Great Britain where there is an unwritten Constitution and fundamental constitutional changes can be made by a simple Bill. The Opposition Leaders regard the safeguard of some effective power of delay by the Second Chamber as vital at all times and especially at the present juncture when political instability is so evident throughout the world. They believe that there is no danger that such a power would be used frivolously. For the very existence of a Second Chamber must depend on its acting with due responsibility. And this would apply with redoubled force in the case of a Second Chamber composed of men and women chosen for their individual wisdom and experience, especially if steps were taken to ensure as far as possible that there is no permanent majority for any one political Party. In this case it could not be said that the procedure would operate differently in the cases of Governments of the Left and of the Right.

Notwithstanding this view, the Opposition Leaders considered that if it had been possible to reach agreement over the whole field of Composition and Powers of the Second Chamber, they might have regarded as acceptable a period of eighteen months from Second Reading in the Commons—halfway between the two years of the Parliament Act and the one year proposed by the Parliament Bill.

Indeed, in order to facilitate such agreement, they would have been prepared to suggest for consideration by their supporters an even shorter period of twelve months from the Third Reading in the Commons. Any further reduction of the period would in their view involve a breach in the spirit and purpose of the Parliament Act. No doubt the time factor would vary with the complexity of a Bill, and the time taken up by Parliamentary debate in both Houses. But a period must be provided which covers all Bills. On the principle to be applied in deciding what that period should be, there is really a fundamental difference between the Government and the Opposition. In the view of the official Opposition, the effect of the Government proposals would be to allow a period sufficient to allow full Parliamentary consideration by both Houses, but little or no more. The Opposition contend that this is not enough; and that the time factor must be sufficient to allow for reflection by the country after discussion in Parliament has been concluded and the matters at issue between the two Houses have been clearly defined.

Failure to provide this period for reflection by the electors would, in the view of the Opposition, curtail the powers of the Second Chamber to a point at which its value as a balancing factor in the constitution would be largely nullified. To this they could not agree in view of the danger to the liberties of the People that would be involved.

10. The Liberal Leaders had originally criticised the Parliament Bill on the ground that it did not provide a sufficient suspensory period. Accordingly, they had suggested that the "period of delay" should run, not from the Second Reading, but from the Third Reading in the Commons.

However, in their view, the alternative proposal made by the Government during the course of the Meetings sufficiently met their original objection, and the Liberal Leaders were prepared to suggest the acceptance by their Party Members of the Government proposal.

Having regard to the measure of agreement in principle on proposals for the revised composition of the Second Chamber, the Liberal Leaders deplored the breaking off of further discussions by reason only of a matter of three months in the suspensory period. This, in their view, is a matter of minor importance, which should have been capable of adjustment.

11. The representatives of all three Parties were united in their desire to see the House of Lords continue to play its proper part in the Legislature; and in particular to exercise the valuable functions of revising Bills sent up by the Commons, and initiating discussion on public affairs. It was regarded as essential, moreover, that there should be available to the country a legislative body composed of men of mature judgment and experience gained in many spheres of public

life. But the Government representatives and the representatives of the Official Opposition considered that the difference between them on the subject of Powers was fundamental, and not related only to the length of the "period of delay."

In these circumstances, the Party representatives concluded that there did not exist between them that basis for further discussions which would warrant carrying negotiations beyond their present stage.

THE FUNCTIONS OF PARLIAMENT, 1951

House of Commons Debates, 13 November 1951; Official Report, c. 842

MR. HAROLD MACMILLAN: Parliament has, of course, three main purposes: first, to vote supplies; second, to deal with legislation, mainly that put forward by the Government of the day; but third, and of equal importance, what Mr. Asquith [*sic*] used to call the "Grand Inquest of the Nation." . . . I think all of us know what it means; it means chivvying the Ministers. . . .

SECTION III

The Executive

EXPERTS AND MINISTERS ON THE WAR COUNCIL, 1915

First Report of the Dardanelles Commission (Cd. 8,490, 1917)

14. From the commencement of the war until November 25th, 1914 . . . no change was made in the machinery for the superior conduct of naval and military operations. That machinery consisted . . . of the Cabinet, assisted by the Committee of Imperial Defence, with the War Office and the Admiralty acting as its executive agents. The Cabinet at that time consisted of twenty-two members. It must have been obvious from the first that it was far too numerous to control effectively the conduct of the war, more especially by reason of the fact that many of the Ministers presided over Departments which, in some cases, were very slightly and, in others, were in no degree concerned with warlike operations. Thus, for four months, during which time events of the utmost importance were occurring, the machinery employed for designing and controlling the higher operations of the war was both clumsy and inefficient. Eventually some improvement was effected. The War Council took the place of the Committee of Imperial Defence.[1]

15. The composition and functions of the War Council did not materially differ from those of the Committee of Imperial Defence. A change of some importance was, however, made in the procedure. It had been the practice to pass round the notes of the proceedings at the meetings of the Committee of Imperial Defence to all the members who had been present, and who were thus able to correct any inaccuracies that might occur in the representation of their views. Owing to the great press of business, this practice was abandoned by the War Council. Longhand notes were, indeed, kept by the Secretary, but these, of course, cannot carry the same authority as corrected minutes. . . .

16. The main change which was effected was, however, in connection with the powers of the Council as compared to those of the Committee of Imperial Defence. Whilst the latter body was in existence, the responsibility for all important decisions remained, theoretically in all, and practically in most cases, with the united Cabinet. The War Council remained, like the Committee of Imperial Defence, a Committee of the Cabinet with some experts added. Theoretically, the powers of the united Cabinet remained the same as before. Practically, they underwent a radical change. It was the Council, and not the united Cabinet, which finally decided the most important matters,

[1] From June, 1915, onwards, the "War Council" was termed the "Dardanelles Committee." After the Coalition Government was formed a "War Committee" was instituted. Its functions did not differ from those of the War Council, but its composition underwent some change.

and gave effect to its decisions without necessarily waiting for any expression of assent or dissent from the Cabinet. The Cabinet appear to have been generally informed of any important decisions which may have been taken by the Council, but not until after the necessary executive steps had been taken to give whole or partial effect to those decisions. . . .

17. It is obvious that the main questions which came under the consideration of the War Council in connection with the Dardanelles operations were of a highly technical nature on which the opinions only of those who were possessed of naval or military knowledge or experience would be of any real value. It is, therefore, essential to ascertain, with as great a degree of accuracy as possible, what was the precise position assigned to the expert members of the Council. . . .

19. . . . Expert naval advice was represented by Lord Fisher, the First Sea Lord. . . . The view taken by Lord Fisher of his own position at the War Council may be gathered from the following extract from his evidence:

The Chairman: I should like you to explain why you thought that at the War Council there were only two alternatives before you, one to yield your opinion absolutely and the other to resign. You were on a consultative body. Is it possible to carry on business with a consultative body on such a basis as that? —*A.* I can make it clear to you. The War Council only consisted of the Cabinet Ministers. We were not members of the War Council. . . . We were the experts there who were to open our mouths when told to.

Q. Nothing else?—*A.* Nothing else. . . .

Conclusions

(*o*) We are unable to concur in the view set forth by Lord Fisher that it was his duty, if he differed from the Chief of his Department, to maintain silence at the Council or to resign. We think that the adoption of any such principle generally would impair the efficiency of the public service.

[Mr. Andrew Fisher and Sir Thomas Mackenzie dissented from this conclusion, Mr. Fisher writing: "I dissent in the strongest terms from any suggestion that the Departmental Advisers of a Minister in his company at a Council Meeting should express any views at all other than to the Minister and through him, unless specifically invited to do so. I am of opinion it would seal the fate of responsible government if servants of the State were to share the responsibility of Ministers to Parliament and to the people on matters of public policy. . . ."]

THE WAR CABINET, 1917

Cd. 9,005, 1918

The most important constitutional development in the United Kingdom during the last year has been the introduction of the War Cabinet system. This change was the direct outcome of the war itself. As the magnitude of the war increased, it became evident that the Cabinet system of peace days was inadequate to cope with the novel conditions. The enlarged scope of Government activity and the consequent creation of several new departments, made a Cabinet consisting of all the Departmental Ministers meeting under the Chairmanship of the Prime Minister, far too unwieldy for the practical conduct of the war. It was extremely difficult for so large a body to give that resolute central direction which became more imperative the more the population and resources of the nation had to be organised for a single purpose —the defeat of German militarism. Even the development of a comparatively small War Committee did not entirely meet the needs of the case, as the final responsibility rested not with them but with the Cabinet.

With the change of government, therefore, a new method of governmental organisation was introduced. The system of the War Cabinet distinguishes between the body which is responsible for the supreme direction of the war and the Ministers who have charge of the great administrative departments of State. The general direction of the policy of His Majesty's Government during the war rests with the War Cabinet, whose members, with one exception, are relieved of the day to day preoccupations of administrative work, and whose time is, therefore, entirely available for initiating policy and for the work of co-ordinating the great Departments of State. The original members of the War Cabinet were: the Prime Minister, the Right Hon. Earl Curzon, the Right Hon. Viscount Milner, the Right Hon. A. Bonar Law, and the Right Hon. Arthur Henderson. Since then the Right Hon. Sir Edward Carson has been added to the War Cabinet, and the Right Hon. G. N. Barnes has taken the place of Mr. Henderson. In addition, in June, 1917, the War Cabinet invited General Smuts, who had attended the meetings of the Imperial War Cabinet as the Representative of the Union of South Africa, to attend the meetings of the War Cabinet during his stay in the British Isles. The only exception to the principle laid down above that the members of the War Cabinet should be free from administrative duties was in the case of Mr. Bonar Law, who filled the office of the Chancellor of the Exchequer, and one of whose principal duties was to act as the chief representative of the Government in the House of Commons.

The method of working the War Cabinet is as follows. At each

meeting the Cabinet begins by hearing reports as to the progress of the
war since the previous day. Unless it wishes to confine its deliberations
to general questions of policy, it then proceeds to deal with questions
awaiting its decision. As these questions in the vast majority of cases
affect one or more of the administrative departments, almost all its
meetings are attended by the ministers and their chief departmental
officials concerned. The majority of the sessions of the War Cabinet
consist, therefore, of a series of meetings between members of the War
Cabinet and those responsible for executive action at which questions
of policy concerning those departments are discussed and settled.
Questions of overlapping or conflict between departments are determined and the general lines of policy throughout every branch of the
administration co-ordinated so as to form part of a consistent war plan.
Ministers have full discretion to bring with them any experts, either
from their own departments or from outside, whose advice they consider would be useful. The extent to which this policy of inviting
expert assistance is carried may be judged from the fact that from
December 9th, 1916, to December, 1917, no less than 248 persons other
than members of the War Cabinet and the Secretariat have attended
its meetings. These include experts on Foreign, Dominion, Indian,
Colonial Affairs, Finance, Man-Power, Labour, Munitions and Industry, Shipping and Shipbuilding, Agriculture, Food Control, Education, Trade, Railways and Local Government, etc. The Secretary of
State for Foreign Affairs, the First Sea Lord of the Admiralty, and the
Chief of the Imperial General Staff attend at every meeting to communicate the latest intelligence in regard to the war and to consult
with the War Cabinet on questions that arise from day to day. Under
this system the War Cabinet has held more than 300 meetings in the
past year. This fact in itself indicates the great change which has taken
place in the work of the Cabinet.

In practice a considerable number of less important, but often
highly complex, questions are referred to individual members of the
War Cabinet or to Committees of Ministers or others. In some cases
the Minister or Committee has power to decide, in others the instruction is to carry out a detailed investigation such as the War Cabinet
itself could not usefully undertake and submit a Report for final
decision to the Cabinet. By this means the War Cabinet is enabled to
carry out exhaustive investigations without the whole of its members
being overburdened with the details of every question.

Apart from the attendance of the Ministers in charge of the Departments concerned, certain other arrangements are made to ensure that
the Government Departments are kept in close touch with the policy
of the Cabinet, and, conversely, that the members of the War Cabinet
are kept in touch with the policy and action of the various Departments. Minutes are kept of the discussions of the War Cabinet.

Complete files of these minutes are sent to the Ministers most closely concerned in the conduct of the war. In addition, copies of the War Cabinet minutes affecting them are sent to all other Departments. Besides this, the Secretariat of the War Cabinet are responsible for preparing weekly reports by arrangement with the Secretaries of State for Foreign Affairs, India and the Colonies on the matters with which they are concerned. These reports are circulated widely to all Ministers. Conversely a number of the Government Departments render weekly reports to the War Cabinet and also to other Ministers who are concerned or interested.

The working of the War Cabinet cannot be fully understood without some reference to the Secretariat which has come into existence in order to enable it to do its work. The Secretariat consists of the Secretary, Lieut.-Colonel Sir M. P. A. Hankey, and of ten Assistant Secretaries, with an office establishment located at 2, Whitehall Gardens. Under instructions from the Prime Minister the principal duties of the War Cabinet Secretariat are as follows:

(1) To record the proceedings of the War Cabinet.

(2) To transmit the decisions of the War Cabinet to those Departments which are concerned in giving effect to them or otherwise interested.

(3) To prepare the agenda papers; to arrange for the attendance of Ministers and other persons concerned; and to procure and circulate the documents required for discussion.

(4) To attend to the correspondence connected with the work of the War Cabinet.

(5) To prepare the Reports referred to in the previous section.

In addition to these primary duties the War Cabinet Secretariat provides the British Section of the Secretariat of the Inter-Allied Conferences, of the Supreme War Council at Versailles, the Secretariat of the Imperial War Cabinet, and the Secretariat of the majority of the Sub-Committees working in connection with the War Cabinet. The War Cabinet Secretariat is built up on the nucleus of the Secretariat of the Committee of Imperial Defence, which provided a system of liaison officers between the Committee and the Admiralty, War Office, India Office, and Colonial Office. This system has now been extended. Additional officers have been added, so that a liaison is now established between the War Cabinet Secretariat and all the Departments of the Government. This provides yet another means of securing touch between the War Cabinet and the various Government Departments. The Secretariat has also developed an organisation for the rapid distribution of documents dealing with inter-departmental matters of all kinds, which is by no means the least important branch of its work.

In addition to the War Cabinet Secretariat there was created a small Prime Minister's Secretariat to assist the Prime Minister in the discharge of the heavy responsibilities which fall upon him under the War Cabinet system.

The introduction of the War Cabinet system has resulted in considerable modifications of the administrative system of the Government. In the first place it has freed the various departmental Ministers from the constant necessity which rested upon them under the old Cabinet system of considering those wider aspects of public policy which often had nothing to do with their departments, but for which they were collectively responsible. They are, therefore, now able to devote a far larger part of their time to those administrative duties, which have become more exacting as the national activities have expanded under the pressure of the war. Secondly, it has made possible an increase in the number of Ministerial officers so as to effect a better distribution of functions. The new Ministries created since the introduction of the War Cabinet are the Ministries of Labour, Shipping, Food, Air, National Service, Pensions and Reconstruction. The method whereby the Ministers are kept in touch with one another and with the War Cabinet has already been described. . . .

THE UNREFORMED CABINET

House of Lords Debates, 19 June 1918; Official Report, cc. 263 sqq.

EARL CURZON OF KEDLESTON: . . . Let me begin by asking, what was the old Cabinet system which the present Government was intended to replace? . . . My noble friends will bear me out when I say that meetings of the Cabinet were most irregular; sometimes only once, seldom more than twice a week. There was no agenda, there was no order of business. Any Minister requiring to bring up a matter either of Departmental or of public importance had to seek the permission of the Prime Minister to do so. No one else, broadly speaking, was warned in advance. It was difficult for any Minister to secure an interstice in the general discussion in which he could place his own case. No record whatever was kept of our proceedings, except the private and personal letter written by the Prime Minister to the Sovereign, the contents of which, of course, are never seen by anybody else. The Cabinet often had the very haziest notion as to what its decisions were; and I appeal not only to my own experience but to the experience of every Cabinet Minister who sits in this House, and to the records contained in the memoirs of half a dozen Prime Ministers in the past, that cases frequently arose when the matter was left so much in doubt that a Minister went away and acted upon what he thought was a decision which subsequently turned out to be no decision at all, or was repudiated by his colleagues. No one will deny that a system, however embedded in the traditions of the past and consecrated by constitutional custom, which was attended by these defects was a system which was destined, immediately it came into contact with the hard realities of war, to crumble into dust at once.

THE MACHINERY OF GOVERNMENT, 1918

Report of the Machinery of Government Committee (of which Lord Haldane was chairman) (Cd. 9,230, 1918)

2. We were appointed "To enquire into the responsibilities of the various Departments of the central executive Government, and to advise in what manner the exercise and distribution by the Government of its functions should be improved."

3. We have endeavoured to define in the first place the general principles which should govern the distribution of the responsibilities in question. . . .

The Cabinet

5. But before dealing . . . with Departmental organisation, some reference must be made to the functions and procedure of the Cabinet, which is the mainspring of all the mechanism of Government. Its constitution and the methods of its procedure must depend to a large extent on the circumstances of the time, on the personality of the Prime Minister, and on the capacities of his principal colleagues. . . .

6. The main functions of the Cabinet may, we think, be described as:

(a) the final determination of the policy to be submitted to Parliament;

(b) the supreme control of the national executive in accordance with the policy prescribed by Parliament; and

(c) the continuous co-ordination and delimitation of the activities of the several Departments of State.

7. For the due performance of these functions the following conditions seem to be essential, or, at least, desirable:

(i) The Cabinet should be small in number—preferably ten or, at the most, twelve; (ii) it should meet frequently; (iii) it should be supplied in the most convenient form with all the information and material necessary to enable it to arrive at expeditious decisions; (iv) it should make a point of consulting personally all the Ministers whose work is likely to be affected by its decisions; and (v) it should have a systematic method of securing that its decisions are effectually carried out by the several Departments concerned.

8. . . . It is sufficient to point out that during the war an entirely new type of Cabinet has been evolved, with new methods of procedure. . . .

Formulation of Policy

12. . . . We have come to the conclusion . . . that in the sphere of civil government the duty of investigation and thought, as preliminary to action, might with great advantage be more definitely recognised. . . .

14. . . . [We] urged strongly (*a*) that in all Departments better provision should be made for enquiry, research, and reflection before policy is defined and put into operation; (*b*) that for some purposes the necessary research and enquiry should be carried out or supervised by a Department of Government specially charged with these duties, but working in the closest collaboration with the administrative Departments concerned with its activities. . . .

16. A Cabinet with such knowledge at its disposal would, we believe, be in a position to devolve, with greater freedom and confidence than is at present the case, the duties of administration, and even of legislation. . . .

Allocation of Functions between Departments

18. . . . Upon what principle are the functions of Departments to be determined and allocated? There appear to be only two alternatives, which may be briefly described as distribution according to the persons or classes to be dealt with, and distribution according to the services to be performed. Under the former method each Minister who presides over a Department would be responsible to Parliament for those activities of the Government which affect the sectional interests of particular classes of persons, and there might be, for example, a Ministry for Paupers, a Ministry for Children, a Ministry for Insured Persons, or a Ministry for the Unemployed. Now the inevitable outcome of this method of organisation is a tendency to Lilliputian administration. It is impossible that the specialised service which each Department has to render to the community can be as high a standard when its work is at the same time limited to a particular class of persons and extended to every variety of provision for them, as when the Department concentrates itself on the provision of one particular service only, by whomsoever required, and looks beyond the interests of comparatively small classes.

19. The other method, and the one which we recommend for adoption, is that of defining the field of activity in the case of each Department according to the particular service which it renders to the community as a whole. Thus a Ministry of Education would be concerned predominantly with the provision of education wherever, and by whomsoever, needed. Such a Ministry would have to deal with persons in so far only as they were to be educated, and not with

articular classes of persons defined on other principles. This method
annot of course, be applied with absolute rigidity. The work of the
Education Department, for example, may incidentally trench on the
phere of Health, as in the arrangements of school houses and care for
he health of scholars. Such incidental overlapping is inevitable, and
ny difficulties to which it may give rise must in our opinion be met
y systematic arrangements for the collaboration of Departments
jointly interested in particular spheres of work. But notwithstanding
uch necessary qualifications, we think that much would be gained if
he distribution of departmental duties were guided by a general
rinciple, and we have come to the conclusion that distribution
ccording to the nature of the service to be rendered to the community as a whole is the principle which is likely to lead to the mini-
num amount of confusion and overlapping. . . .

21. It will be noticed that in certain cases the two principles of dis-
ribution which we have contrasted . . . may lead to an identical concentration of functions. Thus, the great service of National Defence,
which (whether given to one, or to two or to three Ministries) is
ssentially distinct from the function of the other Ministries, is also
marked off by dealing, principally and specifically, with the large
umber of persons employed by the Government in all the various
ranches of the naval, military, and air services. In like manner, if the
ailways and canals should be nationalised, it would be necessary to
nake the administration of this great service of National Transport a
separate Department, whether we had regard to the nature of the
ervice thus rendered to the community, or to the dealings with so
xtensive a staff as would have to be employed. In short, there are, in
elation to such nationalised services, two distinct forms of expert
apacity which it is essential that the organisation should develop.
One of these is ability in the recruitment, promotion, co-ordination,
nd direction of a large body of persons of different grades and capa-
ities, engaged in a common enterprise of a peculiar nature. . . . The
ther form of special ability in such nationalised occupations, certainly
o less important, but of a different nature, is ability for the fulfilment
f the technical requirements of the service which the Department has
o render to the community. . . .

22. We may conclude that where any great enterprise is nationalised
—in the sense of being carried out, in the main, by persons in direct
overnment employment—as is the case with regard to National
efence and the Postal and Telegraph service, and as may possibly be
he case with regard to railways and the coal supply, such an adminis-
ation must form the sphere of a separate Ministry or Ministries. . . .

29. *Financial Control.* . . . [We] think that all Departments should
nclude in their staff an officer of high grade specially charged with
nancial duties, provided with a financial staff sufficiently strong to

enable him to maintain a continuous survey of all proposals for expenditure originating within the Department, and regularly consulted before any decision on a matter of financial importance is arrived at by the Minister.

30. *Intra-Departmental Meetings.* We would draw attention to the arrangements adopted as part of the recent reorganisation of the Board of Trade for holding regular meetings of the Minister, the Parliamentary Secretaries, the permanent Heads of the Department and the principal officers concerned, for the purpose of dealing with questions of policy which affect more than one section of the Board. . .

31. *Organisation and Ministerial Responsibility.* We think that in arrangements of this kind may be found one answer to the objection which are sometimes raised to placing the sole responsibility for the administration of great Departments in the hands of a single Minister. Attempts have been made to distribute the burden of responsibility by other means. In some cases, recourse has been had to the system of administrative Boards. We draw attention to the findings of the Royal Commission on the Civil Service[1] that this system is less effective in securing responsibility for official action and advice than the system followed in Departments where full responsibility is definitely laid upon the Minister; and we think that where, as in the case of the Insurance Commissioners, a Board is set up without explicit statutory provision for a Minister responsible to Parliament for their work, the position is obviously unsatisfactory.

32. But the doctrine of Ministerial responsibility has also been criticised in another way. It has been said that there are certain functions of Government which require for their exercise a judicial temper and a position of independence that cannot be maintained by a Minister who is constantly exposed to criticism in Parliament. . .

33. We are so far from thinking that the importance of a service to the community is prima facie a reason for making those who administer it immune from ordinary Parliamentary criticism, that we feel that all such proposals should be most carefully scrutinised, and that there should be no omission, in the case of any particular service, of those safeguards which Ministerial responsibility to Parliament alone provides.

34. *Advisory Committees.* But the preservation of the full responsibility of Ministers for executive action will not, in our opinion, ensure that the course of administration which they adopt will secure and retain public confidence, unless it is recognised as an obligation upon Departments to avail themselves of the advice and assistance of advisory bodies so constituted as to make available the knowledge and experience of all sections of the community affected by the activities of the Department. . . .

[1] Fourth Report (1914), Ch. IX, paras. 68, 69, 72.

Parliamentary Control

48. . . . Our terms of reference direct us to frame our recommendations with the primary object of promoting the efficient and economical working of the public service. But we have throughout our deliberations borne in mind the fact that any action directed to this end would fail to achieve its purpose if it were to have the effect of disturbing the balance of authority between the Legislature and the Executive.

It would, we think, be generally felt that any improvement in the organisation of the Departments of State which was so marked as substantially to increase their efficiency should have as its correlative an increase in the power of the Legislature as the check upon the acts and proposals of the Executive. . . .

52. We should hesitate to enter . . . upon questions of procedure which Parliament alone can examine or determine with authority, were it not that it has been definitely suggested to us that the efficiency of the public service would be improved if steps were taken to secure the continuous and well-informed interest of a Parliamentary body in the execution by each Department of the policy which Parliament has laid down.

53. It has been suggested that the appointment of a series of Standing Committees, each charged with the consideration of the activities of the Departments which cover the main divisions of the business of Government, would be conducive to this end. Any such Committees would require to be furnished with full information as to the course of administration pursued by the Departments with which they were concerned; and for this purpose it would be requisite that Ministers, as well as the officers of Departments, should appear before them to explain and defend the acts for which they were responsible. . . .

Conclusion

55. If the principle which we have suggested in this Part of the Report, that the business of the various Departments of Government should be distributed as far as possible according to the class of service with which they are concerned, be accepted, the business of Government would fall into one or other of the following main divisions:

I.—Finance. II and III.—National Defence and External Affairs. IV.—Research and Information. V.—Production (including Agriculture, Forestry, and Fisheries), Transport, and Commerce. VI.—Employment. VII.—Supplies. VIII.—Education. IX.—Health. X.—Justice.

Rbg

It does not follow that there would be only one Minister for each of these branches. Some of them would undoubtedly require more than one.

[Part II is concerned with the detailed application of the principles enunciated above to the Departments.]

CO-ORDINATION OF DEFENCE FORCES, 1923

Recommendations of the National and Imperial Defence Committee (Cmd. 1,938, 1923)

The following decisions have been taken by His Majesty's Government on the recommendations of the National and Imperial Defence Committee:

(1) It is undesirable and impracticable to supersede the Ministerial heads of the three Fighting Services by making them subordinates of a Minister of Defence; the alternative plan for an amalgamation of the three Service Departments is equally impracticable.

(2) On the other hand, the existing system of co-ordination by the Committee of Imperial Defence is not sufficient to secure full initiative and responsibility for defence as a whole and requires to be defined and strengthened.

(3) Under the existing system the Committee of Imperial Defence, an advisory and consultative body, enquires into and makes recommendations in regard to the issues of defence policy and organisation which are brought before it. The power of initiative lies with the Government Departments and with the Prime Minister.

(4) This system, though invaluable up to a point, does not make any authority, except the Prime Minister, who can only devote a small part of his time and attention to defence questions, directly responsible for the initiation of a consistent line of policy directing the common action of the three or any two of the three Services, taking account of the reactions of the three Services upon one another.

(5) While, therefore, the existing system of departmental initiative will continue, the responsibility for the wider initiative referred to above in Paragraph (4) will also rest with the Chairman of the Committee of Imperial Defence acting under the general direction of the Committee of Imperial Defence and with the assistance of the three Chiefs of Staff.

(6) In accordance with the terms of the Treasury Minute of 4 May 1904, constituting the Committee of Imperial Defence in its present form, the Committee of Imperial Defence will continue to consist of the Prime Minister as President, with such other members as, having

regard to the nature of the subject to be discussed, he may from time
to time summon to assist him. In pursuance of a decision by the Prime
Minister, the Committee places on record that the following should be
members:

The Chairman (Deputy to the Prime Minister); the Secretary of
State for War; the Secretary of State for Air; the First Lord of the
Admiralty; the Chancellor of the Exchequer, or the Financial Secretary; the Secretary of State for Foreign Affairs; the Secretary of State
for the Colonies; the Secretary of State for India; the Chiefs of Staff
of the three Fighting Services; the Permanent Secretary of the Treasury
as head of the Civil Service. In addition to these, other British or
Dominion Ministers of the Crown and other officials, or persons having
special qualifications, will be summoned as members by the President
according to the nature of the business.

(7) The functions of the Chairman of the Committee of Imperial
Defence will be:

(i) To preside over the Committee of Imperial Defence in the
absence of the Prime Minister.

(ii) To report to the Prime Minister (when he himself has not presided) and to the Cabinet the recommendations of the Committee of
Imperial Defence.

(iii) In matters of detail, to interpret the decisions of the Prime
Minister and the Cabinet thereupon to the Departments concerned.

(iv) Assisted by the three Chiefs of Staff, as laid down in Paragraph
(5) above, to keep the defence situation as a whole constantly under
review so as to ensure that defence preparations and plans and the
expenditure thereupon, are co-ordinated and framed to meet policy,
that full information as to the changing naval, military and air
situation may always be available to the Committee of Imperial
Defence and that resolutions as to the requisite action thereupon may
be submitted for its consideration.

(8) In addition to the functions of the Chiefs of Staff as advisers on
questions of sea, land or air policy respectively, to their own Board or
Council, each of the three Chiefs of Staff will have an individual and
collective responsibility for advising on defence policy as a whole, the
three constituting, as it were, a Super-Chief of a War Staff in Commission. In carrying out this function they will meet together for the
discussion of questions which affect their joint responsibilities.

(9) Questions relating to co-ordination of expenditure may be entertained by the Committee of Imperial Defence when referred to it by
the Cabinet. The Committee (subject to any directions by the Cabinet)
will consider such questions in the light of the general defence policy
of the Government and of the strategical plans drawn up to give effect
to that policy in time of war.

(10) The Secretariat of the Committee of Imperial Defence will

continue to act as liaison officers between the Chairman of the Committee and the Service Departments. The staff of the Committee will be strengthened by the addition of an Assistant Secretary to be nominated by the Prime Minister on the recommendation of the Secretary of State for Air, whose status will be identical with that of the three existing Assistant Secretaries nominated by the Prime Minister on the nomination of the Secretary of State for War, the Secretary of State for India and the First Lord of the Admiralty.

(11) The Standing Defence Sub-Committee is suppressed and its past proceedings will be merged into those of the Committee of Imperial Defence.

THE PUBLIC CORPORATION, 1925

Report of the Broadcasting Committee, 1925 (Cmd. 2,599, 1926)

3. Broadcasting has become so widespread, concerns so many people, and is fraught with such far-reaching possibilities, that the organisation laid down for the British Broadcasting Company no longer corresponds to national requirements or responsibility. Notwithstanding the progress which we readily acknowledge, and to the credit of which the Company is largely entitled, we are impelled to the conclusion that no company or body constituted on trade lines for the profit, direct or indirect, of those composing it can be regarded as adequate in view of the broader considerations now beginning to emerge.

5. . . . we do not recommend a prolongation of the licence of the British Broadcasting Company, or the establishment of any similar body composed of persons who represent particular interests. We think a public corporation the most appropriate organisation. Such an authority would enjoy a freedom and flexibility which a Minister of State himself could scarcely exercise in arranging for performers and programmes, and in studying the variable demands of public taste and necessity. The authority can be set up by Statute or under the Companies Acts. However established, it would hold the licence of the Postmaster-General, and in view of the scale, significance and potentialities of Broadcasting, the proposed corporation should be invested with full authority. Its status and duties should correspond with those of a public service, and its directorate should be appointed with the sole object of promoting the utmost utility and development of the enterprise. We think the "British Broadcasting Commission" would be a suitable title for the new authority. . . .

16. . . . We have framed our report . . . with the knowledge that the

State, through Parliament, must retain the right of ultimate control.
We assume that the Postmaster-General would be the Parliamentary
spokesman on broad questions of policy, though we think it essential
that the Commission should not be subject to the continuing Ministerial
guidance and direction which apply to Government Offices. The progress of science and the harmonies of art will be hampered by too
rigid rules and too constant a supervision by the State. Within well-
defined limits the Commission should enjoy the fullest liberty, wide
enough to mark the serious duties laid upon it, and elastic enough to
permit variation according to technical developments and changes in
public taste. It would discourage enterprise and initiative, both as
regards experiments and the intricate problem of programmes, were
the authority subjected to too much control. The aspirations and the
public obligations of Broadcasting can best be studied by a body
appointed ad hoc, endowed with adequate tenure, and concentrating
on this particular duty. The Commissioners should therefore be
invested with the maximum of freedom which Parliament is prepared
to concede.

THE REPUTATION OF THE CIVIL SERVANT, 1928

(*Cmd. 3,037*)

[In February, 1928, the Prime Minister appointed a Board of Enquiry of
three senior Civil Servants, to examine statements made during the case of
Ironmonger & Co. v. Dyne that three members of the Foreign Office had
been speculating in foreign currency.]

56. The first duty of a Civil Servant is to give his undivided allegiance to the State at all times and on all occasions when the State has a
claim upon his services. With his private activities the State is in
general not concerned, so long as his conduct therein is not such as
to bring discredit upon the Service of which he is a member. But to
say that he is not to subordinate his duty to his private interests, nor
to make use of his official position to further those interests, is to say
no more than that he must behave with common honesty. The Service
exacts from itself a higher standard, because it recognises that the
State is entitled to demand that its servants shall not only be honest
in fact, but beyond the reach of suspicion of dishonesty. It was laid
down by one of His Majesty's Judges in a case some few years ago
that it was not merely of some importance but of fundamental
importance that in a Court of Law justice should not only be done,
but should manifestly and undoubtedly be seen to be done. . . . We
apply without hesitation an analogous rule to other branches of the

public service. A Civil Servant is not to subordinate his duty to his
private interests; but neither is he to put himself in a position where
his duty and his interests conflict. He is not to make use of his official
position to further those interests; but neither is he so to order his
private affairs as to allow the suspicion to arise that a trust has been
abused or a confidence betrayed. These obligations are, we do not
doubt, universally recognised throughout the whole of the Service;
if it were otherwise, its public credit would be diminished and its
usefulness to the State impaired.

57. It follows that there are spheres of activity legitimately open to
the ordinary citizen in which the Civil Servant can play no part, or
only a limited part. He is not to indulge in political or party controversy, lest by so doing he should appear no longer the disinterested
adviser of Ministers or able impartially to execute their policy. He is
bound to maintain a proper reticence in discussing public affairs and
more particularly those with which his own Department is concerned.
And lastly, his position clearly imposes upon him restrictions in matters
of commerce and business from which the ordinary citizen is free.

THE LEGISLATIVE AND JUDICIAL POWERS OF THE EXECUTIVE, 1929-32

[The Committee on Ministers' Powers was appointed by the Lord Chancellor
on 30 October 1929, "to consider the powers exercised by or under the direction of (or by persons or bodies appointed specially by) Ministers of the Crown
by way of (a) delegated legislation and (b) judicial or quasi-judicial decision,
and to report what safeguards are desirable or necessary to secure the constitutional principles of the sovereignty of Parliament and the supremacy of
the law".

The original members of the Committee were: the Earl of Donoughmore
(chairman), Sir John Anderson, the Duchess of Atholl, the Rev. James Barr,
Dr. E. L. Burgin, the Earl of Clarendon, Sir Warren Fisher, Sir Roger Gregory,
Professor H. J. Laski, Sir William S. Holdsworth, Sir W. Ellis Hume-Williams,
Sir Leslie Scott, Mr. Gavin Simmonds, Miss Ellen Wilkinson, and Sir John J.
Withers. The Countess of Iveagh was appointed as an additional member in
January 1930. The Earl of Donoughmore resigned the chairmanship on
grounds of health in April 1931, and was succeeded by Sir Leslie (later Lord
Justice) Scott. The Committee published its report in 1932.]

I

EVIDENCE BEFORE THE COMMITTEE

(A) Sir Maurice L. Gwyer, H.M. Procurator-General and Treasury Solicitor, Called and Examined:

(*The Witness handed in the subjoined memorandum on . . . "delegated legislation."*)

3. . . . [Every] Departmental power, whether of delegated legislation or of judicial functions, has been conferred by Parliament itself. Criticism of the Departments either for possessing or for exercising such powers (as distinct from the manner of their exercise) is in truth a criticism of Parliament itself. It is, however, complained . . . that Ministers on the instigation of their Departments force upon Parliament legislative proposals which are undesirable in the public interest, and that Parliament, faced with the choice either of accepting measures of which it disapproves or of precipitating a political crisis, finds itself compelled to choose what it presumably regards as the lesser evil, and that the Departments take advantage for their own ends of this dilemma. If the dilemma exists . . . the remedy lies with Parliament itself. . . .

4. In the second place, it is trite doctrine that for every official act of his Department the Minister must accept responsibility in Parliament. A Civil Servant is not responsible to Parliament but only to the Minister who presides over his Department, and the responsibility of the Civil Servant is at an end when the Minister has either accepted or rejected the advice which the Civil Servant has tendered to him. To impute responsibility to Civil Servants for legislative proposals accepted by a Minister and enacted by Parliament is as illogical as it is unjust. Those who do so must recognise that their criticism is directed not merely, nor indeed primarily, against the Civil Service but against the system of Cabinet and Parliamentary Government, and is in fact destructive of the whole theory of ministerial responsibility on which that system is based.

5. Thirdly, the popular portrait of the Civil Servant, avid of power and unscrupulous in his manner of attaining it, is to those who know the facts so remote from real life as to be almost laughable. . . . A bureaucracy in the true sense of the word does not and cannot exist in England, or indeed under any system of parliamentary government; for . . . the word is borrowed from Continental systems of the past, where both Ministers and Civil Servants owed a duty to the Monarch alone, and could not be held responsible by any popularly elected body.

6. Fourthly, it is probably realised only by a few how vast is the

mass of business at the present day transacted by Government Departments, and how small a part of it is represented by those powers and
duties which fall within the terms of reference of the Committee. . . .
Civil Servants have not the time, even if they had the desire, to devote
their energies to the acquisition of power for the purpose of harassing
the King's subjects. . . .

25. The Committee will, I hope, permit me in conclusion to suggest
that the subject matter of their investigation is not merely one of the
scope of Departmental powers at the present time. It goes far deeper
and involves the whole philosophy and technique of modern government. The greater the complexity of our civilisation and the wider the
range of our legislation, the more difficult it is for a popularly elected
legislature to exercise complete control over administrative policy.
The utmost under present conditions that it can do in fact is to secure
that competent administrators are chosen and to enforce strictly the
principle of administrative responsibility; and fundamental change
would imply the adoption of a new theory of government. . . .

Sir Leslie Scott

63. One question about the check afforded by putting the regulations
before Parliament. Do you think that that is in practice a check of
any real value?—. . . [64] No, I do not think it is. That merely informs
Parliament of what is going on in the administrative sphere, but the
power of praying for annulment by address is a real check. . . .

68. Take the affirmative form, as distinguished from the negative,
requiring that the regulations should be confirmed by a Resolution of
each House?—With great respect, that does seem to me to be the wrong
method, because it is inviting Parliament to enter the administrative
sphere, because at any rate the making of the Regulations after Parliament has given the power to make them is an administrative act,
and I do not think that Parliament can share with the Executive the
functions of administration. You at once get a divided responsibility,
and the Minister could then throw the whole responsibility on to a
legislative and deliberative body of exercising functions which, with
the greatest respect to it, it really is not within its sphere to exercise. . . .

Sir John Withers

111. Does it not appear to you that there must be two alternative
modes [of exercising control after Regulations have been made] either
by setting up some Parliamentary Committee . . . [112] or to adopt
the system of administrative law and form some sort of administrative
body which should act as a Court of Appeal . . .?—The second suggestion I could answer at once. . . . To form an administrative Court of
Appeal for the purpose of deciding whether a Minister's Orders and

Regulations were suitable or not seems to me to cut at the very root of Parliamentary Government. It is transferring the functions of Parliament to an outside tribunal. . . .

Sir Warren Fisher

165. Assuming that as individuals we do not want to be subject to the arbitrary discretion of the Executive . . . do you really think we have at the present moment as individuals effective safeguards against executive tyranny?— . . . I do not think the control of Parliament over the details of administrative action is always as effective as it possibly ought to be in an ideal State, or possibly as effective as it was 50 years ago in this country, but what the remedy may be, I should be sorry to say.

166. From a parliamentary point of view you would agree that the existence of question time *in terrorem* is about the only safeguard we have?—That is as effective as anything. . . .

Sir Ellis Hume-Williams

399. Well, let me take your definition of quasi-judicial decision (which I accept) as the power of giving a decision on questions or differences of an administrative and non-justiciable character which cannot be determined by reference to any fixed rule of law. . . . [400] Do you think there should be always appeal as of right [to a Court]?— No, certainly not. You would be referring things then to a Court with which the Court has no concern at all. You would be appealing . . . from the rock to the sand.

401. I suppose you mean that the decisions are so shifting?—No, where you have a Court which is administering law, that is the rock. But if you are going to transfer to the Court the duty of deciding things according to discretion where would you get? The appeal in a case like that is to Parliament. It is for Parliament to challenge the Minister's discretion in a matter like that, not the Court. . . . [404] . . . Take . . . the power of the Minister to make an Order extending the boundaries of a municipality. The decision there of the Minister was necessarily a policy decision. There is no principle on which any Court could decide whether the City of Leeds should absorb Morley and Pudsey or not . . . Parliament is the only body that can tackle a matter of that kind. . . .

408. . . . This is section 130 of the Local Government Act [of 1929]:

If any difficulty arises in connection with the application of this Act to any exceptional area or in bringing into operation any of the provisions of this Act the Minister may make such Order for removing the difficulty as he may judge to be necessary for the purpose and any such Order may modify the provisions of this Act so far as may appear to the Minister necessary for carrying the Order into effect.

Do you agree with this, that one result of that section is that there can
be no Orders that are *ultra vires*? If an Order is *ultra vires* the Minister
simply modifies or changes the Act and it becomes *intra vires*?—For a
limited period. . . .

410. Do you think Parliament has gone too far?—No, not a bit.
May I tell you why? We had a similar section in the Insurance Act
of 1911, and I drafted many Orders under that Section, and it is
literally true that the Act could never have started at all but for the
power reserved to the Insurance Commissioners by that Section. . . .

(B) Sir William Graham-Harrison, K.C., First Parliamentary
   Counsel, Called and Examined:

(The Witness handed in the subjoined Memorandum.)

3. . . . speaking from a practical experience, which now extends to
a period of 27 years, of the work of getting legislation through Parliament I have no hesitation in saying that it would be impossible to
produce the amount and the kind of legislation which Parliament
desires to pass, and which the people of this country are supposed to
want, if it became necessary to insert in the Acts of Parliament themselves any considerable portion of what is now left to delegated legislation. As classical examples I would refer to the vast bulk of the National
Health Insurance Regulations and Special Orders, which run to more
than a thousand pages, and to the eight hundred pages of the Orders
setting up trade boards.

I should also like to emphasise a side of the question which appeals
to me particularly as one who has drafted, not only a large number of
Statutes, but also a very large number of Statutory Rules and Orders,
viz. the superiority in form which, as a result of the different circumstances and conditions under which they are respectively prepared and
completed, delegated legislation has over Statutes. In most cases the
time available for drafting Bills is inadequate and their final form when
they have passed both Houses is generally unsatisfactory. On the other
hand, Statutory Rules can be prepared in comparative leisure and
their subject matter can be arranged in a logical and intelligible shape
uncontrolled by the exigencies of Parliamentary procedure and the
necessity for that compression which every Minister (however much in
debate he may use the draftsman as a whipping-boy) invariably
demands in the case of a Bill. . . .

4. . . . In my opinion, one of the most important safeguards against
the improper use of delegated powers (though this applies much more
as respects Regulations of a general character than . . . of a personal
or locally limited character) is the fact that no Minister in his senses
with the fear of Parliament before his eyes would ever think of making
Regulations without (where practicable) giving the persons who will

be affected thereby (or their representatives) an opportunity of saying what they think about the proposal. A large proportion of the Regulations now made, e.g. regulations under the Factories Acts and the Mines Acts, affect two sets of persons who have conflicting interests, viz. the employers and the employed. In these cases the parties on both sides are sufficiently organised to make their views known and felt. It must, however, be admitted that on the other hand there are cases where the persons affected are not sufficiently organised to bring any pressure to bear on the Minister concerned and for them this safeguard does not exist. . . .

5. In conclusion, there are one or two miscellaneous points which deserve the Committee's attention:

(i) At present there are extraordinary and quite indefensible differences in the period for which rules are required to lie before Parliament; in some cases the period is as much as 100 sitting days, in others less than 20. . . .

(ii) The question of the moment at which Statutory Rules and Orders are to take effect requires consideration. . . . As the law stands, there is nothing to secure that the persons affected shall have notice of Rules before they come into operation. Rules may come into force immediately they are made, and the rule-making authority having made them are not under any obligation to publish them but may keep them in a pigeon-hole for any length of time.

(iii) There is one practice which is very popular with some Departments which I think is objectionable, viz. the insertion in Rules of a provision enabling the Minister by whom the Rules are made to revoke or vary some particular provision in the Rules, e.g. a schedule, by a mere direction given by him not in the form of a fresh Rule. I have always taken objection to such proposals and believe them to be illegal; it will be seen that the effect of such a procedure is to withdraw amendments to the Rules from the control of such safeguards as may apply to the making of Rules of the class in question. . . .

Professor Laski

562. Have you thought at all whether the suggestion that has been made from time to time by Members of Parliament and others—consideration of these rules by a Committee or a Joint Committee of the two Houses—would be a valuable way of assuring that Parliamentary attention was drawn to them, in the light of the fact that they are made under powers given by Parliament?—I have only considered the question to this extent. It seems to me quite impossible for any Committee to get through the work within any reasonable limits of time.

563. Supposing instead of a single Committee, or a single Joint Committee, you grouped the different Ministries in some way according to their functions, and had Committees to deal with groups of

subjects. Do you think it would be possible then on the point of time?
—I am rather doubtful about it. But what I feel about any such suggestion is that a large bulk of these rules are very small stuff indeed, and
I really think that Parliament has many more important things to
occupy the attention of its Members. I think the real remedy is that if
Parliament does not like something that a Minister does, it should tell
him so, and take care that he does not do it again. I think it would
really be a great waste of time for Members of Parliament to go
through a great deal of the stuff which appears in a year's volume of
the Statutory Rules and Orders.

564. As an entire outsider, both to Parliament and Ministries, may
I put the kind of problem that a layman like myself feels when you
say that Parliament, when it objects to what the Minister has done,
should tell him so? Can, in fact, Parliament seriously tell a Minister
that it does object, in such a way that a Minister will always take care,
without turning the Government out?—You put a point that I have
thought a great deal about lately. I say it with a good deal of hesitation,
but I think that there is more difficulty about doing that than, according to the theory of the Constitution, there ought to be. I think it is
more difficult now than it was sixty years ago. . . .

Sir Claud Schuster

666. Do you think Departments are so indifferent to what Parliament says as has been suggested?—No.

667. I thought you rather lightly accepted the suggestion that I
understood had been made that Ministers and their Departments
were an impregnable ironclad against which attacks were directed in
vain?—I do not think I meant to say that. . . .

668. The ordinary administrator is a timorous fowl. The one thing
he wants more than anything else is to keep his Minister out of a row?
—Yes.

669. As far as he can manage it?—Certainly.

670. He runs very fast directly a Member of Parliament raises his
voice.
Sir Warren Fisher: Is he not an enthusiast sometimes? . . .

Sir Roger Gregory

695. Will you look at paragraph 5 (ii) of your memorandum. You
refer there to the power of making a rule and not publishing it. Would
it be possible for a person to be prosecuted or penalised under a rule
which has never left the pigeon holes of the Minister who has made
it?—Technically, it would be possible, but I do not know that anybody
would ever be convicted. As soon as it is made, it is the law in force.

696. A Court might have to convict if it was proved it was the law

in force?—There would be some way out of it. He would be a first offender, I should think.

697. That is the fact, that a person can be prosecuted for the infringement of a rule which has never left the office in which it was made?—It might be. There were at one time various provisions that a thing should not come into force until a certain time had elapsed. It is a question worth considering whether there should not be some form of publication. May I mention one case I know in which a statutory rule consisted of nothing more than an interchange of letters between two Departments, and in those letters there was contained a statutory rule?

698. That is a pretty bad case. These things are pretty nearly as bad as Mr. D. . . . , who used to write his rules in a dark place?—That is only what may happen.

699. It is a thing we have to deal with?—I know another case where a statutory rule was forgotten altogether for two years by the person in charge of it. No one knew of it, but there it was, the rule in force. . . .

(C) Mr. C. T. Carr Called and Examined:

(*The Witness handed in the subjoined Memorandum.*)

. . . The advantages of delegating legislative authority—economy of Parliamentary time, availability of expert knowledge, promptness of action and so on—are conspicuous. . . .

It is notorious that during the late war the scale of delegated legislation was beyond all precedent. Indeed, even the figures in the table below do not tell the full tale of D.O.R.A. But it is significant, and perhaps surprising, to find that the tide has now ebbed back to a pre-war mark. In the following table the first column contains the annual totals of all statutory rules and orders registered under Section 3 of the Rules Publication Act since 1894. The second and third columns show these totals split (as prescribed by Treasury regulations) into "general" and "local" rules and orders. The sharpest fluctuations are visible in the "local" class owing to causes susceptible of explanation.

Year	Annual total	General	Local
1894	1,015		
1895	950	246	704
1896	1,229	197	1,032
1897	986	168	818
1898	1,151	200	951
1899	1,000	223	777
1900	995	174	821
1901	1,042	156	886
1902	980	161	819
1903	1,196	170	1,026

Year	Annual total	General	Local
1904	1,899	143	1,756
1905	1,379	162	1,217
1906	986	165	821
1907	1,058	231	827
1908	1,349	256	1,093
1909	1,528	205	1,323
1910	1,368	218	1,150
1911	1,336	172	1,164
1912	1,919	342	1,577
1913	1,406	414	992
1914	1,914	522	1,392
1915	1,241	406	835
1916	941	508	433
1917	1,383	753	630
1918	1,825	1,204	621
1919	2,241	1,091	1,150
1920	2,475	916	1,559
1921	— 2,110	727	1,383
1922	1,450	430	1,020
1923	1,624	366	1,258
1924	1,601	426	1,175
1925	1,461	466	995
1926	1,745	448	1,297
1927	1,349	445	904
1928	1,132	415	717
1929	1,262	391	871

If I may comment first upon the local class, the substantial figures from 1903 to 1905 are due to the Education Act of 1902; the increases in 1908 and 1909 are due to numerous orders for the local application of the Public Health Acts Amendment Act, 1907: similarly the Public Health Act of 1925 swells the local total in 1926 and the following years. Other transitory increases may be caused by epidemics of measles, outbreaks of foot-and-mouth disease, and so on, or, in the post-war period, by floods of "increases of charges" and "extensions of time" orders for public undertakings. The local rules and orders largely consist of some adjustment of local government law or some development of public health for which there has presumably been a local demand, the local standard being often higher than the general. The local Acts of Parliament are a vast uncharted sea. No draftsman framing a measure of general application could confidently cover the possible variations occasioned by local legislation in a matter, for instance, like rating. Hence the need for adjusting general provisions to particular cases by some such machinery as the "removal of difficulties" order. On the whole I doubt whether a student of local rules and orders will discover in them any serious inroad upon liberty or any cause for Parliament to be jealous. . . .

With regard to the total of "general" orders in the second column of the table, it is noticeable that for the first seventeen years the figures fluctuate roughly between 150 and 250. Not till 1912 (the year after the National Insurance Act) do they exceed 300. The total went over 500 in 1914, but the full force of war-time conditions was not felt till 1918. This impetus died away again till in 1922 there was a return to the pre-war figure. After notably steady results from 1922 to 1928, the total dropped last year below the 400 mark, though it is the common opinion that post-war Parliaments are not less generous in delegating legislative power than their predecessors.

The absence of violent fluctuations in the "general" list since 1922 may be evidence that the system is becoming stabilised. . . .

Rules and orders which modify Acts of Parliament are naturally viewed with dislike or suspicion. The mere press-the-button procedure for the operation of a statute on an "appointed day" is of considerable antiquity and proved convenience; but it seems improper that a statute—in the making of which all of us have in theory participated through our representatives—should be interfered with by a body subordinate to Parliament. Two large classes of instances seem unobjectionable. First, there is the case where Parliament, instead of delegating some matter of minor detail to be dealt with by departmental rule or order from the outset, inserts its own ideas of the matter in the text of the Act and then allows the department to modify them from time to time. This matter appears hardly more sinister than if the matter had been entrusted to departmental legislation from the beginning. Subject to proper safeguards, it seems appropriate in such instances as the list of poisons scheduled to the Poisons and Pharmacy Act, 1908; untidy results can be periodically cleaned up by consolidation. The second class contains those cases where Parliament, having changed the law in general terms, allows the consequential modifications to be specifically worked out by rule or order. The use of "legislation by reference," whereby enactments passed for one purpose are applied to a quite different purpose, involves textual adaptations frequently effected (if specified at all) by delegated legislation. Similar adaptation is sometimes permitted when one central authority is substituted for another. . . .

The machinery of registering Statutory Rules and Orders is governed by section 3 of the Rules Publication Act, a provision inserted at the last moment into the Bill which the Law Society had prepared for the different purpose of ensuring prior notice of intention to make rules of court.

Under section 3 the statutory rules must be sent to the King's Printer (who is the controller of H.M. Stationery Office) "forthwith after they are made," and must, in accordance with Treasury regulations, be numbered, printed and put on sale. . . .

A rule-making authority which hid its rules in a pigeon-hole would be breaking the statutory direction. . . . When the 1893 Act first began to operate, it is probable that all departments were not equally alert in sending their rules and orders for registration under section 3, although in October, 1894, the Queen's Printer issued a printed circular asking that copies should be sent him. Occasionally, omissions are still detected, some serious, some trivial. . . .

If it were felt that some drastic step was necessary in order to prevent the possible hushing up of departmental legislation, the Committee might care to consider the suggestion that no rule or order should have any validity until registered. . . .

There is nothing new in the principle of delegated legislation. Plato makes his Athenian Stranger say that, though the lawgiver may write out the laws as precisely as he can, the test of time will show him that he must leave some things over for someone else to put right. . . .

Nor is the principle wrong in itself. If may be a breach of Montesquieu's theory of the separation of powers. If the executive, the legislature and the judiciary are pictured as three independent and self-willed drivers of one vehicle, each of whom can and will apply a powerful brake against the others, the vehicle may not run over any pedestrians but on the other hand it may not move at all. The problem would seem to be one not of right and wrong but of balance of public advantage—is the administrative convenience of delegated legislation outweighed by loss of individual liberty or other disadvantage . . . ?

There are two primary safeguards of individual liberty against the possible menace of delegated legislation. First, in respect of policy and administration, there are various well known methods of bringing home any abuse to a minister responsible to Parliament. . . .

Secondly, in respect of legal validity, there is the judicial power (to be strengthened if necessary) to pronounce upon questions of *vires*. . . .

Another valuable safeguard is preliminary consultation with the interests affected. This course is often prescribed by statute. The Advisory Committee under the London Traffic Act . . . is a miniature Parliament in itself. . . .

(D) Mr. W. A. Robson Called and Examined:

(*The Witness handed in the subjoined memorandum.*)

1. . . . The Separation of Powers is a legendary conception which has at no period of English history accurately described the actual division of authority between the various organs of government.

There is no immutable necessity for any particular division of powers. Nor has any organ of government a vested right to exercise a particular function. It is misleading and unscientific to use language which implies such a right. For example, it is common to speak of the "encroachment" of the Executive on the sphere of the Judiciary. As I shall show, the fields of jurisdiction of which complaint is made concern the newer functions of government. There can scarcely be "encroachment" on territory which has not previously been settled. . . .

2. . . . An opposition exists in England between the ideas of "law" and of "government." . . . The struggle between King and Commons has now become transformed into a conflict between the Executive on the one hand and the Judiciary and the legal profession on the other. The latter no doubt regard themselves as champions of the popular cause; but the existence of a State providing social services on a vast scale is due to the diffusion of voting power on a democratic basis throughout the community.

3. . . . The scope and character of government have changed enormously in the last 50 years. Formerly, government was chiefly regulatory and negative; its main task (apart from defence) was to keep the ring and maintain fair play while private interests asserted themselves freely. To-day, government is largely concerned with the administration of social services, and has become positive in a new sense. A century ago, the State acted mainly as policeman, soldier and judge. To-day, the State acts also as doctor, nurse, teacher, insurance organiser, house-builder, sanitary engineer, chemist, railway controller, supplier of gas, water and electricity, town-planner, pensions distributor, provider of transport, hospital organiser, road-maker, and in a large number of other capacities.

The change from regulatory or *control* activities to *service* activities on the part of Government necessitates new forms of administrative authority. . . .

4. . . . In enquiring into the exercise of judicial powers by Government departments it should not be assumed that the mere existence of legislative enactments conferring powers which preclude review by the Courts of Ministerial determinations is evidence of executive tyranny. Clearly the manner in which the powers are used is more important than the mere existence of statutory provisions.

Nor must we *assume* that access to the Courts is inevitably a guarantee against ministerial oppression. The most tyrannical department of Government appears to be the Inland Revenue, which often threatens the citizen with litigation in the Courts if he ventures to disagree with an administrative decision. . . .

Again, another dangerous and unscientific assumption is the belief that immunity from control by the Courts of Law involves an anarchical absence of all effective restraint whatsoever. New forms of law, legal tissue in the making, always appear at first as manifestations of extra-legal absolutism. . . .

5. . . . It is suggested that criticism directed on *a priori* grounds against the exercise of judicial powers by Government departments,

SBG

etc., usually fails to take account of four important aspects of the situation:—

(1) Limitation as to the suitability of the Courts to act as tribunals of review for certain types of administrative decisions. These limitations may arise from various causes such as (*a*) lack of special knowledge or experience of the subject matter, (*b*) absence of a body of case-law appropriate to the circumstances. The result of this is either a mere transfer of discretion from the Executive to a non-expert judicial body unconcerned with functional ends, or a refusal by the Courts to disturb the administrative determination. (*c*) Existence of a body of hardened legal doctrine unsuited to the unforeseen circumstances which may now have arisen. (*d*) Traditional lack of sympathy with the positive aims of modern government. (*e*) Defects in the procedural machinery and legal forms which must be used in order to obtain access to the Courts. For example, such remedies as *mandamus, prohibition, certiorari*, and *ultra vires* are in many cases useless for the purpose of getting a review of administrative determinations. (*f*) Expense and difficulty of litigation. (*g*) The absence of a body of public law and the concepts appropriate thereto in English jurisprudence. (*h*) Volume of business which would press upon the Courts and produce congestion.

(2) The development of judicial habits of mind and a judicial outlook by administrators and other persons who are called upon to decide practical issues. . . .

(3) The existence of potential control, (*a*) by Ministers over civil servants, (*b*) by Parliament over Ministers.

(4) The potential control exercised by public opinion over administrative officials.

For these and other reasons I do not believe that it is desirable to give in every case a right of appeal to the Courts from the decision of the administrative body. . . .

6. . . . I suggest it is impossible to be satisfied with the existing state of affairs which embodies neither the institutional safeguards of *droit administratif* nor the traditional guarantees of English judicial practice.

Very shortly, the advantages and disadvantages of Administrative Tribunals may be summarised under the following heads:

Advantages of Administrative Tribunals. Cheapness. Rapidity. Conducive to efficient administration. Introduction of special knowledge and experience. Accumulated departmental information is made available for use. Flexibility. Ability to promote a policy of social improvement. Development of new standards. Infusion of new moral ideas.

Disadvantages of Administrative Tribunals. Secrecy or lack of publicity. Poor quality of investigation into questions of fact. Inability to compel production of documents and attendance of witnesses. Anonymity. Exclusion of lawyers. Failure to give reasons for decision. Absence of report of cases. Refusal of oral hearing.

7. . . . *Suggested principles.* An Administrative Tribunal is the appropriate body for deciding questions in dispute: (1) Where a new policy of social improvement is being promoted. (2) Where it is desired to create new standards rapidly in an unexplored field. (3) Where new or existing standards are to be applied or extended throughout the country, and consistency and co-ordination are required. (4) Where special knowledge or experience, or departmental information, are necessary for a good decision. (5) Cheapness and speed are not sufficient justification for an administrative tribunal. (6) Administrative Jurisdiction should not extend to matters already dealt with by the Courts of Law. It should normally be concerned with disputes in which one or both parties are public authorities. (7) An Administrative Tribunal should always have power to act as a Tribunal of first instance. (8) Judicial powers should invariably be exercised by a definite Tribunal consisting of public servants specially nominated for the purpose by the responsible Minister. (9) An aggrieved party should always have a right to an oral hearing. (10) Administrative Tribunals should have power to call for documents and compel the attendance of witnesses. (11) The reasons for a decision and the principles followed should invariably be given. Administrative Tribunals should publish regular reports of their decisions. (12) Great attention should be paid to the qualifications, training and experience of the *personelle* of administrative tribunals. (13) The representation of outside interests on the tribunal is desirable in certain circumstances. (14) The person or persons who enquire into the facts should in all cases also decide the issue. (15) The Ministerial control over the work of an Administrative Tribunal should be strictly confined to directions as to principles to be followed contained in a Letter of Reference addressed to the members. This document should invariably be open to the public. (16) In important questions an appeal should lie to a superior Administrative Appeal Tribunal. (17) The members of Administrative Tribunals should be liable in the ordinary course for malice, negligence, corruption or fraud, committed in the course of their duties. (18) Administrative Tribunals should in no circumstances have power to decide questions involving the liberty of the subject.

(E) MEMORANDUM BY THE MINISTRY OF HEALTH:

PART IV

A. ENACTMENTS CONFERRING POWERS ON THE MINISTER OF HEALTH TO MAKE RULES OR REGULATIONS TO WHICH SECTION I OF THE RULES PUBLICATION ACT, 1893, APPLIES.

1. Public Health (Regulations as to Food) Act, 1907.
2. Rag Flock Act, 1911.

3. Milk and Dairies (Consolidation) Act, 1915 (Section 1).
4. Census Act, 1920.
5. Local Authorities (Financial Provisions) Act, 1921.
6. Milk and Dairies Amendment Act, 1922.
7. Bread Acts Amendment Act, 1922.
8. National Health Insurance Act, 1922.
9. Housing (Financial Provisions) Act, 1924.
10. National Health Insurance Act, 1924.
11. Rating and Valuation Act, 1925.
12. Widows', Orphans' and Old Age Contributory Pensions Act, 1925.
13. Town Planning Act, 1925 (except Sections 6 and 19).
14. Therapeutic Substances Act, 1925.
15. Economy (Miscellaneous Provisions) Act, 1926 (Part I).
16. Poor Law Act, 1927.
17. Local Authorities (Emergency Provisions) Act, 1928.
18. National Health Insurance Act, 1928.
19. Rating and Valuation (Apportionment) Act, 1928.
20. Local Government Act, 1929 (except rules or regulations made under Sections 22, 26 and 59).
21. Agricultural Rates Act, 1929.
22. Widows', Orphans and Old Age Contributory Pensions Act, 1929.

B. ENACTMENTS CONFERRING POWERS ON THE MINISTER OF HEALTH TO MAKE RULES OR REGULATIONS TO WHICH SECTION I OF THE RULES PUBLICATION ACT, 1893, DOES NOT APPLY.

1. Poor Law Amendment Act, 1844.
2. Burial Act, 1852.
3. Vaccination Act, 1867.
4. Gas and Water Works Facilities Act, 1870.
5. Vaccination Act, 1871.
6. Gas and Water Works Facilities Act, 1873.
7. Vaccination Act, 1874.
8. Public Health Act, 1875.
9. Canal Boats Act, 1877.
10. District Auditors Act, 1879.
11. Epidemic and other Diseases Prevention Act, 1882.
12. Public Health and Local Government Conferences Act, 1885.
13. Local Government Act, 1888.
14. Infectious Disease (Notification) Act, 1889.
15. Public Health Acts Amendment Act, 1890.
16. Public Health (London) Act, 1891.
17. Local Government Act, 1894.
18. London (Equalisation of Rates) Act, 1894.
19. Agricultural Rates Act, 1896.

20. Vaccination Act, 1898.
21. Metropolis Water Act, 1902.
22. Midwives Act, 1902.
23. Borough Funds Act, 1903.
24. Public Health Act, 1904.
25. Unemployed Workmen Act, 1905.
26. Alkali, etc., Works Regulation Act, 1906.
27. Public Health Acts Amendment Act, 1907.
28. Small Holdings and Allotments Act, 1908.
29. Housing, Town Planning, etc., Act, 1909.
30. Fishery Harbours Act, 1915.
31. Land Settlement (Facilities) Act, 1919.
32. Nurses Registration Act, 1919.
33. Blind Persons Act, 1920.
34. Unemployment Insurance Act, 1920 (Section 32).
35. Water Undertakings (Modification of Charges) Act, 1921.
36. Education Act, 1921 (Section 135).
37. Local Government and other Officers Superannuation Act, 1922.
38. Rent and Mortgage Interest Restrictions Act, 1923.
39. Housing, etc., Act, 1923.
40. Housing Act, 1925.
41. Town Planning Act, 1925 (Sections 6 and 19).
42. Public Health Act, 1925.
43. Housing (Rural Workers) Act, 1926.
44. Public Health (Smoke Abatement) Act, 1926.
45. Nursing Homes Registration Act, 1927.
46. Food and Drugs (Adulteration) Act, 1928.
47. Local Government Act, 1929 (Sections 22, 26 and 59).

FURTHER MEMORANDUM BY THE MINISTRY OF HEALTH:

3. Emphasis should at the outset be laid on the point . . . that the matters with which regulations made by the Ministry deal (and the same is no doubt true of other Departments) are almost without exception under the continuous scrutiny of powerful associations and bodies representing Local Authorities, manufacturing and trading interests, officers of Local Authorities, and members of the public, whether as owners of property, ratepayers, professional men, insured persons and the like. This is a point of such fundamental importance in connection with the consideration of any rule-making system that at the risk of stating what is familiar it may be well to recall to the Committee some of the more prominent bodies with which to a greater or less extent the Department is in communication, formal or informal, in connection with the exercise of rule-making powers.

Local Government (including Poor Law and Rating).	County Councils' Association; Association of Municipal Corporations; Urban and Rural District Councils' Associations; National Association of Local Government Officers; Association of Poor Law Officers.
Public Health. Housing. Town Planning. Model Byelaws.	Royal Sanitary Institute; Surveyors' Institution; Royal Institute of British Architects; Housing and Town Planning Association; Town Planning Institute.
National Health Insurance.	Approved Societies' Consultative Council; National Association of Approved Societies; National Association of Insurance Committees; British Medical Association.

(F) Sir Arthur Robinson, Secretary to the Ministry of Health, Called and Examined:

Sir Leslie Scott

2225. I should like to ask one question about the reports of persons holding local inquiries. From the general trend of your evidence I gather that perhaps the strongest reason against publishing the reports is, in your view, that the decision of the Minister is in fact made not only on the report but on other considerations as well?— Certainly.

2226. As a matter of practice, does he, or some other person representing him in the Ministry, discuss with the Inspector orally the report and what happened at the inquiry, and his views about it?— Normally discussion of that sort would go on, I think. If there is any point of difficulty or doubt in the report, the Inspector is asked for further explanation of it, and so on, and those further explanations become part of the material on which the decision is finally given.

2227. If the reasons are subsequently published, even in the form of a letter or statement, the reasons given may be reasons which are not specifically mentioned in the report?—Certainly. You have the case where the decision differs from the Inspector's recommendation. I do not say that is a common case, but there are a number of such cases. The Inspector, who I suppose is primarily a technical man acting from a technical standpoint, goes so far, and then you have other sorts of considerations that come in, and you have the final decision which, as I say, in a certain number of these cases differs from the recommendation.

2228. Do these cases often depend in their ultimate result upon a hard fight on disputed facts?— . . . You do get a certain number of cases where there is dispute on the facts, but in the normal case . . . the issues do not turn upon that. . . . [2230] . . . Of course the difficulty always is, . . . what is a fact.

2231. Precisely. Is that difficulty one of the reasons that make you say that it would not do to publish even the report of facts?—I do have difficulty on that, for the reason that it is quite hard to say what is fact and what is opinion. If you take a Slum Clearance Report, you have to say something about a certain house, and what the man finally says is that the house is insanitary for various reasons, a wall may be bulging, or the drains may be all wrong, and so on, but someone else who goes there may take a different view of what the fact is. . . .

Sir John Withers

. . . 2266. *Ex hypothesi*, on your evidence the Minister has before him certain other facts that the Inspector does not report upon?—Not necessarily facts. . . . [2267] . . . What I said was the Minister has to take account of considerations other than those which the Inspector has in his mind.

2268. . . . Don't you think it right that at some stage or another the people interested should have the right to criticise that material?— I do not think so at all. This material is very often pure policy. . . .

II

THE REPORT OF THE COMMITTEE

Cmd. 4,060, 1932.

SECTION I.—INTRODUCTORY

5. . . . We do not doubt that in the exercise of the judicial and quasi-judicial powers of Ministers justice is as a general rule substantially done; but . . . justice is not enough. What people want is security for justice, and the only security for justice is Law, publicly administered.

Great stress has been laid on this public need by the Lord Chief Justice in *The New Despotism*. . . . We regard [this] as a warning against possible dangers of great gravity towards which he discerns an existing tendency to drift. We are very much alive both to the presence of such dangers and to their gravity if not checked . . . But . . . we see nothing to justify any lowering of the country's high opinion of its Civil Service or any reflection on its sense of justice, or any ground for a belief that our constitutional machinery is developing in directions which are fundamentally wrong. Our Report draws attention to certain parts of that machinery which are capable of improvement, and certain aspects of its working where specific safeguards are needed. At the same time we say deliberately that there is no ground for public fear, if the right precautions are taken. . . .

SECTION II.—DELEGATED LEGISLATION

2. . . . It is indeed difficult in theory and impossible in practice to draw a precise dividing line between the legislative on the one hand and the purely administrative on the other. . . .

. . . Indeed, to exclude "administrative" regulations from any system of safeguards to be adopted in regard to delegated legislation would be dangerous; for to do so might let in the very evils against which safeguards are designed. Executive discretion, uncontrolled by safeguards, may easily become a cloak for those very powers of arbitrary legislation or judicial decision feared by those critics who describe our Civil Service as "the Bureaucracy" and think of it as "the new despotism." . . .

4. . . . We doubt . . . whether Parliament itself has fully realised how extensive the practice of delegation has become, or the extent to which it has surrendered its own functions in the process, or how easily the practice might be abused . . .

6. Delegated legislation by Ministers of the Crown invariably takes one of two forms:

> (*a*) the statutory Order in Council;
> (*b*) the Departmental regulations . . .

12. . . . [A] system of delegated legislation is indispensable. Indeed, the critics of the system do not seek to deny its necessity in some form. Their complaint lies rather against the volume and character of delegated legislation than against the practice of delegation itself. . . . We . . . think it may be convenient to summarise the main criticisms. . . .

(1) Acts of Parliament may be passed only in skeleton form and [contain] only the barest general principles. Other matters of principle, transcending procedure and the details of administration, matters which closely affect the rights and property of the subject, may be left to be worked out in the Departments, with the result that laws are promulgated which have not been made by, and get little supervision from Parliament. . . .

(2) The facilities afforded to Parliament to scrutinise and control the exercise of powers delegated to Ministers are inadequate. There is a danger that the servant may be transformed into the master.

(3) Delegated powers may be so wide as to deprive the citizen of protection by the Courts against action by the Executive which is harsh, or unreasonable.

(4) The delegated power may be so loosely defined that the area it is intended to cover cannot be clearly known, and it is said that uncertainty of this kind is unfair to those affected.

(5) While provision is usually made (*a*) for reasonable public notice, and (*b*) for consultation in advance with the interests affected where they are organised, this is not always practicable, particularly where the public affected is general and not special and organised.

(6) The privileged position of the Crown as against the subject in legal proceedings places the latter at a definite disadvantage in obtaining redress in the Courts for illegal actions committed under the authority of delegated legislation.

Each of these criticisms is important, but they do not destroy the case for delegated legislation. . . . What the system lacks is coherence and uniformity in operation. . . .

SECTION III.—JUDICIAL OR QUASI-JUDICIAL DECISION

2. . . . A "quasi-judicial" decision is . . . one which has some of the attributes of a judicial decision, but not all. . . .

A true judicial decision presupposes an existing dispute between two or more parties, and then involves four requisites:

(1) the presentation (not necessarily orally) of their case by the parties to the dispute; (2) if the dispute between them is a question of fact, the ascertainment of the fact by means of evidence . . .; (3) if the dispute between them is a question of law, the submission of legal argument by the parties; and (4) a decision which disposes of the whole matter by a finding upon the facts in dispute and an application of the law of the land to the facts so found, including where required a ruling upon any disputed question of law.

A quasi-judicial decision equally presupposes an existing dispute between two or more parties and involves (1) and (2), but does not necessarily involve (3), and never involves (4). The place of (4) is in fact taken by administrative action, the character of which is determined by the Minister's free choice. . . .

3. . . . [Although] "natural justice" does not fall within those definite and well-recognised rules of law which English Courts of Law enforce, we think it is beyond doubt that there are certain canons of judicial conduct to which all tribunals and persons who have to give judicial or quasi-judicial decisions ought to conform. The principles on which they rest are we think implicit in the rule of law. . . .

(i) The first and most fundamental principle of natural justice is that a man may not be a judge in his own cause. . . .

. . . It goes without saying that in no case in which a Minister has a pecuniary or any other similar interest in a decision, . . . should he exercise either judicial or quasi-judicial functions. . . .

But disqualifying interest is not confined to pecuniary interest. . . . Indeed, we think it is clear that bias from strong and sincere conviction as to public policy may operate as a more serious disqualification than pecuniary interest. . . . [The] bias to which a public-spirited man is subjected if he adjudicates in any case in which he is interested on public grounds is more subtle and less easy for him to detect and resist. . . .

. . . We think that in any case in which the Minister's Department would naturally approach the issue to be determined with a desire that the decision should go one way rather than another, . . . Parliament would do well . . . to provide that the Minister himself should not be the judge, but that the case should be decided by an independent tribunal. . . .

The application of the principle which we have just enunciated as to quasi-judicial decision is not so easy, since a quasi-judicial decision ultimately turns upon administrative policy for which an executive Minister should normally be responsible. . . .

(ii) The second principle of natural justice is one which has two aspects . . . No party ought to be condemned unheard; and if his right to be heard is to be a reality, he must know in good time the case which he has to meet. But on neither branch of this principle can any particular procedure . . . be regarded as fundamental.

(iii) It may well be argued that there is a third principle of natural justice, namely, that a party is entitled to know the reason for the decision, be it judicial or quasi-judicial. . . .

(iv) Some judges have discerned a fourth principle of natural justice . . . : that when Parliament has provided for what amounts to an oral hearing by the method of a "public inquiry," local or otherwise, held before an inspector appointed for the purpose by the Minister, as a means of guidance to the Minister in his decision . . . it is contrary to natural justice that the inspector's report upon the inquiry should not be made available to the parties so heard. . . .

4. Decisions which are purely administrative stand on a wholly different footing from quasi-judicial as well as from judicial decisions and must be distinguished accordingly. . . . [There] is no legal obligation . . . to consider and weigh submissions and arguments, or to collate any evidence, or to solve any issue. The grounds upon which [the person deciding] acts, and the means which he takes to inform himself before acting, are left entirely to his discretion. . . .

But even a large number of administrative decisions may and do involve, in greater or less degree, at some stage in the procedure which eventuates in executive action, certain of the attributes of a judicial decision. Indeed generally speaking a quasi-judicial decision is only an administrative decision, some stage or some element of which possesses judicial characteristics. . . .

9. It is obvious that the separation of powers is *prima facie* the guiding principle by which Parliament when legislating should allocate the executive and judicial tasks involved in its legislative plan. If the statute is in general concerned with administration, an executive Department should be entrusted with its execution; but if the measure is one in which justiciable issues will be raised in the course of carrying the Act into effect, . . . then *prima facie* that part of the task should be separated from the rest, and reserved for decision by a Court of Law— whether ordinary or specialised, as in the circumstances Parliament may think right.

It is only on special grounds that judicial functions should be assigned by Parliament to Ministers or Ministerial Tribunals. . . .

But quasi-judicial decisions stand on a different footing. The presumption as to the correct legislative course is the other way; for a decision which ultimately turns on administrative policy should normally be taken by the executive Minister. . . .

12. We do not think that any will dispute that the jurisdiction of the High Court of Justice to quash the proceedings of inferior courts is important, and that its . . . jurisdiction should be no less vigilantly exercised in the case of a Minister or Ministerial Tribunal. . . .

The scope of the High Court's supervision is well established by law. If a properly constituted inferior tribunal has exercised the jurisdiction entrusted to it in good faith, not influenced by extraneous or irrelevant considerations, and not arbitrarily or illegally, the High Court cannot interfere. When exercising its supervisory powers the High Court is not sitting as a Court of Appeal from the Tribunal, but it has power to prevent the usurpation or mistaken assumption by the Tribunal of a jurisdiction beyond that given to it by law, and to ensure that its decisions are judicial in character by compelling it to avoid extraneous considerations in arriving at its conclusion, and to confine itself to decision of the points which are in issue before it. Likewise a Minister or Ministerial Tribunal is not autocratic but is an inferior tribunal subject to the jurisdiction which the Court of King's Bench for centuries, and the High Court since the Judicature Acts, has exercised over such tribunals. That the jurisdiction extends to quasi-judicial, as well as to judicial functions, was expressly decided by the House of Lords in *Minister of Health* v. *The King* (*on the Prosecution of Yaffe*).

We regard as essential the maintenance of this jurisdiction, and a simple and cheap access to the High Court in order to invoke it. . . .

19. Mr. W. A Robson has put before us detailed proposals for the establishment of a system of administrative Courts and administrative Law independent of Ministers. . . . We have considered their expediency, but interesting as they are, we cannot recommend their adoption; in our view they are inconsistent with the sovereignty of Parliament and the supremacy of the Law. . . .

A regularised system of administrative Courts and administrative Law, such as Mr. Robson proposes, would involve the abolition of both the supervisory and the appellate jurisdiction of the High Court in matters pertaining to administration; and we believe that it would result in the withdrawal to a great extent of those judicial activities, which are inseparable from administration, from the influence of public opinion.

We, therefore, without hesitation advise against its adoption.

The Lord Chief Justice has himself expressed the opinion in Ch. III of *The New Despotism* that "*droit administratif*" is completely opposed to the first principles of our Constitution.

The truth of this observation is clearly illustrated by the history of the system of administrative Law existing in modern France. . . .

ANNEX V

NOTE BY PROFESSOR LASKI ON THE JUDICIAL INTERPRETATION OF STATUTES

I wholly concur . . . that it is undesirable to transfer the interpretation of statutes which define and control the administrative process . . . to special Courts. . . . But this is not to say that the methods of interpretation now used by the Courts are satisfactory. . . .

. . . The canons of the historic method now operative seem to me defective in a number of particulars; (1) they exaggerate the degree to which the intention of Parliament may be discovered from the words of a statute; (2) they underestimate the degree to which the personality of the judge, what Mr. Justice Holmes has called his "inarticulate major premiss", plays a part in determining the intention he attributes to Parliament; (3) they exaggerate both the certainty and the universality of the Common Law as a body of principles applicable, in the absence of statute, to all possible cases; (4) they minimise the possibility that the judge can, in his work of interpretation, fully operate the principle of *Heydon's case* [1584] and consider the evil the statute was intended to remedy so that their construction may suppress the mischief and advance the remedy. They thus make the task of considering the relationship of statutes, especially in the realm of great social experiments, to the social welfare they are intended to promote one in which the end involved may easily become unduly narrowed either by reason of the unconscious assumptions of the judge, or because he is observing principles of interpretation devised to suit interests we are no longer concerned to protect in the same degree as formerly. . . .

. . . Legislation construed by the historic canons of analysis which our Courts adopt is too often so interpreted as to defeat the real intention of the legislator . . . I suggest that the method of interpretation should be less analytical and more functional in character; it should seek to discover the effect of the legislative precept in action so as to give full weight to the social value it is intended to secure. . . .

NOTE BY MISS ELLEN WILKINSON ON DELEGATED LEGISLATION

While agreeing generally with this report I would like to add a note regarding the tone of certain passages which rather give the impression that the delegating of legislation is a necessary evil, inevitable in the present state of pressure on parliamentary time, but nevertheless a tendency to be watched with misgiving and carefully safeguarded.

I feel that in the conditions of the modern state, which not only has to undertake immense new social services, but which before long may be responsible for the greater part of the industrial and commercial activities of the country, the practice of Parliament delegating legislation and the power to make regulations, instead of being grudgingly conceded, ought to be widely extended, and new ways devised to facilitate the process. . . .

TREASURY CONTROL AND THE CIVIL SERVICE, 1931

Report of the Royal Commission on the Civil Service (Cmd. 3,909, 1931)

18. The control exercised by the Treasury over the Service depends on and has developed out of the power of the purse, and in particular out of the responsibility for the presentation to Parliament of the Estimates for the Civil and Revenue Departments. Several other factors have assisted the tendency to centralise in the Treasury a general supervision over the personnel of the Service. Among these factors are the extension of classes common to the Service whose conditions of service must be regulated by some central body, the need for improved organisation in Departments called upon to carry out business of increasing volume and complexity, and the greater attention paid to staff questions generally. Since 1919, staff matters have been dealt with by a special branch of the Treasury, known as the Establishments Department, whose consent is required to the numbers, grading, remuneration and conditions of service of all Civil Service staffs.

19. Further, as a result of its special constitutional position, it has for many years been the practice for the Treasury, of which the Prime Minister as First Lord is the titular head, to deal with matters affecting the Civil Service as a whole. Under the Orders in Council of 22nd July, 1920, power was expressly conferred on the Treasury to make regulations for controlling the conduct of Your Majesty's civil establishments, and providing for the classification, remuneration and other conditions of service of all persons employed therein. . . . Within the limits of such regulations made by the Treasury, Heads of Departments remain free to issue detailed rules for the administration of their own Departments.

20. Another important change was made in 1920, when the Government of the day affirmed the principle of requiring the consent of the Prime Minister to the appointment of permanent Heads of Departments, their deputies, principal financial officers, and principal establishment officers. It is now the duty of the Permanent Secretary to the Treasury, when a vacancy arises in any of these posts, to submit advice for the consideration of the Prime and of the Minister of the Department in which the vacancy occurs.

587. The Staff side of the National Council made the following criticisms of the existing system: that Treasury control in staff matters was severe; that the control was exercised not only at the stage when departmental and ministerial proposals involving expenditure were considered prior to submission to the Cabinet or Parliament, but subsequently in regard to the detailed expenditure of the money; that the Treasury's scrutiny of expenditure was unimaginative and destructive and gave rise to friction between the Treasury and Departments and that this friction militated against efficiency.

589. The criticisms of Treasury control made by the Staff side were not borne out by the official evidence. We were told by permanent Heads of Departments and other official witnesses that, while their proposals were not always agreed to by the Treasury, in general they were satisfied that their proposals received full and fair consideration. We were informed that, whereas not many years ago it was the practice for negotiations between Departments to be carried out mainly in writing, to-day the establishment officers of Departments met and consulted at frequent intervals with their opposite numbers in the Establishments Department of the Treasury. In his evidence before us, the Permanent Secretary to the Treasury claimed that, while in the past there had been a good deal of friction between the Treasury and Departments, matters now worked far more smoothly. He also referred to the close contact between permanent Heads of Departments on all major issues.

590. Our conclusion is that the system of Treasury control in staff matters is, in the main, satisfactory, and that there is no justification for any general relaxation of the present system of control, or for any proposal to remove the control of staff matters from the Treasury to some other Department. . . .

LOCAL GOVERNMENT EXPENDITURE, 1932

Report of the Committee on Local Expenditure (England and Wales) (Cmd. 4,200, 1932)

7. The following table shows the total revenue expenditure of Local Authorities in England and Wales on all services, except trading undertakings, falling on rates and grants. . . .

| | Expenditure falling on rates and grants | | |
Year ending 31 March	Rates £	Grants £	Total £
1920	113,089,416	47,912,453	161,001,869
1921	151,906,718	61,922,356	213,829,074
1922	160,163,899	73,709,956	233,873,855
1923	151,078,001	72,791,346	223,869,347
1924	140,006,325	75,197,868	215,204,193
1925	143,951,377	77,473,905	221,425,282
1926	150,583,323	80,032,595	230,615,918
1927	163,307,732	82,714,444	246,066,176
1928	160,413,911	85,860,680	246,274,591
1929	163,601,196	89,022,042	252,623,238
1930	154,888,952	107,463,251	262,352,203

8. It will be seen . . . that the principal heads of expenditure falling on rates and grants in the year 1929–30 were as follows:

	£
1. Education	79,685,166
2. Highways and Bridges	48,470,092
3. Public Health (including the sanitary services, lunacy and mental deficiency)	42,678,884
4. Relief of the Poor	31,457,884
5. Police	20,899,587
6. Housing	13,927,407

10. . . . The figures . . . show a growth in Local Government expenditure and in Local Government commitments which must call for very serious thought and indicate that a very heavy burden has been placed on the private citizen.

We recognise that both the Central Government and the Local Authorities have to bear responsibility for what has taken place and, if economy is to be effected, it will be necessary not only that the Central Government should refrain from placing fresh burdens on the country but that the Local Authorities themselves should review the whole field of their activities and tighten up their administration.

Since the War there has been a steady stream of legislation giving

Local Authorities fresh powers and imposing fresh duties and obligations upon them. There have been Acts, Orders, or Regulations dealing with Housing, Education, Agriculture, Public Health, Mental Deficiency, Roads, and almost every subject affecting Local Government.

When a new duty is imposed on or a new function assigned to Local Authorities by Parliament under the general jurisdiction of a Government Department, that Department is expected to give effect to the wishes of Parliament, and proceeds to persuade and at times to apply pressure to Local Authorities to take action. In this process there is sometimes a tendency to aim at perfection and uniformity and inadequate allowance is made for local needs and circumstances.

We feel strongly that the time has come when a halt should be called to legislation involving Local Authorities in fresh expenditure. They already have more than enough to do in perfecting their organisation to carry out the many new duties assigned to them in recent years.

Before expenditure can be reduced it is necessary to arrest its growth and this, we are satisfied, is one of the most effective ways to arrest it.

11. The encouragement of increased local expenditure has been most marked in those services where the system of percentage grants prevails, indeed it has been an avowed defence of the system that it does and is designed to induce Local Authorities to develop the services or carry out the works for which the grants are offered. The operation of the unemployment grants illustrates the principle in its extreme form.

It is not suggested that Local Authorities enter upon reckless expenditure merely because a large percentage will be borne by the Exchequer, but they have been encouraged to embark on expenditure they would otherwise have been willing to postpone by the consideration that there are Government grants available which, if not taken, will go to someone else.

A further consequence of the system is that Local Authorities raise loans for expenditure which might with advantage have been defrayed from revenue. This is due to the natural reluctance of the Central Government to increase its demands on the public purse by meeting its due share of the expenditure in one sum instead of spreading it over a period of years. . . .

12. We desire to refer specially to one feature of the percentage grant system, namely, the control exercised by Government Departments over Local Authorities. Here it is not limited to general policy, but extends to matters of lesser moment and even to trivialities.

We recognise that the responsible Ministers must be in a position to satisfy themselves that Local Authorities are doing their work and that the money provided by the Exchequer is being properly expended;

and if the money is being provided on a pound for pound basis—or in extreme cases on a three pound for one pound basis—it may be argued that the scrutiny must be detailed.

However that may be, a substantial expenditure of time and labour is incurred by Local Authorities in preparing detailed particulars of proposals for submission to the Government Departments, dealing with demands for information and statistics or in consultation with reference to matters which might safely be left to the discretion of the Local Authorities. . . .

13. . . . [We are led] to the conclusion that the precedent established in the Local Government Act, 1929, should be followed, and the principle of equitable block grants extended to as many as possible of those services which are at present aided by percentage grants.

This would make for economy, would get rid of much meticulous irritating and wasteful supervision, and would leave Local Authorities free to administer their services in the manner best suited to the particular needs of their area and to their financial resources, subject to general review by the Central Departments of the efficiency and economy of their arrangements. . . .

THE HEADSHIP OF THE CIVIL SERVICE, 1942

House of Lords Debates, 25 and 26 November 1942; Official Report, cc. 223 sqq. and 275 sqq.

THE EARL OF PERTH: . . . I think it would simplify matters if I remind your Lordships of a question which I put to His Majesty's Government about the title and functions of Head of the Civil Service, and of the reply which I received from the noble and learned Viscount on the Woolsack on 4 August last. The question was to ask His Majesty's Government

when and by what instrument the title of "Head of the Civil Service" was first bestowed on the Permanent Secretary to His Majesty's Treasury; whether Parliamentary sanction was or has subsequently been obtained to the bestowal of the title and what are the powers conferred on and the functions performed by the holder of the title.

The answer given was as follows:

The supreme Head of all the Services of the Crown is the Sovereign. The Ministerial Head of His Majesty's Civil Service is the Prime Minister and First Lord of the Treasury. The principal officer of that Service is the Permanent Secretary to the Treasury; that title was introduced in 1867 and the post has since carried with it the official headship of the Service. No formal instrument recording the fact appears then to have been issued, but the position was explicitly reaffirmed in 1919 by the Government of the day in connexion with the reorganisation of the Treasury after the last war. Appointment as "Permanent Secretary to the Treasury and official Head of H.M. Civil Service" is made by the Prime Minister with the approval of His Majesty. The sanction of Parliament to appointments and titles in the Crown Services is not required. The function of the holder of this post is to direct, subject to Ministerial authority, the work of the Treasury, including that part of the Treasury's work which is concerned with the general supervision of the Civil Service and the central oversight of the official machinery of government; his duties in this regard include that of advising the Prime Minister and First Lord, after consultation with any other Minister concerned, on appointments to certain senior posts in the Service which require the Prime Minister's approval, namely: Permanent Heads of Departments, their Deputies, Principal Finance Officers and Principal Establishment Officers. The holder of this post is, of course, in the exercise of his functions, subject to the authority of the Government of the day and he has no powers independent of the Minister to whom he tenders advice and to whom he is responsible.

. . . The Tomlin Report on the Civil Service states that in 1920 the Government of the day affirmed the principle of requiring the consent of the Prime Minister to certain important appointments—namely, Permanent Under-Secretary, Deputy Permanent Under-Secretary, Principal Establishment Officer and Principal Finance Officer. But there was no question here of reaffirmation, and it would appear that these functions were first bestowed on the Permanent Secretary of the Treasury in 1920. Some of us . . . believe that the post of Head of the Civil Service was created only in 1919. . . .

[The Earl of Perth then referred to the duties of the Secretary of the Treasury to advise the Prime Minister on appointments.]

How does this duty, as defined, apply particularly as regards the authority of responsible Ministers of the Crown? If a permanent Secretaryship or Deputy Permanent Secretaryship becomes vacant it is no longer the responsible Minister who will propose to the Prime Minister the names of those whom he regards as best fitted to fill the vacancy. The responsible Minister has, according to the answer, no direct access to the Prime Minister in a matter of such vital concern to his Department. It is true that he is to be consulted by the Head of the Civil Service, but there is no assurance that his advice will be taken, and the appointment might be made contrary to his desires. He has then to accept it or to resign his high office. This seems to me an intolerable position for a Minister of the Crown, and I have grave doubts whether it is in accordance with our constitutional principles. . . .

THE LORD CHANCELLOR (VISCOUNT SIMON): . . . The permanent heads of great Departments do not change nearly as frequently as their political heads; it may even be that in some great Departments the same Permanent Secretary has seen quite a number of "embarrassed phantoms" come and go. But what happens when . . . it is necessary to choose a new Permanent Secretary for a Major Department . . . ?

The first thing to realise is this. . . . The appointment is made by the Minister at the head of the Department. It is he, and nobody but he, who appoints the new Permanent Secretary. . . .

Now we come to the next point. Is it really suggested that the Minister who is at the head of the Department will appoint his Civil Service head at his own will and pleasure without consulting anyone else? . . . [The] Ministerial Head of His Majesty's Civil Service is the Prime Minister and the First Lord of the Treasury. He has got the constitutional responsibility, and that is why it is formally provided— and has been for over 20 years—that the consent of the Prime Minister to these particular appointments must be obtained. . . . Nobody would think of disputing, I imagine, that it is proper that, while the Minister at the head of the Department appoints and announces the appointment, the Prime Minister's approval has to be obtained to it. . . .

Nothing in my previous answer, I would assure my noble friend, was intended to suggest that the Minister cannot discuss the matter with the Prime Minister. . . .

The next step is this. If, then, the Prime Minister has to be consulted, and if his approval has to be given, and in many cases expressed, to the appointment which his colleague makes, is the Prime Minister to be debarred from any advice except the advice of his political colleague? . . . Of course, he is entitled to take advice from anybody, but the natural person to advise him is the Secretary to the Treasury. . . .

I think, if I may say so to my noble friend, that there is a tendency to fall into error here, because it is easily assumed that in matters of public administration in this country we follow a precise formal protocol. There is nothing *très protocolaire* in our methods here. All the better. I should imagine that in some cases the first step that is taken is that the Minister who has to appoint the head of a Department communicates with the Secretary of the Treasury. . . . It is a wise thing if you are going to put a proposal up to the Prime Minister, to take steps, if you can, to see that those who may be called in to advise the Prime Minister know what it is all about beforehand. . . .

. . . I most entirely agree . . . that 1919 or 1920 is the date when these things were put on a perfectly firm and exact basis. What happened was this. After the last war the future constitution of the Treasury was discussed among Cabinet Ministers. They arrived at certain views and the matter was brought before the Finance Committee of the Cabinet. At this distance of time I do [not] think it can be objectionable to speak of this. In 1919 there was a Committee of the Cabinet, consisting of Mr. Lloyd George, Mr. Bonar Law, Mr. Austen Chamberlain, Lord Milner and Sir Auckland Geddes. . . . The main points that were then decided were these: That the Treasury should be reorganised in three main sections dealing respectively with finance, with supply and with establishments, each under an official of the status and with the pay of the head of a First Class Department of State; that the activities of all three Departments of the Treasury were to be co-ordinated and controlled by a Permanent Secretary to the Treasury with a salary superior to that of the head of a first-class Department of State. This last-mentioned individual was to be recognised as Head of the Civil Service. . . .

My noble friend asked two questions. . . . First of all, he wanted to know whether the Permanent Secretary of the Treasury could intervene in questions of policy relating to Departments other than the Treasury. The answer is really this, that questions of policy are not for civil servants at all, either for the Permanent Secretary of the Treasury or for anyone else; they are for Ministers, and especially for Cabinet Ministers, and for the Cabinet. The Prime Minister and the Chancellor of the Exchequer both have a good deal of say in the policy of the Government as a whole. On many matters the Chancellor of the Exchequer exercises, in the nature of things, a considerable and perhaps a preponderating influence; that is why there are so many Ministerial conferences at the Treasury. The Chancellor of the Exchequer's responsibilities in this regard are, or may be, delegated by him within certain limits to his permanent officials; for instance, it is quite common to put a Treasury man on a Committee which is being organised by another Department. These officials, in their different spheres, carry out duties on his behalf and under his general direction; but, if my noble friend is suggesting that the status or title of official Head of the Civil Service confers on the Permanent Secretary some right or power not inherent in his position as Secretary to the Treasury, then I can give him the most explicit assurance on that point. . . . This gentleman enjoys no form of independent authority inconsistent with the constitutional responsibility of Ministers who direct him. . . .

LORD HANKEY: . . . I think it should be understood that the position of the Head of the Civil Service is consultative rather than advisory.

That brings us back to the question whether the Head of the Civil Service should be the same person as the Secretary of the Treasury. There is a strong argument for that because the Treasury, owing to its close financial association with the Departments on all levels, does get a tremendous lot of information about the personnel of Government Departments, and whatever is done in the way of reorganisation it is important that that source of information should be available to the Head of the Civil Service. But I doubt if that advantage overrides the disadvantages of his being the Head of the Treasury. The first and obvious disadvantage is that the Permanent Secretary to the Treasury is supposed, in principle, to help the Chancellor of the Exchequer to run the finances of the country. I do not believe that that was the case after the last war because the occupant of the post became so tremendously absorbed in his duties as Head of the Civil Service. . . .

The second objection, even more important, is that it is unsound from a psychological point of view that the civil servants of all the Departments should feel that their future is almost entirely dependent on the Permanent Head of the Financial Department of the Government. Civil servants of all ranks must always be free to support the policy of their Minister—if necessary to "fight his corner" even against the Treasury—without any lurking doubt in their minds as to any effect this might have on their careers. I used to wonder sometimes whether this was not one of the factors that affected the extraordinary and almost dangerous grip which the financial authorities obtained before the war in at least one of the Fighting Services and to a certain extent in others, and which I believe was a factor in the backwardness of our war preparations. . . .

LORD KENNET: . . . Nothing surely could be more remote from facts than to suppose that the Treasury is only a Ministry of Finance. It is a great deal more; it is in truth three Ministries in one, with only a very slight bond between them. It is a Ministry of Finance in the first place—the financial side. It is, secondly, a Ministry of Supply— watching over the expenditure of the Government Departments, concerned characteristically for the Estimates. That is another Ministry. But there is a third, very little related to these two, the Establishment side of the Treasury, and that is the side which is the central co-ordinating Department of the whole of the Civil Service. . . . It is as head of that Department that the Head of the Civil Service acts, and not as head of the Financial Department; and though the difference may well seem to have a subtlety, it is nevertheless a practical one and well recognised by all concerned. . . .

I fear that the practical conclusion must be that nobody can discharge the functions of the Head of the Civil Service in the more important aspect unless he is at the same time the responsible official chief of the Establishment Department of the Treasury, and thus has the knowledge, experience, and authority to keep him in touch with the qualifications necessary for the office which he discharges. . . .

LORD GEDDES: . . . It so happened that early in 1919, Sir Albert Stanley, as he then was—Lord Ashfield—was President of the Board of Trade. He fell ill, and I was sent to that office as acting President just at the time when that very great and very distinguished civil servant, Sir Hubert Llewellyn Smith, was reaching the end of his time. In the ordinary course I went to the Prime Minister and told him what

I thought would be a good arrangement to make with regard to a successor. He said to me, "Well, I think we should get Lord Milner and Mr. Bonar Law in on this." It was out of that that originated the Committee of which . . . the Lord Chancellor told us. . . . The idea in Lord Milner's mind was that we should get a powerful, strong, central Department to be the Department of the Civil Service, and that is the Establishment Division of the Treasury as it was created. But it became necessary to realise the Civil Service which, when we speak of it here in the area of Westminster, we are apt to regard as a small collection of senior civil servants, is a very big organisation with great problems throughout the country.

In 1919 no one who knew the facts would have maintained that the Government was really a good employer. There were many things lacking. . . . There was a great lack in many parts of the Civil Service, we were told, of real *esprit de corps*. In fact, there was great discontent. . . . Lord Milner worked out the scheme which was finally embodied in the Minute [of 4 September 1919] . . . and in the Circular of 15 September 1919. . . . When it was approved by the Committee and communicated to and accepted by the Cabinet, the purpose of that organisation was to provide a definite central figure who would, if I may put it this way, impersonate the Government as the employer in the vast extents of the Civil Service which are not immediately under observation in Whitehall. The work done by Sir Warren Fisher in the years between 1919 and 1939—because, after all, he was there for 20 years—in building up the employer's side, the modern employer's outlook, on behalf of the Government in relation to the civil servants employed, is a marvellous bit of work for which he has not received anything like the credit he deserves. . . .

There was in my mind, and I have no doubt there was in the minds of every other member of that Committee, the thought that we were making a very definite change in the relations of the Head of the Civil Service to the Service as a whole. We were giving him new responsibilities and giving him new powers. It so happened that immediately after the war . . . there was pressure on the Government from the country and from the Press in the direction of economy. . . . Your Lordships will also remember that there came a period of great financial pressure and strain due to the colossal attempt that we made to pay the American Debt. Then came the return to the gold standard, the coming of the economic blizzard, and all the rest of it.

All that had a profound effect upon the position of the Head of the Treasury as the Head of the Civil Service. During this long period of years all the pressure from the Government was towards cutting down expenditure. . . . [Every] Minister to whom I spoke, other than Chancellors of the Exchequer, always had a grievance that he was not allowed to carry out his policy, while the Chancellors of the

Exchequer . . . always had a grievance that everybody else was spending far too much, or at least trying to do so. That had the effect of putting the head of the Treasury into the position of continually having to bring his influence to bear upon Departments to get them to moderate their demands, not only through Ministers but through those inter-departmental discussions which so often precede the deliberations of Ministers in the preparations of Estimates and so on. That pressure from the Treasury, very often exercised, I am told, by Sir Warren Fisher in interview and discussion, undoubtedly had the effect at times of making certain members of the Civil Service, who were keen to carry out the policy of their Ministers, get a little hot under the collar, and a superstition arose—it would be difficult to find much evidence for it, but that the superstition did exist there is no doubt—that if people made too strong a fight with the Treasury for the policy of their Departments they would not perhaps be quite so lucky in the next turn for promotion. That is inevitable where you have struggle and pressure and where one man is occupying two positions, and having to apply the pressure not necessarily himself directly but through the appropriate controller or possibly at a lower level, that same man being in a position, as would appear to other civil servants . . . to influence their promotion and their reward. . . .

THE CIVIL SERVICE, 1943

House of Commons Debates, 28 January 1943; Official Report, cc. 667 sqq.

MR. WILLIAM BROWN: . . . How far do the defects of the [Civil] Service arise from the character of the relationship between itself, Parliament, and the public; that is to say, how far are they the inescapable consequences of our democratic system of government (in which case we may have to endure them), or how far are they remediable by changes in organisation and control? . . .

Because Civil Service defects are bound to figure largely in the Debate, I hope the House will bear with me if I pay a word of tribute to the Service. I affirm that in three respects the public service of Britain is far and away the best in the world. The first respect is its tradition of probity and incorruptibility. . . .

The second respect is its non-political character. . . .

The third respect—it is time someone paid this tribute—is in the tradition of public service, which it renews from generation to generation. There is a sense in which the Civil Service is a vocation. If its members do not take the vow of chastity, at least they take the vows of poverty and obedience. . . .

Nevertheless, having paid that tribute, I admit that, particularly
in this war, more so than in the last, the Service has not shown itself
to the advantage which I and its other admirers would like to have
seen, and preceding speakers are right when they say there is a good
deal of public criticism of the Service to-day, more than I have been
aware of at any earlier time in my connexion with it. What are the
charges that are made against it? . . . Substantially, there are four
charges. The first is that civil servants run to paper—that there are
all sorts of transactions which in an ordinary commercial office would
be the subject of oral or telephonic decision, but which in the Civil
Service become the subject of meticulous, elaborate, detailed, paper
record.

Criticism No. 2 is that in our accountancy arrangements we carry
checking and cross-checking auditing processes to a quite unnecessary
degree of elaboration. The third charge is that the Civil Service has
developed to a fine art the technique of avoiding individual responsibility or, in popular language, the technique known as "passing the
buck." Fourthly, that as the result of those things, the pace of the
whole machine is slowed up, and we have a static and negative Civil
Service at a time when war conditions demand that we should have
every ounce of possible drive and energy. . . . I am not going to deny
those charges, but I ask . . . how far those defects lie in the nature
of things.

Let me put it another way. If I am a private capitalist, . . . running
a business, it is within my unfettered discretion as to how far I carry
the process of recording and minuting. I am only answerable, at the
end of the year, to a meeting of shareholders, many of whom probably
will not attend. . . . But suppose I had a shareholders' protection committee of 615 members, meeting three days a week, with every member
free to interrogate me on every aspect of my policy and every detail
of any transaction within my control, obviously I should find myself
compelled to maintain records in the same degree of detail that the
Civil Service does, burdensome as that responsibility may be and
costly as it is, and slowing us down as it does. I affirm that democracy
in Britain is never better than it is at Question time in the House of
Commons. And it would be a poor exchange to sacrifice the right of
individual Members to interrogate Ministers in the utmost detail for
the sake of a few hundreds of thousands of pounds which you might
save by taking away that right.

Again, the civil servant when he does a financial transaction, has
not only to think of the accounts section of his own Ministry. He has
to think of the Exchequer and Audit Department, he has to think of
the Chancellor of the Exchequer, he has to think of the Public Accounts
Committee, and he has to think of the Select Committee on National
Expenditure. And if that lot has not bowled him out, there is the

House of Commons as a whole in reserve. Inevitably under those conditions you are bound to have a degree of detail in accountancy which goes much beyond what you might expect to see in private enterprise.

The third criticism, that we "pass the buck," again illustrates this difference between democratic and autocratic government. In a dictatorship you are not obliged to treat all citizens as equal before the law. In a democracy you are. And it follows that the civil servant must not give to one member of the public one sort of treatment and to another different treatment. He has to treat all alike, and he has to consider, in deciding each case, whether he is not creating a precedent which will subsequently be acted on in other cases. In those circumstances there is bound to be a degree of cross-referencing which is much greater than needs to be the case with a private concern. But I notice that, simultaneously with being charged with dodging responsibility, there is a school in Britain, of which Lord Hewart was a very able spokesman, which conceives of the civil servant as being so thirsty for responsibility that he is continually grabbing powers that do not belong to him, and separating and subtracting them from the powers of Parliament. I do not mind which charge we have to face—but they cannot both be true. . . . With regard to the last point, that we are slowed down, I agree. But I hope that what I have said will indicate that to a degree those things are inherent in the democratic structure of government. They are part of the price we have to pay for being able to call Ministers and civil servants to account. . . .

CIVIL SERVICE ORGANISATION AND METHODS

Fifth Report from the Select Committee on Estimates, 1946–47

SURVEY OF EVIDENCE

3. . . . From the history of previous recommendations on the subject . . . the following brief summary can be made:

1914. *The Royal Commission on the Civil Service* (the "MacDonnell Commission") recommended the creation with the Treasury of "a special Section for the general supervision and control of the Civil Service"; this Section was, amongst other duties, "to carry out inquiries and investigations into any matters connected with departmental administration and methods of working."

1918. *The Haldane Committee on the Machinery of Government* urged that the Treasury should undertake more frequent inquiries into the general administration of Departments. . . .

1931. *The Royal Commission on the Civil Service* (the "Tomlin Commission") recommended that provision should be made for the continuous overhaul of the machinery of Government by a small staff, recruited from the Civil Service and specially trained to deal with problems of efficiency and economy in departmental organisation.

1942. *The National Expenditure Committee* stated that in the period between the two wars the response of the Treasury to the demand that expert knowledge and study should be brought to bear on the problems of departmental organisation had been meagre in the extreme. The control of Establishments remained in the hands of Civil Servants whose experience was for the most part limited to the procedure of the Departments in which they served. The only definite action which had been taken to make use of the experience of the outside world was the introduction into the Treasury, in 1919, of a few "Treasury Investigating Officers," versed in the use of office machines and appliances, to control the supply of such equipment to Government Departments. The concern of these officers with organisation seldom rose above the efficient use of the machines which they supplied. . . . In the opinion of the National Expenditure Committee, the period from 1919 to 1939 was marked by an almost complete failure by the Treasury to foster the systematic study of organisation as applied to Government Departments.

4. On the outbreak of war the spread of Government activity was followed by corresponding, but gradual, adjustments in departmental machinery. By July 1940, the Chief Investigating Officer's staff had risen to 22, of whom 16 had been brought in from outside and 6 were Civil Servants. By the end of July 1941, the total strength of the Investigating Section had increased to 35, and by the beginning of June 1942, to 46. The Section was also renamed the "Organisation and Methods Division" in order to give a more accurate description of its enlarged scope.

5. About the middle of 1941 the Treasury decided that the time had come to take stock of the work achieved by their investigating teams, and in order to secure an authoritative and unprejudiced opinion they invited Mr. Reid Young to survey results and advise on future developments. He confirmed the tentative view of the Treasury that, whatever help from outside might be given, it must not lead Departments to think that they were in any way relieved of responsibility for the efficiency of their own organisation. It was therefore decided that the larger Departments should be encouraged to set up O. and M. sections of their own in order to ensure the continuous oversight of their own machinery. But Treasury help was not to be eliminated, and one of the functions of the Treasury O. and M. staff was to be the co-ordinating of the results of investigations carried out in the various Departments, so that experience might be pooled.

6. A further consequence of Mr. Reid Young's inquiries was the creation early in 1942 of a panel of business men on a part-time basis to supervise the work of the O. and M. Division of the Treasury and O. and M. in Departments. This panel was reconstituted as an advisory body in 1943. . . .

9. The purpose of O. and M. in the Civil Service is to secure maximum efficiency in the operation of the Government's executive machinery; and, by the expert application of scientific methods to organisation, to achieve economies in cost and labour. The operations of the O. and M. service, although not directed primarily to securing reductions in staff, almost invariably result in the more economical use of staff. O. and M. is an advisory service; recommendations resulting from a review are a matter for consideration by the Head of a Department and for adoption at his discretion. . . .

11. Of approximately 100 Government Departments, 19 have established their own O. and M. Branches, each under the administrative direction of the Principal Establishments Officer. The remaining Departments, which include the Foreign Office and the Ministry of Health, have so far decided to rely upon the Treasury O. and M. staff for advice on specific problems, for periodical reviews of departmental machinery and, in particular, for the planning of new work undertaken by a Department. At 1 April 1946, the aggregate O. and M. staff (other than clerical) of the Departments, including the Treasury, was 179. By 1 April 1947, the numbers had increased to 224½. . . .

12. On 8 January 1945, the Treasury O. and M. Division issued a memorandum setting out the status and functions of departmental O. and M. Branches and their relations with the Division. This document has become known as "The O. and M. Charter." It states that a Department is to have untrammelled control in O. and M. matters within its own field, and that the creation of an O. and M. Branch is not to relieve departmental officers of their primary responsibility for efficient organisation: the O. and M. Branch is to be responsible to the Establishment Officer, who, it is suggested, should have the word "Organisation" incorporated in the name of his office and of his division. Advice on O. and M. in general, with particular reference to the planning of new work, is specified as the chief function of the Branch, and it is emphasised that advice and not instruction is to be the method of approach. . . . The Charter outlines the functions of the Treasury O. and M. Division as consisting, among other things of working on assignments in those Departments having no O. and M. Branches of their own; and, by the provision of staff, assisting, on request, those Departments possessing O. and M. Branches. The Division should, in addition, maintain contact with departmental O. and M. Branches by encouraging the joint examination of common problems, by conducting courses of training and study groups, and also

by acting as a centre to which departmental O. and M. officers can refer.

13. The Treasury O. and M. Division is now fully incorporated in the Treasury system, and it constitutes the headquarters for O. and M. development throughout the Civil Service. . . .

14. The work of the Division falls, broadly, into two classes; first, service to other Government Departments, and, secondly, general investigations and studies. . . .

18. The Advisory Panel of business men . . . maintain an active interest in the O. and M. service and meet at the Treasury once a month for consultation with the Third Secretary (Establishments and Machinery of Government), the Director and Deputy Director of the O. and M. Division. With their intimate knowledge of the O. and M. service, they are able to supply a valuable contact with important business organisations and to offer advice at the highest level of the Civil Service.

19. In each Department where there is an O. and M. Branch, this has been placed under the authority of the officer in charge of Establishments as a separate unit of his organisation. . . .

21. . . . the status of O. and M. Branches varied considerably in different Departments. Of the 19 departmental O. and M. Branches, 10 were in the charge of Assistant Secretaries, the remaining nine being directed by officers of junior rank. Two of the Assistant Secretaries had had no previous experience of O. and M. work either within or outside the Civil Service. In the greater number of Departments, the O. and M. service is directed to methods of work at the lower levels, or to the investigations of problems as they arise, rather than to the consideration of organisation at the higher levels of administration. This limitation was said to result from the comparatively small numbers of O. and M. staff, whose time is fully occupied with *ad hoc* inquiries. . . .

24. The Treasury undertake the training of officers who are selected for O. and M. work, whether they are on the staff of the Treasury or other Departments. . . .

28. It is the responsibility of the Treasury Division to co-ordinate the activities of departmental O. and M. Branches and to secure that new ideas and experience are made available throughout the Service. . . .

32. The following figures taken from published statements showing the civil staffs in Government Departments in 1939, 1945, 1946 and 1947, are given as an indication of the effect of war and subsequent legislation upon the numbers employed:

1st April	1st July	1st April	1st January	1st April
1939	1945	1946	1947	1947
374,301	666,981	695,950	722,294	716,953

The total figures of Non-Industrial Civil Servants at 1st April, 1947, are analysed by staff groups in the table below:

1st April, 1947	Men	Whole-time Women	Men	Part-time Women	Total
Administrative. .	3,600	595	33	9	4,216
Executive . .	40,479	10,079	255	83	50,727
Clerical and Sub-Clerical .	132,291	128,230	207	8,071	264,660
Professional, Technical and Scientific .	34,242	3,187	481	55	37,697
Minor and Manipulative .	133,030	62,072	24,900	20,288	217,996
Technical Ancillary .	46,829	7,791	164	146	54,775
Inspectorate . .	4,877	720	133	3	5,665
Messengerial, etc .	32,157	13,419	1,018	8,132	50,151
Total . . .	427,609	256,351	27,194	38,792	716,953

These figures indicate that approximately 80 per cent. of those employed in the Civil Service are engaged on work where the application of improved organisation and methods should lead to staff economies. . . .

36. . . . It was suggested by one witness that the re-distribution of the business of Government at the higher levels was a field not yet covered by the O. and M. service, and that improvements could be made if the problem was approached with a view to designing the most effective Government machine instead of applying expedients to a structure designed for a different purpose. In his view, the principles which guided the Civil Service were adequate when Government activities were mainly of a quasi-judicial nature. They were inadequate, however, for the ever-increasing Government activities of a quasi-operational nature; these raise intricate problems when the co-ordination of several Ministries is involved in the achievement of a specific object. The witness considered that such problems had not been satisfactorily solved and that the machinery of Government could be re-designed to operate more efficiently from the top to the bottom. . . .

37. The Permanent Secretary of the Treasury stated in evidence that during the last year or so, the Permanent Secretaries of all the Whitehall Departments had been much concerned with questions of efficiency generally, and there had been a small group at high official level working on some of the problems. That Group had heard evidence from outside business people of great experience, including many who, as a result of some years of war service in Government Departments, not only knew the Government machine from inside, but also had a detached point of view. Suggestions which emerged from that inquiry have led to the setting up of a small committee, consisting chiefly of Permanent Secretaries, of which the Head of the Treasury himself is

likely to be chairman. One of the ways in which this committee is expected to be of most use is to see that accepted recommendations from O. and M. are put into effect.

38. . . . He pointed out that there had been a growth in recent years of machinery for collecting information from all Departments about the economic life and needs of the country; this information finds its way to Ministers and the Cabinet by means of, for example, the Economic Section of the Cabinet Office, the Central Statistical Office and, now, the Inter-department Planning Staff. . . .

CONCLUSIONS

56. Finally, if industry is to be urged to become more efficient, it seems essential that the Government should put its own administration in order. It is clear that insufficient thought has been given to adapting the machinery of Government to its new tasks, and that, as the Prime Minister himself has stated, the administration is strained almost to breaking point. The problem that has to be considered to-day is not identical with that considered by . . . earlier inquiries. The extent of the Government's interest in industry has been permanently widened, and the Civil Service has increasingly been required to take a more direct part in the economic life of the country. New and great responsibilities have been placed upon it, more particularly in regard to the nationalised industries. With this increase in its duties an increase of staff is inevitable. Furthermore, although some new Ministries have been formed and much of the responsibility for the actual conduct of industrial and trading activities is being placed in the hands of quasi-governmental boards, the size of the major Departments of State has of necessity been greatly enlarged. The obvious danger is that those may have become too large and cumbrous to work rapidly and efficiently as single administrative units. It has been argued that a redistribution of functions between existing Departments would not be likely to effect any striking economy in manpower. This may be so; but a reconsideration of the whole pattern of the Government machine in the light of modern conditions might well suggest a re-organisation that would increase the rapidity and efficiency with which the ever growing volume of work is discharged. This might not reduce staff, but it might obviate further increases and should result in economy in the true meaning of that word.

57. The problem is not confined to questions of establishments and machinery for interdepartmental liaison. A pattern has to be worked out by which the new National Boards and other extra-governmental bodies, which nevertheless have responsibilities to the State, can be incorporated in, or satisfactorily linked to, the administrative machinery. . . .

58. . . . Your Committee wish to emphasise their conclusion that little is to be gained by tinkering with a problem of such fundamental importance—a problem which lies at the root of good government, a problem which demands the highest priority among the many tasks now waiting to be done.

WEAKNESSES IN LOCAL GOVERNMENT, 1947

Report of the Local Government Boundary Commission for 1947 (H.C. 86 of 1947–48)

1. . . . Our experience amply confirms the statement made recently in Parliament by the Minister of Health: " . . . Everyone who knows about local government feels that it is nonsense to talk about functions and boundaries separately. They have to be taken together. . . ."

3. . . . In this part of the Report we . . . mention some of the main factors which, in our view, impede local government and give rise to a sense of frustration.

4. *Disparity in Size and Resources.*—A major defect of the present organisation is the disparity between individual counties and individual county boroughs in the matter of population and resources. This disparity is due in part to historical causes, but mainly to the fact that adjustments of the local government structure have not kept pace with changes of population or with changes in functions.

Under the Local Government Act, 1888, the boundaries of administrative counties . . . were based on the ancient county boundaries. These had behind them a wealth of history, tradition and sentiment. Some of them were by no means ideal for local administration of the services of that day and the addition of a large range of new services has added considerably to the number of unsuitable areas. Since 1888 there has been no general review of the area of counties.

By the same Act the status of county borough was granted to certain boroughs, either because they were then "counties of towns," or because they had a population of 50,000 or upwards. In introducing the Bill for the Act of 1888 the Government of the day proposed that only the ten largest cities, all having populations at that date of more than 100,000, should be independent of county government, but this intention was abandoned, not without reluctance, during the passage of the Bill, and 63 towns became county boroughs. In 1926, the minimum population for county borough status was raised from 50,000 to 75,000 and in 1945 it was in effect raised to 100,000 by the Act, but since 1888 no county or county borough has ever lost its status, and the gulf between the greater and smaller authorities in each class has widened.

We set out some significant figures for England and Wales: . . .

Population range	Counties[1]	County boroughs
Less than 50,000	5	4
50,000–75,000	5	16
75,000–100,000	3	13
100,000–150,000	6	23
150,000–200,000	4	11
200,000–500,000	24	12
500,000–1,000,000	8	3
Over 1,000,000	6	1
	61	83

The largest county in population is Middlesex (2,270,000) and the smallest Rutland (18,000).

The largest county borough is Birmingham (1,085,000), and the smallest Canterbury (25,000). . . .

The aggregate population of the 50 smallest counties and county boroughs is approximately equal to the aggregate of the two largest (Middlesex and Birmingham).

Five million persons live in Lancashire and 4½ million in Yorkshire, together nearly a quarter of the population of England and Wales.

Forty-one out of 80 county boroughs (excluding three in Greater London) are in Cheshire, Lancashire, Staffordshire and Yorkshire.

County districts present a similar spectacle of disparity in population and in resources. For example, the largest urban district has a population of 200,000 and the smallest of 700, with 1d. rate products of £8,600 and £16 respectively.

A systematic allocation of functions between the different types of authorities is plainly impossible if units of each type vary within such wide limits. The weakness of the smaller counties and county boroughs has unquestionably been one of the causes of the transfer of functions from local to central government or to other authorities, just as the weakness of the smaller county districts has led to a transfer of functions to the counties. Unless this defect in the system is remedied, Parliament may well hesitate to entrust to local authorities in the future new functions which are in themselves entirely apt for local administration.

5. *Concentrations of Population.*—The failure of the local government system to keep pace with the changing pattern of modern industrial England is seen most strikingly in the huge concentrations of population living in neighbouring towns, which are closely knit as economic

[1] Excluding the County of London.

and industrial units but have little or no connection or cohesion as local government units. Most of these concentrations have grown up without regard to ancient boundaries or to those fixed subsequently. In 1888 Parliament recognised the existence of this problem in the Metropolis and boldly solved it by creating a new county council area —the County of London. . . . No similar action has since been taken elsewhere. There are at least five other areas where large concentrations of population exist—the Black Country, Manchester and District, Merseyside, Tyneside and the West Riding. In smaller degree Teesside, the Potteries and the areas in and near Brighton and Bournemouth present a similar problem.

6. *Central Control.*—Another result due, at least in part, to the weakness of the smaller units in all types of authorities has been the increased central control of local administration which, if carried much further, would cut at the root of local government. In the second half of the nineteenth century public health and local government legislation was content to leave local authorities with a wide measure of discretion in the exercise of their functions. Approval of capital expenditure, periodic audits and the disclosure of defects and abuses by public inquiry formed the main control in the hands of the central Government. Since the close of the century a sharp reversal of this policy has been apparent. This may be seen by comparing the language of the Statute Book in the two periods. In the earlier Acts a local authority was empowered ("may") or directed ("shall") to provide a particular service. The later pattern of legislation directs it to prepare and submit to the appropriate Minister a scheme of arrangements for making the service available and empowers the Minister to accept, modify or reject the scheme as he thinks fit. Moreover, in addition to war and post-war controls, there is now a much more extensive system of supervision over day-to-day operations of local authorities. There are, no doubt, other factors making for this change of policy—the increasing tendency of Parliament to hold Ministers and their Departments responsible for every act or omission on the part of a local authority (a tendency which has contributed to the creation by Departments of large regional staffs), and the increasing share of the taxpayer in the financial burden of local services.

7. *Haphazard Allocation of Functions.*—A development which has tended to distort the shape of local government is the multiplication of Departments charged with the oversight of specialised local government services. Education, health, highways, town and country planning, agriculture and police are six local government services under the supervision of separate Ministers. The result is that no one Department can view local government as a whole. . . . As a consequence the allocation of functions to different types of authorities has been unsystematic and the process has gone on without much reference to local

government as a balanced organism. Much of this legislation was passed in the pressure of wars or of the aftermath of wars. Piecemeal decisions had to be taken on the course of Parliamentary debates and often as the outcome of Parliamentary bargaining; and the fact that each new arrangement has emerged after a struggle between the various types of local authorities has not conduced to fruitful co-operation between them. Another result has been to create a mass of joint boards, joint committees and other combinations for particular purposes.

8. *Conflicts over Boundaries*. Ever since 1888 conflict between counties and county boroughs over boundary extensions and the creation of county boroughs has been a constant feature of local government. . . . The existence of autonomous and ever-growing county boroughs made conflict inevitable. . . .

From 1888 until 1923 . . . 33 proposals for the creation of county boroughs were made, and 23 were ultimately successful. . . . Similarly 165 proposals were made for county borough extensions, of which 110 were successful in full or in part. These creations and extensions transferred from the counties to county boroughs about 3,000,000 population and £14,500,000 rateable value. . . . Other substantial extensions and one creation took place between 1923 and 1939, usually after lengthy and expensive Parliamentary contests.

Since the establishment of this Commission in 1945 we have received applications for the creation and extension of county boroughs which would have removed substantial areas and resources from counties and involved the disappearance of 66 non-county boroughs, 130 urban districts and 11 rural districts, as well as the absorption of parts of 174 other county districts. The attitude of county councils to these demands is normally one of unqualified resistance, and has culminated in counterclaims for the removal of county borough status from most of the existing county boroughs. . . .

It is, in our view, a matter of first importance to the future of local government that this very natural antagonism should cease. . . .

THE MACHINERY OF PLANNING, 1947

House of Commons Debates, 10 March 1947; Official Report, cc. 964 sqq.

THE PRESIDENT OF THE BOARD OF TRADE (SIR STAFFORD CRIPPS): I beg to move,

That this House welcomes the laying before Parliament of a survey of the nation's requirements and resources for 1947. . . .

. . . Let me turn to the first section of the White Paper, dealing with economic planning. . . . There is a wide difference between what may be termed totalitarian planning, and democratic planning. The essence of the former is that the individual must be completely subordinated to the needs of the State, even to the extent of depriving the individual of free choice of occupation. Democratic planning, on the other hand, aims at preserving maximum freedom of choice for the individual while yet bringing order into the industrial production of the country, so that it may render the maximum service to the nation as a whole. We are attempting to make a success of democratic planning, and . . . we have decided . . . not to employ, as a normal matter, methods of direction or compulsion of manpower outside the necessities of defence.

We must, therefore, adapt our methods of planning to our means of control and enforcement. . . . We must . . . attempt to guide production . . . not by direct control of manpower, as with the Services, but with other regulatory controls which are available, such as those of raw materials, capital, investment, machinery allocation, taxation, and so on. But, apart from those various controls, we must also rely upon the individual co-operation of both sides of industry. . . .

There are two important changes which we are making, on the basis of our experience up to date, in connection with the reorganisation of economic planning. . . . First is the strengthening of the staff for economic planning, and the second is the arrangement for ensuring the co-operation of industry in the planning organisation. The foundation of this economic planning work must, of course, be done in the departments concerned with trade, industry and economic affairs. In recent months these Departments have been constituting their planning staff. In future, it will be the recognised practice that each Department will have a whole-time planning staff under a senior officer, charged with special responsibilities in this field.

The most important development on which His Majesty's Government have decided is the strengthening of the inter-departmental planning arrangements. They propose, therefore, to appoint a joint planning staff, somewhat on the lines of the procedure that was so successfully developed in the war, as, for example, in the joint war production staff. The main strength of this staff will be departmental planning officers. But it is essential that the staff should work under effective direction from the centre, and it has been decided to make a new appointment of a full-time executive head of the interdepartmental planning staff. . . . Each of the departmental planning officers will have on his staff at least one officer whose duties are arranged so that, while he does not lose contact with his own Department, he can devote a considerable part of his time on the central work of the joint staff. It is contemplated that these assistants will frequently meet together to work as special groups under the staff. Under these arrangements, the head of the organisation will not himself require to have any large staff of his own, but he will need a small, picked staff of persons with programming experience and a small secretariat.

The function of this inter-departmental staff will cover the whole field of forward planning . . . [and] will, of course, work in the closest relation with the other central organisations, in particular the Economic Section of the Cabinet office and the Central Statistical Office, both of which have important contributions to make towards economic planning. . . .

THE CIVIL SERVICE AND POLITICS, 1949

Report of the [Masterman] Committee on the Political Activities of Civil Servants (Cmd. 7,718)

II. PRESENT POSITION

(i) Parliamentary Candidature and Service

7. Civil servants are generally disqualified by statute from sitting in the House of Commons. . . . The law on the subject of "placemen" and "offices of profit" is complicated and in many respects obscure. It is, however, clear that Parliament's consistent policy has been to prevent members of the House of Commons from holding posts of the kind usually filled by civil servants. This policy has long been accepted as a fundamental feature of the British constitution.

8. Apart from the rules which Parliament has laid down regarding its own composition, the Civil Service also has its disciplinary regulations prohibiting Parliamentary candidature without prior resignation. . . . In 1924 the Chancellor of the Exchequer appointed a committee under the chairmanship of Lord Blanesburgh to inquire into the position. The Blanesburgh Committee unanimously recommended that the existing ban on Parliamentary candidature without prior resignation should be maintained for the whole of the non-industrial Civil Service. . . .

9. The Government adopted those recommendations of the Blanesburgh Report which were unanimous, and to give effect to them the Servants of the Crown (Parliamentary Candidature) Order, 1927, was made, providing that "No person employed by or under the Crown to whom this Order applies shall issue an address to electors or in any other manner publicly announce himself, or allow himself to be publicly announced as a candidate or a prospective candidate for election to Parliament until he has retired or resigned from such employment." . . .

(ii) Other Political Activities

15. The main forms of political activity in the national field, other than Parliamentary candidature, which we have had in mind . . . are: (*a*) holding office in party political organisations, whether national or local; (*b*) speaking on public platforms on party political matters; (*c*) writing letters to the press or publishing books or leaflets on party political matters; (*d*) canvassing.

16. There exists no universal regulation governing these matters comparable with that for Parliamentary candidature. Civil servants may vote and belong to political parties, but the only all-Service rule on the extent to which they may engage in general political activities —apart from the overriding limitations imposed by the Official Secrets Acts—is a general exhortation of long standing that "civil servants are expected to maintain at all times a reserve in political matters and not put themselves forward prominently on one side or the other." This rule applies only to non-industrial staff. . . .

(iii) Local Government Activities

20. The only general instruction on the subject of participation in local government by civil servants refers to candidature and service on local councils and is contained in a Treasury Circular of 1909 which left it to the Head of each Department to determine "whether, and, if so, upon what conditions, an officer of his Department may become a candidate for, or serve on, any local council provided that the duties involved . . . shall not conflict with the personal performance of the officer's duties to his Department." The Blanesburgh Report recommended that the matter remain one for departmental regulation, pointing out that, whilst the objections to Parliamentary candidature did not necessarily apply to local government candidature, it would clearly be wrong to allow candidature in the Departments whose duties consisted largely in the regulation of local authorities. . . .

21. All industrial civil servants are allowed to take part in local government activities without any restrictions. . . .

V. GENERAL PRINCIPLES

37. . . . . There are two such principles which we think vital, the first of which tells in favour of the removal of restrictions on civil servants' political activities, the second in favour of their retention. In framing our recommendations we have constantly tried to find a balance between these two conflicting principles:

(i) In a democratic society it is desirable for all citizens to have a voice in the affairs of the State and for as many as possible to play an active part in public life.

(ii) The public interest demands the maintenance of political impartiality in the Civil Service and of confidence in that impartiality as an essential part of the structure of Government in this country.

38. . . . For the purposes of our enquiry . . . we have been obliged to distinguish between (*a*) the free expression of a man's party-political views in private or through the ballot-box, and (*b*) their expression in public for the purpose of propagating the ideas of a political party.

. . . The second is also a right for the ordinary citizen, but it is in practice relinquished by many. It is not in our view a right which cannot justifiably be limited or withheld in certain circumstances by other considerations if these are sufficiently important to the public interest as a whole. . . . The public interest demands, at least amongst those employees of the State who correspond with the common conception of the Civil Service, a manner of behaviour which is incompatible with the overt declaration of party political allegiance.

39. This incompatibility is obvious in the case of the Administrative Class who are the advisers of Ministers and assist in the making of policy. . . . The Administrative civil servant voluntarily enters a profession in which his service to the public will take a non-political form. It will consist in the wise and accurate estimation of the reasons for and against a particular course of action, formulated not for the purpose of influencing the public mind, but for the benefit of those who actually have to take decisions. . . . It is very unlikely that a civil servant formed by years of training and the exercise of administrative functions would hold clear-cut party views in the sense of being a consistent supporter of the entire programme of one party, even if on the whole his sympathies lay with it. . . .

41. Only a very small proportion of the Service is, however, in close contact with Ministers. . . . The whole Administrative Class numbers only about 3,500 men and women, most of whom are stationed in Headquarters Departments in the Whitehall area. The Departments in which these Administrative staffs work are, however, composed of civil servants organised in divisions or branches, and made up of members of the various classes—Professional, Executive, Clerical and Typing—who work together as teams. All of them are, in differing ways appropriate to the responsibilities of their rank, engaged at different stages on the same blocks of work, and each contributes in varying degree according to this status towards the decisions made by the Administrative officers or towards the submissions made to Ministers. The requirements of the work demand this grouping, and a real sense of unity exists among the members of these different grades who work together as part of a single organisation; we are satisfied that the same basic principles apply to all of them alike.

42. Outside the Whitehall Ministries the Civil Service is a very large and widely spread body of men and women who are engaged not in

advising Ministers but in the conduct of practical business. . . . In these cases, the essential factor is the relation of civil servants with the public rather than their relations with the Minister. First the work of these civil servants must in fact be completely impartial. Secondly, the public as a whole and the Press must be satisfied in their own minds that no suggestion of political bias enters into their treatment of individuals. . . . The importance of these considerations can hardly be exaggerated to-day when vital decisions on claims for social benefits, assessment to tax, liability to various forms of national service, entitlement to certain rationed commodities, and many other aspects of daily life are being taken by officials often of humble rank. . . .

43. There is finally to be considered the harmful effect upon the Service itself if the political allegiance of individual civil servants became generally known to their superior officers and colleagues. . . .

44. It follows, in our opinion, that the principle hitherto observed in the Civil Service, that a civil servant maintains a certain reserve in political matters and does not put himself forward prominently on one side or the other, is plainly right for that part of the Service popularly associated with the phrase "white-collar workers." . . .

48. Our general conclusion is that to preserve the attitude of detachment in all civil servants in whom its absence might adversely affect the public service is so important as easily to outweigh any hardship felt by individuals who are deprived of the freedom to propagate political views among their fellow citizens. It will certainly justify maintaining the deprivation in some cases in which the risk is only slight. The public service should, in our view, consistently be given the benefit of any doubt. Any weakening of the existing tradition of political impartiality would be the first step towards the creation of a "political" Civil Service. . . .

VI. APPLICATION OF GENERAL PRINCIPLES

53. . . . We have come to the conclusion that it is both possible and necessary to draw a horizontal line of demarcation through the whole Service, putting above the line those who, because of the nature of their work, must be excluded from party-political activity, and putting below it those to whom freedom to engage in political activities could be granted without prejudicial consequences. . . .

(E) PARTICIPATION IN LOCAL GOVERNMENT

82. There has been a substantial change in the character of local government since the issue of the Treasury Circular of 1909. . . . Thus local government tends nowadays more and more to be organised on party political lines corresponding to those of national government,

and, if this trend continues, it seems likely that within a few years, all local government may be run on a purely party basis. . . . We doubt, however, whether this position has yet been reached. . . .

86. . . . We feel it impossible in present circumstances to make a recommendation of a permanent nature. . . . We have reached the conclusion that the existing arrangements should continue, for an experimental period of five years, subject to the substitution of a general rule for the whole Service in place of departmental rules. . . .

VIII. SUMMARY OF CONCLUSIONS

3. We . . . recommend that a line of demarcation be drawn below the Administrative, Professional, Scientific, Technical, Executive, Clerical and Typing grades and, apart from certain exceptions, above the Minor and Manipulative and the Industrial grades. Those below the line would be permitted greater liberty than those above it. . . .

5. All members of the grades "below the line" should be permitted to stand for Parliament without resignation unless they are elected. . . .

The existing ban upon Parliamentary candidature should continue to apply to civil servants "above the line." The rule under which civil servants who are peers of Parliament may attend in their place when their official duties permit but may not vote or take part in debate should also be maintained.

6. All grades of the Civil Service "below the line" should be completely free to engage in all other forms of political activity, both national and local, subject only to the maintenance of overriding considerations such as the Official Secrets Acts and the ban on political activities while on duty or in official premises.

7. All the grades "above the line" should continue to maintain a reserve in political matters. In national politics they should abstain from any public manifestation of their views which might associate them prominently with a political party. They should not (a) hold office in any party political association; (b) speak in public on matters of party political controversy; (c) write letters to the Press, publish books or articles, or circulate leaflets setting forth their views on party political matters; (d) canvass in support of political candidatures. . . .

10. Despite the growing tendency of local government to be run on party political lines we are averse from treating it at present in the same way as national politics. . . . Civil servants "above the line" wishing to stand for local office should seek the permission of their Department. Permission should be granted wherever possible, subject to the applicant being able to comply with the convention requiring a reserve in political matters and avoid becoming involved in national

party political controversy; this does not, however, preclude him from speaking in public, writing to the Press, or circulating leaflets setting forth his views, so long as he confines himself to local issues and acts with moderation. . . .

THE POWER OF THE CABINET, 1950

House of Lords Debates, 17 May 1950; Official Report, cc. 237 sqq.

VISCOUNT CECIL OF CHELWOOD rose to move to resolve, That the growing power of the Cabinet is a danger to the democratic constitution of the country. The noble Viscount said: . . . It seems to me that if this state of things goes on, we are bound to have an increasing concentration of power in the hands of the Administration—that is to say, the Cabinet—which will tend more and more to be an oligarchy consisting of individuals who, by political docility, have earned the approval of those who have control of the Party organisation. I know that any argument of the kind I have tried to present to your Lordships is always answered by saying that, after all, the Members of the House of Commons represent the electorate, and if the electorate disapprove of them and of their subservience to the Government they can be rejected. But is that proposition true? In practice, the electorate cannot just choose anyone; they must choose a candidate put forward by some organisation. Moreover, if they dislike the behaviour of their Member, they can do nothing until there is another General Election. The truth is that, under our present Constitution, when the Cabinet is once in power there is no way of effectively controlling it. . . .

So the position really is this. The Cabinet, appointed by the Prime Minister, have dictatorial powers over the whole administrative functions of the Government, and the Prime Minister is answerable only to the majority of the House of Commons. Further, the membership of that majority owe their position to the political organisation of the Party of which the Prime Minister is the chief. If they show any disposition to take an independent line, intimation is conveyed to them that they will not be the Party candidates at the next Election. Even if any of them is supported by the local organisation which originally chose him, experience shows that that support will disappear under pressure from London. . . .

THE LORD CHANCELLOR (VISCOUNT JOWITT): . . . As I conceive it, a democracy must provide the most adequate opportunities for discussion and for criticism, unlike an autocracy under which laws are imposed without the people being given a chance to discuss them. But if a democracy is going to mean mere discussion, if this House or the other place is to become a mere talking shop, then that would be one of the greatest dangers with which we could be confronted. . . .

The complexity of modern life demands inevitably that more and more must the Government of the day interfere with the individual. . . . In every country this has gone on, and in the complexity of life as it exists to-day it is inevitable that it should go on. The Cabinet is not cut off from contact with current opinion. Indeed, it is of the essence of the whole conception that the Cabinet should listen to what the House of Commons and the Members of the House of Commons are thinking and saying, and should listen to what the electorate are thinking and saying. It listens and it learns. In very truth, I may apply to such a body Carlyle's witty saying: "I am the leader, therefore I must follow."

Consider what control Parliament has in making its opinion felt. It has the admirable system of Parliamentary Questions. I am told that there are something like 15,000 to 16,000 Questions every year. There is the Adjournment debate, and there is the possibility of Motions on the Adjournment. It is quite unreal to suppose that the Cabinet shut themselves off from the current or prevalent opinions of the day. I suppose it is common knowledge that one of the most frequent visitors to the Cabinet in this and in all other Governments has been the Chief Whip, in order of course that the Cabinet and the House of Commons may be closely enmeshed. Sir David Maxwell Fyfe wrote an interesting and thoughtful article in the *New English Review* in March of last year, and on this topic of the extent of control which the House of Commons exercises, he points out that although at that date the Government had lost only one by-election, twenty-three Ministers had come and gone. . . .

I believe that the real danger to our system of democracy and freedom lies to-day in the possibility that it may not be prompt and swift in action. By all means let us provide in every way we can the fullest and most adequate discussion but . . . if we find that we have developed a system which is all talk and no action, then the minds of men will turn to some other system which does give them prompt action. The problem before democracy is to combine these two things. I believe that the secret of the successful working of our Constitution . . . consists in the steady confidence which is reposed by Parliament in the Cabinet. If that confidence were withdrawn, we should have a series of short and unstable Governments until we might find that we had prepared the ground for some sort of despotism. . . .

VISCOUNT SIMON: . . . To my mind, the question is not one of Cabinet solidarity, or of the necessity of unity of decision in a Cabinet; it is a question of the extent to which in recent times a Cabinet once in office has felt sure that it can do what it likes without effective challenge; and it is a question as to whether there is not increased

ubmissiveness in the ordinary Member of Parliament to those who
are his leaders, with the result that in fact Ministers possess a greatly
increased power compared with what they used to have. . . .

. . . I wonder whether there is not a development—in my view, an
exaggerated and distorted development—of the doctrine of electoral
mandate. There is nothing we hear so frequently nowadays as: "You
may not like this, but the Government have a mandate from the
electors to do it." Subject to those who know more about our electoral
history than I do, . . . I do not think the practice into which we have
fallen of having at the beginning of every General Election an elaborate
electoral programme, covering all sorts of topical subjects designed to
attract the votes of different sections of the electorate—town and
country, service people, officials, the poor voter, everybody—is of very
ancient date. It is a comparative novelty. . . .

The doctrine is now current . . . that once a Government is installed
in power after a General Election, the Government has an absolute
unquestioned authority in all circumstances to carry out by legislation
every item in that listed programme, however casually it may appear
in the manifesto. . . . I think it is a mistake to treat the electorate, the
sovereign power in this country, as though they acted on the day of a
General Election in putting a particular Government into power, and
that they then went to sleep until there is another General Election,
when they suddenly wake up and, as often as not, reverse the decision
they gave before.

I submit . . . that that is not a proper analysis of our constitutional
arrangements. I submit that the true view is that the electorate is
sovereign all the time and, like other people, is influenced in its judgment by experience, reflection and argument, and, it may be, greater
wisdom. . . . [It] is not the case that, on the true view, the electorate
has put into power a Government which is authorised beyond all
question to operate as it pleases until the next General Election comes
along. That, to my mind, is the real question which is involved in
what we are discussing. . . .

It is not that anyone challenges the constitutional proposition of
Cabinet unity. It is not that anybody seeks to deny the essential rule
that the Cabinet must act together and stand together. That is elementary. The question is: To what extent can this united body act without
any serious consideration of what critics may say, because they think:
"We are dead safe; we have enough people here to vote for us"? Their
supporters may not have heard a word of the argument; they may not
themselves think the Cabinet is right, but, after all, "They vote for us,
every vote counts, and that is all that matters." . . .

. . . Is there not something in the proposition that, if you really
embrace the theory of Socialism, it leads not to democracy but dan-
gerously near to a form of dictatorship? . . . [The] point is, are we

not in fact drifting into a position in which the Cabinet not only is a solid Cabinet of people who act together, as of course they always must do, but can count on a mechanical majority which in no circumstances will desert them whatever be the extravagance to which they propose to go? . . . I cannot help feeling that in earlier days the private Member in fact had much more influence behind the scenes, as well as in the voting Lobby, than the private Member has to-day. . . . I do not at all deny that we must see developments, and it may be that in some ways the developments are good and necessary. There are a great many things which must, because of their nature, be governed by regulation, and which cannot be made the subject of express statutory enactment and amendment. The real question is: Have we not tended to drift into a situation in which the increasing subservience of the private Members of the House of Commons in effect threatens to turn our constitutional system into a system in which the Government feel no restraint at all upon what they propose to do? . . .

CABINET PAPERS, 1951

House of Commons Debates, 5 December 1951; Official Report, c. 2,396.

Mr. Frederick Peart asked the Prime Minister what restrictions are placed on the use of Cabinet papers and Ministerial documents for the purpose of authorship and publication.

The Prime Minister (Mr. Winston Churchill): Former Ministers may at any time have access to Cabinet papers issued to them while they were in office, but no disclosure of the proceedings of the Cabinet may be made without the permission of the King. In view of the provisions of the copyright and the official secrets Acts, no disclosure of other official documents must be made without prior consultation with the Government of the day. . . .

TREASURY CONTROL, 1951

Fourth Report of the Committee of Public Accounts, 1950–51

The Committee of Public Accounts have made further progress in the matters to them referred, and have agreed to the following Fourth Report:—

GENERAL

TREASURY CONTROL

1. Your Committee have devoted considerable attention during the course of the Session to the question of Treasury control of

expenditure. . . . Instances of apparent extravagance and waste of public funds have been brought to their notice . . . and they felt it was their duty to ascertain whether Treasury control is now as effective as it used to be.

2. The field of public expenditure has grown enormously since 1914, both in size and in scope, and the changes which have taken place, especially since 1939, could not fail to have produced some changes in the relations between the Treasury and the spending Departments. Moreover, the Treasury have now assumed responsibility in the sphere of economic planning, and their duties are no longer confined to those of "prudent housekeeping." The Treasury submitted a memorandum in which they explained the changes which were effected in the early 1920's with the full concurrence of the Committee of Public Accounts at that time and set out the scope of Departmental and Treasury responsibility, with particular reference to the responsibilities of Accounting Officers of Government Departments. Since then these appointments have been held by the Permanent Heads of Departments.

3. The Treasury memorandum explains that three separate stages in the expenditure of public moneys by a Department may be recognised. The first is the formulation and submission of a proposal, its approval and the granting of the financial authority. The second is the execution or administration of the project. Though this stage is primarily the responsibility of the Departments and their Accounting Officers, the Treasury have a general responsibility for seeing that any Department is so organised and staffed that it can adequately fulfil this responsibility. They moreover require to be kept in touch with the progress of the expenditure, so that they may keep a watch on the total government spending, both current and prospective; on major schemes, formal periodical reports are rendered to them. The Treasury exercise complete control over all Departments in the salaries and numbers of their staff. The third and final stage is the audit stage, at which the outcome of the expenditure is examined, and both the Accounting Officer and the Treasury appear as witnesses before the Public Accounts Committee.

4. Your Committee enquired as to the detailed means by which the Treasury satisfy themselves that the amount of an estimate is reasonable and as to who in fact carries out the cross-examinations of experts to ensure that any proposal is sound. They were informed that the work is carried out by the whole range of the administrative staff of the Treasury, recruited through open competition and by promotion from lower grades; that officers are in their early years moved about as much as possible from one division to another so as to gain varied experience, which is considered preferable to expert knowledge; and that, in the opinion of the Treasury, control is as effectively maintained now as in the past and, on occasions, Heads of Departments

complain that it is so meticulous and so detailed that work cannot proceed as quickly as it ought. Your Committee give full weight to these facts and contentions.

5. In short, the Treasury accept full responsibility for examining and approving proposals for expenditure, but responsibility for execution and administration is placed primarily on the Accounting Officers. The Treasury claim that, by placing responsibility where it now rests, they have achieved a better understanding with Departments and that control of expenditure is in fact more effective than under the former system. Nevertheless, the Treasury would not claim that control could not be made still more effective by learning from experience how to keep Departments up to the mark without bringing under direct Treasury control a very large mass of relatively small and detailed matters. In particular, the Treasury are developing a system under which their officers keep in constant touch with their "opposite numbers" in the spending Departments on all broad issues of policy which affect finance and seek to influence that policy so as to secure economical expenditure and administration.

6. Your Committee see no reason to differ from the general contention of the Treasury that the present division of responsibility between that Department and the Accounting Officers of other Government Departments is broadly on sound lines, intended to create a proper sense of economy throughout the Civil Service. There are, however, certain observations on the operation of the present method of control which they think might usefully be recorded and considered.

(i) *Position of Public Accounts Committee*

7. In their memorandum the Treasury referred more than once to the position of the Public Accounts Committee and to the duty of each Accounting Officer to be answerable to that Committee. This is an accepted and valuable factor in Parliamentary control of expenditure, but Your Committee wish to make it clear that the procedure of accounting to the Legislature for past expenditure should not be invoked as lessening the need for the fullest control by the Executive of prospective and current expenditure.

(ii) *Position of Accounting Officers*

8. Accounting Officers are appointed by the Treasury, but the Treasury memorandum explained that as Permanent Secretaries they remain responsible to their Ministers for economy and to the Public Accounts Committee for justifying the management of their Departments. The Treasury agreed in evidence that Accounting Officers, though not servants of the Treasury, had a certain responsibility to that Department but that their constitutional responsibility was to their own Ministers. Your Committee recommend that consideration

should be given to the question whether the link between Accounting Officers and the Treasury should not be further defined and strengthened in practice.

(*iii*) *Position of Principal Finance Officers*

9. In their memorandum the Treasury laid some stress on the fact that normally within each Department there is, under the Permanent Secretary and Accounting Officer, a Principal Finance Officer, whose appointment or removal is, like that of the Permanent Secretary, himself, reserved for the consent of the Prime Minister. This fact, the Treasury stated, greatly strengthens the hand and position of these officers. While the officer holding this position should no doubt remain on the staff of the Accounting Officer, Your Committee are glad to note the importance attached by the Treasury to his special position; they take the view that officers holding this post should be graded as among the most important officers of Departments and should be encouraged to put forward their views on all matters of finance to Ministers and Accounting Officers before decisions are reached. It is important, in Your Committee's view, that all Ministers should be aware of the special conditions relating to this post and they were glad to learn that the Treasury felt certain that this was the case. Much of the value of the procedure must depend on general knowledge of its existence.

(*iv*) *Disciplinary Action when Losses occur*

10. In their memorandum the Treasury referred to the financial liability of Accounting Officers for making good deficits which might be disallowed, and Your Committee enquired whether similar disciplinary action was ever taken in the Civil Service against officers responsible by their neglect for losses of public funds. The Treasury were of the opinion that, where responsibility could be brought home for real mismanagement and obvious errors, an undue tolerance was not shown, though it might be that in rather minor matters the public service does not always demand dismissal where an outside employer would. There were other ways of making disapproval known. There are noted in the Appropriation Accounts numerous cases of prosecution of officers for dishonesty, and Your Committee think that some lessons might usefully be drawn from an examination of the practice of other large organisations in dealing with incompetence as well as with fraud.

(*v*) *Treasury's Exercise of Virement*

11. The Treasury have the sole right to approve virement, that is, the transfer of a saving on one subhead of a Vote to meet excess expenditure on another subhead, and have informed Departments that it is

not to be assumed that authority for this procedure will be automatically forthcoming. Whenever it appears probable that a subhead may be exceeded, Treasury authority should forthwith be sought for the excess. They have, moreover, told Departments that savings on subheads which are largely unrelated to the general run of the Vote will not be regarded as available for use to meet excesses elsewhere on the Vote. Cases occur in which the Treasury refuse to sanction virement, but they were unable to give the number of such cases in recent years.

12. Your Committee regard this as an important duty of the Treasury in the field of financial control. Though Parliament appropriates money by Votes which often cover all a Department's activities, the Estimates are presented under numerous subheads and Parliament might well feel that a larger sub-division of Votes would be required if they could not rely on strict Treasury control in this matter. Your Committee trust, therefore, that the Treasury will limit their sanctions, for virement to cases which they feel quite certain that Parliament would approve and will insist on Supplementary Estimates rather than approve virement between subheads providing for services of a different nature.

(vi) Treasury Nominees

13. In recent years an increasing volume of governmental activity has been entrusted, not to Government Departments with their own Accounting Officers, answerable directly to the Committee of Public Accounts, but to independent or semi-independent bodies, generally appointed by Ministers and financed from public moneys, but not directly responsible to Parliament. Your Committee have therefore looked into the question of Treasury control over the expenditure of such bodies, and in particular have enquired whether the Treasury normally appoint a nominee on the governing board of the organisation, as they formerly did on the Boards of the Special Area Trading Estates Companies. The Treasury said that in their experience such appointments were of doubtful value; bankers did not put a bank director on the Board of every company to which they lent money, and the Treasury would regret any general rule that they themselves should do so.

14. It has unfortunately been the experience of Your Committee that there has been some laxity of control of public expenditure in a number of bodies of this type and, while they appreciate the reasons which make the normal departmental system of control inappropriate, they think that some tighter degree of control is called for over the financial transactions of some of these bodies, particularly where the whole of their income is derived from the Exchequer. They suggest therefore that, with this end in view, Treasury nominees should be appointed to some of these bodies, either as full members or as assessors

—not with any power of veto over expenditure but with the duty of advising their colleagues in financial matters and of reporting from time to time to the Treasury on the financial policy and prospects of the body. . . .

(vii) Grants in Aid

15. Many of the bodies referred to in the last paragraph are financed by grants in aid, and the Treasury in their memorandum said that such bodies naturally tend to have considerably greater liberty of action than ordinary Government Departments. The Treasury approve the estimate for the grant in aid, but once the amount of it has been settled no attempt will normally be made to exercise a very detailed control over the organisation's activities. The bodies in receipt of grants in aid differ widely in character and in the degree of Departmental control. They are not generally required to relinquish at the end of the financial year any surplus left unspent, and in many instances the Comptroller and Auditor General has no access to their books and accounts.

16. Your Committee are fully alive to the important functions competently carried out by many of these bodies. They are, however, of the opinion that a too rapid increase of expenditure in this direction is unhealthy; that new bodies should receive grants only after most careful scrutiny and enquiry by the Departments concerned; and that the books and accounts of all bodies which receive the greater part of their income from public funds should be open to inspection by the Comptroller and Auditor General so that he may, if necessary, report on them to Parliament. . . .

(viii) Conclusion

18. . . . Your Committee . . . are aware that the Treasury staff is much larger than it used to be, but they also have in mind that in the last forty-five years Government expenditure has increased nearly forty-fold. The fact that a far larger proportion of the national income is spent by Government Departments obviously makes it desirable that the control of expenditure should be as exact as ever. But the broadening of the functions of the Treasury from those of a Department concerned principally with good housekeeping to one seeking to guide the whole economic trend of the country must mean that it directs proportionately less of its attention to ensuring efficiency and economy in Departmental spending. The question that presents itself is whether this development has been allowed to go too far.

19. Your Committee are impressed by the keen interest shown by senior officers of the Treasury in these problems and are satisfied that the Treasury are as anxious as they are themselves to maintain the traditional authority of Parliament over all expenditure of public

money. Nevertheless, they are not sure that Treasury control is, as that Department claim, more effective than it was thirty years ago. In view of the paramount need for economy, they trust that the Treasury will not only discharge to the full the duties entrusted to them by Parliament of scrutinising and controlling public expenditure, particularly by bodies which are not directly accountable to Parliament, but will also give serious consideration to any changes in organisation which may be called for in the light of modern developments.

POLITICAL ACTIVITIES OF CIVIL SERVANTS, 1953

White Paper presented by the Financial Secretary to the Treasury to Parliament, March 1953 (Cmd. 8,783)

6. On November 1st, 1949, it was announced that the Government would give immediate effect to that part of the [Masterman] Report which proposed to free some 450,000 civil servants from existing restrictions, but for the rest of the Civil Service the practice which prevailed before the Report was received would be maintained in force while further consideration was given to the matter.

7. . . . In coming to the decisions they have now made, the Government have had the benefit of advice from a Committee of the National Whitley Council specially appointed to consider the possibility of extending the area of freedom beyond that recommended in the Masterman Report.

8. This Whitley Committee suggested that it would be reasonable, practicable and consistent with the general principles underlying the Masterman Committee's recommendations, to modify the Masterman scheme by dividing the non-industrial Civil Service, not into the two categories of the completely free and the restricted, as recommended by the Masterman Committee, but into three categories. The third category would be intermediate between the two proposed by the Masterman Committee and would be formed by dividing the Masterman restricted category into two parts: those restricted . . . ; and those who, while not completely free like those below "the Masterman line," would be eligible for very considerable freedom to be granted or withheld by Departments according to the closeness or otherwise of the individual's contact with the public. This freedom, where granted, was to be subject to certain understandings about reserve in public utterances on party political matters. . . .

10. In considering the extent to which civil servants should be free to take part in political activities the Government have had constantly in mind the two conflicting principles which are at the heart of this question. On the one hand—to quote the words of the Masterman

Committee—it is desirable in a democratic society "for all citizens to have a voice in the affairs of the State and for as many as possible to play an active part in public life." On the other, "the public interest demands the maintenance of political impartiality in the Civil Service and confidence in that impartiality as an essential part of the structure of Government in this country."

Having considered the Whitley Committee's proposal, the Government have concluded that the creation of an intermediate class between the two classes proposed by the Masterman Committee represents a fair and reasonable balance between the two fundamental but conflicting principles set out above, and that its introduction would not damage the interests of the State or the reputation of the Civil Service for political impartiality.

The Government have therefore decided to introduce this scheme and it will be brought into force as soon as possible.

11. . . . The Government have decided that the line should be drawn as described in paragraph 18 of the [Whitley] Report and that the junior executive officer and analogous grades should be in the area of restriction.

12. . . . canvassing will be barred to civil servants restricted in their political activities and will be open to those in the intermediate group only by permission.

The Government agree however that the existing Post Office rule permitting canvassing by Post Office staff except where "obviously incompatible with their official position" should be maintained.

13. The practical effect of these decisions is substantially to increase the number of civil servants free to take part in political activities. . . .

When these present decisions are put into effect the position will be that, out of a Civil Service of some 1,000,000 individuals, about 62 per cent. will be completely free; something like another 22 per cent. will, subject to the acceptance of the need for discretion, be free to take part in all activities except Parliamentary candidature; while only some 16 per cent. will be barred from taking part in national political activities—and of these as many as possible of those who seek it will be given permission to take part in local government and political activities in the local field. . . .

15. The Government are satisfied that the scheme . . . imposes restrictions on civil servants only where they are necessary if the confidence of the public in the political impartiality of the Civil Service is not to be impaired. To preserve this confidence political reserve must be maintained not only by those civil servants who work in the spheres where policy is determined: but also by those who work in local offices and deal directly with the individual citizen in relation to his personal circumstances. It is the latter who are "the Civil Service" to the individual citizen. . . .

APPENDIX

CIVIL SERVICE NATIONAL WHITLEY COUNCIL

Report of a Joint Committee . . .

The Intermediate Class

11. Civil Servants of the intermediate class would be eligible for *permission* to engage in all national political activities except Parliamentary candidature.

12. The granting of permission would depend on the acceptance of a code of *discretion*, putting certain limitations on the extent to which, and the manner in which, the civil servant could express views on Governmental policy and national political issues generally. (Hence the exclusion of Parliamentary candidature from permissible activity: it would be impractical to demand discretion of this sort from a would-be Member of Parliament.) . . .

13. In deciding which of their intermediate class staff should be allowed this degree of freedom Departments would be influenced mainly by the criterion of remoteness of contact with the public and anonymity.

14. The grades to be included in the intermediate class would be settled centrally. This having been done, each Department would divide its intermediate class staff as follows:—

(*a*) those to be covered by what might be called an open general licence to take part in all the national political activities open to the intermediate class, this open general licence being given to cover whole blocks of staff, so far as possible;

(*b*) those who must individually seek permission, which would be granted on the merits of the individual case according to the criterion indicated in paragraph 13 above.

The detailed arrangements would be discussed with the departmental staff representatives, but within the machinery centrally laid down the decision would rest with the Department.

15. Subject to certain special rules for those Departments (e.g. the Ministries of Housing and Local Government, Education, Health and Transport) in close official contact with local authorities, intermediate class staff with an open general licence for national political activities would be allowed to take part in *local government and in political activities in the local field* . . . subject to:—

(*a*) the observance of the code of discretion referred to in paragraph 12 above;

(*b*) the notification to their Department of election to a local authority.

Intermediate class staff not covered by open general licence could seek permission to take part in local government activities and in political activities in the local field. Generally speaking, those to whom permission would be given to take part in national political activities would be given permission to take part in local government, etc., activities subject to the code of discretion. . . . Those not allowed to take part in national political activities would nevertheless, in as many cases as possible, be given permission to take part in local government and in political activities in the local field. This permission, which would be subject to a code of discretion requiring them to act with moderation, particularly in matters affecting their own Department —see Annex 2—would cover freedom to hold local party political office, such as Ward Secretary, impinging only or primarily on local government activity, but not any office impinging only or primarily on party politics in the national field.

16. Staff who were neither in the intermediate class nor in the area of complete freedom would not be allowed to take overt part in national political activities. But (subject to what is said in Paragraph 15 about the special position of certain Departments) they would be eligible to seek permission to take part in local government activities and in political activities in the local field. This permission would be given to the maximum extent which the circumstances permitted, subject to the observance of the code of discretion (Annex 2).

17. Apart from a difference of opinion on the Staff Side's proposition that canvassing, in a Parliamentary or a local election, is not such a public manifestation of party political views that it need be forbidden to anyone . . . the two Sides are in agreement on this conception of the intermediate class.

18. The question then is, what grades should be included in this class? The two Sides are agreed that it should include the following:—

(*a*) typists, clerical assistants, clerical officers, and their analogues— general Service and departmental;

(*b*) grades parallel to those in (*a*), i.e. grades of roughly the same status, whether general Service or departmental, e.g. scientific assistant;

(*c*) departmental grades known as the intermediate clerical grades (a very small group);

(*d*) grades parallel to the general Service grade of junior executive officer, i.e. grades which, not being in an executive class, either general Service or departmental, or in a class analogous thereto (e.g. the information officer class) are of roughly the same status, e.g. draughts- men, leading draughtsmen, assistant experimental officer, experimental officer, technical grades 2 and 3;

(*e*) Post Office manipulative supervising officers who, not being within the area of freedom as recommended in the Masterman Report, have salary scales whose maximum is not higher than, or not much higher than the maximum of the junior executive officer scale.

19. So constituted, the intermediate class would include about 290,000 staff. Of these it is estimated that some 185,000 would be given an open general licence (see paragraph 14). Of the 100,000 or so who would have individually to seek permission to take part in national political activities, probably about 45,000 would get it. The great majority of those who would not get it would be in local offices of the Ministry of Labour and National Service, the Ministry of National Insurance, the Inland Revenue, and the National Assistance Board. Those not allowed to take part in national political activities would be given permission to take part in local government activities to the maximum extent which the circumstances of the particular case permitted. . . .

ANNEX I

Code of Discretion for those who, though not completely free politically, are allowed to take part in both national political activities and local government and political activities in the local field.

A certain discretion is required of those civil servants who, not being within the area of complete political freedom, are nevertheless given permission to take part in national political activities (other than Parliamentary candidature) and in local government and local political activities. All such staff should bear in mind that they are servants of the public, working under the direction of Her Majesty's Ministers forming the Government of the day. While they are not debarred from advocating or criticising the policy of any political party, comment should be expressed with moderation (particularly in relation to matters for which their own Minister is responsible) and should avoid personal attacks. They should use every care to avoid the embarrassment to Ministers or to their Department which could result, whether by inadvertence or not, from the actions of a person known to be a civil servant who brings himself prominently to public notice in party political controversy.

ANNEX II

Code of Discretion for those who, though not allowed to take part in national political activities, are allowed to participate in local government and political activities in the local field.

The permission to participate in local government and in political activities in the local field granted to civil servants not free to participate in national political activities is subject to the condition that they act with moderation and discretion, particularly in matters affecting their own Department and that they take care not to involve themselves in matters of political controversy which are of national rather than local significance.

SECTION IV
Judicial Proceedings

LOCAL GOVERNMENT BOARD v. ARLIDGE, 1914

House of Lords, A.C., [1915] 120

Appeal from a decision of the Court of Appeal, reversing a decision of the Divisional Court.

VISCOUNT HALDANE, L.C.: My Lords, the question which has to be decided in this case is whether the appellants, the Local Government Board, have validly dealt with an appeal brought before them under the provisions of s. 17 of the Housing and Town Planning Act, 1909. The respondent is the assignee of a lease of a dwelling house, No. 83, Palmerston Road, in the metropolitan borough of Hampstead. On 12 January 1911, the borough council made an order under s. 17, sub-s. 2, of the Act to which I have referred, prohibiting the use of the house for habitation until in their judgement it had been rendered fit for that purpose. On 7 March 1911, the respondent gave notice of appeal to the Local Government Board. That Board intimated, in accordance with s. 39 of the Act and with the rules which it had made thereunder, that it would not decide the appeal without having held a local inquiry. A public inquiry was, as the result, held on 24 May 1911 before Mr. Edward Leonard, one of the housing inspectors of the Board designated for that purpose, who also made a personal inspection of the house on 2 June following. The respondent had furnished the Board with copies of reports of certain experts whom he had consulted, such reports being to the effect that the house was perfectly habitable, and that there was no justification for the closing order. The respondent had intimated that he should decline to attend the inquiry, and he did not appear or tender evidence. On 6 June the inspector submitted to the Board his report of the inspection, and on 29 July 1911 the Board, after considering the report and the other documents before them, confirmed the closing order. On 11 August, the respondent applied to the Board to state a special case under s. 39, sub-s. 1 (*a*), of the Act for the opinion of the High Court, raising the point that the order of 29 July was invalid, because (*a*) the report of the inspector had been treated as a confidential document and had not been disclosed to the respondent, and (*b*) because the Board had declined to give the respondent an opportunity of being heard orally by the person or persons by whom the appeal was finally decided, in addition to the opportunity which he had had of stating and arguing his case before the inspector. The Board declined to state a case, and the respondent did not, as he could have done under the Act, apply to the High Court for an order calling on the Board to state it.

My Lords, in the meantime the respondent applied to the borough council to determine the closing order having regard to repairs which he had effected, and on 5 October 1911 the council refused on the ground that the premises had not been rendered by such repairs fit for habitation. On 19 October the respondent appealed again to the Board, this time against the refusal to determine the closing order. I pass over certain communications and proceedings relating to the technical points taken by the respondent, inasmuch as these have ceased to be of importance, and I come to 25 November 1911. On this date the Board gave notice to the respondent of their intention to hold a second public local inquiry with respect to his appeal against the refusal of the borough council to determine the closing order. The inquiry was held on 8 December before the same inspector. The respondent was present with his solicitor and witnesses, and the borough council and the London County Council were also represented. The respondent's solicitor argued his case, and the respondent and his witnesses gave evidence. On 13 December the inspector submitted to the Board his report, together with a shorthand note of the evidence and speeches. On 8 January 1912 the Board intimated to the respondent that it would be willing to consider any further statement in writing which he desired to submit to it. The respondent did not avail himself of this opportunity, but applied for writ of certiorari to remove the order of the Board into the King's Bench Division to be quashed, on the ground that the appeal had not been determined in the manner provided by the law. The points taken were that the appeal had been decided neither by the Board nor by any one lawfully authorised to act for them, and that the procedure adopted by the Board was contrary to natural justice in that the respondent had not been afforded an opportunity of being heard orally before the Board. I assume further, what appears to have been the case, that the point was also taken that the report of the inspector on the second inquiry was not disclosed to the respondent. This point was certainly afterwards argued in the Court of Appeal.

The case was heard before Ridley, Coleridge, and Bankes, JJ. Among the affidavits which they had before them was one by Sir Horace Monro, the Permanent Secretary of the Board, who stated that the decision was come to after full and careful consideration of the reports made by the inspector, and of the evidence and documents, including the observations and objections put forward in the correspondence by the respondent's solicitors. He referred to the invitation already mentioned, addressed by the Board to the respondent's solicitors, to place before it in writing any further statement the respondent might desire it to consider. He said that the appeal had been determined judicially on the report of the inspector, and the evidence taken by him (although without any oral hearing of the respondent beyond that of the inquiry), in the same manner in all respects as it had been customary as regards other appeals to the

Board. He referred to a formal order of the Board, signed by the President, and by the assistant secretary, dismissing the appeal.

On these facts the learned judges of the King's Bench Division declined to hold that the appeal had not been properly disposed of, both in form and in substance. . . .

The Court of Appeal, consisting of Vaughan Williams, Buckley, and Hamilton, L.JJ., by a majority took a different view and reversed the decision. Vaughan Williams, L.J., held that the appeal was one inter partes, the respondent and the Hampstead Local Board being the opposing parties. He thought that the duty of the Board was to hear both sides, and to disclose all the evidence of fact placed before them, and the conclusions of law adopted by them as the basis of their decision. He held that the non-production to the respondent of the inspector's reports was contrary to the principles of natural justice, and that, in the absence of a plain direction in the statute abrogating the necessity of observing these principles in dealing with the reports, the principles of English justice had been violated. He appeared further to think that the absence of any statement by or on behalf of the Board as to which of its members considered the appeal was a further objection to the validity of the Board's order.

Buckley, L.J., thought the importance of the general question which was raised very great. It was increasingly common for statutes to empower Government departments to decide questions affecting rights of property, and it was of the first importance that their proceedings should be so conducted as to command the confidence of the public, and that the principles applicable in their conduct should be well understood. A mere power to make rules determining the procedure in such appeals did not obviate the necessity of such rules being in accordance with natural justice. It was essential that each of the parties should know the case the other made and should be heard in the other's presence. Assuming that it could be validly provided that the original hearing should assume the form of a statement in writing, it was not clear that a party who subsequently desired to be heard orally could be debarred from claiming to be so heard.

The learned Lord Justice thought that as the local authority was the authority against which the appeal to the Board was brought, it was in one sense not a party litigant, but, as it could be ordered to make a counter-statement and to pay or receive costs, for all material purposes it was not to be distinguished from a party litigant, and therefore the other party ought to know the case it made. Having regard to the terms of s. 5 of 34 & 35 Vict., c. 70, which constituted the Board and provided that anything to be done on its behalf might be done by the President or any member, or by a secretary or assistant secretary authorised by its General Order, the inspector was not within the class of persons who could decide anything. If he made a report on

a public inquiry held by him it should be made public. A case could
not be argued before one man and decided by another. The respondent
had therefore no real opportunity of presenting his case when he was
invited by the letter of 8 January 1912 to do so, for he was not permitted
to see the report.

Hamilton, L.J., was of a different opinion. The practice, he said,
of the Board, like that of its predecessor the Poor Law Board, had
always been to dispose by correspondence of appeals even in important
matters such as an auditor's disallowance of items, and in treating the
inspector's report as confidential it was only following an old and well-
known practice. The question was whether, if the statute itself did not
in terms authorise the practice, it was contrary to natural justice, "an
expression sadly lacking in precision." He referred to several prece-
dents, and came to the conclusion that it was a sound inference, to be
drawn as matter of construction, that the Legislature, aware, as he
took it to have been, of the practice as to these inquiries and its incidents, intended that the local inquiry which it prescribed should be
the usual local inquiry, and that the usual incidents should attach in
default of any special enactment, including the incident that the
Board should treat the report as confidential. He was of opinion that
what had been done was in accordance with the Act of 1909.

My Lords, I have thought it important to set out with some fulness
the conflicting views in the Court of Appeal. It is obvious that two of
the judges there based their conclusions on the principle that in the
absence of a direction to the contrary, which they could not find in the
statute, the analogy of the procedure in a Court of justice must guide
them. Hamilton, L.J., on the contrary, thought that he found in the
statute a scheme of procedure that excluded this analogy. Which of
these opinions was right can only be determined by referring to the
language of the Legislature. Here, as in other cases, we have simply
to construe that language and to abstain from guessing what Parliament had in its mind, excepting so far as the language enables us to
do so. There is no doubt that the question is one affecting property and
the liberty of a man to do what he chooses with what is his own. Such
rights are not to be affected unless Parliament has said so. But Parliament, in what it considers higher interests than those of the individual,
has so often interfered with such rights on other occasions, that it is
dangerous for judges to lay much stress on what a hundred years ago
would have been a presumption considerably stronger than it is
to-day. . . .

The closing of dwelling-houses as being dangerous or injurious
to health, or unfit for habitation, is no new jurisdiction. The Housing
of the Working Classes Act, 1890, gave to the local authority the
power to take proceedings to enforce penalties and closing orders
before Courts of summary jurisdiction, to be followed, in certain

circumstances, by demolition orders. Under that Act the owner of the house had an appeal to quarter sessions. The power of closing was somewhat extended by the Housing of the Working Classes Act, 1903, but the principle of the application being to a Court of justice remained the same. A change of this principle was introduced in the Housing and Town Planning Act, 1909. The local authority was empowered itself to make the closing order, certain conditions having been complied with, and it was given power to determine the closing order if satisfied that the house in respect of which the order had been made had subsequently been rendered fit for habitation. In respect of both a closing order and a determining order the owner was given a right of appeal. But the appeal was to be, not as before to quarter sessions, but to the Local Government Board. Stringent powers of inspection were given to both the local authority and the Local Government Board. In the case of an appeal, the procedure as to everything, including costs, was to be such as the Board might by rules determine. The Board was to have power to make such order on any appeal as it should think equitable. It could state a case, but only on a question of law, for the opinion of the High Court, and could be compelled by the High Court to do so. The rules were to provide that the Board should not dismiss any appeal without having first held a public local inquiry. . . .

My Lords, it is obvious that the Act of 1909 introduced a change of policy. The jurisdiction, both as regards original applications and as regards appeals, was in England transferred from Courts of justice to the local authority and the Local Government Board, both of them administrative bodies, and it is necessary to consider what consequences this change of policy imported.

My Lords, when the duty of deciding an appeal is imposed, those whose duty it is to decide it must act judicially. They must deal with the question referred to them without bias, and they must give to each of the parties the opportunity of adequately presenting the case made. The decision must be come to in the spirit and with the sense of responsibility of a tribunal whose duty it is to mete out justice. But it does not follow that the procedure of every tribunal must be the same. In the case of a Court of law, tradition in this country has prescribed certain principles to which in the main the procedure must conform. But what that procedure is to be in detail must depend on the nature of the tribunal. In modern times it has been increasingly common for Parliament to give an appeal in matters which really pertain to administration, rather than to the exercise of the judicial functions of an ordinary Court, to authorities whose functions are administrative and not in the ordinary sense judicial. Such a body as the Local Government Board has the duty of enforcing obligations on the individual which are imposed in the interests of the community. Its character is that of an organisation with executive functions. In

this it resembles other great departments of the State. When, therefore, Parliament entrusts it with judicial duties, Parliament must be
taken, in the absence of any declaration to the contrary, to have
intended it to follow the procedure which is its own, and is necessary
if it is to be capable of doing its work efficiently. I agree with the view
expressed in an analogous case by . . . Lord Loreburn. In *Board of
Education* v. *Rice*[1] he laid down that, in disposing of a question which
was the subject of an appeal to it, the Board of Education was under a
duty to act in good faith, and to listen fairly to both sides, inasmuch
as that was a duty which lay on every one who decided anything. But
he went on to say that he did not think it was bound to treat such a
question as though it were a trial. The Board had no power to administer an oath, and need not examine witnesses. It could, he thought,
obtain information in any way it thought best, always giving a fair
opportunity to those who were parties in the controversy to correct or
contradict any relevant statement prejudicial to their view. If the
Board failed in this duty, its order might be the subject of certiorari
and it must itself be the subject of mandamus.

My Lords, I concur in this view of the position of an administrative
body to which the decision of a question in dispute between parties
has been entrusted. The result of its inquiry must, as I have said, be
taken, in the absence of directions in the statute to the contrary, to be
intended to be reached by its ordinary procedure. In the case of the
Local Government Board it is not doubtful what this procedure is. The
Minister at the head of the Board is directly responsible to Parliament
like other Ministers. He is responsible not only for what he himself
does but for all that is done in his department. The volume of work
entrusted to him is very great and he cannot do the great bulk of it
himself. He is expected to obtain his materials vicariously through his
officials, and he has discharged his duty if he sees that they obtain
these materials for him properly. To try to extend his duty beyond this
and to insist that he and other members of the Board should do everything personally would be to impair his efficiency. Unlike a judge in a
Court he is not only at liberty but is compelled to rely on the assistance
of his staff. When, therefore, the Board is directed to dispose of an
appeal, that does not mean that any particular official of the Board
is to dispose of it. This point is not, in my opinion, touched by s. 5 of
33 & 34 Vict., c. 70, the Act constituting the Local Government Board
to which I have already referred. Provided the work is done judicially
and fairly in the sense indicated by Lord Loreburn, the only authority
that can review what has been done is the Parliament to which the
Minister in charge is responsible. The practice of the department in the
present case was, I think, sufficiently shown by Sir Horace Monro's
affidavit to have been followed. In accordance with that practice the

[1] A.C., [1911] 179.

Board, in order to obtain materials with which to decide, appointed one of its health inspectors to hold a public inquiry. This was in accordance with the rules it had made under the section of the statute which I have quoted and with its usual practice. It is said that the report of the inspector should have been disclosed. It might or might not have been useful to disclose this report, but I do not think that the Board was bound to do so, any more than it would have been bound to disclose all the minutes made on the papers in the office before a decision was come to. It is plain from Sir Horace Monro's affidavit that the order made was the order of the Board, and so long as the Board followed a procedure which was usual, and not calculated to violate the tests to which I have already referred, I think that the Board was discharging the duty imposed on it in the fashion Parliament must be taken to have contemplated when it deliberately transferred the jurisdiction, first, from a Court of summary jurisdiction to the local authority, and then, for the purposes of all appeals, from quarter sessions to an administrative department of the State. What appears to me to have been the fallacy of the judgement of the majority in the Court of Appeal is that it begs the question at the beginning by setting up the test of the procedure of a Court of Justice, instead of the other standard which was laid down for such cases in *Board of Education* v. *Rice*. I do not think the Board was bound to hear the respondent orally, provided it gave him the opportunities he actually had. Moreover, I doubt whether it is correct to speak of the case as a lis inter partes. The Hampstead Borough Council was itself acting administratively, although it had the right to appear, and did appear, before the inspector and on the appeal, and might have to pay or receive costs.

For the reasons I have given, I have arrived at the conclusion that the judgements of the Divisional Court and of Hamilton, L.J., in the Court of Appeal were right, and that this appeal should be allowed with costs here and in the Court of Appeal, and that the order of the Divisional Court should be restored.

Lords Shaw of Dunfermline, Parmoor and Moulton concurred.

Order of the Court of Appeal reversed and order of the King's Bench Division restored.

ROBERTS v. HOPWOOD AND OTHERS, 1924

House of Lords, [*1925*] *A.C. 578*

Appeal from an order of the Court of Appeal reversing an order of the Divisional Court.

LORD BUCKMASTER: My Lords, the appellant in this case is the district auditor originally appointed by the Local Government Board (now represented by the Minister of Health) for the purpose of auditing year by year the accounts of the metropolitan borough councils. In the performance of this duty he has surcharged the respondents, who are certain aldermen and councillors of the Poplar Borough Council, with the sum of £5,000 for the year between April 1, 1921, and April 1, 1922. The question on this Appeal is whether that surcharge has been lawfully made.

Before considering the facts it would be well to examine the powers with which the district auditor is invested. These are to be found in s. 247 of the Public Health Act of 1875, a section rendered applicable to the accounts of the metropolitan borough councils by s. 14 of the London Government Act of 1899 and s. 71 of the Local Government Act of 1888. Sub-sect. 7 of s. 247 contains the directions imposing upon the auditor the duty of making disallowances and surcharges . . . : "Any auditor acting in pursuance of this section shall disallow every item of account contrary to law, and surcharge the same on the person making or authorising the making of the illegal payment, and shall charge against any person accounting the amount of any deficiency or loss incurred by the negligence or misconduct of that person, or of any sum which ought to have been but is not brought into account by that person, and shall in every such case certify the amount due from such person, and on application by any party aggrieved shall state in writing the reasons for his decision in respect of such disallowance or surcharge, and also of any allowance which he may have made." It is to be observed that this sub-section consists of two branches; the first deals with the disallowance of every item contrary to law and surcharging the sum as therein provided, and the second with the deficiency or loss incurred by negligence or misconduct which is to be charged against the person who is accounting. It is suggested that this latter provision is really applicable to the officers or assistants of any local authority whose accounts, by s. 250 of the Public Health Act, are also to be audited by the auditors. It is quite possible that this is the true explanation of the different branches of the sub-section, but its determination is unnecessary in the present case, because it is not alleged that there has been negligence or misconduct in any person. It is said that the amounts disallowed are contrary to law, and that the making of them constituted the making of an illegal payment, so that it is the first branch of the section alone with which this Appeal is concerned. . . . The power of revising the decision of the auditor is to be found in sub-s. 8, which enables a person aggrieved to apply for a writ of certiorari to remove the disallowance to the King's Bench Division, where the whole matter is subject to revision. This is the course that has been adopted. An order nisi was obtained on June 26, 1923, calling upon the district auditor to show cause why a writ should not issue against him, and upon the rule being heard the Divisional

Court, on November 21, 1923, dismissed the order calling upon the district auditor to show cause, and this decision was reversed by the Court of Appeal, Bankes, L.J., dissenting from the other members of the Court.

The relevant facts which induced the district auditor to make the surcharges in question are as follows:—

During the years 1920 and 1921 the ordinary rates of wages, whether measured by taking as a standard wages for the same work paid immediately before the war and adding thereto the percentage representing the increased cost of living, or by taking the amounts fixed by the Joint Industrial Councils' award as the proper sum to be added to the pre-war wage, showed violent oscillations. . . . The three classes of wages in respect of which the surcharges have been made were women (Grade A), general labourers, and men to whom the trade union scale for masons and paviors applied. So far as the women were concerned they were paid throughout from April 1, 1920, to April 1, 1923, at a level weekly wage of 80s., the pre-war wage being 23s. 6d., brought up by considering the added increased cost of living to 54s. 6d. on April 1, 1921, and descending to 43s. on April 1, 1922. The Joint Industrial Councils' award gave for the month of April, 1921, 69s. 6d.; for May, June and July, 62s. 6d.; for August, September and October 57s. 6d., from which level it descended by steps to 51s. 6d. on April 1, 1922 and continued to descend to April 1923.

. . . The district auditor, in determining the line above which he regards the payments as illegal, has taken the pre-war rate, increased it by the cost of living and added to that a sum of 20s. a week by way of margin. . . . If the powers of the district council are limited to the payment of fair and even full wages, measured not actually in but by reference to the terms of standard rates fixed either by trade unions or by joint councils, there could, I think, be little objection to what the auditor has done, but the real difficulty in the present case lies in determining what is the limit of discretionary power given to the district council with regard to payment of wages. Now these powers are to be found in s. 62 of the Metropolis Management Act of 1855, which runs as follows: "The Metropolitan Board of Works, and (subject to the provisions herein contained) the board of works for every district under this Act, and the vestry of every parish mentioned in Schedule (A) to this Act, shall respectively appoint or employ, or continue for the purposes of this Act, and may remove at pleasure, such clerks, treasurers, and surveyors, and such other officers and servants as may be necessary, and may allow to such clerks, treasurers, surveyors, officers, and servants respectively such salaries and wages as the board or vestry may think fit." . . .

. . . The discretion thus imposed is a very wide one, and I agree with the principle enunciated by Lord Russell in the case of *Kruse* v.

XBG

Johnson,[1] that when such a discretion is conferred upon a local authority the Court ought to show great reluctance before they attempt to determine how, in their opinion, the discretion ought to be exercised.

Turning now to what the borough council have done, the reason for their action is to be found in the affidavit sworn by Mr. Scurr, Mr. Key, Mr. Lansbury and Mr. Sumner. In para. 6 of that affidavit they make the following statement: "The council and its predecessors the district board of works have always paid such a minimum wage to its employees as they have believed to be fair and reasonable without being bound by any particular external method of fixing wages, whether ascertainable by Trade Union rate, cost of living, payments by other local or national authorities or otherwise." And if the matter ended there it would be my opinion that a decision so reached could not be impeached until it were shown that it was not *bona fide*, and absence of *bona fides* is not alleged in the present proceedings. Para. 9, however, of the same affidavit puts the matter in a different form. It is there said: "9 . . . The Council did not and does not take the view that wages paid should be exclusively related to the cost of living. They have from time to time carefully considered the question of the wages and are of the opinion, as a matter of policy, that a public authority should be a model employer and that a minimum rate of £4 is the least wage which ought to be paid to an adult having regard to the efficiency of their workpeople, the duty of a public authority both to the ratepayers and to its employees, the purchasing power of the wages and other considerations which are relevant to their decisions as to wages."

Now it appears that on August 31, 1921, a resolution was passed by the borough council to the effect that no reduction of wage or bonus should be made during the ensuing four months, and this was acted upon for the following twelve months. It was, I think, well within their power to fix wages for a reasonable time in advance, and there are cogent reasons why this should be done, but that decision should be made in relation to existing facts, which they appear to have ignored. In August, 1921, the cost of living had been continuously falling since November of the previous year, and it continued to fall, so that it is difficult to understand how, if the cost of living was taken into account in fixing the wages for adult workers at a minimum basis of £4, the sharp decline in this important factor should have been wholly disregarded by the borough council. But the affidavit contains another statement, which I think is most serious for the council's case. It states that £4 a week was to be the minimum wages for adult labour, that is without the least regard to what that labour might be. It standardised men and women not according to the duties they performed, but according to the fact that they were adults. It is this that leads me to

[1] [1898] 2 Q.B. 91, 99.

think that their action cannot be supported, and that in fact they have not determined the payment as wages, for they have eliminated the consideration both of the work to be done and of the purchasing power of the sums paid, which they themselves appear to regard as a relevant though not the dominant factor. Had they stated that they were determined as a borough council to pay the same wage for the same work without regard to the sex or condition of the person who performed it, I should have found it difficult to say that that was not a proper exercise of their discretion. It was indeed argued that this is what they did, but I find it impossible to extract that from the statement contained in the affidavit. It appears to me, from the reasons I have given, that they cannot have brought into account the considerations which they say influenced them, and that they did not base their decision upon the ground that the reward for work is the value of the work reasonably and even generously measured, but that they took an arbitrary principle and fixed an arbitrary sum, which was not a real exercise of the discretion imposed upon them by the statute.

It is for these reasons that I think the Appeal should succeed. . . .

LORD SUMNER: . . . Passing now to s. 62 of the Metropolis Management Act, 1855, the respondents found themselves upon its final words, "such salaries and wages as the board or vestry may think fit," and contend that, in effect, they remove the amount of wages paid beyond the scope of effective criticism. The council may pay in good faith what wages they please. It is not said that they can pay, if they please, unreasonable wages, but that, for all purposes, what they please is what is reasonable. Their reason is substituted as the test of reasonableness for that of the auditor or of the Courts of law. All the same the result is that expenditure, which is in fact wholly unreasonable, is on this view not contrary to law, if the council *bona fide* choose to incur it. This is a pure paradox. . . .

The purpose, however, of the whole audit is to ensure wise and prudent administration and to recover for the council's funds money that should not have been taken out of them. . . . [The auditor] has to restrain expenditure within proper limits. His mission is to inquire if there is any excess over what is reasonable. I do not find any words limiting his functions merely to the case of bad faith, or obliging him to leave the ratepayers unprotected from the effects on their pockets of honest stupidity or unpractical idealism. . . .

Much was said at the Bar about the wide discretion conferred by the Local Government Acts on local authorities. In a sense this is true, but the meaning of the term needs careful examination. What has been said in cases, which lie outside the provisions as to audit altogether, is not necessarily applicable to matters, which are concerned with the expenditure of public money. There are many matters, which the Courts are indisposed to question. Though they are the ultimate judges of what is lawful and what is unlawful to borough councils, they often accept the decisions of the local authority simply because they are themselves ill equipped to weigh the merits of one solution of a practical question as against another. This, however, is not a recognition of the absolute character of the local authority's discretion, but of the limits within which it is practicable to question it. There is nothing about a borough council that corresponds to autonomy. It has great responsibilities, but the limits of its powers and of its independence are such as the law, mostly statutory, may have laid down, and there is no presumption against the accountability of the authority. Everything depends on the construction of the sections applicable. . . .

Order of the Court of Appeal reversed and order of the King's Bench Division restored.

THE KING v. MINISTER OF HEALTH, EX PARTE YAFFE, 1930

[1930] 2 K.B. 98

SWIFT, J.: This case raises an important point of constitutional law, which so far as I know has never yet been decided, although there are dicta to be quoted on one side or the other. . . .

The question raised may I think be stated thus: When Parliament delegates its powers of legislation to a Minister of the Crown, and enacts that in certain circumstances he may make "an Order," and that his Order "when made" shall have effect as if enacted in the Act, is it open to the Judiciary, if that alleged Order be challenged, to consider whether in fact "an Order" has been made?

By s. 40, sub-s. 3, of the Housing Act, 1925, it is provided that the Minister of Health in certain circumstances "may by Order" confirm a scheme. The Minister in this case alleges that he has made "an Order." That fact is challenged, and it is said that he could not have made and did not make the alleged Order—Can the Courts of law interfere?

The question arises in this way: Part II of the Housing Act, 1925, imposes upon local authorities the duty of making schemes for the improvement of unhealthy areas in their district. Such schemes recognised by the Act are either "improvement" or "reconstruction" schemes.

By s. 40, sub-s. 3, the Minister of Health may by order confirm those schemes, and by sub-s. 5 "the order of the Minister when made shall have effect as if enacted in this Act."

This case comes before the Court on a rule nisi calling upon the Minister of Health to show cause why a writ of certiorari should not issue to remove into this Court an alleged Order made by the said Minister and dated on or about November 23, 1928, purporting to confirm a scheme known as "The Liverpool (Queen Anne Street) Improvement Scheme, 1928."

The answer of the Minister is that this Court has no power to canvass his Order, as under s. 40, sub-s. 5, it is of statutory effect; and he also contends that if there is power in the Court to discuss it the Order is intra vires; and he further contends that in the circumstances of this case the discretionary writ ought not to go in favour of the applicant.

Where an Order has been made by the Minister of Health in pursuance of s. 40, sub-s. 3 of the Act of 1925, it clearly has effect by virtue of sub-s. 5 as if in fact it were in the Act, and it may be that it is not competent for any Court to inquire into its validity or to question its propriety; but it seems to me that whether an Order has been made by the Minister so as to become a statutory enactment must be a question of fact; it cannot be enough that it should be said that the Minister has made an Order under the Act and therefore the jurisdiction of the Courts is ousted; there must always arise the question whether in fact the Minister has in fact made an Order, which must depend upon the antecedent question whether he was in fact ever in a position to make the Order which he purports to have made. . . .

Before . . . a local authority approaches the Minister of Health with regard to an improvement scheme it is necessary: (1) that an official representation shall have been made to the local authority; (2) that the local authority shall pass a resolution to the effect that the area is an unhealthy area and that an improvement scheme ought to be made in respect of the area; (3) that after passing such a resolution they shall forthwith proceed to make a scheme for the improvement of the area; (4) that maps, particulars and estimates shall accompany such scheme: s. 38, sub-s. 1; and (5) that as soon as an improvement or reconstruction scheme has been prepared the local authority shall publish and serve the notices prescribed by s. 39.

Until these things have all been done the local authority cannot approach the Minister, and there is no power in him to make an Order on the local authority. His power is limited to confirming with or without conditions or modifications the scheme which the local authority has prepared. . . .

The words of sub-s. 5 of s. 40 of the Act are: "The Order of the Minister when made shall have effect as if enacted in this Act."

I think that the words "when made" must be given effect to, and that they mean in this Act "when made in sequence with the events which the Act prescribes shall lead up to them," and if any of the steps required by the Act are omitted, in my view, the Minister has not made an Order within the meaning of sub-s. 3 of 3. 40 (although indeed he may have purported to do so), and sub-s. 5 of 3. 40 does not apply. . . .

It appears that on January 18, 1928, the medical officer for the City of Liverpool made an official representation to the local authority, the result of which was that on March 7 at a council meeting the Common Seal . . . was affixed to what was alleged to be a scheme . . . and that the alleged scheme was on April 4 sent . . . to the Minister of Health.

The Minister thereupon directed a local inquiry to be held . . . and that inquiry took place on May 1, 2 and 3, 1928. On November 23, 1928, the Minister purported to make an Order.

Now it is quite clear that the scheme embodied in the Order of November 23 is not the scheme which was forwarded . . . to the Minister on April 4, and it is equally clear that what was forwarded . . . was not a scheme at all. And it is equally clear that when the local inquiry was held on May 1, 2 and 3 no valid scheme was in existence or was inquired into, and it is further quite plain that after the scheme which is embodied in the Order of the Minister of November 23 came into existence no local inquiry was held.

It is admitted by the Attorney-General on behalf of the Minister of Health that the scheme sent to him on April 4 was a scheme which was void and of no effect. . . . It has been quite recently held in the Court of Appeal, affirming the decision of this Court, that a scheme in these terms is not an improvement scheme at all: *Rex* v. *Minister of Health, ex parte Davis.*[1] The Attorney-General admitted that if a writ of prohibition had been applied for before the Minister made what purports to be an Order on November 23 there would have been no answer.

It seems to me therefore that as a matter of fact certain essential steps before the Minister could make an Order were lacking. There was no "scheme," there was no "local inquiry" after a scheme had been prepared, and I do not think the time ever came when as a matter of fact he could make an Order.

Having come to the conclusion that the Minister in this case did not make an Order and never was in a position in which he could make an Order I am faced by the argument that he has purported to make an Order and that this Court cannot inquire into the validity of what he has done. . . .

. . . We are bound, I think as part of the common law of England, to treat the Order of the Minister made under sub-s. 5 "when made" as statutory—but does that justify us in accepting or compel us to accept his mere ipse dixit that he has made "an order"? In my opinion, No. If we know, as in this case on the evidence we clearly do know,

[1] [1929] 1 K.B. 619.

that he could not have made the Order, I believe that it is my duty to say he has not made the Order. . . .

If once an Order is made it becomes part of the Act of Parliament. It has all the strength and virtue of the Act, it is incorporated in it and nobody can question it, but in my view it is open to any citizen adversely affected to inquire "Is this in truth an Order made under the Act or is it something which has without justification obtained the semblance of such an Order?" And if upon investigation this Court is satisfied that the "thing" which is purporting to be an Order of the Minister is not, and cannot in fact be, an Order within the meaning of s. 40, sub-s. 3, of the Act, ought it not to say so?

For these reasons I think the purported Order should be removed into this Court to be quashed. . . .

TALBOT, J.: I regret I am not able to take the same view of this case as my brother. . . .

. . . We were asked to make this rule for certiorari absolute on the ground that inasmuch as the Minister might have been prohibited from considering the scheme because he had no jurisdiction under the Housing Act, 1925, to confirm it, the Order confirming it is not an Order made under the Act, and is therefore ultra vires. In fact the Order very materially altered the scheme submitted to the Minister, and it is not suggested that as the scheme now stands it is not one which might have been lawfully submitted and confirmed. We are asked therefore in effect to annul a scheme which, if it had been originally drawn in the shape in which it now is, could not have been complained of in a Court of law. . . .

LORD HEWART, C.J.: I have come to the conclusion, not without doubt and reluctance, that this rule ought to be discharged. . . . [It] seems to me that the words of s. 40, sub-s. 5, of the Act, . . . are sufficient to cover the irregularities which preceded the making of the Order. . . .

Rule discharged.

The applicants appealed. On April 10 the following judgments were read:

SCRUTTON, L.J.: . . . Before the Court of Appeal, the Attorney-General, having reconsidered the matter, did not admit that the proposed scheme and Order were ultra vires, and it is therefore necessary to consider this point, as to which are bound by the principles laid down in this Court in *Davis's* case. . . . Shortly, the Act provides that where a housing area is in a condition dangerous to health, it may be cleared, and rebuilt or rearranged, that is, improved, by a scheme submitted to the Minister of Health and, after a public inquiry, after advertisement of the proposals adopted with or without modifications and promulgated in an Order by the Minister of Health. In *Davis's* case the Corporation of Derby submitted a scheme which did not include any specific plans for improvement or reconstruction but authorised the Corporation, having cleared the whole area, to "sell, lease or otherwise dispose of it, as the Council may think fit, or to appropriate or use it for any purpose approved by the Minister of Health." Lord Hanworth, M.R., states the problem thus in *Davis's* case: "Do these proposals embody a good improvement scheme within Part II of the Housing Act, 1925? . . ." and he answers the question thus: "After carefully surveying and examining the sections of Part II of the Act, I can find no warrant for holding that a scheme for mere demolition without any proposal for replacement or reconstruction, or for substitution, is within the Act," and: "For these reasons I have come to the conclusion that an 'improvement scheme' or 'scheme for the improvement of the area' must contain provisions for the user of the land where it has been acquired, and that a proposal to acquire sites in an area, leaving open the question as to its subsequent user till after the Minister has given expression to the purpose for which it shall be used, is not a scheme that complies with the Act." . . .

In my opinion, on the principles laid down in *Davis's* case, such a scheme [as that made in Liverpool] does not comply with the provisions of the Housing Act, and the Corporation and the Minister before the Order was made could have been prohibited from proceeding with it, as a scheme ultra vires his powers as conferred by the Act. One ventures to hope that local authorities and the Ministry will note and comply with the views of the Courts as to these limitations of their powers under the existing Act. . . .

The Parliamentary history on this particular subject begins in 1890 . . . [and] shows a gradual increase in the powers of the Ministry, and greater freedom from the control of Parliament. The strongest clause is that repeated in Schedule III, s. 2, of the Housing Act, 1925, from Schedule I, s. 2, of the Housing Act, 1909. That clause runs: "Shall, save as otherwise expressly provided by this schedule, become final and have effect as if enacted in this Act; and the confirmation by the Minister shall be conclusive evidence that the requirements of this Act have been complied with, and that the Order has been duly made and is within the powers of this Act." This apparently is intended to prevent any question of ultra vires being raised however flagrantly the Order in question may exceed the powers of the Act. . . .

The present Act enables a Minister to take away the property of individuals without compensation on certain defined conditions. In my view those conditions must be strictly complied with, and only the very clearest words can give final validity to an Order which does not comply with the prescribed statutory conditions. . . . [An] order which goes beyond the statutory conditions under which alone it can be made, an Order which for that reason the Minister could be prohibited from making, if he announced his intention of making it, is not an Order which when made can by reason of s. 40, sub-s. 5, have statutory effect. . . .

I have considered the authorities cited. . . . The case which has given me most anxiety is *Institute of Patent Agents* v. *Lockwood*[1]. . . . It was [there] unnecessary for the House of Lords to determine what would be the position if the rules had been ultra vires . . .

. . . But as a matter of constitutional importance, I hope that Members of Parliament and Ministers and Parliamentary draftsmen will consider whether this form of legislation is really satisfactory. It may be convenient for Ministers not to have to consider carefully whether the powers they are purporting to exercise are within their statutory authority and the powers delegated to them by statute. Parliamentary draftsmen may have got into the habit of inserting this kind of Star Chamber clause either on the instructions of a Minister or as a matter of habit without his instructions. Members of Parliament may not trouble to consider what the sections to which they are giving legislative authority really mean, but simply follow the authority of the Minister and the Government Whip. But I cannot think it desirable that when Parliament delegates authority to affect property and persons only if certain statutory conditions are observed, it should then pass clauses which, it may be contended, allow their delegates to contravene these conditions, and make ultra vires orders which cannot be controlled by the Courts which have to administer the laws of the land.

Greer, L.J., and Slesser, L.J., concurred.

Appeal allowed.

Appeal to the House of Lords, March 23, 1931, [1931] A.C. 494

VISCOUNT DUNEDIN: . . . The first question, and it is a very important and far-reaching one, is, therefore, as to the effect of s. 40, sub-s. 5. Has it the effect of preventing any inquiry by way of certiorari proceeding of a scheme confirmed by the Minister? It is evident that it is inconceivable that the protection should extend without limit. If the Minister went out of his province altogether, if, for example, he proposed to confirm a scheme which said that all the proprietors in a scheduled area should make a per capita contribution of £5 to the municipal authority to be applied by them for the building of a hall, it is repugnant to common sense that the order would be protected, although, if there were an Act of Parliament to that effect, it could not be touched. Now the high water mark of inviolability of a confirmed order is to be found in . . . the case of the *Institute of Patent Agents* v. *Lockwood*. That case arose under the Patents, Designs, and Trade Marks Act. By that Act the Board of Trade was empowered to pass

[1] [1894] A.C. 347.

such general rules as they thought expedient for the purposes of the Act. Such rules were, "subject as hereinafter prescribed," to be of the same effect as if they were contained in the Act, and were to be judicially noted. The "as hereinafter prescribed" was that the rules were to be laid before Parliament for forty days, and if, within forty days, either House disapproved of any rule, it was to be of no effect. . . . The House of Lords held that the provision as to the rules being of like effect as if they had been enacted in the Act, precluded inquiry as to whether the rules were ultra vires or not.

Now, there is an obvious distinction between that case and this, because there Parliament itself was in control of the rules for forty days after they were passed, and could have annulled them if motion were made to that effect, whereas here there is no Parliamentary manner of dealing with the confirmation of the scheme by the Minister of Health. Yet I do not think that that distinction, obvious as it is, would avail to prevent the sanction given being an untouchable sanction. I think the real clue to the solution of the problem is to be found in the opinion of Herschell, L.C., who says this: "No doubt there might be some conflict between a rule and a provision of the Act. Well, there is a conflict sometimes between two sections to be found in the same Act. You have to try and reconcile them as best you may. If you cannot, you have to determine which is the leading provision and which the subordinate provision, and which must give way to the other. That would be so with regard to the enactment, and with regard to rules which are to be treated as if within the enactment. In that case, probably the enactment itself would be treated as the governing consideration and the rule as subordinate to it."[1]

What that comes to is this: The confirmation makes the scheme speak as if it was contained in an Act of Parliament, but the Act of Parliament in which it is contained is the Act which provides for the framing of the scheme, not a subsequent Act. If therefore the scheme as made, conflicts with the Act, it will have to give way to the Act. The mere confirmation will not save it. It would be otherwise if the scheme had been, *per se*, embodied in a subsequent Act, for then the maxim to be applied would have been "Posteriora derogant prioribus." But as it is, if one can find that the scheme is inconsistent with the provisions of the Act which authorises the scheme, the scheme will be bad, and that only can be gone into by way of proceedings in certiorari.

I doubt if prohibition will ever be found to be an appropriate remedy. . . . In the meantime, I only wish to say that I think the Court of Appeal, was right in refusing to decide the case on the ground taken by the Divisional Court.

Now there arises the second question, and it must be apparent that, in accordance with the opinion which I have just expressed, the limits

[1] [1894] A.C. 360.

are narrow within which objections may be found. The respondent . . . can only object with success if he can show that the scheme is a scheme which is not such a scheme as is contemplated and provided for by the Act. . . .

To turn now to the objections urged. They are really two in number. The first is that the scheme, as submitted to the Minister, did not include a lay-out plan, and the second is that in clause 5 of the scheme, as originally presented, the Council was given untrammelled powers, a defect which the Minister had no right to cure. . . .

My view of the matter is that there is no cut and dried form in which a scheme must be propounded. The essentials are that it should clearly show the area which, in its present condition, is treated as the unhealthy area, and that, further, it should show that the municipality have bona fide proposals in sight, but that all particulars, and the precise form that reconstruction may take, are left over for the decision of the Minister, who can impose such conditions as he desires.

Now, when I apply this view to the facts in the present case, so far from finding something which resembles *Davis's* case, I find a very definite proposal. . . . It is clear therefore that the Minister was fully aware of the general scheme as to how the cleared area was to be dealt with, when he granted the confirmation. . . .

As confirmed, the scheme seems to be unassailable. . . . [It] is clearly my opinion that, if the Minister finds a good scheme, but disfigured by a blot upon it which would make it possible to call the legality of the scheme in question, he is absolutely entitled to remove that blot. . . .

Order of the Court of Appeal reversed and judgment of the King's Bench Division restored.

DUNCAN v. JONES, 1935

[1936] 1 K.B. 218

[Mrs. Katherine Duncan was one of four speakers who, it was announced, would address a meeting outside an unemployment training centre in Deptford on 30 July 1934. She was told by the chief constable of the district that the meeting might not take place there, but might be held in another street 175 yards away. Nevertheless, Mrs. Duncan began her speech, and was at once arrested by Inspector Jones. She was convicted at Tower Bridge Police Court of obstructing the inspector when in the execution of his duty, under the Prevention of Crimes Acts, 1871 and 1885, and fined 40s. During the hearing of her appeal to London Quarter Sessions, it was shown that a disturbance had followed a previous meeting, in May 1933, which Mrs. Duncan had addressed outside the training centre. The deputy-chairman of quarter sessions, in dismissing the appeal, held that the police had reasonable cause to believe that a breach of the peace would follow the meeting called in July, and that it was therefore their duty to prevent the meeting from being held.]

LORD HEWART, C.J.: There have been moments during the argument in this case when it appeared to be suggested that the Court had to do with a grave case involving what is called the right of public meeting. I say "called," because English law does not recognise any special right of public meeting for political or other purposes. The right of assembly, as Professor Dicey puts it, is nothing more than a view taken by the Court of the individual liberty of the subject. If I thought that the present case raised a question which has been held in suspense by more than one writer on constitutional law—namely, whether an assembly can properly be held to be unlawful merely because the holding of it is expected to give rise to a breach of the peace on the part of persons opposed to those who are holding the meeting—I should wish to hear much more argument before I expressed an opinion. This case, however, does not even touch that important question.

Our attention has been directed to the somewhat unsatisfactory case of *Beatty* v. *Gillbanks*.[1] . . . In my view, *Beatty* v. *Gillbanks* is apart from the present case. . . .

The present case reminds one rather of the observations of Bramwell, B., in *Reg.* v. *Prebble*,[2] where, in holding that a constable, in clearing certain licensed premises of the persons thereon, was not acting in the execution of his duty, he said: "It would have been otherwise had there been a nuisance or disturbance of the public peace, or any danger of a breach of the peace."

The case stated which we have before us indicates clearly a causal connection between the meeting of May 1933, and the disturbance which occurred after it—that the disturbance was not only post the meeting but was also propter the meeting. In my view, the deputy-chairman was entitled to come to the conclusion to which he came on the facts which he found and to hold that the conviction of the appellant for wilfully obstructing the respondent when in the execution of his duty was right. . . .

HUMPHREYS, J.: I agree. I regard this as a plain case. It has nothing to do with the law of unlawful assembly. No charge of that sort was even suggested against the appellant. The sole question raised by the case is whether the respondent, who was admittedly obstructed, was so obstructed when in the execution of his duty.

It does not require authority to emphasise the statement that it is the duty of a police officer to prevent apprehended breaches of the peace. Here it is found as a fact that the respondent reasonably apprehended a breach of the peace. It then, as is rightly expressed in this

---

[1] [1882] 9 Q.B.D. 308.   [2] [1858] I. F. & F. 325.

case, became his duty to prevent anything which in his view would cause that breach of the peace. While he was taking steps to do so he was wilfully obstructed by the appellant. I can conceive no clearer case within the statutes than that.

Singleton, J., concurred.

Appeal dismissed.

LIVERSIDGE v. SIR JOHN ANDERSON AND ANOTHER, 1941

House of Lords, [1942] A.C. 206

[Regulation 18 B of the Defence (General) Regulations, 1939 stated: "If the Secretary of State has reasonable cause to believe any person to be of hostile origin or associations or to have been recently concerned in acts prejudicial to the public safety or the defence of the realm or in the preparation or instigation of such acts and that by reason thereof it is necessary to exercise control over him, he may make an order against that person directing that he be detained." In May 1940, the Home Secretary, Sir John Anderson, made an order for the detention of Robert Liversidge. Liversidge applied for particulars of the grounds on which the Home Secretary had reasonable cause to believe him to be a person of hostile associations over whom control should be exercised.]

Appeal from the Court of Appeal affirming an order of the King's Bench Division refusing the appellant's application for particulars of defence in an action by him against the Home Secretary for false imprisonment.

VISCOUNT MAUGHAM: . . . I propose, first, to deal with the important question of the construction of the words in the regulation, "If the Secretary of State has reasonable cause to believe, etc.," that is, the question whether, as the appellant contends, the words require that there must be an external fact as to reasonable cause for the belief, and one, therefore, capable of being challenged in a court of law, or whether, as the respondents contend, the words, in the context in which they are found, point simply to the belief of the Secretary of State founded on his view of there being reasonable cause for the belief which he entertains. . . .

. . . The appellant's counsel truly say that the liberty of the subject is involved. They refer in emphatic terms to Magna Carta and the Bill of Rights, and they contend that legislation dealing with the liberty of the subject must be construed, if possible, in favour of the subject and against the Crown. Adopting the language of Lord Finlay, L.C., . . . in the case of *Rex* v. *Halliday*, I hold that the suggested rule has "no relevance in dealing with an executive measure by way of preventing a public danger" when the safety of the state is involved. . . .

. . . My Lords, I am not disposed to deny that, in the absence of a context, the prima facie meaning of such a phrase as "if A. B. has reasonable cause to believe" a certain circumstance or thing, it should be construed as meaning "if there is in fact reasonable cause for believing" that thing and if A. B. believes it. But I am quite unable to take the view that the words can only have that meaning. It seems to me reasonably clear that, if the thing to be believed is something which is essentially one within the knowledge of A. B. or one for the exercise of his exclusive discretion, the words might well mean if A. B. acting on what he thinks is reasonable cause (and, of course, acting in good faith) believes the thing in question.

In the present case there are a number of circumstances which tend to support the latter conclusion. . . .

. . . I am of the opinion that the arguments . . . in favour of the construction for which the Attorney-General contends must greatly outweigh any arguments . . . on the other side and that his construction must prevail. The result is that there is no preliminary question of fact which can be submitted to the courts and that in effect there is no appeal from the decision of the Secretary of State in these matters provided only that he acts in good faith. . . .

In my opinion, the present appeal should be dismissed. . . .

LORD ATKIN: . . . It is surely incapable of dispute that the words "if A has X" constitute a condition the essence of which is the existence of X and the having of it by A. If it is a condition to a right (including a power) granted to A, whenever the right comes into dispute the tribunal whatever it may be that is charged with determining the dispute must ascertain whether the condition is fulfilled. In some cases the issue is one of fact, in others of both fact and law, but in all cases the words indicate an existing something the having of which can be ascertained. And the words do not mean and cannot mean "if A thinks that he has." "If A has a broken ankle" does not mean and cannot mean "if A thinks that he has a broken ankle." "If A has a right of way" does not mean and cannot mean "if A thinks that he has a right of way." "Reasonable cause" for an action or a belief is just as much a positive fact capable of determination by a third party as is a broken ankle or a legal right. If its meaning is the subject of dispute as to legal rights, then ordinarily the reasonableness of the cause, and even the existence of any cause is in our law to be determined by the judge and not by the tribunal of fact if the functions deciding law and fact are divided. Thus, having established, as I hope, that the plain and natural meaning of the words "has reasonable cause" imports the existence of a fact or state of facts and not the mere belief by the person challenged that the fact or state of facts existed, I proceed to

show that this meaning of the words has been accepted in innumerable
legal decisions for many generations, that "reasonable cause" for a
belief when the subject of legal dispute has been always treated as an
objective fact to be proved by one or other party and to be determined
by the appropriate tribunal. I will go further and show that until
June or July of this year in connection with this reg. 18B, there never
has been any other construction even submitted to the courts in
whatever context the words are found. . . .

. . . [The] original form of the regulation issued in September, 1939,
gave the Secretary of State the complete discretion now contended for:
"The Secretary of State if satisfied, etc." But it was withdrawn and
republished in November, 1939, in its present form. It is not competent to us to investigate what political reasons necessitated this
change, but it is at least probable that it was made because objection
had been taken to the arbitrary power and it was seen that Parliament
might intervene. What is certain is that the legislators intentionally
introduced the well known safeguard by the changed form of words.

. . . No one doubts that the Emergency Powers (Defence) Act, 1939,
empowers His Majesty in Council to vest any minister with unlimited
power over the person and property of the subject. The only question
is whether in this regulation His Majesty has done so.

. . . It is said that it could never have been intended to substitute
the decision of judges for the decision of the minister, or, as has been
said, to give an appeal from the minister to the courts. But no one
proposes either a substitution or an appeal. A judge's decision is not
substituted for the constable's on the question of unlawful arrest, nor
does he sit on appeal from the constable. He has to bear in mind that
the constable's authority is limited and that he can only arrest on
reasonable suspicion, and the judge has the duty to say whether the
conditions of the power are fulfilled. If there are reasonable grounds,
the judge has no further duty of deciding whether he would have
formed the same belief any more than, if there is reasonable evidence
to go before a jury, the judge is concerned with whether he would
have come to the same verdict. . . .

I view with apprehension the attitude of judges who on a mere
question of construction when face to face with claims involving the
liberty of the subject show themselves more executive minded than the
executive. Their function is to give words their natural meaning, not,
perhaps in war time leaning towards liberty, but following the dictum
of Pollock, C.C., in *Bowditch* v. *Balchin*,[1] cited with approval by my
noble and learned friend Lord Wright in *Barnard* v. *Gorham*:[2] "In a
case in which the liberty of the subject is concerned, we cannot go
beyond the natural construction of the statute." In this country, amid
the clash of arms, the laws are not silent. They may be changed, but

[1] [1850] 5 Ex. 378.   [2] [1941] A.C. 378, 393.

they speak the same language in war as in peace. It has always been one of the pillars of freedom, one of the principles of liberty for which on recent authority we are now fighting, that the judges are no respecters of persons and stand between the subject and any attempted encroachments on his liberty by the executive, alert to see that any coercive action is justified in law. In this case I have listened to arguments which might have been addressed acceptably to the Court of King's Bench in the time of Charles I. . . .

LORD MACMILLAN: . . . In the first place, it is important to have in mind that the regulation in question is a war measure. This is not to say that the courts ought to adopt in wartime canons of construction different from those which they follow in peace time. . . . But in a time of emergency when the life of the whole nation is at stake it may well be that a regulation for the defence of the realm may quite properly have a meaning which because of its drastic invasion of the liberty of the subject the courts would be slow to attribute to a peace time measure. The purpose of the regulation is to ensure public safety, and it is right so to interpret emergency legislation as to promote rather than to defeat its efficacy for the defence of the realm. . . .

In the next place, it is relevant to consider to whom the emergency power of detention is confided. The statute has authorised it to be conferred on a Secretary of State, one of the high officers of State who, by reason of his position, is entitled to public confidence in his capacity and integrity, who is answerable to Parliament for his conduct in office and who has access to exclusive sources of information. In a question of interpreting the scope of a power it is obvious that a wide discretionary power may more readily be inferred to have been confided to one who has high authority and grave responsibility. . . .

LORD WRIGHT: . . . All the courts to-day, and not least this House, are as jealous as they have ever been in upholding the liberty of the subject. But that liberty is a liberty confined and controlled by law, whether common law or statute. It is, in Burke's words, a regulated freedom. It is not an abstract or absolute freedom. Parliament is supreme. . . . I have ventured on these elementary and obvious observations because it seems to have been suggested on behalf of the appellant that this House was being asked to countenance arbitrary, despotic or tyrannous conduct. But in the constitution of this country there are no guaranteed or absolute rights. The safeguard of British liberty is in the good sense of the people and in the system of representative and responsible government which has been evolved. If extraordinary powers are here given, they are given because the emergency is extraordinary and are limited to the period of the emergency. . . .

LORD ROMER: . . . It is also to be noticed that the words of para. 1 are not "if there *is* reasonable cause to believe," but, "if the Secretary of State *has* reasonable cause to believe." It is, of course, true, as has been said by my noble and learned friend Lord Atkin, that the words "if a man has a broken ankle" do not and cannot mean "if he thinks he has a broken ankle," but the regulation is not dealing with the state of a man's body. It is dealing with the state of man's belief, in other words with the state of his thoughts. The words "if a man has a belief that a certain thing exists" necessarily mean "if he thinks that the thing exists," and the word "has" may well have been used in the regulation to indicate that it is throughout concerned with the impression that is created on the mind of the Secretary of State and not with the impression they may produce on a court of law. Not only is the belief to be his. The estimate of the reasonableness of the causes that have induced such belief is also to be his and his alone. . . .

Appeal dismissed.

POINT OF AYR COLLIERIES, LTD. v. LLOYD GEORGE, 1943

Court of Appeal, [*1943*] *2 All E.R. 546*

LORD GREENE, M.R.: The object of the action out of which this appeal arises was to impugn the validity of an Order made on Feb. 5, 1943, entitled: "The Point of Ayr Collieries Limited Control Order, 1943." That Order was made by the Minister of Fuel and Power under the Defence (General) Regulations, reg. 55 (4). That paragraph, the relevant parts of which I will quote, is as follows:

If it appears to a competent authority that in the interests of the public safety, the defence of the realm, or the efficient prosecution of the war, or for maintaining supplies and services essential to the life of the community, it is necessary to take control on behalf of His Majesty of the whole or any part of an existing undertaking, and that, for the purpose of exercising such control, it is expedient that the undertaking or part should be carried on in pursuance of an order made under this paragraph, the competent authority may by order authorise any person . . . to exercise, with respect to the undertaking or any part thereof specified in the order, such functions of control on behalf of His Majesty as may be provided by the order. . . .

. . . In the present case the appellants have led a quantity of evidence. . . . It may be summed up by saying that the appellants' case is that there were no adequate grounds upon which the Minister could find as he says he found, namely, that it appeared to him that it was necessary to take control.

If one thing is settled beyond the possibility of dispute, it is that, in construing regulations of this character expressed in this particular form of language, it is for the competent authority, whatever Ministry that may be, to decide as to whether or not a case for the exercise of the powers has arisen. It is for the competent authority to judge of the adequacy of the evidence before it. It is for the competent authority to judge of the credibility of that evidence. It is for the competent authority to judge whether or not it is desirable or necessary to make further investigations before taking action. It is for the competent authority to decide whether the situation requires an immediate step, or whether some delay may be allowed for further investigation and perhaps negotiation. All those matters are placed by Parliament in the hands of the Minister in the belief that the Minister will exercise his powers properly, and in the knowledge that, if he does not so do, he is liable to the criticism of Parliament. One thing is certain, and that is that those matters are not within the competence of this court. It is the competent authority that is selected by Parliament to come to the decision, and, if that decision is come to in good faith, this court has no power to interfere, provided, of course, that the action is one which is within the four corners of the authority delegated to the Minister.

In the present case let me assume that every statement in the appellants' evidence is correct, and that there is nothing to be said on the other side, in other words that there are no additional facts outside those set out in the appellants' evidence. In my opinion, the appellants' evidence does not establish any circumstances which give this court power to interfere with what is admittedly the *bona fide* decision of the Minister. We cannot investigate the adequacy of his reasons. We cannot investigate the rapidity or the lack of investigation, if it existed, with which he acted. We cannot investigate any of those things because Parliament in its decision has withdrawn those matters from the courts and has entrusted them to the Ministers concerned, the constitutional safeguard being, as I have said, the supervision of Ministers exercised by Parliament. That being so, that is an end of the case. The Minister put in no evidence. He was not bound to put in any evidence, because his case rested on the basis that, even accepting the evidence put in by the appellants, there was no case for him to answer. In my opinion, that view was perfectly correct. . . .

Lords Goddard and du Parcq agreed.

Appeal dismissed.

RE HURLE-HOBBS, 1944

1 All E.R., [1944] 249

TUCKER, J.: . . . In the spring of 1940, the Lambeth Borough Council had a contract with two years still to run . . . for the collection and disposal of house, street and trade refuse in the Borough of Lambeth. . . . The contract had originally been entered into in 1932, and had been renewed for a further five years from 1937.

. . . In February 1940 [the contractor] applied to the Lambeth Borough Council for additional remuneration on the ground of increased prices due to the war. His application was referred to a sub-committee who, after considering a report from the borough engineer, recommended the payment of £7,000 in each of the two remaining years of the contract. This recommendation was adopted by the council on 25 April, 1940, and the sums in question were subsequently paid to the contractor. At an audit held by the district auditor in the autumn of 1942 these items were disallowed as being contrary to law, and 48 councillors who took part in the decision to make the payments were surcharged in respect thereof. From this decision of the district auditor the 48 councillors appeal to this court under the Local Government Act, 1933, s. 229.

Before referring further to the circumstances of this case it is, I think, essential to endeavour to ascertain the guiding principles to be applied in order to decide whether or not the payments impugned were unlawful. In this connection most assistance is, I think, afforded by a study of *Roberts* v. *Hopwood*.[1] It must however be remembered that that was a decision under the Metropolis Management Act, 1855, s. 62, dealing with wages. . . . It must also be kept in mind that the payments in question had been made in pursuance of a decision to pay a minimum wage of £4 a week for all adult labour, young and old, male and female, skilled and unskilled, it not having been shown, to use the words of Lord Sumner, that the women's work was the same or comparable with the men's, or that the women *inter se*, or the men *inter se*, were engaged in equivalent tasks. It was a decision held to have been made on social and political grounds rather than economic considerations. This being the position, much consideration was given to the question whether the word "reasonable," which did not appear in the section, was to be introduced for the purposes of construction. . . . [The House of Lords] made it clear that it is not for the district auditor, or the court, to substitute their discretion for that of the council if there are any grounds upon which the council could reasonably have exercised their discretion as they did. . . .

In the result, their Lordships were of opinion on the facts of that case that the council had given what amounted to gratuities to their servants without any compensatory benefits to the ratepayers and accordingly had not reasonably exercised their discretion but acted arbitrarily. . . .

In the present case we have to consider two payments made to a contractor who was already bound to perform the necessary services for the council for the collection and disposal of refuse until March 1942. It is not suggested that there was any consideration in law for these payments, and they were, therefore, in a sense gratuities and

[1] See above, p. 315.

voluntary payments. None the less, counsel for the district auditor does not contend that such lack of legal consideration will of itself render the payments "contrary to law." He says the payments were unlawful because the council considered extraneous matters, ignored much relevant matter, acted without real evidence of hardship on the part of the contractor or probability that the service would suffer, and failed to investigate his claim with proper care. In considering such contentions as these it is desirable to formulate with precision the test to be applied, and it is for this reason that I have set out in some detail the observations of their Lordships in *Roberts* v. *Hopwood*.

It appears to me that that case, although dealing with wages and a different section of the governing Act, indicates the broad principles which should be applied in the present case. It appears to me that the proper test to be applied in the circumstances of this case is contained in the following questions: (i) Did the councillors who have been sur-charged apply their minds to the relevant considerations in deciding to make these payments? (ii) Was there material upon which they could reasonably come to the conclusion that there was a danger that without the payments the services might be impaired? (iii) Was there material upon which they could reasonably fix the amount at £7,000? Their *bona fides* is not in question, so I omit what would otherwise be a material matter for consideration. These questions may perhaps be put more shortly thus: Was their decision arrived at solely in the interests of the ratepayers upon reasonable materials, or was it a mere arbitrary decision to pay away the moneys of the ratepayers as a gratuity to the contractor so that he should suffer no diminution of his profits?

Judged by this test I find that the propriety of the original contract and its price has never been questioned; that prices had admittedly risen to the extent of the percentages shown in the borough engineer's report upon which the council acted; that it was a time of war when it is more than usually difficult to foresee the probable course of events; that the council had received a letter from the contractor . . . which, I think, contains an implication that failing any increase he may no longer be able to maintain his services . . .; that the contractor occupied a unique position, and that failing him the only alternative would have been for the council hastily to improvise some system of their own at a time of labour shortage and rising prices; that the council had received a favourable recommendation from their experienced borough engineer; that they had received an undertaking from the contractor that he would ask for no further increase (including increases due to rises in wages) for the remainder of the contract period; and that the town clerk had advised them that such payments were lawful.

Taking all these matters into consideration and having regard to [various affidavits], all of which go to show that these gentlemen were applying their minds to the proper question, namely, the interests of the ratepayers and the likelihood of the services being impaired, I think there was material upon which the councillors could reasonably come to the conclusion that the services might suffer, and that they did in fact apply their minds solely to this consideration.

. . . I pass to consider the district auditor's reasons as set out in his report, to all of which I have given careful consideration before arriving at my decision already indicated. His reasons may be summarised as follows: (i) There was no consideration in law for the payments. (ii) The contract had not been frustrated. (iii) The contractor had not made out a *prima facie* case for increase. (iv) No evidence was provided as to the contractor's costs. (v) The council neglected to refer to their own records which would have shown that by March 1940 the services were diminishing in volume. (vi) Failure to consult other borough councils with whom the contractor had contracts. (vii) Failure to ask for expert advice from the borough treasurer. (viii) The council never in fact apprehended any danger of the service breaking down, and were never in real doubt as to the contractor's financial stability.

As to those, (i) and (ii) were not relied upon by counsel for the district auditor as sufficient *per se* to justify the disallowance. This is important, because it appears as if the district auditor took the view that these matters would of themselves have justified his decision apart from the other circumstances upon which he relied. (iii) to (vii) inclusive, deal with matters which are all relevant to the issue, but I do not think it necessary to deal with them *seriatim* in detail, because after giving them due weight as against the considerations previously set out, I have come to the conclusion that they do not turn the scale in favour of the disallowance. As to (iii), I ought perhaps to say that I am not in agreement with the district auditor's conclusion. (v) I reject. The figures show that by March 1940 there had been a slight drop in refuse collected, but the curve shown in the graph put in evidence was quite in accordance with seasonal fluctuations in previous years. . . . I can see no reason at all why the council should have anticipated any appreciable variation in the volume of the services to be rendered in the future, and I think this argument was born of wisdom acquired from after events.

The lack of evidence as to costs, and the failure to consult other borough councils, are in my view much the most serious objections. The absence of information as to costs, persisting until the present time, I have already referred to. The failure to consult the other boroughs was, I think, an unfortunate mistake, but if *bona fide* cannot, in my view, be considered as fatal to the contentions of the applicants. The borough treasurer, although not actually consulted, was throughout conversant with what was taking place, and never raised any objection.

With regard to (viii), I do not think it necessary that the councillors should actually anticipate a complete breakdown in the services or the bankruptcy of the contractor before sanctioning any increase. If the district auditor took this view, I think he was applying too severe a test. If he did not take such a narrow view, but is intending merely to say that the councillors had no material before them upon which they could reasonably anticipate any likelihood of some impairment in the services, then I take a different view on the evidence before us.

In the result, I am of opinion that this appeal succeeds, and that the disallowances and surcharges should be quashed.

Viscount Caldecote, L.C.J., and Atkinson, J., concurred.

Appeal allowed.

BLACKPOOL CORPORATION v. LOCKER, 1947

Court of Appeal, [*1948*] *1 K.B. 349*

[The Defence (General) Regulations, 1939, reg. 51, provided: "(1) A competent authority, if it appears . . . to be necessary or expedient to do so [for any purpose specified in s. 1 (1) of the Supplies and Services (Transitional Powers) Act, 1945] may take possession of any land, and may give such directions as appear . . . to be necessary or expedient in connection with the taking of possession. . . . (5) A competent authority may, to such extent and subject to such restrictions as it thinks proper, delegate all or any of its functions under paras. (1) to (3) of the regulation to any specified persons or class of persons."

The Minister of Health delegated his power to take possession of houses to local authorities by means of "circulars," which contained conditions, among others, that (i) no chattel might be requisitioned, and the requisition notice should give direction as to the disposal of chattels; and (ii) where the owner, within 14 days, notified his intention of occupying his house, the authority should not proceed further in the matter unless it were satisfied that this would result in serious under-occupation.

A prospective buyer of the defendant's house in Blackpool paid a deposit on 18 June 1946. Two days later, a requisition notice was served on the defendant under reg. 51 (1), stating that the town clerk of Blackpool had taken possession of the premises. This notice contained no direction as to the disposal of the defendant's furniture. The prospective buyer withdrew his offer; and on 26th June the defendant occupied the house himself, notifying the town clerk that he intended to live there. On 29th July, in the course of correspondence, the town clerk stated that the Minister of Health wished him to emphasise that the defendant had committed an offence under the Defence Regulations, that he was a trespasser, and that the premises must be vacated at once. On 20 August, the Minister purported to confirm the town clerk's decision, and on 28 November the Minister purported to ratify all the town clerk's actions in the matter.]

Appeal by the defendant from an order of the Blackpool County Court, granting the plaintiffs an injunction restraining the defendant from continuing to occupy his house, and awarding nominal damages for trespass. The county court judge held that, while the original requisitioning of the house was unauthorised, subsequent letters from the Minister had validated the town clerk's excess of authority.

SCOTT, L.J.: This appeal raises several important questions about the delegated legislation enacted by the Ministry of Health. . . . There is one quite general question affecting all such sub-delegated legislation and of supreme importance to the continuance of the rule of law under the British constitution, namely the right of the public affected to know what that law is. That right was denied to the defendant in the present case. . . .

The delegation of powers, both executive and legislative, was effected by what the Minister of Health styled "circulars." The instruments of delegation were justly entitled to that name as they were on their face addressed to all councils with powers of local government above the level of parish councils. . . .

Before I approach the history of the ways in which in the present case the corporation, on the one hand, and the Ministry on the other, sought to use or misuse the provisions of the circulars, it is necessary to consider their true legal effect. . . . The startling feature of the whole story before the court is that both the corporation and the officers of the Ministry of Health, when writing the letters in the correspondence and taking the views and actions therein appearing, radically misunderstood their own legal rights and duties, and appear to have been oblivious of the rights of the private householder. That the Minister's "circulars" were not mere executive directions but delegated legislation with statutory force, conferring powers on the corporation which they would not otherwise have possessed and imposing on them duties for the reasonable protection of the individual house-owner, does not seem to have entered the minds of either the corporation or the Ministry of Health. . . . I cannot help thinking that much of the legal misconceptions in the minds both of the Ministry of Health and of the corporation about the extent and scope of powers remaining vested in the Minister after he had delegated almost all of them to the corporation was due to the mistaken belief that he was, under para. (1), still retaining a general power of supervision. . . .

The Rules Publication Act, 1893, and the Statutory Instruments Act, 1946, which repealed the former and re-enacted an amended edition of it, had publicity as well as control by Parliament as a main object; but both have what seems to me the grave defect of not being applicable to any but primary delegated legislation. They are both expressly limited to such delegated legislation as is made under powers conferred by Act of Parliament, whether on His Majesty in Council or on a Minister of the Crown. Such primary delegated legislation has . . . to be printed forthwith by the King's Printer and published as a statutory rule or order, etc.: but for delegated legislation made under powers conferred *by a regulation or other legislative instrument not being itself an Act of Parliament,* there is no general statutory requirement of publicity in force to-day. Of such secondary or "sub-delegated" legislation as I call it for clarity, neither the general public . . . nor the legal adviser of an affected member of the public, however directly he may be affected, has any source of information about his rights, to which he can turn as of right and automatically. The modern extent of sub-delegated legislation is almost boundless; and it seems to me vital to the whole English theory of the liberty of the subject, that the affected person should be able at any time to ascertain what legislation affecting his rights has been passed under sub-delegated powers. So far as I know, this is the first case where that aspect of delegated legislation has come before the courts for direct consideration.

. . . The defendant's solicitor had the greatest difficulty in ascertaining from either the corporation or the Ministry what his client's rights were. . . . [In] order to bring out clearly the really monstrous character of some of the contentions and allegations of both corporation and Ministry, I want to analyse a little the legal relationships created by the circulars as sub-delegated legislation . . .; because it is only on understanding what those legal relations were that one realises the full gravity of this almost incredible case . . .

. . . [The] circulars contained . . . ministerial legislation with statutory force, transferring to the local authorities concerned the Minister's legal power to override the common law rights of individual members of the public, for the purposes defined in the circulars, and limited by their conditions. In any area of local government, where the Minister had by his legislation transferred such powers to the local authority, he, for the time being, divested himself of those powers, and, out of the extremely wide executive powers, which the primary delegated legislation contained in reg. 51, para. 1 had conferred on him to be exercised at his discretion, retained only those powers which in his sub-delegated legislation he had expressly or impliedly reserved for himself. The constitutional justification for the delegation permitted by para. 5 was obviously that local needs and opportunities relevant to the housing problem would necessarily be infinitely more within the local knowledge of the local authorities than in the Ministry whether central or regional. The letter of 28 November presumably sent upon direction from London was, in my opinion, *ultra vires* the Minister, and legally a nullity.

My conclusions on the whole case are as follows: (1) The original attempt at requisition on 20 June was inoperative for these reasons: (*a*) because the notice purported to requisition the house and its contents, whereas the corporation was by the terms of the sub-delegated legislation forbidden to requisition furniture . . .; (*b*) because a similar illegal usurpation of power was attempted in the corporation's omission to have the furniture contents put into a separate room at the time of requisition, or immediately after it. Thus, the notice, combined with the taking of the keys *colore officii*, involved an actual taking possession of both house and furniture, which in law was a trespass by the corporation. (2) On the notification by the defendant on 22 June and again on 27 June, of his intention himself to occupy, the corporation ought to have taken their hands right off ("shall not proceed further in the matter"). The house was never in fact "occupied" by the corporation and when the defendant entered, he entered an unoccupied house, of which the corporation never had any such possession in law as would make him then or thereafter a trespasser. . . .

Appeal allowed.

FRANKLIN AND OTHERS v. MINISTER OF TOWN AND COUNTRY PLANNING, 1947

House of Lords, [*1948*] *A.C. 87*

[The Minister of Town and Country Planning, after a public local inquiry had been held, made an order under the New Towns Act, 1946. The appellants applied to the High Court to have the order quashed, on the grounds: "(1) That the said order is not within the powers of the New Towns Act, 1946, or alternatively that the requirements of the said Act have not been complied with and the interests of the (appellants) have been thereby substantially prejudiced in that—(A) before considering the objections of the (appellants) the Minister stated that he would make the said order, and was thereby biased in any consideration of the said objections; and (B) the Minister did not before making the said order cause a public local inquiry to be held with respect thereto; and (2) that the New Towns Act, 1946, impliedly requires that the objections of the (appellants) should be fairly and properly considered by the Minister and that the Minister should give fair and proper effect to the result of such consideration in deciding whether the said order should be made and that such implied requirements were not complied with." Henn Collins, J., quashed the order, holding that, though the Minister had not acted ultra vires, he had not fulfilled his duty to act judicially in considering the objections. The Court of Appeal reversed this decision, holding that the appellants had not discharged the onus of proving that the Minister was biased when he made the order.]

LORD THANKERTON: My Lords, the appellants, who are the owners and occupiers of dwelling-houses and land situate at Stevenage, challenge the validity of the Stevenage New Town (Designation) Order,

1946, made on November 11, by the respondent, under the New Towns Act, 1946, which had received the Royal Assent on August 1, 1946. This challenge is made under s. 16 of the Town and Country Planning Act, 1944, which provides by sub-s. 1 (*b*) that the court "if satisfied that the order or any provision therein . . . is not within the powers of this Act or that the interests of the applicant have been substantially prejudiced by any requirement of this Act or of any regulation made thereunder not having been complied with, may quash the order or any provision contained therein . . . either generally or in so far as it affects any property of the applicant." The relevant provisions of the New Towns Act, 1946, are as follows: "1. (1) If the Minister is satisfied, after consultation with any local authorities who appear to him to be concerned, that it is expedient in the national interest that any area of land should be developed as a new town by a corporation established under this Act, he may make an order designating that area as the site of the proposed new town. (2) The provisions of sch. I to this Act shall have effect with respect to the procedure to be followed in connexion with the making of orders under this section; and ss. 16 and 17 of the Town and Country Planning Act, 1944, . . . shall apply to an order made under this section as they apply to an order made under s. 1 of that Act." The relevant provisions of sch. I as to orders under s. 1 are as follows: "1: Where the Minister proposes to make an order under s. 1 of this Act, he shall prepare a draft of the order describing the area to be designated as the site of the proposed new town. . . . 3. If any objection is duly made to the proposed order and is not withdrawn, the Minister shall, before making the order, cause a public local inquiry to be held with respect thereto, and shall consider the report of the person by whom the inquiry was held. 4. Subject to the provisions of the last foregoing paragraph the Minister may make the order either in terms of the draft or subject to such modifications as he thinks fit: Provided that, except with the consent of all persons interested, the Minister shall not make the order subject to a modification including in the area designated as the site of the proposed new town any land not so designated in the draft order." . . .

There does not appear to be much dispute as to the facts, but a great deal rests on the proper inference to be drawn from these facts. . . . On January 21, 1946, a committee appointed by the respondent, . . . and the Secretary of State for Scotland, known as the "Reith Committee" . . . recommended: "Arrangements should be made for setting up immediately a public corporation for the development of a new town at Stevenage to proceed with the necessary work in advance of legislation." The New Towns Bill was introduced by the respondent in the House of Commons on April 17, 1946, and was ordered to be printed. . . . On May 6, 1946, the respondent attended and spoke at a public meeting in Stevenage Town Hall, called to consider a proposal for designating an area of land in the neighbourhood of Stevenage as the site of a new town. The appellants base their case mainly on the statements made in an advance press notice issued by the respondent prior to the meeting, and statements made by the respondent in the course of his speech, as evidence that the respondent had by that time completely made up his mind that the designation of Stevenage as a new town would be carried through, whatever was said at the meeting or subsequently.

The New Towns Bill received a second reading in the House of Commons on May 8, 1946, and received the Royal Assent on August 1, 1946. The statutory duty of carrying out the designation of new towns thus became imposed on the respondent as Minister of Town and Country Planning. Under para. 1 of sch. I to the Act, the respondent prepared, on August 3, 1946, a draft order for the designation of the Stevenage area. . . . Objections were thereafter received, and, on the instructions of the respondent, a public local inquiry was held by Mr. Morris on October 7 and 8, 1946, and Mr. Morris made a report to the respondent on October 25, 1946. . . . On November 8, 1946, the respondent caused a letter to be sent to the objectors, in which, after stating that he had considered Mr. Morris's report, and that, after giving careful consideration to the various submissions made to him on behalf of interested local authorities and statutory undertakers and by private individuals affected by the proposals, he had decided to make the order. The respondent, in fourteen paragraphs, dealt in turn with the main objections raised. The appellants sought to maintain that, in para. 13, the respondent had not effectively dealt with the objections raised by the Metropolitan Water Board, the Lee Conservancy Board and the Lee Conservancy Catchment Board as to water supply and sewage disposal, which the appellants contended were vital to the practicability of the whole proposal, but only stated that he had appointed a consultant to examine the possibilities of a scheme which will apply to a much wider area than that of the immediate vicinity of Stevenage. In my opinion this contention . . . was correctly disposed of by Lord Oaksey, L.J., [in the Court of Appeal], who pointed out that none of these authorities had ever suggested that it was an entirely unpracticable scheme, and that it really raised a question of expense. . . . It appears to me that the respondent's letter of November 8 not only does not support the appellants' contention, but that it is evidence that the Minister had properly considered the objections.

. . . Henn Collins, J., upheld the first contention of the present appellants on the ground that the respondent's functions in considering the report of Mr. Morris's inquiry were quasi-judicial, that he did not consider the objections with an open mind, and that "he did not consider or decide the question aye or no should the order be confirmed with an open mind, but that he meant to confirm it whatever the force of the objections might be, trusting that some solution would be found." The learned judge based his view on the respondent's speech of May 6, 1946, and on para. 13 of the respondent's letter of November 8. As regards the former, he says: "If I am to judge by what he said at the public meeting which was held very shortly before the Bill, then published, became an Act of Parliament, I could have no doubt but that any issue raised by objectors was fore-judged. . . . But when he made that speech . . . he had no administrative functions in relation to the Act in question, for the Act had not then been passed. Though that was his attitude two days before the Bill received the second reading, it is upon the objectors to prove that the Minister was in a like mind, or at least had not an open mind, from and after, at latest, the inception of the public inquiry, which was held in October, 1946." As regards the letter of November 8, 1946, the learned judge says: "In this case . . . the Minister has dealt, in writing, with the substance of the objections—with one exception, namely, that directed to the difficulties of water supply and sewage disposal. It is obvious that those difficulties must be met before the scheme can go through. The Minister acknowledges that they have not been met, and that he is taking advice as to how it can be done. Non constat that any way will be found. And yet, with that fundamental problem still outstanding, the Minister confirms his order. How can it be said that he weighed the objection with an open mind when he acknowledges that he did not and does not know the force of it? When, therefore, I ask myself whether the objectors have satisfied me that from and after the inception of the inquiry up to and including the moment at which the Minister decided to confirm his order, he had not an open mind, my answer is that they have." It is clear that had the learned judge appreciated, as was pointed out in the Court of Appeal, that no witness had suggested that the scheme could not go through, unless the suggested difficulties of water supply and sewage disposal had been met, and had he realised that he had put a wrong construction on para. 13 of the letter of November 8, he would not only have been left without any evidence that from and after the inception of the inquiry up to and including the confirmation of the order the respondent had not an open mind, but he would have had the evidence of the letter . . . that the respondent had so considered the report, and he should also have taken account of the unchallenged affidavit of the respondent on January 21, 1947, referred to by the Court of Appeal that "before causing the said order to be made, I personally carefully considered all the objections made by the objectors including the present applicants, together with the submissions made and evidence given on their behalf as appearing in the said transcript. I also carefully considered the report of the said Arnold Morris." . . . In that aspect of the evidence it appears that the learned judge in view of his reasoning, as above quoted, would not have quashed the order. The Court of Appeal accepted this view of the reasoning of the learned judge, and, while assuming that his inference from the respondent's speech of May 6, that the respondent had not then an open mind and that any issue raised by the objectors was fore-judged was well-founded, held that the learned judge's statement of the evidence of the objectors as to water supply and sewage disposal was incorrect, it not having been suggested that the scheme was entirely impracticable, and on his erroneous construction of the letter of November 8, set aside the decision of Henn Collins, J., and restored the Stevenage New Town (Designation) Order of the present respondent.

My Lords, I agree with the decision of the Court of Appeal, but I am of opinion that an incorrect view of the law applicable in this case was taken by the learned judge, and I feel bound, despite the assumption of its correctness by the Court of Appeal, to examine the correctness of the learned judge's view as to the proper inference from the respondent's speech of May 6. . . . In my opinion, no judicial, or quasi-judicial, duty was imposed on the respondent, and any reference to judicial duty, or bias, is irrelevant in the present case. The respondent's duties under s. 1 of the Act and sch. I thereto are, in my opinion, purely administrative, but the Act prescribes certain methods of, or steps in, discharge of that duty. It is obvious that, before making the draft order, which must contain a definite proposal to designate the area concerned as the site of a new town, the respondent must have made elaborate inquiry into the matter and have consulted any local authorities who appear to him to be concerned, and obviously other departments of the Government, such as the Ministry of Health, would naturally require to be consulted. It would seem, accordingly, that the respondent was required to satisfy himself that it was a sound scheme before he took the serious step of issuing a draft order. It seems clear also, that the purpose of inviting objections, and, where they are not withdrawn, of having a public inquiry, to be held by someone other than the respondent, to whom that person reports, was for the further information of the respondent, in order to the final consideration of the soundness of the scheme of the designation; and it is important to note that the development of the site, after the order is made, is primarily the duty of the development corporation established under s. 2 of the Act. I am of opinion that no judicial duty is laid on the respondent in discharge of these statutory duties, and that the only question is whether he has complied with the statutory directions to appoint a person to hold the public inquiry, and to consider that person's report. On this contention of the appellants no suggestion is made that the public inquiry was not properly conducted, nor is there any criticism of the report by Mr. Morris. In such a case the only ground of challenge must be either that the respondent did not in fact consider the report and the objections, of which there is here no evidence, or that his mind was so foreclosed that he gave no genuine consideration to them, which is the case made by the appellants. Although I am unable to agree exactly with the view of the respondent's duty expressed by the learned judge, or with some of the expressions used by the Court of Appeal in regard to that matter, it does appear to me that the issue was treated in both courts as being whether the respondent had genuinely considered the objections and the report, as directed by the Act.

My Lords, I could wish that the use of the word "bias" should be confined to its proper sphere. Its proper significance, in my opinion, is to denote a departure from the standard of even-handed justice which the law requires from those who occupy judicial office, or those who are commonly regarded as holding a quasi-judicial office, such as an arbitrator. . . . But, in the present case, the respondent having no judicial duty, the only question is what the respondent actually did, that is, whether in fact he did genuinely consider the report and the objections.

Coming now to the inference of the learned judge from the respondent's speech on May 6, that he had not then a mind open to conviction, . . . [it] seems probable that the learned judge's mind was influenced by his having already held that the respondent's function was quasi-judicial, which would raise the question of bias, but, in any view, I am clearly of opinion that nothing said by the respondent was inconsistent with the discharge of his statutory duty, when subsequently objections were lodged, and the local public inquiry took place, followed by the report of that inquiry, genuinely to consider the report and the objections. The only passages in the speech quoted in the appellants' case are contained in the third quotation I have made . . .: "I want to carry out in Stevenage a daring exercise in town planning. (*Jeers.*) It is no good your jeering: it is going to be done. . . . After all this new town is to be built in order to provide for the happiness of sixty thousand men, women and children. . . . The project will go forward, because it must go forward. . . ." The only two additional passages . . . were . . . "In anticipation of the passage of the Bill— and I have no doubt that it will go through," and . . . "But we have a duty to perform, and I am not going to be deterred from that duty. While I will consult as far as possible all the local authorities, at the end, if people become fractious and unreasonable, I shall have to carry out my duty—— (*Voice:* Gestapo!)" My Lords, these passages in a speech, which was of a political nature, and of the kind familiar in a speech on second reading, demonstrate (1) the speaker's view that the Bill would become law, that Stevenage was a most suitable site and should be the first scheme in the operation, and that the Stevenage project would go forward, and (2) the speaker's reaction to the hostile interruptions of a section of the audience. In my opinion, these passages are not inconsistent with an intention to carry out any statutory duty imposed on him by Parliament, although he intended to press for the enactment of the Bill, and thereafter to carry out the duties thereby involved, including the consideration of objections which were neither fractious nor unreasonable. I am, therefore, of opinion that the first contention of the appellants fails, in that they have not established either that in the respondent's speech he had fore-judged any genuine consideration of the objections or that he had not genuinely considered the objections at the later stage when they were submitted to him.

The remaining contention of the appellants is that the inquiry held by Mr. Morris did not comply with the statutory requirements for such a local public inquiry, in respect that no evidence in support of the draft order was led on behalf of the respondent. . . . As I have already pointed out, the object of the inquiry is further to inform the mind of the Minister, and not to consider any issue between the Minister and the objectors; that is for the Minister thereafter to consider and decide. Accordingly, I am of opinion that this contention of the appellants also fails.

In my opinion, the appeal should be dismissed and the judgment of the Court of Appeal should be affirmed . . .

Lords Porter, Uthwatt, du Parcq and Normand, concurred.

Appeal dismissed.

R. v. TRONOH MINES, LTD., AND OTHERS, 1952

Central Criminal Court, [*1952*] *1 A11 E.R. 697*

[After writs had been issued for the General Election of 1951, a company published in a national newspaper an advertisement headed "Tronoh-Malayan Tin Group of Companies. Interim statement on dividend limitation", which contained criticisms of the Labour Party's financial policy and included these words: "The coming general election will give us all the opportunity of saving the country from being reduced, through the policies of the Socialist government, to a bankrupt 'Welfare State'. We need a new and strong government with Ministers who may be relied upon to encourage business enterprise and initiative. . . ." The company, the secretary, and the proprietors of *The Times* newspaper were jointly charged with unlawfully incurring expenses with a view to promoting or procuring the election of a candidate other than the Labour candidate at the parliamentary election to be held in the constituency in which the company had its office and the

newspaper was published, contrary to s. 63 (1) (b) and s. 63 (5) of the Representation of the People Act, 1949. On a second count, it was alleged that the
expenses were incurred with a view to promoting or procuring the election
of the Conservative candidate in this constituency.]

McNAIR, J.: On the view I take of the construction of s. 63 (1) of
the Representation of the People Act, 1949, this is not a case which I
can properly leave to jury. . . .
    . . . So far as is material, s. 63 (1) provides:

"No expenses shall, with a view to promoting or procuring the election of a
candidate at an election, be incurred by any person other than the candidate,
his election agent and persons authorised in writing by the election agent on
account—(a) of holding public meetings or organising any public display; or
(b) of issuing advertisements, circulars or publications; or (c) of otherwise
presenting to the electors the candidate or his views or the extent or nature
of his backing or disparaging another candidate. . . ."

    . . . It seems to me that (c) necessarily imports that the particular
items specified in (a) and (b) must also, if they are to be caught by
the prohibition, be items which have the effect of "presenting to the
electors the candidate or his views or the extent or nature of his backing or disparaging another candidate." If this result had not been
intended, it seems to me that para. (c) would have run: "of presenting
to the electors, whether by means specified in para. (a) or para. (b),
or in any other way, the candidate or his views . . ." Furthermore,
the Interpretation Act, 1889, s. 1 (1), provides that, unless the context otherwise requires, words importing the singular include the
plural, and I think that the context here does necessarily require that
references to the election of a candidate at an election means a candidate at a particular election and not candidates at elections
generally. . . .
    I have reached the decision that on the evidence no reasonable jury
could find that the advertisement in question was presenting to the
electors of any constituency any particular candidate, still less presenting to the electors of the cities of London and Westminster either
the Conservative candidate or any candidate other than a Socialist
candidate or his views.
    . . . If expenses incurred on account of the items specified in (a), (b)
and (c), being supported in writing by the election agent, are permissible and authorised by the election agent, then, by virtue of
sub-s. (2) the person who incurs them has to make a return to the
returning officer of the amount of those expenses, stating the election
at which and the candidate in whose support they were incurred. . . .
[It] is clear that [the prescribed] form is inappropriate for making a
return of expenses of the kind with which we are here concerned.
There is no way in which the expenditure, on the hypothesis I have

stated, incurred in relation to all elections can be apportioned for the purpose of any particular return for a particular election. That consideration alone seems to me to lend strong support to the view that the section is not intended to prohibit expenditure incurred on advertisements designed to support, or having the effect of supporting, the interest of a particular party generally in all constituencies, at any rate at the time of a general election, and not supporting a particular candidate in a particular constituency. . . .

Verdict: "Not Guilty" on both counts.

The Parties and the Electorate

THE CONSTITUTION OF THE LABOUR PARTY, 1918

1.—NAME

The Labour Party.

2.—MEMBERSHIP

The Labour Party shall consist of all its affiliated organisations,[1] together with those men and women who are individual members of a Local Labour Party and who subscribe to the Constitution and Programme of the Party.

3.—PARTY OBJECTS

NATIONAL

(*a*) To organise and maintain in Parliament and in the country a Political Labour Party, and to ensure the establishment of a Local Labour Party in every County Constituency and every Parliamentary Borough, with suitable divisional organisation in the separate constituencies of Divided Boroughs;

(*b*) To co-operate with the Parliamentary Committee of the Trades Union Congress, or other Kindred Organisations, in joint political or other action in harmony with the Party Constitution and Standing Orders;

(*c*) To give effect as far as may be practicable to the principles from time to time approved by the Party Conference;

(*d*) To secure for the producers by hand or by brain the full fruits of their industry, and the most equitable distribution thereof that may be possible, upon the basis of the common ownership of the means of production and the best obtainable system of popular administration and control of each industry or service;

(*e*) Generally to promote the Political, Social, and Economic Emancipation of the People, and more particularly of those who depend directly upon their own exertions by hand or by brain for the means of life.

INTER-DOMINION

(*f*) To co-operate with the Labour and Socialist organisations in the Dominions and the Dependencies with a view to promoting the purposes of the Party and to take common action for the promotion of a higher standard of social and economic life for the working population of the respective countries.

---

[1] Trade Unions, Socialist Societies, Co-operative Societies, Trades Councils, and Local Labour Parties.

INTERNATIONAL

(*g*) To co-operate with the Labour and Socialist organisations in other countries and to assist in organising a Federation of Nations for the maintenance of Freedom and Peace, for the establishment of suitable machinery for the adjustment and settlement of International Disputes by Conciliation or Judicial Arbitration, and for such International Legislation as may be practicable.

4.—PARTY PROGRAMME

(*a*) It shall be the duty of the Party Conference to decide, from time to time, what specific proposals of legislative, financial, or administrative reform shall receive the general support of the Party, and be promoted, as occasion may present itself, by the National Executive and the Parliamentary Labour Party, provided that no such proposal shall be made definitely part of the General Programme of the Party unless it has been adopted by the Conference by a majority of not less than two-thirds of the votes recorded on a card vote.

(*b*) It shall be the duty of the National Executive and the Parliamentary Labour Party, prior to every General Election, to define the principal issues for that Election which in their judgment should be made the Special Party Programme for that particular Election Campaign, which shall be issued as a manifesto by the Executive to all constituencies where a Labour Candidate is standing.

(*c*) It shall be the duty of every Parliamentary representative of the Party to be guided by the decision of the meetings of such Parliamentary representatives, with a view to giving effect to the decisions of the Party Conference as to the General Programme of the Party.

5.—THE PARTY CONFERENCE

1. The work of the Party shall be under the direction and control of the Party Conference, which shall itself be subject to the Constitution and Standing Orders of the Party. The Party Conference shall meet regularly once in each year, and also at such other times as it may be convened by the National Executive.

2. The Party Conference shall be constituted as follows:—

(*a*) Trade Unions and other societies affiliated to the Party may send one delegate for each thousand members on which fees are paid.

(*b*) Local Labour Party delegates may be either men or women resident or having a place of business in the constituency they represent, and shall be appointed as follows:—

In Borough and County Constituencies returning one Member to Parliament, the Local Labour Party may appoint one delegate.

In undivided Boroughs returning two Members two delegates may be appointed.

In divided Boroughs one delegate may be appointed for each separate constituency within the area. The Local Labour Party within the constituency shall nominate and the Central Labour Party of the Divided Borough shall appoint the delegates. In addition to such delegates, the Central Labour Party in each Divided Borough may appoint one delegate.

An additional woman delegate may be appointed for each constituency in which the number of affiliated and individual women members exceeds 500.

(*c*) Trades Councils under Section 8, clause *c*, shall be entitled to one delegate.

(*d*) The members of the National Executive, including the Treasurer, the members of the Parliamentary Labour Party, and the duly-sanctioned Parliamentary Candidates shall be *ex officio* members of the Party Conference, but shall, unless delegates, have no right to vote.

6.—THE NATIONAL EXECUTIVE

(*a*) There shall be a National Executive of the Party consisting of twenty-three members (including the Treasurer) elected by the Party Conference at its regular Annual Meeting, in such proportion and under such conditions as may be set out in the Standing Orders for the time being in force, and this National Executive shall, subject to the control and directions of the Party Conference, be the Administrative Authority of the Party.

(*b*) The National Executive shall be responsible for the conduct of the general work of the Party. The National Executive shall take steps to ensure that the Party is represented by a properly constituted organisation in each constituency in which this is found practicable; it shall give effect to the decisions of the Party Conference; and it shall interpret the Constitution and Standing Orders and Rules of the Party in all cases of dispute subject to an appeal to the next regular Annual Meeting of the Party Conference by the organisation or person concerned.

(*c*) The National Executive shall confer with the Parliamentary Labour Party at the opening of each Parliamentary Session, and also at any other time when the National Executive or the Parliamentary Party may desire such conference, on any matters relating to the work and progress of the Party, or to the efforts necessary to give effect to the General Programme of the Party.

7.—PARLIAMENTARY CANDIDATURES

(*a*) The National Executive shall co-operate with the Local Labour Party in any constituency with a view to nominating a Labour Candidate at any Parliamentary General or Bye-Election. Before any Parliamentary Candidate can be regarded as finally adopted for a constituency as a Candidate of the Labour Party, his candidature must be sanctioned by the National Executive.

(*b*) Candidates approved by the National Executive shall appear before their constituencies under the designation of "Labour Candidate" only. At any General Election they shall include in their Election Addresses and give prominence in their campaigns to the issues for that Election as defined by the National Executive from the General Party Programme. If they are elected they shall act in harmony with the Constitution and Standing Orders of the Party in seeking to discharge the responsibilities established by Parliamentary practice.

(*c*) Party Candidates shall receive financial assistance for election expenditure from the Party funds on the following basis:—

Borough Constituencies, £1 per 1,000 electors.

County Divisions, £1 15*s.* per 1,000 electors.

8.—AFFILIATION FEES

1. Trade Unions, Socialist Societies, Co-operative Societies, and other organisations directly affiliated to the Party (but not being affiliated Local Labour Parties or Trades Councils) shall pay 2*d.* per member per annum to the Central Party Funds with a minimum of 30*s.*

The membership of a Trade Union for the purpose of this clause shall be those members contributing to the political fund of the Union established under the Trade Union Act, 1913.

2. The affiliation of Trades Councils will be subject to the following conditions:—

(*a*) Where Local Labour Parties and Trades Councils at present exist in the same area, every effort must be made to amalgamate these bodies, retaining in one organisation the industrial and political functions, and incorporating the constitution and rules for Local Labour Parties in the rules of the amalgamated body.

(*b*) Where no Local Labour Party is in existence and the Trades Council is discharging the political functions, such Trades Council shall be eligible for affiliation as a Local Labour Party, providing that its rules and title be extended so as to include Local Labour Party functions.

(*c*) Where a Local Labour Party and a Trades Council exist in the same area, the Trades Council shall be eligible to be affiliated to the

Local Labour Party, but not to the National Party, except in such cases where the Trades Council was affiliated to the National Party prior to November 1st, 1917. In these cases the Executive Committee shall have power to continue national affiliation on such conditions as may be deemed necessary.

(*d*) Trades Councils included under Section (*c*) shall pay an annual affiliation fee of 30*s.*

Local Labour Parties must charge individual enrolled members, male a minimum of 1*s.* per annum, female 6*d.* per annum; and 2*d.* per member so collected must be remitted to the Central Office with a minimum of 30*s.*, as the affiliation fee of such Local Labour Party.

In addition to these payments, a delegation fee of 5*s.* to the Party Conference or any Special Conference may be charged.

(*Constitution as adopted by the Party Conference held in London on February 26th, 1918.*)

THE CONSERVATIVE PARTY AND THE COALITION, 1922

Report of a meeting of Conservative Members of the House of Commons at the Carlton Club on 19 October, 1922.

THE CHAIRMAN (MR. AUSTEN CHAMBERLAIN): . . . I do not think it is necessary to read any of the letters of apology [for absence], except one which I have received from Lord Curzon . . . :—

MY DEAR CHAMBERLAIN,

I have been a good deal concerned at the idea of members of the House of Lords, and particularly myself, as leader, being present, and very likely being called upon to speak, at the meeting of the members of the House of Commons at the Carlton Club tomorrow. As you may have learned, considerable feeling has been aroused at the limitation of the meeting to members of one House of Parliament alone, and although the situation is quite clear as it affects yourself and your leadership of the party in your House, since you are appealing to the body by which you were elected, it is different as regards myself and my House.

I have received several protests from peers against my taking part, as leader of the House of Lords, in a meeting from which peers are excluded, and seeking to influence by anything that I may say the members of the House of Lords, and I think in the circumstances that it will be better that I should abstain.

I am,

Yours very sincerely,

CURZON OF KEDLESTONE.

My lords and gentlemen: I have asked you and my friends in the Cabinet to meet me because it was you who elected me as your leader in the House of Commons, and in so doing practically appointed me to my present position. I have asked you to meet at this moment because it is a moment fraught with grave issues for our party and for our country. . . .

For months past the task of Government has been increasingly difficult, and the strain placed upon your leaders has been almost indefinitely increased by the failure of unanimity of support from the party behind them. . . .

It is not only in foreign policy that criticism has become increasingly frequent and increasingly difficult. Whatever might have happened, you all know that an election could not be long postponed; and instead of occupying our energies in healing our differences and trying to unite as firmly and as closely as possible our ranks in view of the coming fight, the party has been discussing in groups and sections what course it will pursue, what support it will give to its leaders, what notice it shall give to its allies.

No Government can be conducted with credit to itself or with security for the country in the continuation of circumstances such as those. There often comes a moment in the lives of parties and of Governments when they must take a critical decision. Either they must hang on and go steadily downhill more and more discredited to eventual disaster, or they take the bolder resolve and they seek from those who put them in their position a renewal of the mandate that they hold. We are at one of those moments now, and for my friends and myself I say we have come to the conclusion that it is impossible to continue as we are and that we must seek the earliest appeal to those who are our masters.

I want to ask you to consider under what condition and in what form that appeal is to be made. What are the forces and the policies which stand face to face with one another upon which the country must give its verdict? . . . The old party issues are dead; new problems, new phases, new issues confront us, to-day, new issues, new problems of a different character. They are not the old political questions so often fought out in our long political history; they are social and economic questions. There is, for the first time, by quite the second largest party in the State, a direct challenge to all these fundamental principles of society which hitherto both the great parties in the State have encouraged. . . .

That is the real issue that has to be fought out at the next election. The real issue is not between Liberals and Conservatives. It is not between the old Liberal policy and the old Conservative policy. It is between those who stand for individual freedom and those who are for the socialisation of the State; those who stand for free industry and those who stand for nationalisation, with all its controls and all its inefficiencies. And it is at this moment . . . I am bidden to give notice to quit to the allies with whom I have worked.

My friends and I have carefully . . . considered this situation. . . . To us it appears that this is not a moment to break with old friends, and scatter the forces which can be united in the defence of a cause which is common to us all. . . .

Under the circumstances, my friends and I have come to the conclusion that the advice which, on the eve of an election, we ought to tender to you is that we should maintain the closest, most cordial co-operation in the constituencies and throughout the fight, and after the fight, with the men who have stood by us in the difficult years. We think, we hope, that every Unionist and Conservative, every Liberal-Coalitionist, should stand under his own party name and should retain his party loyalty unimpaired. . . .

. . . If the result of such co-operation gives to the two parties so co-operating the victory, a reconstruction of the Government as the result of the changes of the election will, of course, be necessary; but I submit to you . . . that what the nature of that reconstruction is to be cannot and ought not to be determined until the result of the election is known. . . .

. . . It is you, deriving your authority from the electors, who conferred my authority upon me and made me what I am, and in such a matter as this I can accept no appeal from you to any other authority than that of the electors, who are the masters of us all.

MR. STANLEY BALDWIN: . . . it is my duty at this moment to put before you . . . the views of the minority in the Cabinet—that is, of myself and of Sir Arthur Boscawen. . . .

. . . The Prime Minister . . . is a dynamic force, and it is from that very fact that our troubles, in my opinion, arise. A dynamic force is a very terrible thing; it may crush you, but it is not necessarily right.

It is owing to that dynamic force, and that remarkable personality, that the Liberal Party, to which he formerly belonged, has been smashed to pieces; and it is my firm conviction that, in time, the same thing will happen to our party. . . . We have already seen, during our association with him in the last four years, a section of our party hopelessly alienated. I think that if the present association is continued, . . . the process must go on inevitably until the old Conservative Party is smashed to atoms and lost in ruins. . . .

CAPTAIN PRETYMAN: . . . I propose to move a resolution . . . :

That this meeting of Conservative Members of the House of Commons declares its opinion that the Conservative party, whilst willing to co-operate with Coalition-Liberals, fights the election as an independent party, with its own leader and its own programme.

MR. BONAR LAW: . . . This is a question in regard to which our system . . . has hitherto gone on this principle: that the party elects a leader, and that the leader chooses the policy, and if the party does not like it, they have to get another leader. The question that has to be decided at this meeting is not something that affects the House of Commons alone. It is something which affects every Unionist in every constituency. If it were possible, even at this last moment (I am afraid it is not), I would say: "Let Mr. Chamberlain and those who think with him, and those who disagree with him, submit to the party the question: 'Shall we or shall we not continue the Coalition?' and let us abide by their decision." If that is possible, I would gladly adopt that. But if it is not possible, then what is the position? I am, I suppose, more of a party man than some people. I was leader of our party for a number of years. During the war I really did not think much of the party, but I did always have at the back of my mind, the earnest desire to keep it as a united party, whatever happened. . . . Now we are faced with, I am sorry to say, an inevitable split, and I am afraid the suggestion I have put forward cannot be adopted. I confess frankly that in the immediate crisis in front of us I do personally attach more importance to keeping our party a united body than to winning the next election. I would not say that if I thought there were a danger, as the result of that election, of a Labour Government coming into power. . . .

Now, what is the position? . . . If Mr. Chamberlain's view is carried at this meeting, what happens? It is very wrong that the party should be driven by the minority, but this is certain: that the feeling against the continuance of the Coalition is so strong that our party will be broken—that a new party will be formed; and, not the worst of the evils of that is this, that on account of those who have gone, who are supposed to be more moderate men, what is left of the Conservative Party will become more reactionary; and I for one say that though what you call the reactionary element in our party has always been there, and must always be there, if it is the sole element, our party is absolutely lost. Therefore, if you agree with Mr. Chamberlain in this crisis, I will tell you what I think will be the result. It will be a repetition of what happened after Peel passed the Corn Bill. The body that is cast off will slowly become the Conservative Party, but it will take a generation before it gets back to the influence which the party ought to have . . .

. . . For these reasons, very reluctantly, I shall vote in favour of no Coalition. . . .

The resolution was put to the meeting, and the votes were as follows;

Ayes	.	.	.	*187*
Noes	.	.	.	*87*

CONFERENCE ON ELECTORAL REFORM, 1929-30

Letter from Viscount Ullswater to the Prime Minister (Cmd. 3,636, 1930)

DEAR PRIME MINISTER,

The Conference over which you invited me to preside was formed . . . from three panels of names submitted to me by the Labour, the Conservative and the Liberal parties. . . . Three peers were also added, one from each party. . . .

No terms of reference were given, but it was arranged that the Conference should itself determine the subjects which it would consider, in the light of the suggestions made by the parties, and the order in which they would be taken. . . .

The Conference held its first meeting on 4 December 1929, when it was decided that the first matter to consider was the suggestion of the Liberal section that some system should be adopted with a view to "securing that the composition of the House of Commons shall properly reflect the views expressed by the electorate." It appeared to the Conference that not only was this the most important of the subjects suggested for discussion, but that consideration of any other changes in the law relating to Parliamentary elections might be materially affected by any decision to alter the present system of election.

During ten sittings we thoroughly examined and debated the merits of proportional representation and of the alternative vote as compared with each other and with the existing system. . . .

After a time it became clear that there would be great difficulty in obtaining any general agreement in answer to the question whether any, and if so what, system of election could be recommended in place of the existing system. It was therefore decided, in order to obtain an indication of the direction which further debate should take, to take a provisional vote on the proposals put forward by the Liberal section, which were moved in the form of four Resolutions.

Resolution I.—Any change in the present system of Parliamentary elections should include the adoption of Proportional Representation with the single transferable vote.

This resolution received the support of the Liberal and Conservative sections, together numbering thirteen, but was opposed by the Labour section, eight in number. The support of most of the Conservative section was conditional upon it being decided that a change of some character must be made.

Resolution II.—Certain divisions should remain as single-member constituencies.

This resolution was carried by 11 votes to 8, the minority being composed of the Labour section.

Resolution III.—In the said single-member constituencies, the method of the Alternative Vote should be adopted.

This resolution was negatived by 13 votes to 5, the minority being composed of the Liberal section, one of the Labour section abstaining from voting.

Resolution IV.—Special provision should be made in P.R. constituencies to permit bye-elections being held in divisions of a constituency.

This resolution was carried by 8 votes to 0, nine members abstaining from voting.

The Liberal section explained that, in the event of proportional representation not being finally accepted, they would be prepared to consider the adoption of the alternative vote generally as being preferable to the present system.

The Conservative section indicated that they were not prepared to agree to the alternative vote in any circumstances.

The Labour section explained that none of them was willing to support the alternative vote *per se*, but that some of them were prepared to accept it on conditions that other reforms were adopted at the same time.

Those reforms were as follows:

(1) *Reduction of Election Expenses*

The reduction of a Candidate's expenses at a Parliamentary Election from 6*d.* to 5*d.* per elector in Counties, and from 5*d.* to 4*d.* in Boroughs.

(2) *Party Election Expenditure*

The Publication of Accounts by Political Parties nationally and locally, and a provision to prevent Political Parties spending money on Elections except such expenditure appears in the Election Returns of Candidates and their Agents.

(3) *Speakers' Expenses*

Alteration of the Law to make the payment of Speakers and their travelling expenses legal, providing they are included in the Returns of Candidates and their Agents.

(4) *Motor Cars*

Making the use of Motor Cars illegal for the purpose of bringing people to the Poll, except under suitable regulations laid down by the Returning Officer in the case of persons infirm, sick and disabled.

(5) *Plural Voting*

Abolition of all plural voting, and the repeal of the Business Premises qualification and the University qualification for the Franchise.

(6) *Half-Yearly Registers*

A revision of the Law to enable Returning Officers to compile two Registers of Electors per annum, viz., Spring and Autumn.

(7) *Returning Officers' Deposits*

An amendment of the Law to reduce the quota of Electors from one-eighth to one-tenth, below which the Returning officer's deposit becomes forfeited.

(8) *Double-Membered Constituencies*

The division of Double-membered Constituencies into two Single-membered Constituencies.

(9) *Election Petitions*

Alteration of the Law so as to reduce costs and simplify procedure.

I had already informed the Conference that in my judgment some of the above-mentioned matters were beyond the scope of our enquiry, as they did not arise from experiences gained since the passing of the Representation of the People Act, 1918.

The Conservative section had expressed the view that if questions of Corrupt Practice at elections were to be raised, the enquiry should extend to the whole question of Corrupt and Illegal Practices at elections, including all kinds of expenditure incurred, and all services rendered in connection with elections; also intimidation and persona-tion, rowdyism at meetings or during the election, and slander of candidates or party leaders.

At this stage I consulted you as to the desirability of the Conference proceeding further. Your reply left it to the Conference to decide for itself whether it should continue its sittings. Thereupon the Conference applied itself to the list of topics proposed by the Labour Section.

. . . It was obvious to me at the conclusion of our fifteenth meetings that those discussions might still be very prolonged, whilst the chances of agreement . . . were very remote. . . . I therefore proposed that the Conference should come to a close and, after discussion, this was agreed to.

I was of opinion that no good purpose would be served by prolonga-tion of our labours. The main purpose of the Conference, viz. some general agreement as to the amendment of our electoral laws—had failed, as no agreement had been reached or was likely to be reached. The Conference could only, at the best, submit to you a few resolutions carried on party lines. These would not fulfil the purpose which was in view when the Conference was appointed.

I have therefore to inform you, with regret, that our proceedings have been discontinued. . . .

Yours very truly,

ULLSWATER.

PARLIAMENTARY REPRESENTATION, 1931

House of Commons Debates, 16 March 1931; Official Report, cc. 1721 sqq.

LORD HUGH CECIL: . . . University Representation is attacked, not with any bitter reflection on the Members who actually represent the universities, but in deference to a particular theory of representation, a theory which may be called the theory of equalitarian democracy.

As far as I understand it, the theory comes to this: That all the electors have a right to a vote, and that that right is a political power which must be proportionately shared among the whole 20,000,000 odd people who share in the electoral franchise. Each man has this 20,000,000th share in the representation of the Commons of England; that is the right, and for anyone to have more than a 20,000,000th share is unfair; and that since university Members are elected, first by persons who have two votes, a university vote and an ordinary vote, and, secondly, are elected by a number of votes smaller than is commonly entrusted with the choice of a Member, there is an injustice, and in the name of justice University Representation is to be abolished.

At the outset, of course, that is a mistaken theory. Voting is not a right; voting is a public function. No one has any more right to be a voter than he has to be, let me say, a policeman, or a judge, or a Prime Minister, or a Home Secretary. There is only one good argument for anyone having a vote, and that is the argument that it is in the public interest that he should have a vote; he is merely performing a public function, and, if it is the interest of the public that he should perform that function, that is the only good and sufficient argument why he should perform it. The function which voters exercise is not really a function that gives to each voter an equal share or anything like an equal share in the Government of the country. . . . Everything depends, for example, on a thing so irrelevant to political right as where you happen to live, not in respect of your own opinions but in respect of the opinions of the other voters who share the franchise.

If you are a Liberal and live in the Home Counties, you vote always in a minority, which, though it may be thought of as the exercise of a public right, is a very unsatisfactory right. Even if you are a Liberal living in Wales, where you are a part, not of a minority, but of an assured majority, you still do not matter. But if you are a person who by chance lives where the balance of voters is very nearly equal between the contending parties, you begin to find yourself a very important person, exercising considerable political influence; and, if you combine with a small number of other people of the right way of thinking, you may become one of those organised minorities which make their voices heard with tremendous effect—a small body of people where the constituency is balanced. How can anyone who thinks clearly say that this is a political right which in the name of justice must always be equal?

There are inequalities much more subtle than these obvious inequalities. There are all those inequalities which arise from the system of choosing candidates. In a representative system the choice of the candidate is quite as important as the choice of the Member at the poll, and in many respects more important. Lately, wealthy individuals have run candidates in the name of one cause or another, . . . but, in general, candidates are run by political parties and not by the enterprise of wealthy individuals. However those candidates are chosen, they are not chosen democratically. They are not chosen by the people for the people. . . .

Let me . . . ask how a person desiring to become a Member of Parliament would set out to achieve that object. He would not, I think, present himself to the democracy. If he did, he would almost be thought a lunatic; it would be so eccentric. He would try to get, in modern times perhaps, the support of a wealthy and powerful owner of newspapers, but, in more normal circumstances, he would try to get the support of a political party. . . . He would find that in connexion with the party there was a body called the association, which would be a tolerably numerous body. When he came to close quarters with this body, he would find that the function of the association was not really more discriminative than the function of the electorate at large. He would find that the real authority lay in a small body probably called the executive committee, or by some such title, and when he went to the executive committee he would find that two or three individuals of great energy and force of character really controlled the whole affair. It will be seen at once that all that system is oligarchic, and not democratic. The association which professes to represent the party is an oligarchy drawn from the larger oligarchy. The executive committee which professes to represent the association is a still smaller oligarchy drawn from the other oligarchy, and the two or three people who really decide the matter are the smallest and most powerful oligarchy of all. . . .

First, there is the mechanical difficulty. In the case of a motor car one person must hold the wheel. That is a matter of mechanism, and directly you have an organisation, only a few people can be concerned with directing it, because, without hopeless confusion, a larger number cannot be consulted. Secondly, there is in human nature undoubtedly a perpetual unceasing trend towards oligarchy. People always prefer to let the few control the many. . . .

. . . There is a theory, and a true theory, of representation which is quite different from the theory which I have been criticising. That is a theory which descends to us, I suppose, for 200 or 300 years and which was made classical by the genius of Burke. That theory does not seek to trace political power from each of the 20,000,000 voters . . . up to this House or to the Government of the day. It views representation from another aspect. It seeks to have a House of Commons which shall be representative because it is a microcosm of the whole people. We sit here, on that theory, not as being each man with so many thousand voters' political power to exercise, but as being typical commoners, who are so chosen that the decision we come to is likely to be the decision of the whole people. . . . That vast body of opinion we represent, in the sense that a map represents the country over which the traveller wishes to travel. What is found here will be found, in experience, in the commonalty at large. That is the true theory of representation. It is a reality. It is not this dreadful, artificial argument which everyone knows is untrue and which breaks down in a thousand ways directly you begin to test it. It is the truth. What this House says, whether there is a Labour, or a Conservative, or a Liberal majority, will broadly speaking be more or less acceptable to the whole people, because we are the commons by representation, and what seems to us typical commoners to be right will not, on the whole, seem to be wrong to the commoners outside. . . .

PROPORTIONAL REPRESENTATION, 1933

House of Commons Debates, 6 December 1933; Official Report, cc. 1744 sqq.

MR. ATTLEE: . . . It is said that one great argument for proportional representation is that it saves the able men of various parties from being defeated. I agree that it is a misfortune to lose able men, but there is another danger in that you get a condition in which people do not know their Member at all, and, what is far worse, it makes for the domination of the machine. It makes for the selection of the Member not by the electors but by the machine, and far from freeing this House, such a system would tend to make the House fall more and more into the hands of an outside body.

I recognise that there are very strong points from a theoretical point of view for proportional representation. I think that for certain purposes it is a useful instrument, but I do not think it is an instrument that is at all useful when applied to a Constitution such as ours, because the essential thing to be done at a General Election is to decide what set of opinions and persons is to carry on the government of the country. It is suggested that you may get a minority dominating the majority. It has not often happened in this country, and a government in that position is generally too weak to do very much and does not last very long. . . .

. . . I do not believe it is really worth while discussing electoral systems in theory. I find that all parties, possibly we ourselves, tend to adopt the electoral system which suits their political position in any country for the time being. Minority groups naturally ask for the system that suits them, and majority groups probably have a dangerous tendency to squeeze out minorities. You get a party that thinks it is going to run second on the poll out of three and find it very keen on the alternative vote. On the other hand, the party which runs third moves away from the alternative vote and decides that its only chance is in proportional representation. . . . I have never concealed the point that I dislike the system, although I am perfectly willing to admit that some 20 years ago, when our party were in an even worse position than the Liberal Party, I thought there might be something in proportional representation. I am not considering this question in a theoretical sense, but from the point of view of what is useful. What is needed at any election is a decision for a definite course of action. I do not believe it is for the good of the country that a party with a definite political or economic theory should take office and have to tone down that theory for some third group. I would much rather that the Conservatives, for instance, should have carried out their full policy than allow themselves to be hampered by Liberals. On the whole, unless there is a broad two-party system in this country the machine does not work particularly well. . . .

. . . We believe that the majority in the country should rule, and that the country should return a majority to this House, and our immediate concern is that there is always a danger that the majority opinion will be thwarted by another unrepresentative House. We believe that is quite a serious danger. We have always been of the opinion that it was the great merit of the British Constitution that it was so flexible that you could make great changes without breaking the whole machine, and there is a danger of an endeavour to depart from the flexibility of the machine and to try to put in a special bridle directed to restraining the Labour Party. . . .

. . . I think the idea that we should make this House an exact replica of opinions held in the country is, first of all, quite impossible, and, if it were possible, that it would be undesirable. I do not think that a mosaic of various opinions, with all kinds of cross-currents, combined, by some kind of cabal inside the House, to make one of those shifting Governments such as we get on the Continent, where groups are always changing, is an effective form of Government for this country, certainly not in times like this. Though I admit that the machine has many imperfections, I think it functions better with a clear majority, even when the swing of the pendulum goes over too far, so long as there is an effective Government, because the real defence of democracy is not in abstract theories, but in the practical working of government. ...

MR. ISAAC FOOT: ... There are some things that it is very difficult to define. It is very difficult to define liberty or to define democracy, but whatever definition of democracy there may be, two fundamental things we are entitled to look for in a democratic system. First of all under your system, if it is democratic, the will of the majority for the time being as it is expressed at the polls shall prevail. The other fundamental thing is that substantial minorities shall have a representation that corresponds approximately with their influence and their power. Judged by that test our system stands condemned, and to the extent that it falls short of that it ought to be improved if it is within our power. ...

... under the present system the electorate has no free choice as to the candidates who are placed before it. An idyllic picture has been drawn of a constituency selecting the man of its choice, but 999 people out of 1,000 in a constituency have no voice at all as to the people who submit themselves for election. Generally, as we know, the executives of associations decide who are to be candidates. Reference was made just now to the machine. This system is precisely the system that will give the individual a chance. Suppose that in a constituency where all three parties have strong party machines, they put up three subservient candidates who are ready to toe the party line. Under a system of proportional representation, a fourth man who, as a result of apprenticeship in the local service has gained the confidence of his fellows, could go forward as a candidate and stand side by side with those party nominees and beat them, even though they were smothered with party labels. The system will give the individual in this country an opportunity he has not had before. ...

THE NATIONAL COUNCIL OF LABOUR, 1941

CONSTITUTION

The National Council of Labour shall represent the General Council of the Trades Union Congress, the Executive Committee of the Labour Party, the Executive Committee of the Parliamentary Labour Party, and the Central Board of the Co-operative Union, Ltd.

It shall be constituted as follows:

Representing the Trades Union Congress: The Chairman and six members of the General Council.

Representing the Labour Party: The Chairman and two members of the National Executive Committee, together with the Chairman and three members of the Executive Committee of the Parliamentary Labour Party.

Representing the Co-operative Union, Ltd.: The Chairman and six persons nominated by the Executive Committee.

The Secretaries of the three bodies shall be Joint Secretaries of the National Council.

The Chairman of the General Council of the Trades Union Congress, the Chairman of the National Executive Committee of the Labour Party, and the Chairman of the Central Board of the Co-operative Union, Ltd., shall be Chairman of the National Council, and shall preside at meetings in rotation, as circumstances allow.

DUTIES OF THE COUNCIL

The National Council shall

(*a*) Consider all questions affecting the Labour and Co-operative Movements as a whole, and make provision for taking immediate and united action on all questions of national emergency.

(*b*) Endeavour to secure a common policy and joint action, whether by legislation or otherwise, on all questions affecting the workers as producers, consumers, and citizens.

(*c*) Consult, when necessary, a Joint Conference, consisting of the General Council of the Trades Union Congress, the Labour Party Executive, together with a number of Parliamentary Members (which, with the Labour Party Executive, will be equal in number to the numbers of the General Council of the Trades Union Congress), and the members of the National Authority of the Co-operative Union.

(*d*) Submit an Annual Report to each of the national bodies' members of the Council.

(*e*) Only make pronouncements on matters of national policy after agreement thereto has been signified by the bodies' members of the Council, but this shall not prevent the Council in matters of urgency and where the members are unanimous from so doing. Such pronouncements on emergency matters shall not, however, be binding on the respective constituent bodies unless and until such bodies have ratified them.

FINANCE

The expenditure incurred by the Council shall be met in equal proportion by the General Council of the Trades Union Congress, the Executive Committee of the Labour Party, and the Co-operative Union.

MEETINGS

The National Council shall meet once a month, and emergency meetings shall be called at the request of one of the Secretaries, or any three members of the Council, such meeting to be held within a period of six days from the receipt of the request.

THE ELECTORAL SYSTEM, 1944

Conference of Electoral Reform and Redistribution of Seats: Letter from Mr. Speaker to the Prime Minister, 24 May 1944 (Cmd. 6,534)

My Dear Prime Minister,

On 2 February, the House of Commons, after a two days' Debate, agreed to a Resolution welcoming "the proposal of His Majesty's Government to set up a Conference on Electoral Reform and Redistribution of Seats and to invite Mr. Speaker to preside." . . .

The conclusions so far reached by the Conference are set out in the following series of Resolutions. . . .

I. REDISTRIBUTION OF SEATS

GENERAL

1. The Conference are in favour of a general redistribution of seats as soon as practicable. . . .

PERMANENT RULES

6. The total number of Members of the House of Commons for Great Britain shall remain substantially as at present (i.e. 591, excluding University seats).

7. There shall be no reduction in the present number of Members of the House of Commons for Scotland or for Wales and Monmouthshire.

8. Redistribution shall be effected on the basis of qualified electorate.

9. The standard unit of electorate for each Member of the House of Commons for Great Britain shall be a quota ascertained by dividing the total electorate in Great Britain by the total number of seats in

Great Britain (other than University seats) existing at the time the Boundary Commissioners report.

10. The Boundary Commissioners shall not be required to modify an existing constituency if its electorate falls short of or exceeds the quota by more than approximately 25 per cent.

11. Constituencies at present returning two Members shall be abolished, except where after local enquiry by the Boundary Commissioners it is found in any particular case that abolition is not desirable.

Provided that no county or borough shall continue to return two Members if the electorate falls short of double the quota by more than approximately 15 per cent.

12. The boundaries of Parliamentary constituencies shall, where convenient, coincide with the boundaries of local government administrative areas.

13. The City of London shall continue, as at present, to return two Members. (This Resolution was passed by a majority—Ayes 15; Noes 13.)

14. It shall be an Instruction to the Boundary Commissioners for Northern Ireland, in applying the foregoing rules, that there shall be no change in the present number of Members of the House of Commons for Northern Ireland, and that the quota for Northern Ireland shall be ascertained by dividing the total electorate by twelve (that is, the number of Northern Ireland seats, other than the University seat).

15. The Boundary Commissioners may depart from the strict application of these rules if special geographical considerations (including the area, shape and accessibility of a constituency) appear to them to render such a course desirable.

16. Nothing in the foregoing rules shall apply to University constituencies. . . .

MACHINERY OF REDISTRIBUTION

17. There should be four separate Boundary Commissions: one for England; one for Scotland; one for Wales and Monmouthshire; and one for Northern Ireland.

18. The Speaker should be ex-officio Chairman of all four Commissions.

19. The Speaker should nominate one of the members of each Commission as Deputy-Chairman of the Commission.

20. Each separate Boundary Commission should sit (its Deputy-Chairman presiding) to hear any representations from the Chief or National Officers of the Party organisations with respect to the Commission's provisional proposals for redistribution.

21. Each Boundary Commission should be required to undertake, at intervals of not less than three years and not more than seven years,

a general review of the representation in the House of Commons of that part of the United Kingdom with which it is concerned.

22. The Boundary Commissions should, in addition, have authority to submit special reports at any time recommending changes in respect of any particular constituency or group of constituencies.

23. The reports of the Boundary Commissions should be submitted to the Secretary of State concerned, and the Secretary of State should be required to lay every such report before Parliament, together with a draft Order in Council giving effect to any recommendations (with or without modification) for redistribution, and providing for any consequential or incidental matters. Any such draft Order should be subject to affirmative resolutions. . . .

II. REFORM OF FRANCHISE (BOTH PARLIAMENTARY AND LOCAL GOVERNMENT)

24. The local government franchise shall be assimilated to the Parliamentary franchise and Parliamentary and local government elections shall be held on the same Register.

Provided that Peers shall not lose their right to vote in local government elections.

25. The business premises qualification shall be retained.

Provided that no person shall be entitled to be registered as an elector by reason of the fact that he or she is the husband or wife of a person having a business premises qualification.

26. The existing University representation and methods of election shall be maintained.

Provided that every person who has received or receives a degree (or its equivalent) shall be automatically registered and that no fees shall be charged for registration expenses.

27. A person shall be entitled to be registered for not more than one residence qualification and for not more than one business qualification, provided that such an arrangement is administratively practicable.

(This Resolution was passed by a majority—Ayes, 21; Noes, 8.)

III. METHODS OF ELECTION

28. The system of election known as Proportional Representation shall not be adopted in respect of any constituencies where it does not apply at present.

(This Resolution was passed by a majority—Ayes, 24; Noes, 5.)

The conclusions set out in this Report, and the amount of general agreement that we have achieved, undoubtedly represent for all a subordination of personal opinions sincerely held which would not have been possible unless all members of the Conference had been determined, from the first, to tackle without bias the thorny problems which confronted us. . . .

Yours very sincerely,

D. CLIFTON BROWN.

APPENDIX

4. The following comprehensive Resolution on the subject of Proportional Representation was rejected by the Conference:

"(i) That the Conference reaffirming the Resolution of the Speaker's Conference of 1917, accepts as governing any scheme of redistribution the principle that each vote recorded shall, as far as possible, command an equal share of representation in the House of Commons.

"(ii) That the Conference considers that this principle should apply to methods of elections equally with schemes of redistribution.

"(iii) That the present method of election fails to produce results fully and truly representative of the views of the voters.

"(iv) That the principal reason for this failure is the distribution of the country into single-member constituencies (or double-member constituencies in which each elector has two votes), under which it may be observed,

"(*a*) there can be and has in fact been in the years 1922–3, 1924–9, and 1935 to date a majority in the House of Commons of one party based on a minority of votes for that party in the country;

"(*b*) coalition government has prevailed during the years 1918–22, and 1931 to date, and government by a single party, having no majority in the House of Commons, during the years 1923–4 and 1929–31;

"(*c*) there has not been at any time since the Speaker's Conference of 1917 a government formed by any one party supported by a majority of the voters.

"(v) That the best remedy for the shortcomings of the present method of election is the adoption of some system of Proportional Representation whereunder each elector has a single transferable vote and constituencies return several members, a method which in the words of the present Prime Minister, 'is incomparably the fairest, the most scientific, and on the whole the best in the public interest.'

"(vi) That the Conference accepts the principle of Proportional Representation with the single transferable vote and recommends that it be applied to all constituencies save those affected by special geographical considerations."

Ayes—4. *Noes*—25.

STANDING ORDERS OF THE PARLIAMENTARY LABOUR PARTY, 1945

The Parliamentary Party have the authority to withdraw the Whip on account of things said or done by Members of the Party in the House, such decision to be reported to the National Executive Committee.

Outside activities, whether in writing or speech, which are contrary to the discipline or constitution of the Party shall be dealt with by the National Executive Committee.

STANDING ORDERS

1. For the purpose of securing concerted action in the House, Members shall consult the Officers of the Parliamentary Party before tabling any Motion, Amendment or Prayer, or other proposal which may involve Party policies or decisions, and shall not vote for any Motion, Amendment or Prayer contrary to the decision of the Party Meeting.

2. Where there is persistent refusal to observe the decisions of the Parliamentary Party, it shall be the duty of the Liaison Committee to bring a recommendation to the Party Meeting to report the Member to the National Executive Committee, who shall consider the matter in its constituency and other aspects with which the National Executive Committee is concerned. The Member concerned shall have the right to be heard both by the Parliamentary Party and by the National Executive Committee.

3. It is recognised that on certain matters, for example religion and temperance, Members may have good grounds for conscientious scruples, and in such cases they may abstain from voting.

NOTE.—Members should take advantage of Party Meetings in suitable instances to raise questions of Party policy concerning which they may have doubts.

THE CONSERVATIVE PARTY, 1949

Report of the Maxwell Fyfe Committee on Party Organisation, 1948–9

CHAPTER II.—THE PRESENT ORGANISATION OF THE PARTY

2. In its constitution and organisation three elements go to make up the Conservative Party—(a) the Parliamentary Party in both Houses of Parliament, (b) the Conservative and Unionist Associations for each Constituency, organised in the National Union, and (c) the Conservative and Unionist Central Office.

3. The basis of the Conservative Party is the Constituency Association. Every Association is an autonomous body. It appoints its own Officers, adopts its own Candidate, selects its own Agent and runs its organisation in its own way.

4. Essential sub-divisions in each Constituency Association are the Ward or Polling District Branches, each having its own Committee and Officers and each being represented on the Central Executive Committee of the Constituency Association. These Branch Associations are careful to preserve their own identity and this individualism is often a source of healthy rivalry within the Constituencies.

Each Constituency Association appoints representatives to the Council of the Provincial Area in which it is situated, to the Central Council of the National Union and to the Party Conference. Each Provincial Area appoints four representatives to the Executive Committee of the National Union, with one additional representative for every additional ten Constituencies above the number of thirty.

5. The National Union has had provincial organisations since 1878, either on an Area or a County basis. In 1930 it was decided to create Provincial Areas in those parts of the country which had only county organisations, and at the same time the Provincial Areas and Central Office Areas were made identical. The twelve Provincial Area Councils and Executive Committees, in addition to their advisory functions, enjoy complete power to organise Area activities such as mass demonstrations, conferences, week-end schools, etc.

During recent years there has been a tendency to devolve more and more financial responsibility upon the Areas. The Central Office no longer makes grants direct to Constituencies. All Areas have funds at their disposal and a majority of them have linked their finances with those of the Centre under budgetary arrangements which guarantee that the agreed financial requirements of the Area shall be forthcoming. We commend this development, for the Area organisation is best qualified to assess the needs of poorer Constituencies and to administer the funds which enable them to put forth their maximum effort.

6. The National Union was founded in 1867 and is built upwards from the Constituencies. The Provincial Area Councils consist mainly of representatives appointed by the Constituencies. Such Constituency representatives form the largest element in the Central Council and the Party Conference. The officers of the National Union are elected by the Central Council and consist of a President, a Chairman and three Vice-Chairmen.

7. In the Conservative Party the Constituency Association has direct access to the Centre. However, the size and complexity of modern political organisations would make it impossible for the whole of the detailed business of over 500 Parliamentary Constituencies to be transacted direct with Central Office, so Constituencies are constantly urged to deal with the Area Office whenever possible rather than to bring all their problems to Central Office.

8. The functions of the National Union are primarily deliberative and advisory. Its various representatives in the Areas and at the Centre

enable the collective opinion of the Party to find expression. Its views are conveyed to the Leader of the Party or the Chairman of the Party Organisation as may be necessary and convenient. The opinions of the Executive Committee are sought from time to time on matters of policy connected with organisation, political education and propaganda.

The Executive Committee elects its own Chairman and appoints an Honorary Secretary and a Secretary of the National Union. The Executive Committee consist mainly of members elected by the Areas, who can be regarded as representative of the Constituencies at one remove. The Executive has the following Advisory Committees, the members of which consist mainly of representatives appointed at Area level:

> Central Women's Committee
> Young Conservative and Unionist Central Committee
> Central Trade Union Committee
> Local Government Committee

There is also an Advisory Committee on Policy and Political Education, which is not representative of the Areas, the members being chosen by reason of their special knowledge of the questions to be considered. The Central Committees of the Federation of University Conservative and Unionist Associations (Undergraduates) and of the Conservative and Unionist Teachers' Association are also recognised as Advisory Committees.

9. In order to facilitate regular contact with Constituencies and to ensure that their requirements are promptly and sympathetically met, the Central Office has a branch office in each of the twelve Areas of England and Wales under an official known as the Central Office Agent. It should be understood that, although the Central Office keeps in close touch with the Areas through the Area offices, no orders can be given to Constituency Associations either by the Central Office or by the Area offices. The co-operation of Constituencies is generally assured through the personal relationships between the Association officers and the Central Office Agent.

10. The Central Office organisation is closely linked with that of the National Union both at the Centre and in the Areas. The General Director is the principal official in charge of the Central Office, and he is customarily appointed Honorary Secretary of the National Union. The Central Office Agents are usually appointed Honorary Secretaries of their Provincial Area Councils and Committees. There are regular consultation and exchange of information about all major enterprises which affect the Constituencies, and the Provincial Areas play an indispensable part in putting such schemes into operation.

11. The Central Office was founded in 1870 and in 1911 it was decided to create the post of Chairman of the Party Organisation, to

take over the duties at Central Office previously discharged there by the Chief Whip. The Chief Whip was thus enabled to devote himself to the Party in Parliament. The Chairman, as head of the Central Office, is responsible to the Leader of the Party for the efficiency of the organisation throughout England and Wales. In addition to the Chairman, the Leader appoints two Vice-Chairmen and two Treasurers. The role of the Central Office is to guide, inspire and co-ordinate the work of the Party throughout the country, to advise and assist Constituency Associations and Area Councils and to provide such services as can best be organised centrally.

12. From what has been written in this Chapter it should be clear that the object for which the Headquarters of the Party exists is to assist Associations in the furtherance and success of the Conservative cause. . . . Nevertheless we regret the attitude which still survives in a few quarters, where Central Office is still regarded as a remote body which exercises an unsympathetic control over the Party. The purpose of Central Office and the Area Offices, to which certain functions have been devolved, is to provide all possible help.

CHAPTER III.—THE ELECTION OF THE LEADER

1. At the head of the Party there is the Leader, sustained by the loyalty of the members of the Party to whom he owes his position. He is normally the Leader of His Majesty's Opposition or the Prime Minister in His Majesty's Government. When the Party is in office, he is the main fountain and interpreter of policy and he is charged with the task of advising the Sovereign on appointments to the various offices in his Cabinet and the remainder of the Administration.

2. Originally the election of the Leader rested with the Conservative and Unionist Members of the House of Commons. . . .

It is interesting to note how the system has worked in practice and the stages by which the number electing the Leader has been enlarged. When Lord Salisbury retired, King Edward VII sent for Mr. A. J. Balfour, who was elected Leader of the Party after he became Prime Minister. In 1912 Mr. Bonar Law succeeded Mr. Balfour as Leader of the Party. In 1922 the Leader of the Party was Mr. Austen Chamberlain, having been so elected in 1921, when Mr. Bonar Law resigned because of ill-health. Mr. Austen Chamberlain wished the Party to adhere to the Coalition, but at the Party Meeting his point of view was defeated. King George V sent for Mr. Bonar Law to be Prime Minister and he was subsequently elected Leader of the Party in 1922. An invitation to attend the meeting which confirmed him as the head of the Party was extended to Conservative Peers and Parliamentary Candidates. When Mr. Bonar Law retired in 1923 the King sent for Mr. Stanley Baldwin to be Prime Minister, and, after he became

Prime Minister, he became the Leader of the Party. When Mr. Stanley Baldwin retired in 1937, King George V sent for Mr. Neville Chamberlain, who also became Leader of the Party after becoming Prime Minister. Mr. Neville Chamberlain resigned in 1940 and the King sent for Mr. Churchill, but Mr. Chamberlain remained Leader of the Party till October, 1940, when Mr. Churchill was elected Leader. Thus, since 1902, except for the elections of Mr. Bonar Law in 1912 and Mr. Austen Chamberlain—who never became Prime Minister—in 1921, the election of a Leader of the Conservative Party has actually followed his accession to the Premiership.

3. The number of those eligible to elect the Leader was further increased in 1937, at the election of Mr. Neville Chamberlain, by the addition of the Executive Committee of the National Union. As a majority of that Committee is elected by the Provincial Area Councils, and as those Councils are themselves largely based on representation of the Constituency Associations, the democratic element was further strengthened when the Executive Committee of the National Union was brought in.

The present position is that the following elements constitute the body which can elect a new Leader: the Conservative and Unionist Members of the House of Commons and the House of Lords, all prospective Conservative and Unionist Parliamentary Candidates in the United Kingdom of Great Britain and Northern Ireland, and the Executive Committee of the National Union of Conservative and Unionist Associations. . . .

4. The office of the Chairman of the Party Organisation is and should remain a direct personal appointment by the Leader of the Party. This arrangement is necessary because he must enjoy the full confidence of the Leader; it also gives the Leader an opportunity of recruiting to this office an outstanding personality, not necessarily already related to the Party Organisation.

Similarly the offices of the Vice-Chairmen of the Party Organisation and the Treasurers of the Party are personal appointments of the Leader. . . .

CHAPTER V.—THE PARTY AND POLICY

2. The Party Programme contains the Party's specific proposals whereby its policy can be given practical effect. The preparation of the Programme must be a continuing process; but, as the final document has to be related directly to circumstances existing immediately before a General Election, the final proposals are normally presented in a Party Manifesto by the Leader on the eve of a General Election, and are his responsibility.

3. . . . The specific plans for the application of policy are contained

in the Party Programme. Endorsements and pronouncements on Party policy are the prerogative and responsibility of the Leader, who is served by the various policy committees. These in their turn are influenced by the views of the Party as revealed in the various resolutions at the Party Conferences. . . .

CHAPTER X.—NATIONAL UNION STANDING ADVISORY COMMITTEE ON PARLIAMENTARY CANDIDATES

1. This Committee is a Committee of the National Union, and came into being in 1935. The purpose of the Committee is to assess on broadest grounds the suitability of men and women who are desirous of becoming approved Candidates. A list of approved Candidates, together with brief biographies, is sent on request to Constituency Associations which are selecting a Prospective Candidate. When one of these Candidates is subsequently adopted, he or she becomes an official Conservative Prospective Candidate. . . .

2. The Committee at present consists of the following: The Chairman of the Central Council of the National Union, the Chairman of the Executive Committee of the National Union, the Chairman of the Central Women's Advisory Committee, the Chairman of the Young Conservative Central Committee, the Chairman of the Central Trade Union Advisory Committee, the Chairman of the Party Organisation, the Chief Whip of the Party in the House of Commons and the Honorary Secretary of the National Union (Honorary Secretary). . . .

THE CONSTITUTION AND STANDING ORDERS OF THE LABOUR PARTY, 1950

CLAUSE I. NAME
The Labour Party.

CLAUSE II. MEMBERSHIP

1. There shall be two classes of members, namely:

(a) Affiliated Members
(b) Individual Members

2. Affiliated Members shall consist of:

(a) Trade Unions affiliated to the Trades Union Congress or recognised by the General Council of the Trades Union Congress as *bona fide* Trade Unions.

(*b*) Co-operative Societies.

(*c*) Socialist Societies.

(*d*) Professional Organisations which, in the opinion of the National Executive Committee, have interest consistent with those of other affiliated organisations.

(*e*) Constituency Labour Parties and Central Labour Parties in divided Boroughs.

(*f*) County or Area Federations of Constituency Labour Parties hereinafter referred to as Federations.

3. Political Organisations not affiliated to or associated under a National Agreement with the Party on 1 January 1946, having their own Programme, Principles and Policy for distinctive and separate propaganda, or possessing Branches in the Constituencies or engaged in the promotion of Parliamentary or Local Government Candidatures, or owing allegiance to any political organisation situated abroad, shall be ineligible for affiliation to the Party.

4. Individual Members shall be persons of not less than 16 years of age who subscribe to the conditions of membership, provided they are not members of Political Parties or organisations ancillary or subsidiary thereto declared by the Annual Conference of the Labour Party (hereinafter referred to as "the Party") or by the National Executive Committee in pursuance of Conference decisions to be ineligible for affiliations to the Party.

5. British citizens temporarily resident abroad may become Individual Members, or retain such membership of the Party, by enrolment with the Head Office provided they accept the conditions of membership in Clause III.

CLAUSE III. CONDITIONS OF MEMBERSHIP

1. Each affiliated organisation must

(*a*) Accept the Programme, Principles and Policy of the Party.

(*b*) Agree to conform to the Constitution and Standing Orders of the Party.

(*c*) Submit its Political Rules to the National Executive Committee.

2. Each Constituency Labour Party, Central Labour Party, and Federation must, in addition to the conditions mentioned in Section I of this Clause, adopt the Rules laid down by the Party Conference.

3. Each individual Member must

(*a*) Accept and conform of the Constitution, Programme, Principles, and Policy of the Party.

(*b*) If eligible, be a member of a Trade Union affiliated to the Trades Union Congress or recognised by the General Council of the Trades Union Congress as a *bona fide* Trade Union.

(*c*) Unless temporarily resident abroad, be a member of a Constituency Labour Party either (i) where he or she resides or (ii) where he or she is registered as a Parliamentary or Local Government elector.

CLAUSE IV. PARTY OBJECTS

NATIONAL

1. To organise and maintain in Parliament and in the country a Political Labour Party.

2. To co-operate with the General Council of the Trades Union Congress, or other Kindred Organisations, in joint political or other action in harmony with the Party Constitution and Standing Orders.

3. To give effect as far as may be practicable to the principles from time to time approved by the Party Conference.

4. To secure for the workers by hand or by brain the full fruits of their industry and the most equitable distribution thereof that may be possible, upon the basis of the common ownership of the means of production, distribution, and exchange, and the best obtainable system of popular administration and control of each industry or service.

5. Generally to promote the Political, Social, and Economic Emancipation of the People and more particularly of those who depend directly upon their own exertions by hand or by brain for the means of life.

INTER-DOMINION

6. To co-operate with the Labour and Socialist organisations in the Dominions and the Dependencies with a view to promoting the purposes of the Party, and to take common action for the promotion of a higher standard of social and economic life for the working population of the various countries.

INTERNATIONAL

7. To co-operate with the Labour and Socialist organisations in other countries and to assist in organising a Federation of Nations for the maintenance of Freedom and Peace, for the establishment of suitable machinery for the adjustment and settlement of International disputes by Conciliation or Judicial Arbitration, and for such International Legislation as may be practicable.

CLAUSE V. PARTY PROGRAMME

1. The Party Conference shall decide from time to time what specific proposals of legislative, financial or administrative reform shall be included in the Party Programme.

No proposal shall be included in the Party Programme unless it has been adopted by the Party Conference by a majority of not less than two-thirds of the votes recorded on a card vote.

2. The National Executive Committee and the Executive Committee of the Parliamentary Labour Party shall decide which items from the Party Programme shall be included in the Manifesto which shall be issued by the National Executive Committee prior to every General Election. The joint meeting of the two Executive Committees shall also define the attitude of the Party to the principal issues raised by the Election which are not covered by the Manifesto.

CLAUSE VI. THE PARTY CONFERENCE

1. The work of the Party shall be under the direction and control of the Party Conference which shall itself be subject to the Constitution and Standing Orders of the Party. The Party Conference shall meet regularly once in every year and also at such other times as it may be convened by the National Executive Committee.

2. The Party Conference shall be constituted as follows:

(a) Delegates duly appointed by each affiliated Trade Union or other organisation to the number of one delegate for each 5,000 members or part thereof on whom affiliation fees were paid for the year ending 31 December preceding the Conference.

(b) Delegates duly appointed by Constituency Labour Parties (or Trades Councils acting as such) to the number of one delegate for each 5,000 individual members or part thereof on whom affiliation fees were paid for the year ending 31 December preceding the Conference; where the individual and affiliated women's membership exceeds 2,500 an additional woman delegate may be appointed.

(c) Delegates duly appointed by Central Labour Parties or Trades Councils acting as such in Divided Boroughs not exceeding one for each Central Labour Party.

(d) Delegates duly appointed by Federations not exceeding one for each Federation.

(e) *Ex-officio* Members of the Party Conference as follows:

(i) Members of the National Executive Committee.

(ii) Members of the Parliamentary Labour Party.

(iii) Parliamentary Labour Candidates whose candidatures have been endorsed by the National Executive Committee.

(iv) The Secretary of the Party.

(v) The Chairman and one delegate appointed by the Annual Conference of the Labour Party League of Youth held next preceding the Annual Party Conference.

Ex-officio Members of the Party Conference shall have no voting power unless they are also duly-appointed delegates.

(*f*) Any special Party Conference shall be called on the same basis of representation as that upon which the last Annual Party Conference was convened.

3. In the event of a duly appointed delegate being elected as Treasurer or as a member of the National Executive Committee, the Affiliated Organisation responsible for his or her appointment as a delegate may claim authority at subsequent Party Conferences during his or her period of office, to appoint a delegate additional to the number applicable to it under paras. (*a*), (*b*) and (*c*) of Section 2 of this Clause, provided the delegate elected as Treasurer or as a member of the National Executive Committee:

(i) Remains qualified to be appointed as a delegate under Clause VII; and

(ii) Continues to be duly appointed as a delegate by the Affiliated Organisation claiming authority to appoint an additional delegate within the provisions of this Section.

CLAUSE VII. APPOINTMENT OF DELEGATES TO THE PARTY CONFERENCE

1. Every delegate must individually accept and conform to the Constitution, Programme, Principles, and Policy of the Party.

2. Delegates must be *bona fide* members or paid permanent officials of the organisation appointing them, except in the case of Members of the Parliamentary Labour Party or duly-endorsed Parliamentary Labour Candidates appointed to represent Constituencies in accordance with Section 4 of this Clause.

3. Delegates appointed by Federations or Central Labour Parties must be resident within the area of the organisation concerned or be registered therein as Parliamentary or Local Government electors.

4. Members of the Parliamentary Labour Party and duly-endorsed Parliamentary Labour Candidates may be appointed as delegates by Constituency Labour Parties responsible for their candidatures; otherwise, delegates appointed by Constituency Labour Parties must be resident in the Constituency appointing them, or registered as Parliamentary or Local Government electors therein.

5. No person shall act as a delegate for more than one organisation.

6. No person shall act as a delegate who does not pay the political levy of his or her Trade Union.

7. Members of Parliament not members of the Parliamentary Labour Party are ineligible to act as delegates.

8. The following are also ineligible to act as delegates:

(*a*) Persons acting as candidates or supporting candidates in opposition to duly-endorsed Labour Candidates.

(*b*) Persons who are members of political parties or organisations ancillary or subsidiary thereto declared by the Annual Party Conference or by the National Executive Committee in pursuance of the Conference decisions to be ineligible for affiliation to the Labour Party.

CLAUSE VIII. THE NATIONAL EXECUTIVE COMMITTEE

1. There shall be a National Executive Committee of the Party consisting of 25 members and a Treasurer, elected by the Party Conference at its regular Annual Meeting in such proportion and under such conditions as may be set out in the Standing Orders for the time being in force. The Leader of the Parliamentary Labour Party shall be an *ex officio* member of the National Executive Committee. The Executive Committee shall, subject to the control and directions of the Party Conference, be the Administrative Authority of the Party.

2. The duties of the National Executive Committee shall include the following:

(*a*) To ensure the establishment of, and to keep in active operation, a Constituency Labour Party in every Constituency, a Central Labour Party in every Divided Borough, and a Federation in every suitable area, in accordance with the rules laid down by the Party Conference for the purpose.

(*b*) To enforce the Constitution, Standing Orders, and Rules of the Party and to take any action it seems necessary for such purpose, whether by way of disaffiliation of an organisation, or expulsion of an individual, or otherwise. Any such action shall be reported to the next Annual Conference of the Party.

(*c*) To confer with the Parliamentary Labour Party at the opening of each Parliamentary Session, and at any other time when it or the Parliamentary Party may desire a Conference on any matters relating to the work and progress of the Party.

(*d*) To see that all its officers and members conform to the Constitution and Standing Orders of the Party.

(*e*) To present to the Annual Party Conference a Report covering the work and progress of the Party during its year of office, together with a Financial Statement and Accounts duly audited. The Report, Financial Statement and Accounts shall be sent to affiliated organisations at least two clear weeks before the opening of the Annual Party Conference.

(*f*) To propose to the Annual Party Conference such amendments to the Constitution and Standing Orders as may be deemed desirable,

and to submit to the Annual Party Conference, or to any Special
Party Conference called in accordance with the Standing Orders, such
resolutions and declarations affecting the Programme, Policy and
Principles of the Party as in its view may be necessitated by political
circumstances.

(*g*) To organise and maintain a Fund to finance Parliamentary
Bye-Elections.

(*h*) To organise an Insurance Scheme against the forfeiture of
Returning Officers deposits at every Parliamentary General Election.

3. The decision of the National Executive Committee, subject to any
modification by the Party Conference, as to the meaning and effect
of any rule or any part of this Constitution and Standing Orders, shall
be final.

4. The National Executive Committee shall have power to adjudicate
in disputes that may arise between affiliated and other Party organisations, and in disputes which occur within the Party's Regional,
Federation, or Constituency Machinery, and its decisions shall be
binding on all organisations concerned.

CLAUSE IX. PARLIAMENTARY CANDIDATURES

1. The National Executive Committee shall co-operate with the
Constituency Labour Party for each Constituency in selecting a Labour
Candidate for any Parliamentary Election.

2. The selection of Labour Candidates for Parliamentary Elections
shall be made in accordance with the procedure laid down by the
Annual Party Conference in the Rules which apply to Constituency
and Central Labour Parties.

3. The selection of Labour Candidates for Parliamentary Elections
shall not be regarded as completed until the name of the person
selected has been placed before a meeting of the National Executive
Committee, and his or her selection has been duly endorsed.

4. No Parliamentary Candidature shall be endorsed until the
National Executive Committee has received an undertaking by one
of its affiliated organisations (or is otherwise satisfied) that the election
expenses of the Candidate are guaranteed.

5. Labour Candidates for Parliamentary Elections duly endorsed by
the National Executive Committee shall appear before the elections
under the designation of "Labour Candidate" only. At any Parliamentary General Election they shall include in their Election Addresses
and give prominence in their campaigns to the issues for that Election
as defined by the National Executive Committee in its Manifesto.

6. At a Parliamentary Bye-election a duly-endorsed Labour Candidate shall submit his or her Election Address to the National Executive

Committee for approval. The National Executive Committee, whenever it considers it necessary, shall give advice and guidance on any special issue to be raised, or in the conduct of the campaign during such Bye-election.

7. No person may be selected as a Parliamentary Labour Candidate by a Constituency Labour Party, and no Candidate may be endorsed by the National Executive Committee, if the person concerned:

(*a*) Is not an Individual Member of the Party and, if eligible, is not a member of a Trade Union affiliated to the Trades Union Congress or recognised by the General Council of the Trades Union Congress as a *bona fide* Trade Union; or

(*b*) is a member of a Political Party or organisation ancillary or subsidiary thereto declared by the Annual Party Conference or by the National Executive Committee in pursuance of Conference decisions to be ineligible for affiliation to the Labour Party; or

(*c*) does not accept and conform to the Constitution, Programme, Principles, and Policy of the Party; or

(*d*) does not undertake to accept and act in harmony with the Standing Orders of the Parliamentary Labour Party.

8. Any Candidate who, after election, fails to accept or act in harmony with the Standing Orders of the Parliamentary Labour Party shall be considered to have violated the terms of this Constitution.

CLAUSE X. AFFILIATION AND MEMBERSHIP FEES

1. Each affiliated organisation (other than Federations, Constituency and Central Labour Parties) shall pay an affiliation fee of 6*d.* per member per annum to the Party.

2. Each Constituency Labour Party shall pay an affiliation fee of 6*d.* per annum on each individual member attached to the Party directly or indirectly through its local Labour Parties, Polling District Committees, Ward Committees, and Women's Sections, subject to a minimum payment of £6 per annum.

3. Each Central Labour Party in a Divided Borough shall pay an affiliation fee of £6 per annum.

4. Each County Federation shall pay affiliation fees in accordance with the following scale:

Federations of 2, 3 or 4 Constituency or Central Labour Parties, £1 per annum;

Federations of 5 or 6 Constituency or Central Labour Parties, £1 10*s.* per annum;

Federations of 7, 8 or 9 Constituency or Central Labour Parties, £2 per annum;

Federations of 10, 11, 12 or 13 Constituency or Central Labour Parties, £3 per annum;

Federations of over 13 Constituency or Central Labour Parties, £4 10s. per annum.

5. Each Individual Member of the Party shall pay a minimum membership fee of 6d. monthly to the Party to which he or she is attached in the manner laid down in Constituency and Local Labour Party Rules except Old Age Pensioners who have retired from work and they shall be allowed Individual Membership of the Party on the minimum payment of 1s. per annum. These contributions shall be entered on membership cards supplied by the National Executive Committee to Constituency and Local Labour Parties at 6d. per card, which sum shall include the affiliation fee payable by such organisation to the Party in respect of such members.

CLAUSE XI. PARTY CONFERENCE ARRANGEMENTS COMMITTEE

1. There shall be appointed in accordance with the Standing Orders at each Annual Party Conference a Party Conference Arrangements Committee of Five Delegates for the Annual Party Conference in the year succeeding its appointment, or for any Party Conference called during the intervening period. A member of the Head Office staff shall act as Secretary to the Committee.

2. The duty of the Party Arrangements Committee shall be:

(a) To arrange the order of the Party Conference Agenda.

(b) To act as Standing Orders Committee.

(c) To appoint Scrutineers and Tellers for the Annual Party Conference from amongst the Delegates whose names have been received at the Head Office of the Party two clear weeks prior to the opening of the Conference and submit them for approval to the Conference. In the case of a special Party Conference called under Clause VI, the National Executive Committee may appoint a date prior to which such names must be received.

CLAUSE XII. AUDITORS

There shall be appointed in accordance with the Standing Orders at each Annual Party Conference two delegates to act as Auditors of the Party Accounts to be submitted at the Annual Party Conference next succeeding that at which they are appointed.

CLAUSE XIII. ALTERATION TO CONSTITUTION

The existing Constitution, or any part thereof, may be amended, rescinded, altered, or additions made thereto, by Resolution carried on a card vote at any Annual Party Conference (in manner provided

in the Standing Orders appended hereto) held in every third year
following the year 1950, unless the National Executive Committee
advises that amendments shall be specially considered at any Annual
Party Conference. Notice of Resolutions embodying any such proposals must be sent in writing to the Secretary at the Offices of the
Party, as provided in Standing Orders.

CLAUSE XIV. STANDING ORDERS

The Standing Orders of the Party Conference shall be considered
for all purposes as if they form part of this Constitution and shall have
effect accordingly. New Standing Orders may be made when required,
or the existing Standing Orders amended, rescinded, or altered by
Resolution in the same manner as provided for alterations in the
Constitution itself.

STANDING ORDERS

STANDING ORDER I.—ANNUAL PARTY CONFERENCE

1. The National Executive Committee shall convene the Annual
Party Conference during October in each year, in accordance with the
conditions laid down in the Constitution and these Standing Orders.
It may also convene Special Sessions of the Party Conference when it
deems necessary.

2. When a Party Conference is called at short notice, the Secretaries
of affiliated organisations shall, on receiving the summons, instantly
take steps to secure representation of their organisations, in accordance with the Constitution and these Standing Orders.

3. Any Session of the Party Conference summoned with less than
ten days' notice shall confine its business strictly to that relating to
the emergency giving rise to the Special Session.

4. A delegation fee of £1 per Delegate shall be payable by affiliated
organisations sending Delegates to the Party Conference. *Ex officio*
members of the Party Conference in attendance shall pay a fee of 10s.
Such fees must be paid to the Secretary of the Party before credentials
are issued.

5. To secure the publication of an Official List of Delegates attending the Annual Party Conference, the names and addresses of Delegates
appointed by affiliated organisations must be sent to the Secretary
not later than two clear weeks before the opening of the Annual
Party Conference. In the case of a Special Conference called under
Clause VI, the National Executive Committee may appoint a date
prior to which such names and addresses shall be sent to the Secretary.

6. The National Executive Committee shall make arrangements
each year for the pooling of railway fares in respect of delegations

appointed by Federations, Central Labour Parties, and Constituency Labour Parties.

STANDING ORDER 2.—AGENDA

1. Notice of Resolution for the Annual Party Conference, not exceeding one from any one affiliated organisation, shall be sent in writing to the Secretary at the offices of the Party not later than 12 clear weeks before the opening of the Conference, for inclusion in the first Agenda which shall be forthwith issued to the affiliated organisations. At any Annual Party Conference at which Amendments to the Constitution are to be considered each affiliated organisation may submit one Resolution in addition to a Resolution proposing to amend the Constitution. In the case of a Special Conference called under Clause VI, the National Executive Committee may appoint a date prior to which such notices shall be sent to the Secretary.

2. Notice of amendments to the Resolutions in the First Agenda, not exceeding one from any one affiliated organisation (consequential amendments to a main amendment shall not be counted), and nominations for the National Executive Committee, Treasurer, Auditors, and Annual Conference Arrangements Committee, shall be forwarded in writing to the Secretary not later than six clear weeks before the opening of the Conference, for inclusion in the Final Agenda of the Conference. In the case of a Special Conference called under Clause VI, the National Executive Committee may appoint a date prior to which such notices shall be forwarded to the Secretary.

3. No business which does not arise out of the Resolutions on the Agenda shall be considered by the Party Conference, unless recommended by the National Executive Committee or the Conference Arrangements Committee.

4. When the Annual Party Conference has, by Resolution, made a declaration of a general Policy or Principle, no Resolution or motion concerning such Policy or Principle shall appear on the Agenda for a period of three years from the time such declaration was made, except such Resolutions or motions as are, in the opinion of the National Executive Committee, of immediate importance.

STANDING ORDER 3.—VOTING

Voting at the Annual Party Conference shall be by cards on the following basis:

(*a*) National and Constituency Organisations: One voting card for each 1,000 members or part thereof on whom affiliation fees were paid for the year ending 31 December preceding the Conference.

(*b*) Federations and Central Labour Parties: One voting card each. Voting at any Special Party Conference shall be on the same basis as those upon which voting took place at the preceding Annual Party Conference.

1. For the purpose of nomination and election the National Executive Committee shall be divided into four Divisions:

Division I shall consist of 12 members, to be nominated by Trade Unions, and elected by their delegations at the Annual Party Conference.

Division II shall consist of one member, to be nominated by Socialist, Co-operative, and Professional Organisations, and elected by their delegations at the Annual Party Conference.

Division III shall consist of seven members, to be nominated by Federations, Constituency Labour Parties, and Central Labour Parties, and elected by their delegations at the Annual Party Conference.

Division IV shall consist of five women members, to be nominated by any affiliated organisation, and elected by the Annual Party Conference as a whole.

2. The election for each Division shall be made by means of ballot vote on the card basis as provided in these Standing Orders.

3. Nominations for the National Executive Committee shall be made in accordance with the following conditions:

(*a*) Except in the case of Members of Parliament and duly-endorsed Candidates representing Constituency Labour Parties, nominees must be *bona fide* paying members of the organisations submitting their nominations.

(*b*) Except where a Constituency Labour Party desires to nominate its Member of Parliament or its duly-endorsed Candidate, the nominees of Federations, Constituency Labour Parties, and Central Labour Parties must either reside in or be registered as Parliamentary or Local Government Electors in the area of the Federation or Party submitting the nomination.

(*c*) Only persons appointed to attend the Annual Party Conference as Delegates shall be eligible for nomination for a seat on the National Executive Committee. Nominees who do not attend the Annual Party Conference shall be deemed to have withdrawn their nominations, unless they send to the Secretary on or before the day on which the Conference opens an explanation in writing of their absence, satisfactory to the Conference Arrangements Committee.

(*d*) Members of the General Council of the Trades Union Congress are not eligible for nomination to the National Executive Committee.

(*e*) Before sending in nominations, affiliated organisations must secure the consent in writing of their nominees. Unless such consent is obtained and is attached to the nomination paper, nominations will be rendered null and void.

(*f*) Each affiliated organisation may make one nomination for its appropriate Division of the National Executive Committee. Where an affiliated organisation pays fees on 500,000 members or more it may make one additional nomination (either man or woman) for such Division.

(*g*) Each affiliated organisation may make one nomination for Division IV of the National Executive Committee.

STANDING ORDER 5.—ELECTION OF OFFICERS

1. The National Executive Committee shall elect its own Chairman and Vice-Chairman at its first meeting each year.

2. The Treasurer shall be nominated and elected separately by the Annual Party Conference. Every affiliated organisation may nominate a person for Treasurer who is a duly-appointed Delegate to the Annual Party Conference.

3. The Secretary shall be elected by the Annual Party Conference, on the recommendation of the National Executive Committee, and be *ex officio* a member of the Conference. He shall devote his whole time to the work of the Party and shall not be eligible as a Candidate for, or a Member of, Parliament. He shall remain in office so long as his work gives satisfaction to the National Executive Committee and Party Conference. Should a vacancy in the office occur between two Annual Party Conferences the National Executive Committee shall have full power to fill the vacancy, subject to the approval of the Annual Party Conference next following.

4. Every affiliated organisation may nominate one duly-appointed Delegate for a seat on the Party Conference Arrangements Committee, who, if elected, must be a Delegate to any Party Conference held during his or her period of office. In the event of a member of the Party Conference Arrangements Committee being unable to fulfil his or her duties, the Delegate who received the highest number of votes amongst those not elected shall be called upon, but should the voting list be exhausted the affiliated organisation to which the elected Delegate belonged shall nominate a substitute.

5. Every affiliated organisation may nominate one duly-appointed Delegate to act as Auditor. In the event of an Auditor being unable to perform the duties, the same procedure shall be followed as in the case of the Party Conference Arrangements Committee.

STANDING ORDER 6.—RESTRICTION OF NOMINATIONS

No delegate shall be eligible for nomination to more than one position to be filled by election at any Annual Party Conference. In the event of any Delegate being nominated for more than one such position, the Delegate shall be requested to select the position for which he or she desires to remain nominated. After the selection has been made the Delegate's name shall be omitted from the nominations for all other positions. Should no selection of position be made not later than six clear weeks before the opening of the Conference, all nominations made on behalf of the Delegate shall become null and void.

INSURANCE AGAINST THE FORFEITURE OF RETURNING OFFICERS' DEPOSITS AT A GENERAL ELECTION

At the General Election, 1929, the National Executive Committee imposed upon Parliamentary Candidates an obligation to contribute the sum of £10 to an Insurance Fund, and in return guaranteed Candidates against the forfeiture of their Deposits.

By passing the attached paragraph in the National Executive Committee's Report at the Annual Party Conference at Brighton, 1929, authority has been given to the Committee to make the payment of a premium to a Scheme of Insurance a condition of endorsement:

"The National Executive Committee desire to continue the principle of insurance at future Elections, either on the same basis or in some modified form. In order to make future funds effective, it proposes to make it a condition of endorsement that Candidates must contribute their quotas to the Fund."

Henceforth the National Executive Committee will not endorse the selection of a Parliamentary Candidate until the obligation to pay a premium is acknowledged and agreed to by an affiliated organisation on behalf of its Candidate.

The continuance of this scheme of insurance is now one of the duties placed on the National Executive Committee by Clause VIII, 2 (*h*) of the Party Constitution.

PARTY FIELD FORCES, 1950

H. G. Nicholas, The British General Election of 1950 (*Macmillan & Co.*, London, *1951*), pp. 22 sqq.

The most evident and probably the most important development in party electoral organisation in 1950, compared with previous general elections, was in the recruitment and training of constituency agents. The election agent is a distinctive figure in British political life, and one whose history well deserves writing. His ancestry goes back to

shady beginnings in the service of aristocratic borough patrons, but
to-day he enjoys the esteem which attaches to a profession and accom-
panies legal recognition. . . .

The establishment of one of these paragons in each of the parliamentary constituencies of the country has become one of the ideal
goals of party endeavour. In this the role played by the central offices
is crucial. The problem for each was essentially the same. An agent
works for, as well as in, a constituency; "strong" constituencies can
best afford an agent, but it is "weak" constituencies which will probably most need one. Only the central organisation can resolve the
discrepancy between means and need. But in doing this it must also
have a care that it does not offend local susceptibilities or stifle local
enterprise. Each party solved the problem in its own way.

. . . Between October 1945 and February 1950 the number of fully
qualified Conservative agents was more than doubled. In England and
Wales by the time of the general election 527 out of the 542 constituencies had full-time party officials in charge. . . . Of these 527, 428
were fully qualified agents, 46 were "Certificated Organisers" and the
remaining 53 were unqualified organisers. . . .

The different terms employed for the various grades of party
officials reflect different levels of training and proficiency and indicate,
incidentally, how much the political worker's occupation has acquired
the internal differentiation proper to a profession. The lowest rung of
the profession is occupied by the uncertificated organiser. Next comes his
certificated counterpart. Then comes the Certificated Agent. In large
cities with an organisation embracing several constituencies there will
be a Chief Agent, while at the Regional level there will be a Central
Office Agent and at the Central Office itself the General Director. . . .

The Labour Party's electoral organisation shows several interesting
differences from that of the Conservatives. Its agency strength, in the
first place, was less. For the 1945 election the party succeeded in
mustering about 250 paid agents, but these were largely temporary
recruits who fell away after the election was over. . . . By November
1949 there were 245 full-time agents. By the eve of the election there
were 279 for England, Wales and Scotland.

The inferiority in numbers which this still represented compared
with Conservative strength was in some degree made up by the greater
powers of direction which Transport House possessed over its limited
forces. . . .

It can hardly be doubted that it is the recruitment and maintenance
of a permanent field force of organisers, agents, etc., such as I have
been describing, that constitutes the major financial problem for a
modern party. Election expenses have been successively scaled down

by law until they are now fixed at what is an extremely modest limit. Moreover, a parliamentary election campaign, if a proper amount of enthusiasm is evoked, can be made self-supporting, or even positively profitable, by a constituency association which uses it as an excuse for a fund-raising drive. But the maintenance of a fully-trained field force in the constituencies, with permanent offices for them to work in and the necessary tools for their job—the whole operating even in electoral "peace-time" and ready for complete mobilisation whenever electoral "war," either parliamentary or municipal, threatens—this is the load which most constituencies find too heavy to carry unaided and for which central offices distribute the bulk of the funds they succeed in raising. . . .

The 1950 election campaign thus manifested, to a degree greater than ever before, the concentration of power in the hands of the central offices and the development of a class of full-time, paid, professional political workers. The battle analogies so spontaneously evoked by the contemplation of an election contest had here a precise applicability. The campaign maps studded with flags, before which each party manager was photographed in his office, did indeed indicate to an unprecedented degree troop movements controlled from a headquarters, and troops, moreover, who were regulars, in training, temperament and conditions of service. To fight without the assistance of the regulars was difficult; to defy the directions of the commander-in-chief was dangerous. To do so meant, for a constituency association, going into the battle in most cases with inadequate funds, propaganda or technical and legal advice, quite apart from the psychological discomfort that goes with being out of step with the battalion. Furthermore, this did not apply simply to the period of the election campaign proper. Increasingly, its shadow fell before it, and the peace-time organising and propaganda which were the precondition of success in battle called for a similar direction and control by the centre in the period between campaigns.

This spread in the functions of the constituency association from the mere fighting of an occasional parliamentary election to the maintenance of an all-the-year-round condition of political activity, or at the least of political vigilance, is the concomitant, and in the part the cause of the spread of the modern professional agent. Even within modern times his role has changed. His legal responsibilities under the 1883 Act still remain, but they are lightened by the expert legal assistance and advice furnished to him by his central office. With the disappearance of the limited franchise his registration duties have been reduced to a routine trickle. No longer, therefore, does he need the legal training which, even as late as the thirties, was still a desirable qualification. Such law as he needs to know he can fairly easily acquire through the party's training course, or find embodied in simple language in his election handbook. . . . But to a degree that more than offsets this lightening of his labours there has come the increasing burden of organisation. To keep the association going in dull times as well as in lively, to help the candidate or member to "nurse" his constituency, to direct the whist drives or arrange the fête, to edit the association's "news-letter," to collect the subscriptions, to interest the Press, to hire the halls and the best poster sites, to keep the canvass up to scratch, to find harmless outlets for the enthusiasms of his junior branch, to extract professional standards of performance out of volunteer assistants—all this he must learn to do—and to do it in such a way that the organisation so created can be quickly switched to the conduct of a concentrated election campaign which has to be fought on a modest, and often a tight, budget. It is not surprising that to do this he has become a professional, and that he needs and welcomes all the assistance a central office can give him. Moreover, with his professionalisation has come some of the detachment of the technician. Along with his political devotion to this party's cause goes a craftsman's interest in his work, such as will enable him in the heat and fury of a campaign to admire dispassionately the smoothness of his opponent's machine, or to argue disinterestedly the relative merits of the "marked register" and the "card index" systems of canvassing. Between him and his opposite numbers there will often develop the *camaraderie* of the expert, the respect—and sometimes even the indulgence—which grows up between men who use a common technique although for opposite ends. To only one can it be given to be the organiser of victory, but in the kingdom of means there can be any number of kings. . . .

STANDING ORDERS OF THE PARLIAMENTARY LABOUR PARTY, 1952

1. The privilege of membership of the Parliamentary Labour Party involves the acceptance of the decisions of the Party Meeting. The Party recognises the right of individual Members to abstain from voting on matters of deeply held personal conscientious conviction.

2. The Parliamentary Party have the right to withdraw the Whip on account of things said or done by Members of the Party in the House. The Member or Members concerned shall have the right to be heard at the Party Meeting before the Whip is withdrawn.

3. The National Executive Committee shall be informed of any decision to withdraw the Whip.

4. It is the duty of the Parliamentary Committee to bring before the

Party Meeting cases of serious or persistent breaches of Party discipline, and in appropriate cases to recommend to the Party Meeting that the Member or Members concerned shall be reported to the National Executive Committee. The Member or Members concerned shall have the right to be heard by the Parliamentary Committee and the Parliamentary Party.

5. For the purpose of securing concerted action in the House, Members shall consult the Officers of the Parliamentary Party before tabling any motion, amendment or prayer, or other proposal which may involve Party policies or decisions.

These Standing Orders may be amended, rescinded, altered, added to, suspended or reinstated for such period and under such conditions as may be determined, after due notice, by a duly constituted meeting of the Parliamentary Labour Party.

Standing Orders, as revised in March, 1952.

THE NATIONAL UNION OF CONSERVATIVE AND UNIONIST ASSOCIATIONS

Rules adopted at the Annual Meeting of the Central Council, 13 March, 1947, including amendments made up to 19 March, 1953

NAME

I. The name of this organisation of Conservative and Unionist Associations shall be "The National Union of Conservative and Unionist Associations," hereinafter referred to as "The National Union."

FUNCTIONS

II. The functions of the National Union shall be:

(1) To promote the formation and development of a Conservative and Unionist Association in every Constituency in England, Wales and Northern Ireland, and to foster thought and effort in furtherance of the principles and aims of the Party.

(2) To form a centre of united action, and to act as a link between the Leader of the Party and all organisations of the Party in England, Wales and Northern Ireland.

(3) To maintain close relationship with the Conservative and Unionist Central Office.

(4) To work in close co-operation with the Scottish Unionist Association and the Ulster Unionist Council.

For the attainment of the above functions the work of the National Union shall be dealt with through Provincial Area Councils, a Central Council, an Executive Committee, and a Conference.

MEMBERSHIP

III. The Association of the Party in each Constituency in England, Wales and Northern Ireland, and the Central Association for each Borough with two or more Constituency Associations, subscribing annually direct to the National Union not less than Two Guineas, shall, subject to the approval of the Executive Committee, be Members of the National Union.

The approval of the Executive Committee in respect of the membership of any such Association may be withdrawn at any time at the discretion of the Executive Committee whereupon such Association shall immediately cease to be a Member of the National Union.

Subscriptions, which shall not be returnable either in whole or in part in the case of cessation of membership shall be due on the 1st January in each year and unless paid, together with arrears (if any), the privileges of membership shall be forfeited.

OFFICERS

IV. The Central Council, at its Annual Meeting, shall elect a President, a Chairman and three Vice-Chairmen, who shall be known as the Officers of the National Union.

PROVINCIAL AREA COUNCILS

CONSTITUTION

V. The Council of each Provincial Area in England and Wales shall be constituted annually as follows:

(1) The Officers of the Provincial Area, and the Officers of each County Organisation (if any) within the Provincial Area.

(2) The Officers of each duly constituted and approved Provincial Area Advisory Committee.

(3) The members of the Provincial Area Executive Committee, and members of the Executive Committee of the National Union representing, or resident within, the Provincial Area.

(4) Representatives of each Constituency Association within the Provincial Area, as follows:

(*a*) The members of the National Union Central Council, i.e.:

(i) Two representatives (one of each sex) including the Chairman (or a deputy) of the Association.

(ii) The Chairman (or a deputy) of the Young Conservative and Unionist Divisional Committee.

(iii) The Chairman (or a deputy) of the Divisional Council of Conservative Trade Unionists.

(*b*) Such numbers of representatives as the Provincial Area Council may decide, one-third to be men, one-third to be women, and one-third to be Young Conservatives.

(*c*) The Certificated Agent.

(*d*) The Certificated Organiser.

(5) Representatives of the Central Association for each Borough with two Constituency Associations, as follows:

(*a*) The members of the National Union Central Council, i.e.:

(i) Two representatives (one of each sex), including the Chairman (or a deputy) of the Association.

(ii) The Chairman (or a deputy) of the Young Conservative and Unionist Committee.

(*b*) Such numbers of representatives as the Provincial Area Council may decide, one-third to be men, one-third to be women, and one-third to be Young Conservatives.

(*c*) The Certificated Agent.

(*d*) The Certificated Organiser.

(6) Representatives of the Central Association for each Borough with three or more Constituency Associations as follows:

(*a*) The members of the National Union Central Council, i.e.:

(i) Four representatives (two of each sex) including the Chairman (or a deputy) of the Association.

(ii) Two representatives of the Young Conservative and Unionist Committee, including the Chairman (or a deputy).

(iii) The Chief Certificated Agent.

(*b*) Such numbers of representatives as the Provincial Area Council may decide, one-third to be men, one-third to be women, and one-third to be Young Conservatives.

(*c*) The Chief Certificated Organiser.

(7) Not more than two representatives of each Subscribing Organisation and Club within the Provincial Area.

(8) Vice-Presidents and Honorary Members elected by the Provincial Area.

(9) Four representatives of each University or University College Conservative and Unionist Association within the Provincial Area.

(10) The Conservative and Unionist Members of the House of Lords resident within the Provincial Area, who are in receipt of the Party Whip.

(11) The Conservative and Unionist Members of the House of Commons representing Constituencies within the Provincial Area, who are in receipt of the Party Whip.

(12) The prospective Conservative and Unionist Candidates approved by the Standing Advisory Committee on Candidates and officially selected by Constituency Associations within the Provincial Area.

(13) The Chairman of the National Union, the Chairman of the Executive Committee, and the Honorary Secretary and the Secretary of the National Union.

(14) The Central Office Area Agents.

ELECTION OF OFFICERS AND REPRESENTATIVES

VI. The Council of each Provincial Area in England and Wales shall, under Rules adopted by such Council, elect annually the following:

(1) The President, Chairman, Vice-Chairmen, Honorary Treasurer and Honorary Secretary.

(2) The representatives of the Provincial Area on the Central Council and Executive Committee of the National Union, as provided for under the terms of Rules IX (7) and XIII (3).

PROVINCIAL AREA EXECUTIVE COMMITTEES

CONSTITUTION

VII. An Executive Committee of each Provincial Area in England and Wales shall be constituted annually as follows:

(1) The Officers of the Provincial Area, and the Officers of each County Organisation (if any) within the Provincial Area.

(2) The Officers of each duly constituted and approved Provincial Area Advisory Committee.

(3) Such number of other members as the Provincial Area Council may decide—one-third to be men, one-third to be women, and one-third to be Young Conservatives.

(4) The Central Office Area Agents.

POWERS AND DUTIES

VIII. The powers and duties of the Executive Committee of each Provincial Area in England and Wales shall include the following:

(1) To promote, superintend, and carry through such work of organisation and political education within the Provincial Area as may be considered necessary.

(2) To receive reports from the Provincial Area Advisory Committees and to take such steps thereon as may be deemed proper.

(3) To advise the Executive Committee of the National Union.

(4) To keep the Chairman of the Party Organisation in touch with the needs of every Constituency within the Provincial Area.

(5) To obtain local views on public questions, and transmit them to Headquarters, or to Members of Parliament representing Constituencies within the Provincial Area.

(6) To be a channel of inter-communication between the particular Constituencies within the Provincial Area for the purpose of rendering mutual assistance, and of arranging concerted action.

(7) To administer the funds of the Provincial Area.

(8) To co-opt such number of additional members as may from time to time be deemed advisable by the Provincial Area Council.

(9) To appoint such Sub-Committees and to delegate to them such powers as may from time to time be considered necessary.

(10) To summon the Provincial Area Council at such times as may be deemed necessary, and to draw up the Agenda for the Council Meetings.

(11) To submit a Report of the acts and proceedings of the Committee at every ordinary meeting of the Provincial Area Council.

(12) To frame By-laws for its own guidance, provided always that they are in accordance with the Rules of the National Union.

THE CENTRAL COUNCIL

CONSTITUTION

IX. The Central Council shall be constituted annually as follows:

(1) (*a*) The Leader of the Party, and the Leader of the Party in the House of Lords.

(*b*) The Officers of the National Union.

(*c*) The Chairman and Vice-Chairmen of the Party Organisation, and the Treasurers of the Party.

(*d*) The Chief Whip of the Party in each House of Parliament.

(*e*) The Chairman of the Party's Advisory Committee on Policy.

(*f*) The Chairman of the Central Board of Finance.

(*g*) The General Director, the Chief Organisation Officer, and the Chief Publicity Officer of the Central Office.

(2) The Chairman and the Secretary of each National Advisory Committee.

(3) The members of the Executive Committee of the National Union, and the co-opted members of the Women's and the Young Conservative and Unionist National Advisory Committees.

(4) Representatives of each Constituency Association, as follows:

(*a*) Two representatives (one of each sex) including the Chairman (or a deputy) of the Association.

(*b*) The Chairman (or a deputy) of the Young Conservative and Unionist Divisional Committee.

(*c*) The Chairman (or a deputy) of the Divisional Council of Conservative Trade Unionists.

(5) Representatives of the Central Association for each Borough with two Constituency Associations, as follows:

(*a*) Two representatives (one of each sex) including the Chairman (or a deputy) of the Association.

(*b*) The Chairman (or a deputy) of the Young Conservative and Unionist Committee.

(6) Representatives of the Central Association for each Borough with three or more Constituency Associations, as follows:

(*a*) Four representatives (two of each sex) including the Chairman (or a deputy) of the Association.

(*b*) Two representatives of the Young Conservative and Unionist Committee, including the Chairman (or a deputy).

(*c*) The Chief Certificated Agent.

(7) Representatives of each Provincial Area of the National Union, as follows:

(*a*) The President, Chairman, Honorary Treasurer and one other representative of the Provincial Area Council.

(*b*) The Chairman (or a deputy) and one other representative of each duly constituted and approved Provincial Area Advisory Committee.

(8) Representatives of the University (Graduates) Associations as follows:

(*a*) Eight representatives each of the Oxford, Cambridge and Combined English Universities (Graduates) Conservative and Unionist Associations.

(*b*) Four representatives of the London University (Graduates) Conservative and Unionist Association.

(9) Four representatives of the City of London Conservative and Unionist Association.

(10) Representatives appointed by other Organisations as follows:

(*a*) The Chairman and two other representatives of the Federation of University Conservative and Unionist Associations; and one representative appointed by each University or University College Conservative and Unionist Association.

(*b*) The Chairman, Secretary, and three other representatives appointed by the Governing Body of the Association of Conservative Clubs.

(*c*) The Chairman, Secretary, and one other representative appointed by the Headquarters of the Young Britons.

(*d*) The Chairman of the Conservative and Unionist Films Association.

(*e*) The Chancellor, Secretary, and four other representatives appointed by the Headquarters of the Primrose League.

(*f*) The Chairman and Honorary Secretary of the National Society of Conservative and Unionist Agents; and the Chairman and one other representative of each Provincial Area Branch.

(11) The Conservative and Unionist Members of the House of Lords in receipt of the Party Whip; provided that all of these who desire membership shall so signify their desire not later than fifty-six clear days before the date of the Annual Meeting of the Central Council.

(12) The Conservative and Unionist Members of the House of Commons in receipt of the Party Whip.

(13) The prospective Conservative and Unionist Candidates approved by the Standing Advisory Committee on Candidates and officially selected by Constituency Associations in England and Wales.

(14) The Central Office Agents for each Provincial Area.

(15) Representatives of the Scottish Unionist Association as follows:

(*a*) The President for the time being; the Conveners of the Eastern and Western Divisional Councils; the Conveners of the Women's Committees of the Eastern and Western Divisional Councils.

(*b*) Ten members each of the Eastern and Western Divisional Councils.

(*c*) The Secretaries of the Eastern and Western Divisional Councils, and the Secretaries of the two Women's Committees.

(*d*) The prospective Unionist Candidates approved by the Chairman of the Unionist Party in Scotland and officially selected by Constituency Associations in Scotland.

(16) The Chairman of the Unionist Party in Scotland, and the Political Secretary to the Chairman.

(17) Representatives of the Ulster Unionist Council as follows:

(*a*) Ten members of the Council.

(*b*) The Secretary of the Council and the Secretary of the Women's Council.

(*c*) The prospective Unionist Candidates approved by the Chairman of the Ulster Unionist Party at Westminster and officially selected by Constituency Associations in Northern Ireland.

ANNUAL MEETING

X. The Annual Meeting of the Central Council shall be held at such time and place as the Executive Committee shall appoint, and the procedure for summoning such meeting shall be as follows:

(1) A preliminary notice shall be sent to every member of the Council not later than forty-nine clear days before the date appointed for such meeting.

(2) Notice of any special business for inclusion in the Agenda shall be sent so as to reach the Secretary not later than thirty-five clear days before the date of the meeting. This may be submitted in the form of a Notice of Motion provided it has first received the endorsement of either a Provincial Area, a Constituency Association, or a Central Association for a Borough with two or more Constituency Associations, and authority has been given for it to be moved at the meeting by a representative nominated for that purpose.

(3) A Notice of Motion may also be submitted by any of the following Committees of the National Union: Executive Committee, General Purposes Committee, National Advisory Committees.

(4) The General Purposes Committee shall decide and arrange the order of the business to be brought before the Council.

(5) Fourteen clear days before the date appointed for the meeting the Secretary shall send by post to every member of the Council:

(*a*) A Report of the Executive Committees.

(*b*) An Agenda Paper stating the business to be transacted.

SPECIAL MEETINGS

XI. The Executive Committee may, and if required by not less than one hundred members of the Central Council shall forthwith, summon a Special Meeting of the Council. Fourteen clear days' notice at least shall be given of any such special meeting, and the Agenda Paper shall accompany such notice. No business other than the business specified in the notice convening the meeting shall be transacted at such special meeting.

ATTENDANCE AT MEETINGS

XII. Attendance at Meetings of the Central Council shall be strictly confined to those entitled to be present under the terms of Rules IX.

THE EXECUTIVE COMMITTEE

CONSTITUTION

XIII. The Executive Committee shall be constituted annually as follows:

(1) (*a*) The Leader of the Party, and the Leader of the Party in the House of Lords.

(*b*) The Officers of the National Union.

(*c*) The Chairman and Vice-Chairmen of the Party Organisation, and the Treasurers of the Party.

(*d*) The Chief Whip of the Party in each House of Parliament (when the Chief Whip of the Party in either House is unable to attend his place may be taken by a junior Whip).

(*e*) The Chairman of the Party's Advisory Committee on Policy.

(*f*) The Chairman of the Central Board of Finance.

(*g*) The General Director, the Chief Organisation Officer and the Chief Publicity Officer of the Central Office.

(2) The Chairman of each National Advisory Committee.

(3) (*a*) Six representatives appointed by each Provincial Area—the Chairman, the Treasurer, the Chairman of the Women's Advisory Committee, one Young Conservative, one Trade Unionist, and one elected representative. N.B. The Trade Unionist representative shall be one of the two Area representatives elected to the Trade Unionists' National Advisory Committee.

(*b*) Where a Provincial Area comprises more than thirty Constituencies there shall be one additional representative for each additional ten Constituencies (or a broken number of less than ten but more than five). The Northern Provincial Area shall be entitled to one additional representative so long as it comprises not less than thirty-four Constituencies.

(4) (*a*) One representative of the Conservative and Unionist Peers.

(*b*) The Chairman, a Secretary and two members of the Executive Committee of the Conservative and Unionist Members' Committee. (All four may be represented on occasion by alternates provided that those alternates are members of the Executive of that Committee.)

(*c*) Two representatives of the University (Graduates) Conservative and Unionist Associations.

(*d*) The Chairman and two representatives of the Association of Conservative Clubs.

(*e*) The Chairman of the Young Britons.

(*f*) The Chairman of the Conservative and Unionist Films Association.

(*g*) The Chairman of the National Society of Conservative and Unionist Agents.

(5) Five representatives of the Scottish Unionist Association, viz.: The President for the time being, the Conveners of the Eastern and Western Divisional Councils, and the Conveners of the Women's Committees of the Eastern and Western Divisional Councils.

(6) The Chairman of the Unionist Party in Scotland, and the Political Secretary to the Chairman.

(7) Three representatives of the Ulster Unionist Council—at least one of whom shall be a woman.

(8) Additional members not exceeding twelve, who shall, subject to the Standing Orders of the Executive Committee, be co-opted either wholly at the first meeting of the Committee after it has been annually constituted or from time to time throughout the year as the Committee may determine.

POWERS AND DUTIES

XIV. The powers and duties of the Executive Committee shall be:

(1) To recommend annually to the Central Council for election a President, Chairman and three Vice-Chairmen of the National Union.

(2) To elect annually its own Chairman, who shall be deemed to be an Officer of the National Union.

(3) To appoint an Honorary Secretary and a Secretary of the National Union.

(4) To fill any casual vacancies that may from time to time occur among the Officers of the National Union.

(5) To elect the representatives of the National Union on the Party's Advisory Committee on Policy and other bodies on which it is deemed necessary for the National Union to be represented.

(6) To exercise under Rule III powers of approval and withdrawal of approval in relation to membership of the National Union.

(7) To give decisions upon or take such steps as it shall think fit to bring about a settlement of any dispute or difference submitted by the Executive Council of a Constituency Association (being a Member of the National Union) after the officers of the appropriate Provincial Area shall have failed to bring about a settlement acceptable to all parties to the dispute or difference.

(8) To set up, under Rule XVII, such other National Advisory Committees as may be considered necessary.

(9) To consider reports from the General Purposes Committee and from the Consultative Committee on Party Finance.

(10) To consider any matter or motion submitted by any member of the Committee.

(11) To submit a report to the Central Council, and an Annual Report to the Conference.

(12) To make Standing Orders for its own guidance.

GENERAL PURPOSES COMMITTEE

CONSTITUTION

XV. There shall be a General Purposes Committee constituted annually as follows:

(1) (*a*) The Officers of the National Union (the Chairman of the Executive Committee to be Chairman of the Committee).

(*b*) The Chairman and Vice-Chairmen of the Party Organisation, and the Treasurers of the Party.

(*c*) The Chief Whip of the Party in each House of Parliament (when the Chief Whip of the Party in either House is unable to attend, his place may be taken by a junior Whip).

(*d*) The Chairman of the Party's Advisory Committee on Policy.

(*e*) The General Director, the Chief Organisation Officer and the Chief Publicity Officer of the Central Office.

(2) The Chairman of each National Advisory Committee.

(3) (*a*) The Chairman of each Area Council (when a Chairman is unable to attend his place may be taken by one of the Area representatives on the Executive Committee).

(*b*) Three Men, three Women, three Young Conservatives and three Trade Unionists elected annually by the Executive Committee from amongst its members by postal ballots, nominations being invited from all members of that Committee.

(4) (*a*) The Chairman of the Conservative and Unionist Members' Committee (when the Chairman is unable to attend his place may be taken by a member of the Executive of that Committee).

(*b*) The Chairman of the Association of Conservative Clubs (when the Chairman is unable to attend, his place may be taken by one of the two representatives on the Executive Committee).

(c) The Chairman of the National Society of Conservative and Unionist Agents.

(5) The President of the Scottish Unionist Association and the Chairman of the Unionist Party in Scotland.

(6) One representative of the Ulster Unionist Council (to be chosen from the three representatives on the Executive Committee).

(7) Co-opted members not exceeding five in number.

POWERS AND DUTIES

XVI. The powers and duties of the General Purposes Committee shall be:

(1) To perform all ordinary and emergency acts on behalf of the National Union, except those reserved by Rule XIV, to the Executive Committee.

(2) To consider reports of the National Advisory Committees, and to circulate them to members of the Executive Committee for information.

(3) To consider resolutions passed by Area Councils and by Central and Constituency Associations.

(4) To consider any matter or motion submitted by any member of the Committee, or referred to it by the Executive Committee.

(5) To prepare the Agenda for the Central Council and the Conference.

(6) To prepare an Annual Report for approval by the Executive Committee before submission to the Conference.

(7) To submit a report to each meeting of the Executive Committee.

(8) To make Standing Orders for its own guidance.

NATIONAL ADVISORY COMMITTEES

XVII. (1) There shall be National Advisory Committees of the Executive Committee as follows:

Women's, Young Conservatives', Trade Unionists', Local Government, Political Education, Publicity and Speakers, Federation of University Associations, Teachers' Association.

(2) Each Advisory Committee shall have power to make Rules for its own composition and management, provided such Rules are approved by the Executive Committee.

(3) The Executive Committee shall have power to set up such other Advisory Committees as may be considered necessary, and to give them similar recognition.

THE CONFERENCE

CONSTITUTION

XVIII. The Conference shall be constituted annually as follows:

(1) The members of the Central Council provided for by Rule IX.

(2) Three additional representatives appointed by each Constituency Association (one of each sex and a Young Conservative), including the Honorary Treasurer (or a deputy).

(3) Six additional representatives each of the Oxford, Cambridge and Combined English Universities (Graduates) Conservative and Unionist Associations; and three representatives of the London University (Graduates) Conservative and Unionist Association.

(4) Three additional representatives of the City of London Conservative and Unionist Association.

(5) Each Constituency Association, and the Central Association for each Borough with two or more Constituency Associations, shall be entitled to nominate its Certificated Agent to attend.

(6) Each Constituency Association, and the Central Association for each Borough with two or more Constituency Associations, employing a Certificated Organiser shall be entitled to nominate him or her to attend.

ANNUAL CONFERENCE

XIX. There shall be an Annual Conference which shall be held at such time and place as the previous Annual Conference shall, upon the recommendation of the Executive Committee, appoint; and the procedure for summoning such Conference shall be as follows:

(1) A preliminary notice shall be sent to every member of the Conference, not later than forty-nine clear days before the date appointed for such Conference.

(2) Notice of any special business for inclusion in the Agenda shall be sent so as to reach the Secretary not later than thirty-five clear days before the date of the Conference. This may be submitted in the form of a Notice of Motion provided it has first received the endorsement of either a Provincial Area, a Constituency Association, or a Central Association for a Borough with two or more Constituency Associations, and authority has been given for it to be moved at the Conference by a representative nominated for that purpose.

(3) A Notice of Motion may also be submitted by any of the following Committees of the National Union: Executive Committee, General Purposes Committee, National Advisory Committees.

(4) The General Purposes Committee shall decide and arrange the order of the business to be brought before the Conference.

(5) Fourteen clear days before the date appointed for the Conference the Secretary shall send by post to every member of the Conference:

(*a*) An Annual Report prepared by the Executive Committee.
(*b*) An Agenda Paper stating the business to be transacted.

SPECIAL MEETINGS

XX. The Executive Committee may, and if required by not less than fifty Associations or by five Provincial Areas shall forthwith, summon a Special Meeting of the Conference. Fourteen clear days' notice at least shall be given of any such Special Conference, and the Agenda Paper shall accompany such notice. No business other than the business specified in the notice convening the meeting shall be transacted at such special meeting.

ATTENDANCE AT MEETINGS

XXI. Attendance at Meetings of the Conference shall be strictly confined to those entitled to be present under the terms of Rule XVIII.

AGE LIMIT FOR YOUNG CONSERVATIVE REPRESENTATIVES

XXII. The Young Conservative and Unionist representatives appointed under these Rules must not be over 30 years of age; provided that in exceptional circumstances the Executive Committee may otherwise decide.

STANDING ORDERS

XXIII. The Central Council shall have power to make Standing Orders for the Central Council and Conference.

ALTERATION OF RULES

XXIV. No new Rule of the National Union shall be adopted, nor shall any existing Rule be altered or repealed, except at a Meeting of the Central Council and with the support of not less than two-thirds of the votes of those present and entitled to vote.

Notice of the proposed adoption, alteration, or repeal shall be given with the notice convening the Meeting of the Central Council at which such proposed adoption, alteration, or repeal is to be considered.

INDEX